Strategic Information Systems

Forging the Business and Technology Alliance

Strategic Information Systems

Forging the Business and Technology Alliance

Henry Eric Firdman

FIRST EDITION
FIRST PRINTING

© 1991 by **McGraw-Hill, Inc.**

Library of Congress Cataloging-in-Publication Data

Firdman, G. R. (Genrikh Romanovich)
   Strategic information systems : forging the business and
technology alliance / by Henry Eric Firdman.
     p.   cm.
   Includes index.
   ISBN 0-8306-7723-2
   1. Strategic planning—Data processing. 2. Information
technology—Management. 3. Management—Data processing.
4. Management information systems.   I. Title.
HD30.28.F57 1991
658.4'038'011—dc20   91-9315
                                    CIP

For information about other McGraw-Hill materials, call 1-800-2-MCGRAW in the
U.S. In other countries call your nearest McGraw-Hill office.

Vice President & Editorial Director: Larry Hager
Book Editor: Kay Maloney
Production: Katherine G. Brown
Book Design: Jaclyn J. Boone
              EL2

Contents

Part II
Computer networks:
A foundation for the
information infrastructure

Part III
Information management and protection

Part IV
Human infrastructure

Acknowledgments

Many people contributed to this project, and they all have a full right to share its success. As usual, the author is the only one responsible for all shortcomings, errors, incorrect or short-living ideas, and other mishaps. My only excuse is that I tried to reduce their number to minimum.

Some people contributed to this book without even knowing it. I want to thank Charles Wiseman for his pioneering work on strategic information systems that was my inspiration in working on this project. I also want to thank Michael Porter for teaching me strategic advantage and Andrew Tanenbaum for teaching me computer networks. Their influence on this book is undeniable and enthusiastically acknowledged.

This book has grown out of my executive seminars on strategic information systems at California Institute of Technology's Industrial Relations Center. With their feedback and constructive criticism, the seminar students taught me what issues are more important than others and thus significantly helped me in shaping the book. Thank you all. My thanks also go to Nick Nichols, Valerie Hood, and other friends at Caltech's Industrial Relation Center for their trust and continuing support.

I thank Ray Straka of Pacific Bell for support and endorsement of the ideas presented in this book. His support has gone so far that I have written this book as an independent consultant, but am now writing these acknowledgments as Director of Strategic Information Systems at Pacific Bell. Thank you, Ray, for letting me practice what I have been preaching.

I am grateful to Jerry Papke of TAB McGraw-Hill for encouraging me to write this book and Kay Maloney for making the book much better than the original manuscript.

Thank you, my children, for being patient with me, always finding something to do on your own, and not breaking my computer and laser printer while I was writing this book. For these reasons, I was able to submit the manuscript on time.

Last, but not the least, I want to thank my wife, Larissa, for being **the** major inspiration in my life and in all our ventures and adventures for the last 18 years.

Introduction

Information technology (IT) has commonly been recognized as a ubiquitous strategic weapon necessary to succeed in fierce global competition. There is no doubt that in this decade strategic information systems (SIS) will be used by companies in virtually all industries as a competitive necessity. Some companies, such as American Airlines, Federal Express, McKesson, and Banc One, have already redefined their businesses in the context of SISs and gained a decisive competitive advantage because of the strategic use of IT.

However, in too many cases, huge investments in factory automation and management information systems (MIS) have simply given rise to fiefdoms and multiple islands of automation but have not produced expected strategic benefits and promised tangible paybacks.

One major lesson learned by the winners and losers is that IT by itself does not guarantee success if it is not understood in the context of the enterprise's corporate-specific strategic objectives (CSOs) and the ways in which a certain combination of ITs can help achieve these objectives. In order to compete successfully, every enterprise, big or small—whether it is a vendor, a system integrator, or a potential user of information systems (ISs)—must develop the strategic vision of its future and match that vision with in-house expertise in IT.

Complex decisions about how to achieve proficiency in IT and merge it into the enterprise's business can no longer be left to the IS organization or staff alone. These decisions will affect the future of the enterprise and thus have to be made by decision makers, the ultimate beneficiaries of SISs. In order to make these decisions properly and timely, the decision makers must understand what IT brings to the table and what its current state and future trends are.

Senior management must also understand that even the best possible combination of advanced ITs will not solve all problems by itself. Technologies are only as good as the people who apply them daily in their businesses. What the enterprise really needs to succeed in the strategic use of IT is the ongoing cooperation of people who (1) have a vision of its future and understand CSOs, (2) understand ITs and can apply them to attain CSOs, and (3) can make SISs a reality. In order for the enterprise to build an SIS that provides a sustainable competitive advantage, it desperately needs initiators and agents of such cooperation.

This book will help you become such an agent, no matter which groups you represent. It will help you understand the concept of an SIS and the major enabling technologies involved in SIS development. The book provides a comprehensive, up-to-date analysis of the current state of IT, its future trends, and its implementation in the context of the corporate strategic planning process. It also provides valuable information on cross-fertilization of IT and the work environment.

The book is divided into four parts. Part I, "Linking Business Strategies and Information Technology," includes chapters 1 through 6. Part II, "Computer Networks: A Foundation for the Information Infrastructure," consists of chapters 7 through 9. Part III, "Information Management and Protection," includes chapters 10 through 14. Finally, Part IV, "Human Infrastructure," consists of chapters 15 and 16.

Linking business strategies and IT is one of the most challenging problems businesses face today, but the rewards for those who succeed will be handsome. Part I addresses this question: "How can we reduce the risks and enjoy all the rewards of using IT?"

Chapter 1 describes the five-step strategic planning/plan execution (SPPE) process, which is necessary and sufficient to redefine an enterprise as an information management system (IMS) and thus reap all the benefits of IT. The chapter analyzes problems commonly experienced by business executives when they face IT and discusses possible solutions. It then describes the SPPE process, its organization, and expansion of strategic plans into an action program. Finally, it states three elements of corporate success and shows how SISs support these elements.

In order to build an SIS that supports attainment of the enterprise's strategic objectives, three critical issues must be addressed:

- How to make an SIS relatively stable in the face of imminent changes in strategic objectives and plans, market conditions, IT, and application portfolio
- How to define a basic strategy for SIS design and development (i.e., determine which tasks will be done by the enterprise and which will be outsourced, or developed by outside contractors)
- How to evaluate the effect of the resulting SIS on the enterprise, especially its human infrastructure.

Although these issues are highly interdependent and can hardly be addressed in any specific order or in isolation from one another, each issue implies following a specific set of design philosophies.

The problem of insensitivity to changes can be resolved by adhering to the open systems and downsizing philosophies as well as building the SIS on top of an application-independent corporate information infrastructure.

Chapter 2 discusses the open systems philosophy. Open systems pursue standardization of increasingly higher-level SIS components, gradually turning them into commodity products. The effect is potential plug-out/plug-in compatibility between consecutive generations of computer and networking hardware and software. The entire IS industry becomes a buyer's market.

Chapter 3 discusses the downsizing philosophy. Downsizing appeared first as an issue of economics: the same computational power can be obtained cheaper by moving from mainframes and minicomputers to multiple workstations and personal computers (PC) connected with a local area network (LAN). However, downsizing quickly became a system architecture issue, too. As such, downsizing significantly contributes to building change-insensitive SISs.

The in-house vs. outsourcing problem can be resolved by adhering to the system integration philosophy and the set of guidelines on, and conditions for, outsourcing.

Chapter 4 discusses the system integration philosophy. System integration is a method of providing turnkey solutions to business problems that cut across the enterprise's functional boundaries. One major problem of system integration is striking up a balance between SIS requirements and specifications, which may be very complex, and available financial and human resources, which are usually limited. A good system integration philosophy should provide the set of guidelines for determining what part of the SIS has to be designed and developed by the enterprise itself, or in-house, and what part should be outsourced, or contracted to an outside system integrator.

As stated previously, the SIS should be built on top of an application-independent corporate information infrastructure. The corporate information infrastructure is an organized collection of information sources, storages, processors, and users, along with communication systems connecting them, that supports CSOs and company operations. In addition, it reflects product, information, and transaction flows within the enterprise that are necessary to run its business.

The concept of an application-independent information infrastructure is as important for SISs as the concept of an application-independent database is for data management. It makes a major contribution to SIS stability in face of changing markets, business conditions, CSOs, and IT. Combined with the concepts of open systems, downsizing, and system integration, an information infrastructure promises to eliminate continuous patching of existing systems until they become unmaintainable and to provide stability of information assets and computational resources as well as smooth transition between generations of technology.

The application-independent information infrastructure also provides a corporate-wide view of, and tools for, information integrity preservation and security protection. Finally, it provides a technological foundation for a new human infrastructure required by the new ways of doing business in this decade and beyond.

It is worth mentioning that this book is not about IS design and development per se; rather, it is about making IS design and development easier through the design and development of an application-independent corporate information infrastructure. Because the concept of a corporate information infrastructure is so fundamental, the major part of the book is dedicated to this topic.

Chapter 5 discusses basic requirements for the corporate information infrastructure as well as factors determining it. The chapter includes a blueprint for information infrastructure development.

Chapter 6 defines elements of an information infrastructure—basic hardware and system software, and LANs—and discusses major market trends in each area. It also introduces information infrastructure building blocks and configurations based on four factors:

- Where information resides
- Where applications run
- How information is used and disseminated
- How information is updated

Chapter 6 shows how different combinations of these factors result in a variety of basic configurations and describes their use, including information update regimes. It also presents a client/server model that encompasses some of the basic configurations.

Chapter 7, the first chapter of Part II, introduces computer networks as a foundation for the information infrastructure. It defines network architecture and its major elements. The main part of chapter 7 is dedicated to an overview of the Open Systems Interconnection (OSI) Reference Model, an international networking standard that affects network planning, design, operation, and maintenance today and will continue to do so for years to come. Chapter 7 describes the layered OSI architecture and services offered by its layers. The discussion in this chapter relies on the material in Andrew Tanenbaum's excellent textbook on computer networks (1988).

Chapter 8 introduces the concept of internetworking. The important lesson from the past is that the corporate information infrastructure should not necessarily be homogeneous, but it must be flexible. Internetworking is a powerful technological solution that may provide a valuable combination of end-user freedom, overall infrastructure flexibility, and transparent information sharing and exchange. Chapter 8 presents the rationale for, and the OSI view of, internetworking and describes various kinds of relays that can be used to interconnect heterogenous networks.

Chapter 9 is dedicated to network management, an issue of major concern for both corporate executives and IS managers. Network management is necessary to provide an adequate quality of network service and network adaptability to changing user needs and technology without service disruption. Chapter 9 discusses the organizational, technical, and functional facets of network management. It also provides the OSI approach to network management, an extension of the basic OSI Reference Model.

Chapter 10, the first chapter of Part III, discusses basic requirements for information management; five kinds of information (voice, data, knowledge, text, and images); and basic properties of information (relevance, completeness, timeliness, accuracy, and conciseness).

Chapter 11 is dedicated to data management, the most mature part of information management. It presents the detailed architecture of a database management system, with emphasis on relational databases and the underlying relational data model. The discussion of distributed databases is based on C.J. Date's 12 rules for distributed databases (1987). Chapter 11 also describes limitations of the relational data model and data management and presents the short overview of object-oriented databases as a future direction of data management progress.

Chapter 12 discusses transaction management in databases. It covers data recovery, concurrency control, and integrity preservation.

Chapter 13 is dedicated to specifics of knowledge, text, and image management that complement data management in the entire IMS. It first describes specifics of knowledge and then presents knowledge management as a process. Chapter 13 continues with a discussion of scenarios for text and image management and provides examples of their use.

Chapter 14 is dedicated to security protection of both the infrastructure and the information it manages against deliberate or accidental threats. The security protection is viewed as a techno-managerial problem that should be solved on a system level. Chapter 14 defines security protection as a set of provisions for application and information integrity and for availability of the information infrastructure and ISs running against it.

Part IV addresses the human infrastructure problem. This problem can be resolved through adhering to new personnel development philosophies that close the gap between ISs and employees and affect the organizational structure; education and training; work in small groups; and performance evaluation, incentive, and reward systems.

IT by itself does not give the enterprise a competitive advantage. People who properly use this technology do. Thus, a magic equation for developing SISs is not complete unless one understands how IT and people should work together in a synergistic and mutually enhancing way.

Chapter 15 discusses four important human aspects that affect, and are affected, by the use of IT and SISs: organizational structure; teamwork and work groups; performance evaluation, incentive, and reward systems; and reduction of the proficiency gap between IT and people's ability to use it.

Chapter 16 presents the corporate information management/system development (IM/SD) policy. It outlines a generic IM/SD policy with the understanding that each enterprise will end up with its own unique policy matching its vision and culture. The outline consists of a set of questions to be answered by the IM/SD policy.

Finally, chapter 17 (conclusion) describes plausible changes in the workforce and how they may affect and be affected by IT.

Summarizing, the main goal of the book is to prepare you for meeting the challenges of global competition through integrating human and IS resources to provide products and services of the highest quality faster at the lowest price. And this is exactly what SISs are for.

Part I

Linking business strategies and IT

1

From strategic vision to action programs

Executive summary

There is no question in anyone's mind that linking business strategies, people, and information technology (IT) is one of the most challenging problems businesses face today. An enterprise that provides a successful solution to this problem will find itself in excellent position vis-à-vis its competition. Building effective linkages between business strategies and IT and creating the synergy between SISs and people are high-risk endeavors, but the rewards for those who succeed will be handsome.

Thus, the obvious question is: "How can we reduce the risks and enjoy the rewards of using IT?" Chapter 1 addresses this question by describing the five-step SPPE process, which is necessary and sufficient to redefine an enterprise as an IMS and thus reap all the benefits of IT.

We start with an analysis of problems commonly experienced by business executives when they face IT and describe their implications and possible solutions. We then discuss the strategic planning process, its organization, and the expansion of a strategic plan into an action program. Finally, we show how SISs support three critical success factors.

In my more than six years of IT consulting, I have met many business executives who complained about problems they consistently have had applying IT to their business problems. The complaints typically regard three topics (FIG. 1-1):

- There is a gap between a business problem as formulated by a business executive and a technological solution to this problem, which is provided by IS people. Neither business executives nor IS people seem to be able to fill this gap.

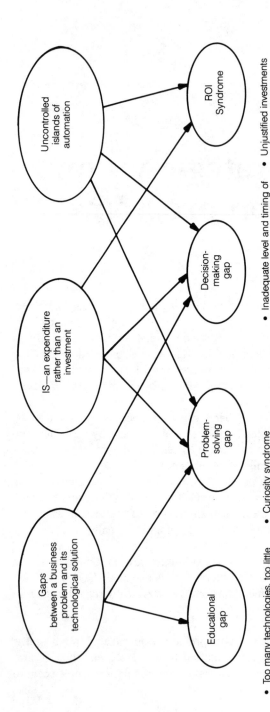

Fig. 1-1. Key problems of IT implementation.

- Funding IS development projects starts out as an investment but ends up as another expenditure. Optimistic return-on-investment (ROI) predictions seldom materialize.
- IS activities often result in the uncontrolled birth of islands of automation— that is, isolated ISs that neither contribute significantly to the bottom line nor communicate and cooperatively work with other, later-built, ISs to increase their contribution in the future. The contradiction between islands of automation and always-limited resources that do not allow one to build an all-embracing IS in one shot seems to be unresolvable.

Problems executives have with IT

The three complaint topics of business executives are implications of deeper problems that must be solved if the enterprise is to succeed in its quest for the strategic use of IT. Let us look at these problems in more detail.

Gaps between a business problem and its technological solution

Three gaps that I call an *educational* gap, a *problem-solving* gap, and a *decision-making* gap are common problems. All three gaps must be eliminated, or at least reduced, if executives are to be able to manage IT effectively.

Educational gap   The essence of the educational gap is that many executives have insufficient understanding of IT. Here are some reasons why they may be short of the required IT proficiency:

- There are too many new technologies and too little time (sometimes insufficient background) to learn them all.
- Technologies change so fast that short-term technical solutions may not be the best (or even good) in the long run.
- Not all technologies are equally important for all executives in all industries. However, many educators and vendors fail to recognize this fact, partly because they have vested interests in teaching technologies they know and/or market.
- The importance of understanding the interrelationships among technologies rather than only isolated technologies is not widely recognized.

Here is a good illustration of the last point.

WAR STORY 1-1. THE "NEW TECHNOLOGY"

A company decides to buy a document imaging system (DIS). No corporate infrastructure for imaging applications exists. No preliminary study of document traffic has been made, and no system architecture has been developed or even suggested. The only justification for making a purchasing decision was that "it is a new technology that other guys are already using, and therefore it should be practically tested."

The company spends about $1.5 million for the DIS and installs it in corporate headquarters, intending to provide access to the system for the users from all other corporate sites. Then the company makes two unpleasant, but important, discoveries:

- One document page imaged at 400 dots per inch (dpi) resolution requires about 250K bytes of memory (as opposed to 2K to 3K bytes required for one page of ASCII text).
- It takes about 35 seconds (!) to pass one page of imaged document through a 56-kilobit-per-second (kbps) fractional T1 line. Thus, using the DIS on a routine basis would immediately bring a corporate network to its knees!

As a result, the company faces some hard choices:

- Leave the purchased DIS alone or use it only as a technology exploration vehicle
- Build a dedicated network for document image transmission only (a very expensive proposition that would cost the company several times the DIS price)
- Develop an imaging infrastructure based on a study of plausible document transmission patterns, number of people involved, and kinds of documents to be transmitted (it's better later than never!)

To summarize, the company has not looked at the specific interrelationships between the imaging and networking technologies, and now it has to pay the price.

The problems resulting from the educational gap can be eliminated by establishing a continuous executive education program that satisfies the following requirements:

- The program must emphasize enabling technologies that are crucial for the enterprise's business and individual executives.
- The program must feature relatively short, but regular, technology updates. Each update should reflect actual changes in both the IT and its perception by executives.
- Technology updates must feature both the current state and the future trends in IT. To provide important continuity, each subsequent technology update should check out the state of forecasts made in the previous ones. Although sometimes embarrassing for forecasters, this process will guarantee that executives understand the reasons why a certain prediction has not come true.
- Since seminars are only as good as the people who conduct them, instructors for the executive education program should be carefully selected. Among many requirements for an instructor's quality, the top two are deep knowledge of a subject and the ability to explain it in an executive's, rather than a "techie's," language.

Problem-solving gap   The problem-solving gap most typically arises in the corporate culture that permits or encourages inventing "solutions looking for the problems." Typical examples of these phenomena include:

- The *curiosity syndrome*. Some technical people interested in a new technology become its missionaries and push it regardless of existing business needs. If they are doing their jobs well (and in most cases they are), they eventually get funding to look for a problem that fits into the solution they promote.
- The *let's-explore-this-new-technology syndrome*. The only difference between this and the previous phenomenon is that technology exploration is initiated by an executive. Unfortunately, technology exploration too often results in putting the cart before the horse. Executives who have authorized technology exploration encourage people who explore it to find applications, and they find applications that are dictated by no existing business need. Thus, the business need is invented.
- The *organizational zeal syndrome*. Some businesses make up for the educational gap by putting new slots in the organizational corporate structure. Two typical slots are chief technology officer (CTO) and technology assessment group (TAG). CTOs and TAGs may be very helpful. However, the problem with them is that if their status, scope of activities, and responsibilities are not well defined, they may quickly turn into self-serving fiefdoms.

The problem-solving gap can be eliminated by establishing an adequate continuous process for translating a business problem into its technological solution. Organizations such as TAGs should serve as temporary, multidisciplinary task forces dedicated to finding a solution to the identified business problem. If the enterprise is short of technological expertise in a certain area, it is usually less expensive to hire "expensive" outside consultants than to keep "inexpensive" technologists in-house if they are not required full time. An underutilized full-time technologist is like a time bomb: at some point this person will certainly say: "Let's explore this new technology."

Decision-making gap The essence of a decision-making gap is that the enterprise is concerned more about the cost-effectiveness of hardware and software acquisition than about the cost-effectiveness of a process that results in the decision of what IS, if any, should be developed.

The obvious psychological reason for this situation is blowing up the "cost" part of cost-effectiveness out of proportion. Purchase of expensive hardware and software seems more important than making a decision that sometimes takes only a few minutes of a senior executive's time. It comes as no surprise that most discussions and questions about a new IT are usually concentrated around hardware and software tools and their comparison rather than if, when, and how the technology should be used. A correct decision of this kind will affect the bottom line much more than correct selection of hardware and software, especially with the advent of open systems (see chapter 2).

The decision-making gap typically can be caused by:

- Inadequate level and timing of decision making. The level at which IS-related decisions are made is usually too low, and concerns hardware and software choices rather than strategic directions and partnerships, market and vendor assessment, system architecture and integration, etc. The timing is inadequate if senior executives get involved too early, when information necessary to make a decision is insufficient, or too late, when all low-level decisions have already been made.
- Inadequate scope of decision making. Not all parties that have to be involved may actually be involved, or some of the parties may be involved for too short a time, or decisions may not be made by consensus of all parties involved. Any of these inadequacies may have grave consequences at the stage of IS development.
- Inadequate principles and process of resource allocation. Because of the lack of a comprehensive top-down strategic plan, limited resources are all too often allocated to those who have a greater clout or even a bigger mouth rather than to those who have a real need or can make the biggest contribution to the overall bottom line.

The decision-making gap can be eliminated by establishing a proper decision-making process. This process, combined with the process for translating a business problem into its technological solution makes up the SPPE process.

Information systems: Investment or expenditure?

The second typical executive complaint pertaining to effective IS use is that IS development is advertised as a worthwhile investment but often ends up as just another expenditure. The problem-solving and decision-making gaps are two major problems that cause this complaint. If the corporate culture encourages inventing "solutions looking for the problems," or the enterprise does not care about the properly organized decision-making process, an IS will likely be an expenditure rather than an investment. At best, the IS will be an investment with a much lower ROI than it could have been otherwise.

Conversely, if the enterprise defines and establishes a proper SPPE process that includes the process for translating a business problem into its technological solution and the decision-making process, the IS will likely be an investment. The better the SPPE process, the higher the expected ROI.

The third reason for the investment vs. expenditure problem is what I call the *ROI syndrome*. The paradox is that pessimistic (that is, realistic) ROI forecasts never get funded, while optimistic ones almost never get materialized. Traditional ROI assessments, however, are still considered sacred.

Naive or excessive faith in traditional ROI assessments can result in:

- Unjustified investments
- Inflated expectations

- Preference for ISs that contribute little to the bottom line
- Undermining of the strategic impact of IS on the business because it is always harder to estimate than the impact of other elements, such as cost elimination or reduction. Figure 1-2 illustrates the intrinsic reverse dependency between the impact at each level (strategic, operational, cost elimination) and our ability to quantify the benefits at that level.

The IS must always be looked at as an investment. This statement implies that:

- Investment objectives must be clearly stated before any investment decisions are made.
- A qualitative view of ROI equal to the quantitative one must be adopted.
- Benefit/risk analysis must be provided at strategic, operational, and cost elimination levels rather than only at the cost elimination level.
- Resource allocations must be made according to the overall impact of a given IS on the business problem in question.

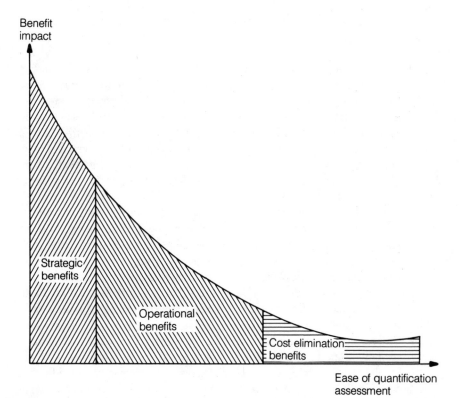

Fig. 1-2. High-impact benefits are hard to quantify.

Islands of automation

The third typical executive complaint pertaining to the effective use of IS is the uncontrolled birth of islands of automation. All three reasons for this complaint have already been discussed: the problem-solving gap, the decision-making gap, and the ROI syndrome.

If the corporate culture encourages inventing "solutions looking for the problems," or the enterprise does not care about the decision-making process, or resources are not allocated on the basis of the impact of IS on the business, the soil for islands of automation and their growth in number is exceptionally fertile.

Unplanned islands of automation can be eliminated by defining and establishing a proper SPPE process that includes (1) the process for translating a business problem into its technological solution and (2) the decision-making process that uses qualitative benefit/risk analysis methods and resource allocation based on an overall IS impact on the corporate business. The following paragraphs discuss the SPPE process in more detail.

SPPE process

The SPPE process or the resulting strategic plan must satisfy at least four conditions:

- The resulting strategic plan must encompass both the enterprise and its immediate business environment (suppliers, distributors, customers, competition, etc.). I call an enterprise along with its immediate business environment a virtual enterprise (FIG. 1-3). The concept is close to the concept of forces driving industry competition developed by Michael Porter (1980). Each enterprise may be a member of many virtual enterprises, being a competitor in one of them, an entrant in another, a supplier in a third, etc. A collection of virtual enterprises forms a *global industrial infrastructure*.
- The SPPE process must be a continuing effort rather than just a one-shot effort. The only way the enterprise can be flexible enough to react quickly to imminent changes is to have a top-down, easily updated strategic plan with deferred low-level decisions.
- The resulting strategic plan must account for the future, rather than the present, state of the enterprise. All IS-related endeavors must take into account the directions in which the enterprise's business will develop in the next three to five years.
- The resulting strategic plan must be top-down rather than bottom-up. I strongly argue for a "Think Big—Start Small" rather than just a "Start Small" strategy. In other words, all tactical, short-term, resource-limited decisions have to be made in the broader context of the overall long-term corporate strategic plan.

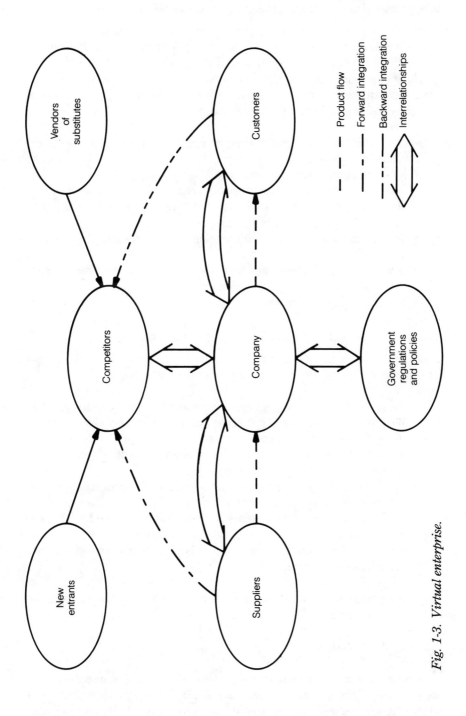

Fig. 1-3. Virtual enterprise.

Why must the strategic planning process be continuing?

Both the virtual enterprise and the global industrial infrastructure are continuously changing. Thus, the strategic plan cannot be developed for the isolated enterprise. For the same reason, the SPPE process cannot be a one-shot effort. The strategic plan developed in such a way would soon become obsolete and could hurt the enterprise more than help it. Possible changes in the virtual enterprise and global industrial infrastructure include:

- Old competitors implement their strategic plans and thus change the virtual enterprise.
- New competitors enter the industry.
- Substitutes of the company's products and services are developed.
- Former suppliers join the competition through forward integration (FIG. 1-3).
- Former customers join the competition through backward integration (FIG. 1-3).
- Government regulations and policies in different countries change, resulting in new, or lost old, opportunities.
- Technology rapidly changes.

Why must a strategic plan account for the future?

There are two convincing practical reasons why a strategic plan must account for the future rather than the present state of the enterprise:

- Implementation of a strategic plan can take three to five years, and during this period the global industrial infrastructure may change significantly. An IS with specifications based on the view of an enterprise as it is today may turn out to be obsolete three to five years down the road. Figure 1-4 illustrates this situation.
- By virtue of a typical corporate capital equipment budgeting process, expensive hardware and software have to be ordered (and sometimes even purchased) one to two years prior to field use in the IS. The only way to make this process meaningful is to have a strategic plan with milestones for future IS release and to base all hardware and software purchases on this plan.

The strategic plan that accounts for the future state of the enterprise is based on the corporate.

INTERLUDE 1-1. VISION.

A vision of direction, long-term objectives, and ways of attaining these objectives is absolutely necessary for the company's survival and prosperity. "Where the vision lacks, people perish!" The source of the vision is a corporate leader who has both the mental power to cre-

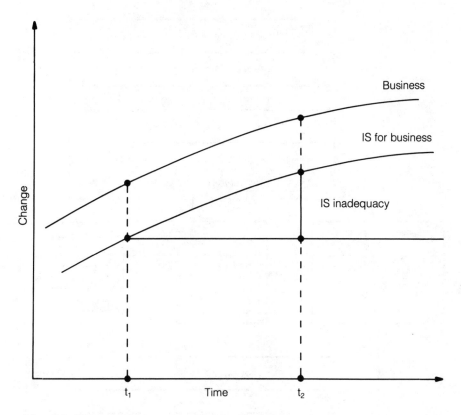

Fig. 1-4. Strategic plan must account for the future.

ate a vision and the practical abilities to make it a reality. However, this leader will be unlikely to create the vision without a management team to supply the necessary information, support, and critical feedback.

Vision is not a property of á small selected group of people. On the contrary, vision must be disseminated across the company to make sure that everyone has the same one. But just dissemination is not enough. Vision must be a source of motivation for everyone. Barbara Lind of Nolan Norton says that vision implies three messages sent by the leader to the troops:

- There is a good place to go.
- This is your personal share of that good place.
- I am the guy who will take you there.

Thus, vision is both practical and mystical. No significant corporate objective can be attained without vision. Nor can any SIS be built without it.

Five-step SPPE process

The corporate vision of the future may be translated into a set of implementable action programs through the following five-step SPPE process (FIG. 1-5).

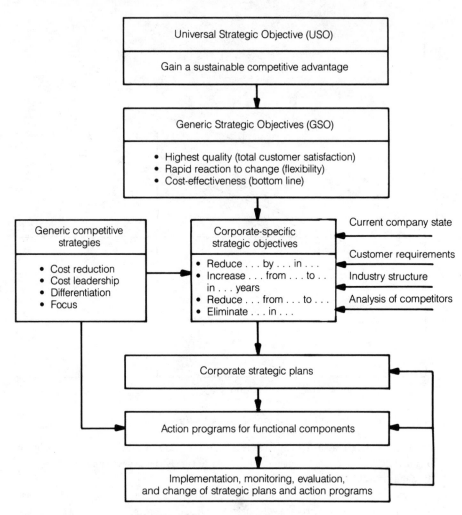

Fig. 1-5. From strategic objectives to action programs.

1. Formulating the list of CSOs consisting of a few easy-to understand statements of what the enterprise wants to accomplish
2. Putting together a capable strategic planning team responsible for translating CSOs into an implementable action program
3. Developing a set of alternative strategic plans with rough estimates of their cost-effectiveness
4. Expanding the selected strategic plan into a hierarchy of increasingly detailed action programs
5. Implementing and monitoring action programs, evaluating their ongoing results, and changing them if necessary

Why must the strategic plan be top-down?

The last two steps of the five-step SPPE process explain why the resulting strategic plan must be top-down (FIG. 1-6).

First, since changes are more likely to happen at the most detailed action level, and in order to reduce the plan's sensitivity to imminent change, its expansion into action programs must be deferred as much as possible. Ideally, plan expansion down to the level of detailed actions should be accomplished right before its execution.

Second, if, as a result of monitoring action programs, the strategic plan should be changed, the change should be accomplished at the lowest possible level of detail. This approach will minimize total changes and contribute to plan stability at the higher level.

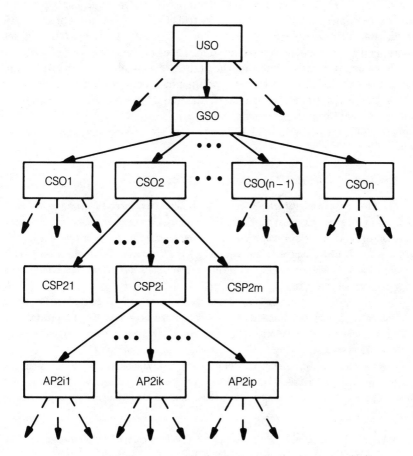

Fig. 1-6. Top-down expansion of strategic objectives.

Third, if changes do occur at the high level (such as the change of strategic direction), a top-down strategic plan provides an unambiguous path pointing out changes that need to be made at lower levels. As soon as the change is announced, all people in charge of plan execution immediately know who is affected and how.

Fourth, the top-down strategic plan allows planners to provide flexible resource allocation and leverage subsequent projects by the successful completion of previous ones. This plan is a "Think Big—Start Small" strategy in action!

Formulating CSOs

Let us discuss FIG. 1-5 in more detail. At the top is a single universal strategic objective (USO): to gain a sustainable competitive advantage. I call it universal because any company in any industry tries hard to attain this objective. All traditional strategic objectives, such as profitability, growth, ROI, market share, and social responsiveness, are derivatives of the USO.

Each company has to interpret the phrase "sustainable competitive advantage" in its unique business context and then translate the obtained interpretation into the requirements for quality, flexibility, and cost-effectiveness that comprise generic strategic objectives.

The following interlude clarifies the concept of sustainable competitive advantage.

INTERLUDE 1-2. SUSTAINABLE COMPETITIVE ADVANTAGE

Slightly paraphrasing Charles Wiseman's definition of *competitive advantage* (1988), I define it as a certain combination of abilities, resources, and environmental factors that a superior performer possesses uniquely or to a greater degree than any of its competitors. The relationship "X has a competitive advantage over Y in Z" means that company X possesses a combination of abilities, resources, and environmental factors that makes it superior to company Y in virtual enterprise Z.

Thus, competitive advantage is relative to the company's virtual enterprise. The direct implication of this statement is that the same company may need different strategies for competing in different virtual enterprises. Needless to say, any common features or components of these strategies have to be carefully identified and implemented only once.

In its absolute sense, sustainability of competitive advantage is a myth. Sustainability exists in time, so one can speak about a duration of sustained competitive advantage. Then for each strategy aimed at gaining a sustainable competitive advantage, the company has to assess:

- What is the minimum duration (period) of sustained competitive advantage the company needs to reap all or most benefits of having it?
- Is competitive advantage effectively sustainable during this period (in other words, how vulnerable is it to changes in the virtual enterprise and competitive attacks)?

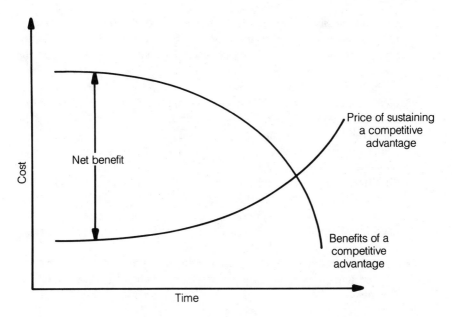

Fig. 1-7. Is sustaining a competitive advantage worth it?

- What is the sustainability price as a function of time (in other words, when will sustaining the competitive advantage begin to cost more than the gains obtained from having it)? (FIG. 1-7)
- Is the sustained competitive advantage worth this price? (FIG. 1-7)

In its assessment of sustained competitive advantage, the company should take into account the following important factors:

- Dynamics of the virtual enterprise; that is, the likelihood of changes and competitive attacks in a certain period of time (for example, compare the computer and mining industry)
- Interrelationships between the given and other virtual enterprises in the company's global industrial infrastructure (identify the commonalities of strategies in different virtual enterprises)
- Flexibility of a competitive strategy and its adaptability to change
- Ease of implementing the competitive strategy

The process of formulating the CSOs require the following input information:

- Generic strategic objectives (GSO). I call them generic because each enterprise has these three objectives in decreasing order of importance: quality measured as the degree of total customer satisfaction, flexibility measured as the time of reaction to change, and cost-effectiveness measured as the company's profitability. However, each enterprise must interpret these objectives in its own context. Who are the customers, and what do they want, in both the short and the long run? What important changes can be expected? Can the enterprise affect and control them and how? What does it mean to conduct the corporate business cost-effectively? These are just a few questions that must be answered in order to translate GSOs into CSOs.

- Generic competitive strategies. The enterprise has to select the basis on which it will compete. Options include (1) competing on the cost basis, (2) differentiating itself from the competition; and (3) focusing on niche markets and competing in those markets on the cost basis or by differentiation. A theory of generic competitive strategies has been developed by Michael Porter (1985). Criticism of Porter's theory is given in Charles Wiseman's book on SISs (1988).
- Current company state. Company assessment is an effort to understand where the company is now and where it has to be to achieve the GSOs. It is also an effective tool for the senior management education necessary to achieve a consensus about CSOs.

The classic approach to company assessment, a theory of value system and value chain, developed by Michael Porter and described in his book *Competitive Advantage* (1985), provides only an initial framework rather than a comprehensive solution to the company assessment problem.

The ultimate solution is to build a formal enterprise model (FEM). The FEM should represent all activities and their interrelationships along with intra- and inter-corporate product, information, and transaction flows (see Interlude 5-1). Once developed, the FEM will be used by corporate management as a simulation tool to play "what-if" games regarding resource allocation, implications of critical decisions, cost reduction, and alternative scenarios of the future.

- Customer requirements. Nothing is more important than gathering feedback from the enterprise's customers and understanding the current state and future trends in the customer industry. The results of customer requirements analysis form the core of CSOs.
- Industry structure. Forces driving industry competition are presented in the virtual enterprise scheme (FIG. 1-3). An analysis of these forces is important for the following reasons:

  a. It shows basic strengths and weaknesses of the enterprise relative to the entire industry.
  b. It shows how industry trends can affect the enterprise's current position.
  c. It gives clues as to how the company can take advantage of the current situation in the industry.

    d. It determines the scope of appropriate strategies and defensive or offensive action programs.

    e. It shows whether the enterprise can influence the virtual enterprise's forces to its advantage and how.

A theory of competitive forces that shape the industry structure has been developed by Michael Porter (1985).

- Analysis of competitors. Business intelligence is a powerful and mandatory management tool that has been used for a long time by trading companies, including the Japanese "sogo shosha" (Mitsubishi, Mitsui, Sumitomo, etc.) (Meyer 1987). Its function is to sort out, collect, and package relevant information about:

    a. What is going on in the virtual enterprise

    b. What is likely to happen to the enterprise in the near future

    c. Events that can potentially affect the virtual enterprise and thus change CSOs

    d. Plausible consequences of, and reactions to, the enterprise's actions in the virtual enterprise and how the enterprise must prepare itself for these reactions

Getting CSOs: an iterative process

Unfortunately, it is impossible to take the six inputs in the previous section, put them into some magic equation, and get CSOs as an output. The CSO formulation process involves judgmental reasoning and is intrinsically iterative. Given an initial set of CSOs, iterations are driven by three studies that have to be done by the company in order to formulate final CSOs:

- Feasibility study, which answers the question: "Are the currently analyzed CSOs attainable?" The feasibility study uses the results of the company's current state assessment and generic competitive strategies as its inputs. The essence of the feasibility study is to eliminate unrealistic CSOs and to obtain reasonable estimates of the resources that have to be allocated to achieve realistic ones as soon as possible or as planned.
- Completeness study, which answers the question: "Are the currently analyzed CSOs those that the market demands us to achieve?" The completeness study uses customer requirements as its main input. The rationale behind the completeness study is to make sure that all customer requirements are accounted for in CSOs and the corporate strategic plan.
- Adequacy study, which answers the question: "Will achievement of the currently analyzed CSOs provide us with a competitive advantage?" The adequacy study is based on the results of competitive analysis. The rationale behind the adequacy study is to make sure that all the CSOs

are analyzed in the context of global competition. It makes no sense to set CSOs whose attainment in two to four years will still leave the company behind its competitors.

Figure 1-8 illustrates an iterative process of CSO formulation. GSOs and the results of an industry structure analysis provide sufficient information to formulate an initial set of CSOs. If the feasibility, completeness, and adequacy studies support the CSOs, the CSOs are approved as inputs for strategic planning. Otherwise, initial CSOs are modified in accordance with the results of the three studies, and another iteration of CSO evaluation begins.

The templates in FIG. 1-5 imply quantitative CSO format (for example, "reduce total inventory by 30 percent in two years"). However, not all CSOs can be expressed this way. Some of them will certainly be in the qualitative format (for example, "improve the corporate image as a provider of high-quality customer service"). Qualitative CSOs are not any worse (or better) than quantitative ones, provided they can be translated effectively into implementable action programs and corporate management is convinced that they effectively support the corporate vision and GSOs.

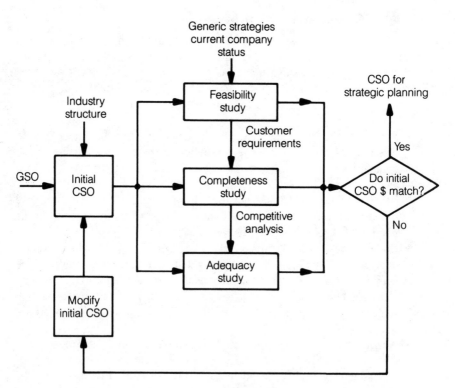

Fig. 1-8. Formulating CSOs is an iterative process.

Selecting CSOs: a negotiation process

The feasibility, completeness, and adequacy studies play an important role in the entire SPPE process. They represent a mechanism for localization of iterations within the CSO formulation process which provides early CSO analysis checkpoints and thus decreases the time span from CSO formulation to strategic plan execution. An undesirable alternative would be to select the initial set of CSOs purely intuitively and then to go through the whole SPPE process only to realize that the selected CSOs are impossible to attain, incomplete, or inadequate.

The three studies take the personal and emotional elements out of the CSO formulation process. As you will see later, both the inputs for the studies and the studies themselves are provided by different individuals and approved on a consensus basis. Actually, CSO selection is a negotiation process fed by the six inputs discussed previously in "Formulating CSOs." Subsequent strategic planning relies heavily on this process.

Organizing the strategic planning process

To provide the strategic planning process that satisfies the four conditions noted in "SPPE Process" earlier in this chapter, a team of people permanently essary. I call this team a *planning task force*. The crucial difference between strategic planning as a permanent and a full-time job should be stressed here. It is unlikely that full-time professional strategic planners can do the job without line people who work actively in their respective professional areas and permanently dedicate part of their time to the strategic planning process as members of the planning task force.

The planning task force must be selected by the chief executive officer (CEO) and should consist of four closely collaborating groups (FIG. 1-9):

- Executive planning group
- Working group
- Business intelligence group
- Outside consultants group

Executive planning group

The executive planning group's functions include:

- Developing an outline of the industry structure through analysis of the global industrial infrastructure
- Determining the set of initial CSOs necessary for the iterative process of getting the final CSOs (FIG. 1-8)
- Directing the working group's activities concerning the development of CSOs, a strategic plan, and action programs

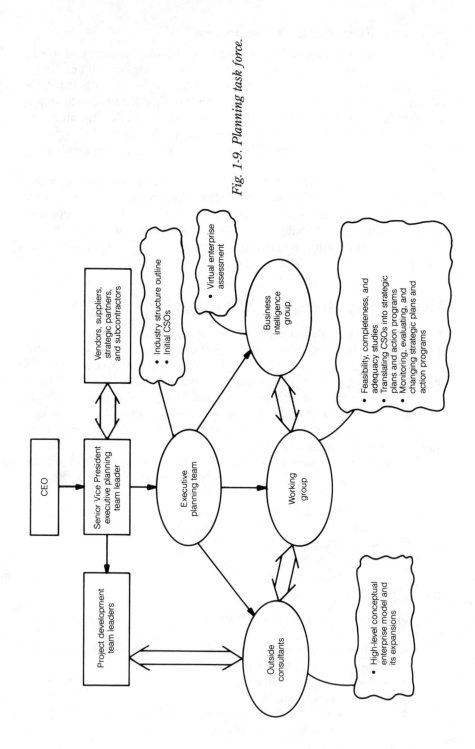

Fig. 1-9. Planning task force.

- Directing the business intelligence group's activities concerning assessments of the company's global industrial infrastructure

The executive planning group has to meet on a regular basis (at least once a month for one day) and may include 5 to 10 key senior managers running or representing major corporate functions, programs, and activities.

Members of the executive planning group should be selected on the basis of:

- Established political power, credibility, and respect within the enterprise
- Knowledge of the enterprise's business
- Openness to, and readiness to learn, new ideas, methodologies, and solutions

The ultimate success of the SPPE process critically depends on who manages the executive planning group. The executive planning group's leader must be at the top corporate level, such as a senior vice president who reports directly to the CEO. However, this person must not be an enforcer. The leader of the group must provide synergy of allocated human and information system resources and create consensus and commitment necessary to make the corporate vision a reality.

In order to accomplish these objectives, the executive planning group's leader should possess the professional qualities of a visionary and trendsetter, an agent of change, a strategic planner, a technology consultant and educator for top management and the board, a translator of business needs and requirements into technological solutions, and a system integrator.

Needless to say, the executive planning group's leader should also possess an unusual combination of personal qualities, including an open conceptual and analytic mind, a broad scope of knowledge, fast learning capabilities, a high energy level, and love for risk taking.

Working group

The working group's functions include:

- Participating in the development of an FEM based on:
  a. Analysis of the product, information, and transaction flows both within the company and across the virtual enterprise
  b. Identification of interrelationships among functional components and corporate activities

- Initiating and participating in competitive analysis efforts undertaken by the business intelligence group
- Performing the feasibility, completeness, and adequacy studies neces-

sary to match initial CSOs against the company's current state, customer requirements, and competition performance and plans (FIG. 1-8)
- Modifying, if necessary, initial CSOs based on results of the feasibility, completeness, and adequacy studies
- Translating resulting CSOs into a strategic plan and then into action programs for each company component
- Proving feasibility and benefits of the strategic plan to the executive planning group and justifying the risks and costs involved
- Selling the strategic plan to employees with the goal of getting early feedback and consensus before the plan is put into action
- Monitoring, evaluating, and (if necessary) changing the strategic plan and action programs

The working group has to meet regularly (at least twice a month for two days per meeting) and should include 10 to 20 members (managers, engineers, system analysts, etc.) who represent major corporate functions, programs, and activities.

Members of the working group should be selected on the basis of:

- Deep knowledge of particular business components and the way they are currently operated
- Eagerness to change the current way of doing business (both mavericks and skeptics should be welcome)
- Balance of experienced veterans and young, aggressive rookies who want to prove themselves
- No participation in political factions or special-interest groups

Business intelligence group

The business intelligence group's functions include:

- Supplying the executive planning group with analyses and recommendations regarding the company's global industrial infrastructure, based on CSOs provided by the executive planning group
- Sending the executive planning group early warning signals about events that require immediate executive interference and actions
- Providing the working group with competitive assessments necessary for developing a strategic plan and action programs
- Collaborating with the working group in monitoring, evaluating, and (if necessary) changing the strategic plan and action programs

Unlike the executive planning and working groups, whose members have to meet on a permanent basis but may also have other responsibilities, the business intelligence group should consist of full-time professionals. A typical business intelligence group may include three to five members (for example, an intelligence professional, an industry watcher and analyst, a market researcher, and an economic forecaster).

Outside consultants group

Functions of the outside consultants group include:

- Initiating, leading, and facilitating the development of an FEM (see "Working Group," earlier in this chapter, and Interlude 5-1)
- Expanding the FEM down to the level of detail required to develop action programs for each company component
- Analyzing the FEM, having in mind the enterprise's simplification, streamlining, and only then automation

The outside consultants group should include two or three outside consultants having combined background in management consulting, operation research, business and data modeling, and structured and object-oriented analysis.

Consensus and commitment

Obtaining consensus and commitment is absolutely indispensable for success of the SPPE process. To obtain consensus about, and commitment to, the set of CSOs outlined in the strategic plan, the planning task force should give the company's employees sufficient time to absorb new ideas in a group environment. Given this time, people will come up with new ideas and better ways of attaining CSOs or implementing the strategic plan and action programs. The planning task force documents have to be considered as straw men for people to study, discuss, and constructively criticize.

Once discussions are over and consensus has been achieved, the chances for genuine corporate-wide commitment to the strategic plan and corresponding action programs are much higher. In turn, obtaining people's commitment builds team spirit, one of the few practical tools capable of breaking through rigid functional and political barriers.

Aggregate strategic plan (ASP)

Once CSOs have been formulated, they can be used as goals in the SPPE process. Thus, a strategic plan describes how the set of CSOs can be attained. Since there may be more than one way to achieve the set of CSOs, a strategic plan conceptually represents a configuration of alternative (but not necessarily mutually exclusive) "hows" for the set of "whats"—that is, CSOs.

Relationships between the sets of CSOs and strategic plans that are to attain these CSOs may be represented by a graph model depicted in FIG. 1-10. (Figure 1-10 shows only one alternative for achieving each CSO.) The set of

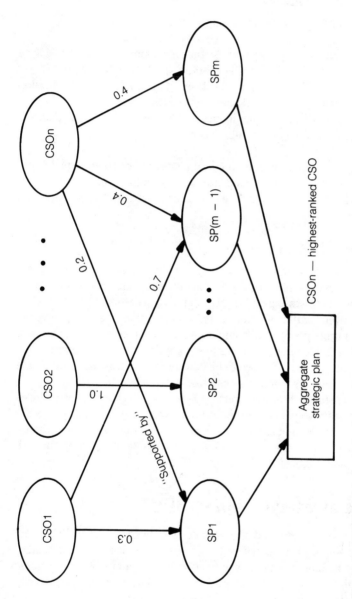

Fig. 1-10. Network of CSOs and strategic plans.

strategic plans, $\{SPj, j = 1, 2, \ldots, m\}$, supports the set of CSOs, $\{CSOi, i = 1, 2, \ldots, n\}$.

Each strategic plan, SPj, $1 \leq j \leq m$, may support some subset of the whole set of CSOs. In FIG. 1-10, for example, $SP(m - 1)$ supports CSO1 and CSOn. Conversely, each CSO, $CSOi$, $1 \leq i \leq n$, may be supported by some subset of the set of strategic plans. In FIG. 1-10, CSOn is supported by SP1, $SP(m - 1)$, and SPm.

The relationship "supported by" is represented by a directed link, L_{ij}, that connects the corporate-specific objective CSOi with the strategic plan SPj contributing to its attainment. The degree of contribution is represented by a number d_{ij}, $0 \leq d_{ij} \leq 1$, attached to the link L_{ij}. In FIG. 1-10 the degree of contribution to CSOn by SP1 is 0.2, by $SP(m - 1)$ is 0.4, and by SPm is 0.4.

We assume that each corporate-specific objective, $CSOi$, $i = 1, 2, \ldots, n$, must be fully supported by some subset of the set of strategic plans. (Otherwise, it would be infeasible.) In other words, the sum of all degrees of contribution to CSOi must be equal to 1.

Some of the CSOs may be conflicting; for example, they may compete for limited resources of money, personnel, or time. Although all CSOs have gone through the feasibility, completeness, and adequacy tests, some of them may be postponed or even excluded because of limited resources available for their attainment. Consequently, two things must be added to the graph model (FIG. 1-10):

- CSOs must be ranked in terms of their relative importance, and CSOs that conflict with CSOs of higher priority must be removed unless other ways of conflict resolution are found. One way or another, the graph model will contain only unconflicting CSOs so that all strategic plans supporting them will be independent or cooperating. In FIG. 1-10 we assume that CSOs are ranked in accordance with their numbers, with CSOn having the highest and CSO1 the lowest rank.
- Each strategic plan, SPj, must be supplied with a rough estimate of the cost necessary to execute it. (Cost estimates are not shown in FIG. 1-10.) Cost estimates can be obtained by analyzing SPj's alternative expansions into an action program and figuring out the cost of each action involved in SPj execution. Figure 1-6 illustrates the expansion of CSO2 into the set of supporting strategic plans, CSP21, ..., CSP2m, and then the expansion of CSP2i into the action program AP2i1, ..., AP2ip.

As mentioned previously, the graph (FIG. 1-10) shows only one possible alternative for achieving each CSO. Strategic planners can build a set of such graphs, each representing such an alternative, or combine all graphs into a single *network* of SCOs and supporting strategic plans. Such a network (FIG. 1-11) includes both an AND-part ("In order to achieve CSOn, SP1 AND SP(m - 1) AND SPm must be executed") and an OR-part ("In order to achieve CSOn, either SP1, SP(m - 1), and SPm OR SP$^{(1)}$1 and SP$^{(1)}$m must be executed").

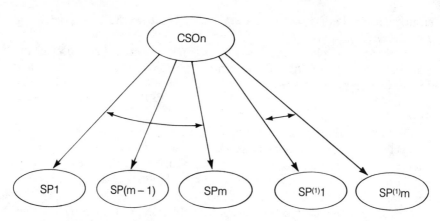

Fig. 1-11. Alternative strategic plans.

After the network of SCOs and supporting strategic plans has been built, the strategic planner can put together an ASP. An ASP is a union of fully utilized and feasible strategic plans. A *fully utilized* strategic plan is a plan that is actually used to support all selected CSOs it can support. A *feasible* strategic plan is a plan that is justified financially through a benefit/risk analysis.

A simple illustration may help to clarify this concept. The corporate-specific strategic objective CSO*n* in FIG. 1-10 is selected first as the highest ranked. Strategic plans supporting it—SP*1*, SP(*m* – *1*), and SP*m*—are selected as components of an ASP. Then CSO*1* may be preferred to CSO*2*, even though the latter has a higher rank, because two out of three already selected strategic plans, SP*1* and SP(*m* – *1*), also support CSO*1*. If we did not select CSO*1*, these two strategic plans would not be fully utilized.

An example of an ASP, adapted from Thomas Gunn's *Manufacturing for Competitive Advantage* is shown in TABLE 1-1. The ASP is further expanded into an action program for each participating corporate component.

Action program

An *action program* is an expansion of the ASP in depth and across all involved corporate components. A single ASP may be expanded into many alternative action programs (FIG. 1-12).

Expansion across corporate components should be determined by the results of the company's assessment, based on the FEM-level analysis. Specifically, actions have to concentrate on:

- Eliminating redundant operations
- Streamlining operations with overcomplicated product, information, and transaction flows
- Finding common activities and operations as a basis for sharing

Table 1-1. Example of a Strategic Plan.

CSOs	Strategic Plan
Reduce quality costs from 10% of sales to: • 5% in one year • 1% in three years	Integrate design engineering and manufacturing engineering functions. Improve production equipment accuracy and availability. Implement and install statistical quality control program in production.

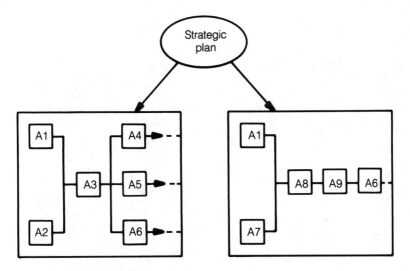

Fig. 1-12. Alternative action programs for a strategic plan.

- Educating and training management and staff
- Developing new methodologies, policies, and procedures
- Promoting automation after simplification

An example of the action program corresponding to the CSO and ASP in TABLE 1-1 is given in TABLE 1-2, adapted from Thomas Gunn's *Manufacturing for Competitive Advantage*.

There is a big difference between (1) approaching the expansion of the ASP into an action program as a conceptual process aimed at understanding the available ASP execution options and their cost (with feedback to cost estimates of strategic plans comprising the ASP); and (2) approaching the expansion of the ASP into an action program as an ASP execution process. While the second approach must be deferred as much as possible, the first one should be encouraged as a necessary part of the SPPE process.

Table 1-2. Example of an Action Program.

CSOs	Strategic Plan	Action Program
Reduce quality costs from 10% of sales to: • 5% in one year • 1% in three years	Integrate design engineering and manufacturing engineering functions.	Develop and install an intelligent computer-aided design system that supports design for manufacturability in fabrication. Introduce group technology for all major fabricated parts. Develop a knowledge-based process planning system. Reorganize product and process design functions within the company. Train design and process engineers to use a new methodology and systems. Improve production equipment accuracy and availability. Replace production equipment repair with preventive maintenance. Develop diagnostic expert systems for all critical units of production equipment. Eliminate production bottlenecks. Underutilize critical units of production equipment. Implement and install statistical quality control program in production. Launch an education and training program in statistical quality control. Certify gauging and measuring tools. Allow a "stop work until fixed" program. Introduce Taguchi methods to reduce the degree of variability for part sizes.

Deferring ASP execution is essential as the most effective way of coping with permanent changes in the virtual enterprise. Viewing the expansion of the ASP into an action program as a conceptual process should be encouraged for the following reasons:

- Senior management must understand the amount of money, time, effort, and cultural changes necessary to implement the ASP.
- Each corporate component that will be involved in ASP execution must understand what it is supposed to do in which alternative action program, how it is going to do that, and in what time frame.
- As a result of such an understanding, each corporate component must commit itself to certain alternative action programs. Commitment is indispensable for successful ASP implementation.

Constraints to actions and how they should be used

After the action programs are put together, constraints to individual actions should be analyzed and taken advantage of. Constraints can be divided into two broad categories: *external* constraints and *internal* constraints. External constraints are the constraints that the enterprise can predict and take into account but cannot fully control or affect. Internal constraints are the constraints that the enterprise can predict, affect, and control.

Examples of external constraints include:

- Industry standards, codes, and regulations
- Market restrictions, such as those determined by cultural factors or imposed by the United States or foreign governments

Examples of internal constraints include:

- Corporate culture
- Social and cultural values
- Organizational structure
- Resource constraints, such as perceived and real financial constraints; shortage of personnel; and shortage of basic management, engineering, manufacturing, and IS skills

A remarkable thing about constraints is that they may not necessarily be obstacles to actions. In some cases constraints may certainly have to be eliminated, if possible. However, in many other cases, constraints may be used to reduce the number of alternative strategic plans and action programs, especially if they cannot be easily controlled or affected.

Here are some recommendations for using constraints to actions to prune or reselect action programs and, if necessary, even ASPs:

- Do not start executing the action program until you understand constraints to planned actions.
- Remember that eliminating or reducing the influence of constraints to actions costs time and money. Estimate the amount of time, money, and effort required.
- Based on constraints to actions, correct (if necessary) your risk/benefit estimates.
- See if one of the alternative action programs is more appropriate than the others in the light of constraint analysis.
- Always approve the action program along with additional actions necessary to eliminate, reduce the influence of, or account for constraints to actions.
- If constraints to actions are difficult to overcome, reconsider the ASP rather than risk the success of the entire SPPE process.

Actions and projects

Each approved action or few closely associated actions make up a project. In order to be successful, a project has to be well defined, limited in scope, and clearly bounded. To achieve this goal, a project description should be developed. In addition to standard project specifications and schedules, a typical project description should include:

- Project goals
- Expected benefits along with explicitly stated assumptions that underlie the expectations
- Cost estimates along with the explicitly stated assumptions that underlie them
- Assessment of possible risks along with contingency actions
- Assessment of basic skills and technologies necessary to implement the project and their current availability
- Estimates of hiring and/or training efforts as well as procurement necessary to acquire basic technologies

As in all previous stages, flexibility is the name of the game. Sufficient flexibility must be built into a project description in order to be able to:

- Change expectations, estimates, and underlying assumptions with minimal damage to investments that already have been made
- Figure out the effect of these changes on entire cost justifications and cash flow requirements across all projects

Assigning priorities to projects

As long as the hierarchical structure of CSOs, strategic plans, and action programs is maintained and monitored on a regular basis, any changes in the global industrial infrastructure, the virtual enterprise, or within the company can be acted upon at the lowest possible level. This is exactly the idea of the "Think Big" part of the "Think Big—Start Small" strategy: to react to an external change with the least possible effort and effect on the ASP and CSOs.

What about the "Start Small" part? It may well be the case that the total number of projects resulting from the strategic planning process will exceed the maximum that can be supported with the enterprise's limited financial and human resources.

The beauty of the hierarchical structure of CSOs, strategic plans, and action programs is that the individual projects may be implemented in a bottom-up, incremental fashion. One will still be able to see a bigger CSO-driven picture and understand the global context of project implementation. Obviously, the situation is different from islands of automation, the brainchild of the infamous "Think Small—Start Small" strategy.

In order to be implemented incrementally, the individual projects have to be assigned relative priorities. Priority assignment rules are determined by the CSO rank and the degree of contribution of the strategic plan to the CSO and are quite straightforward:

- The higher the rank of the CSO supported by a given project, the higher the project's priority.
- The more a given project contributes to CSO attainment, the higher the project's priority.
- Projects that provide a higher ROI in a shorter run are given higher priorities. The idea is that these projects may pay off earlier and provide leverage for longer-term or more expensive projects.

For the CSO with a given rank, starting with the highest one, the set of projects that fully supports it and has the highest total priority is selected for implementation. As soon as the resource estimate for the CSOs selected thus far exceeds the total available resources, the project selection terminates and attainment of lower-ranked CSOs gets postponed.

Planning process

One important corollary of our discussion is that the strategic planning process is much more important than the resulting strategic plan. The strategic plan will imminently change, and even the effects of successful plan execution will never be exactly the same as the planned ones. The real value of a strategic plan is in:

- The experience of its development
- The new horizons people achieve through the education and training necessary to develop and execute the plan
- The process of team building and obtaining consensus and commitment
- Breaking through organizational, political, and turf barriers
- Making the permanent monitoring of strategic plan execution a conventional practice

People who believe that the strategic plan has to be developed quickly and then executed for a long time unchanged are fundamentally wrong. Strategic planning is not a blitzkrieg. It is the sum of planning and plan execution time that really counts. Figure 1-13 illustrates this point.

Hasty planning results in implementation failures, delays, and reworks because the enterprise does not understand well enough what it is really doing and spends too much time in a trial-and-error mode. As a result the corporate vision becomes a reality much later than if enough time were spent in planning, with an obvious effect of more predictable and less risky implementation.

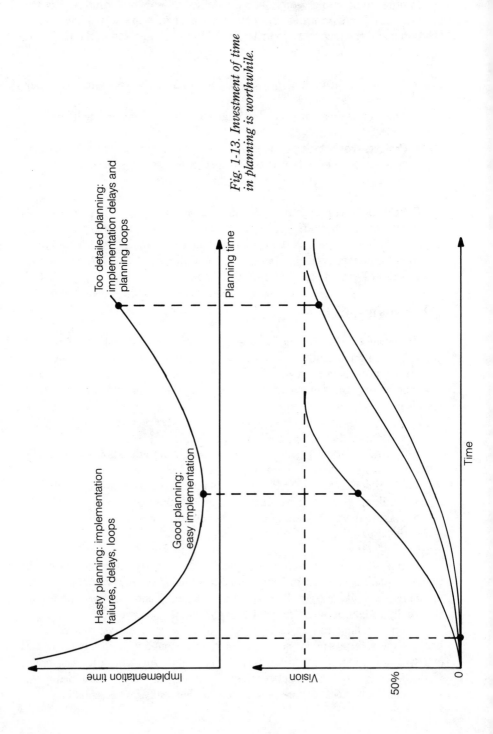

Fig. 1-13. Investment of time in planning is worthwhile.

How much planning is enough? As shown in FIG. 1-13, too much (meaning too detailed) planning is not good either. Like hasty planning, too detailed planning results in implementation delays and reworks, but for another reason. Attempts to predict the future precisely at the detailed level will hardly succeed, and a lot of time will be spent in replanning low-level actions. Most likely, the vision of the future will be lost in the sea of unnecessary detail.

Figure 1-13 shows that an optimal level of planning gives the enterprise general direction and, at the same time, leaves enough freedom and flexibility for it to react to imminent change at the lowest possible level and with the least change in the strategic plan.

The Japanese seem to learn and master the art of optimal planning much better than we Americans. They plan slowly, but more than make up for the initial delays by executing their plans quickly. We can (and must) master this art, too.

If an enterprise is to reap all the benefits of IT, it has to work very hard. "There's many a slip 'twixt the cup and the lip."

Critical success factors

Let us look at the factors that generally affect strategic plans and show how IT can help in their implementation. In his excellent book *Real-World Intelligence*, Herbert Meyer (1987) defines three key factors that characterize our world today:

- Global environment. All businesses operate in the global environment. Transportation, communication systems, modern weapon systems, global scale of banking and manufacturing, and fierce competition for markets and resources, such as labor force and raw materials, all contribute to this factor.
- Change. Change in economy, politics, markets, work force, and technology is actually the only permanent thing we can count on.
- Information glut. Business executives have raw data that have never been available before, and effective management requires information management and refinement.

Thus, in order to compete successfully in today's world, an enterprise must be able to:

- Operate in the global environment
- Adapt to imminent change
- Select information relevant to a current business problem and make proper decisions rapidly

The first ability implies that the enterprise must be integrated, both inside and within its global industrial infrastructure. The second ability implies that the enterprise must be flexible at all levels. The third ability implies that effective and efficient information management is critical to the enterprise's survival and prosperity.

No matter what industry the enterprise is in, or what CSOs it is pursuing, integration, flexibility, and effective and efficient information management must always be considered as three critical success factors and be appropriately reflected in its strategic plans.

Let us look at integration, flexibility, and effective and efficient information management in more detail.

Integration

From the business viewpoint, one may single out three basic kinds of enterprise integration:

- Functional integration, or integration of two or more functional areas within the enterprise. An example of functional integration in the manufacturing industry is integration of design and manufacturing engineering.
- Geographical integration, or integration of dispersed components within the enterprise or its functional area, such as divisions in conglomerates, marketing and sales offices, or field service organizations.
- Interorganizational integration, or integration within the virtual enterprise or even the global industrial infrastructure.

Different kinds of integration may require very different ISs for implementation. As a part of its SPPE process, the enterprise should find out what kind of integration is most critical to meet its SCOs and then implement it.

Flexibility

Two types of flexibility are important to provide corporate adaptability to imminent change. (Compare them with the two types of constraints to actions discussed in "Constraints to Actions and How They Should Be Used" earlier in this chapter.)

- Flexibility necessary to react to a change that the enterprise can predict, affect, and control. Examples include changes in markets, technology, and customer requirements and tastes.
- Flexibility necessary to react to a change that the enterprise can predict and take into account but cannot control or affect. Examples include changes in economy, political situation, and labor force demography.

IT can effectively address both kinds of flexibility. However, in its SPPE effort the enterprise must clearly identify the changes that it deems most important, the ways of affecting and/or predicting these changes, and the degree of flexibility necessary to react to the changes.

Information management

Effective and efficient information management affects both integration and flexibility. Properly planned, executed, and organized information management is the most significant tool for building integration and flexibility into corporate ISs.

Information management includes the following activities:

- Representing and protecting information in an IS
- Determining what information is essential for solving a certain business problem
- Determining where and how to get the information relevant to the business problem
- Disseminating, sharing, interpreting, and processing information necessary to solve the business problem

SIS definition

An information system can be called *strategic* to the extent that it provides integration, flexibility, and effective and efficient information management dictated by its current CSO. With this concept in mind, I define an SIS as an information system that is (1) an inherent part of the business definition (the company's business cannot exist without the SIS); or (2) a prerequisite for the company's long-term survival (the company cannot compete effectively without the SIS); or (3) a prerequisite for the corporate growth or expansion into new markets (the company cannot achieve its CSOs without the SIS).

We can also formulate four main features that distinguish SISs from conventional information systems known as MISs:

- SISs are essentially based on deep understanding of the virtual enterprise and global industrial infrastructure in which the company operates.
- SISs address and affect all three major aspects of corporate business:
  a. Products and services
  b. Internal corporate processes
  c. Relationships with other members of the virtual enterprise
- SISs may determine as well as be determined by CSOs.
- SISs can make a significant impact on the enterprise's competitiveness and bottom line without having to be used directly by top managers. In other words, an SIS is not necessarily an executive information system, and vice versa.

Conclusion

To build SIS that will support the attainment of your company's strategic objectives, you must first address four critical issues:

- How to make the SIS relatively insensitive to imminent changes in strategic objectives and plans, market conditions, IT, and application portfolio.
- Who will design and develop the SIS; that is, which parts will be developed in-house and which will be outsourced or developed by outside contractors.
- How to define the SIS in terms of its ultimate functionality (what the SIS will be able to do) and presentation (how users will interact with the SIS)
- How the resulting system will affect the organization and its human infrastructure

Although these issues are highly interdependent and can hardly be addressed in any specific order or in isolation from each other, each issue implies following a specific set of design philosophies and guidelines.

The problem of sensitivity to changes can be resolved by adhering to the open systems and downsizing philosophies as well as building the SIS on top of the application-independent corporate information infrastructure.

Open systems pursue standardization of increasingly higher-level SIS components, gradually turning them into commodity products. Open systems are discussed in chapter 2.

Downsizing appeared first as an issue of economics: the same computational power can be obtained at a lower cost by moving from mainframes and minicomputers to multiple workstations and PCs connected with a LAN. Most recently, however, downsizing became an issue of a system architecture philosophy and, as such, contributes to building change-insensitive SISs. Downsizing is discussed in chapter 3.

Corporate information infrastructure is an organized collection of information sources, storages, processors, and users, along with communication systems connecting them, that supports CSOs and company operations. The major part of this book (chapters 5 through 14) is dedicated to the corporate information infrastructure.

The in-house vs. outsourcing problem can be resolved by adhering to the system integration philosophy and the set of guidelines on, and conditions for, outsourcing.

System integration is a philosophy of providing turnkey solutions to business problems that cut across the enterprise's functional boundaries. One major part of system integration is the set of guidelines that facilitates users' choice of balance between their own and outside contractors' involvement in SIS development. System integration is discussed in chapter 4.

The SIS design and development problem can be resolved by adhering to the new design philosophy based on software reuse and computer-aided software engineering (CASE) as well as by extensively using new application development technologies, such as intelligent application generation and knowledge-based systems.

Finally, the human infrastructure problem can be resolved through adhering to new personnel development philosophies that close the gap between ISs and employees and affect the organization structure, education and training, work in small groups, incentive and reward systems, and intracorporate communications. Human aspects of SIS are discussed in chapters 15 and 16.

2

Open systems

Executive summary

For many years IS customers were at the mercy of computer vendors that successfully tried to lock them into their proprietary architectures. With the advent of PCs and a significant increase in IS users' level of computer proficiency, the situation is rapidly changing. The IS customer's wish list is diametrically opposite to what the vendor community has nurtured for years and includes the following:

- Integration of a new IS into the installed base of old ones
- Flexibility in selecting vendors and low switching costs if the customer decides to change
- Easy and incremental expandability of existing ISs and applications
- Graceful transition between generations of IT that are replaced too rapidly

To resolve this conflict, customers and vendors had to find a compromise solution: the *open system*.

Open systems are not limited to operating systems or network protocols. They influence the industry progress at all levels of IS components, including software.

Open systems pursue the following goals: (1) standardization of increasingly higher-level IS components, turning them into commodity products; and (2) protection of the IS customer's initial investment in hardware and system/application software. In other words, the center of gravity in IS projects has dramatically shifted from purchasing and putting together various pieces of hardware and system software to developing application software on top of standardized hardware/system software that is easily obtained and installed at a minimal cost.

Open systems have to be well understood because they are championed by IS customers, including United States and European governments, as well as by far-sighted computer vendors. The momentum of open systems is so strong that no serious SIS project can ignore the issues discussed in this chapter.

What is an open system? Few IT concepts cause hotter discussions or obtain more press coverage than open systems. Several international organizations promote them, with Corporation for Open Systems, X/Open Corporation, Open Software Foundation, Unix International, and International Standards Organization (ISO) being the most prominent.

In spite of this publicity (or maybe because of it), the concept of open systems is still poorly understood, and massive confusion prevails. As one example, open systems were defined in *Business Week* (May 23, 1988) as "those that rely on a common set of software that can be easily transferred from one brand of computer to another."

Does this mean that Fortran-77 is an open system just because one can write a program in Fortran-77 on DEC VAX 11/780 and then "easily transfer" it to Cray-2? Are there any differences, then, between open systems and portable software?

Why is "a common set of hardware" not included in the definition? For instance, if an Intel 80386 chip "can be easily transferred" from Compaq's Deskpro to Sun Microsystems' 386i, why don't we call this chip an open system?

Questions like these abound. In this chapter, I will develop a general and, hopefully, unifying concept of an open system, looking first at the conflict between vendors and IS customers as a natural source of open system movement. I will then define an open system and illustrate the concept at different levels of SIS hierarchy. I will proceed with the discussion of potential advantages of open systems and political obstacles to their proliferation. Finally, I will recommend to IS customers some plausible options for now and the foreseeable future.

IS customers against vendors: An intrinsic conflict

One side effect of the IS industry progress over the years has been the growing conflict between hardware/software vendors and their customers. In order to have a growing and stable business, vendors want the following:

- To encourage their customers to go as much as possible for a single-vendor environment
- To lock the customer into the single-vendor solution and thus increase switching costs for the customer and entry barriers for the vendor's competitors
- To expand the customer's existing ISs and applications by offering more hardware and software

- To provide transition between generations of IT through upgrading the customer's installed base and thus further locking the customer into a single-vendor environment

As recently as the early 1980s, customers had practically no other choice than to be at the mercy of computer vendors. The breakthrough came in the mid-1980s. The same microprocessor chips became available to many start-up companies; competition in the vendor community increased significantly; and customers realized that, with many more choices available, they no longer had to be tied to one vendor's proprietary architecture.

With help from such far-sighted vendors as Sun Microsystems, Inc., the customer community formulated its wish list for future ISs and became convinced that it is realistic and implementable. The wish list includes:

- Integration of a new IS into the installed base of old ones
- Flexibility in selecting vendors and low switching costs if the customer decides to change one
- Easy and incremental expandability of existing ISs and applications
- Graceful transition between IT generations that are replaced too rapidly

One can easily see that the customers' wish list is diametrically opposite to what the vendor community has nurtured for years. This conflict is intrinsic to the nature of the computer industry and information systems, and the only way to resolve it is to find a compromise solution equally acceptable to both vendors and their customers. This compromise solution is what I call an *open system*.

The compromise solution, however, is by no means stable. It changes in time, and at any given time is different for different vendors. For example, the compromise solution at IBM or DEC would be very different from the one at NCR or Sun Microsystems.

Thus, the first important feature of an open system is that it is a moving target. Rather than waiting for the advent of a perfectly open system, the customer community has to take advantage of what is available now and will undoubtedly be available a few years from now. At the same time, customers should become more active and influence the course of open system events.

Hierarchy of IS components

The second important feature of an open system is that it is not limited to only operating systems or any other IS component. On the contrary, the open system philosophy permeates all nine hierarchical levels of IS implementation:

- Chips
- Computers

- Operating systems
- Other system software (database management systems, languages, development and performance evaluation tools, etc.)
- Networks
- Software applications (mostly isolated programs)
- Subsystems (software solving a specific facet of the business problem)
- Systems (functional part of entire IS)
- User interface (presentation part of entire IS)

This hierarchy is depicted in FIG. 2-1 with the tenth level added, the level of a business problem that you want to solve in the first place and that is always unique.

Proprietary solutions, de facto standards, and open systems

Let us look at hierarchical levels in FIG. 2-1 in more detail. At the chip level is a spectrum of potential solutions with four points of main interest (listed in increasing order of standardization):

- Proprietary chips, such as reduced instruction set chips (RISC) developed by IBM for RS/6000 or by Hewlett-Packard for its Vectra family.
- Microprocessor chips, such as an Intel 80386 or a Motorola 68030. Many different companies can build their computers based on such a chip. (To name a few, IBM and Compaq use the 80386, while Apple uses the 68030.) Thus, microprocessor chips are less proprietary than proprietary chips. However, a certain chip, such as the 80386, is produced, or at least controlled, by only one company.

    Using a microprocessor chip sometimes (but not always) implies using a certain operating system. For instance, the 68000 series is Unix-oriented, while the 80000 series is MS/DOS-oriented. However, some 80386 computers also run under Xenix, a PC-based version of Unix.
- Memory chips that can be used in any kind of computer—PC, workstation, or mainframe. Since there are several vendors of memory chips, they are less proprietary than microprocessor chips.
- Scalable Processor Architecture (SPARC), a RISC-based architecture proposed by Sun Microsystems that can be implemented in various configurations and semiconductor technologies. At the time of this writing, eight semiconductor companies produce different versions of SPARC, and many SPARC-based systems have been developed or are under development.

Of the four chip solutions, only SPARC deserves to be called a truly open system. (In a somewhat trivial sense, memory is also an open system but by

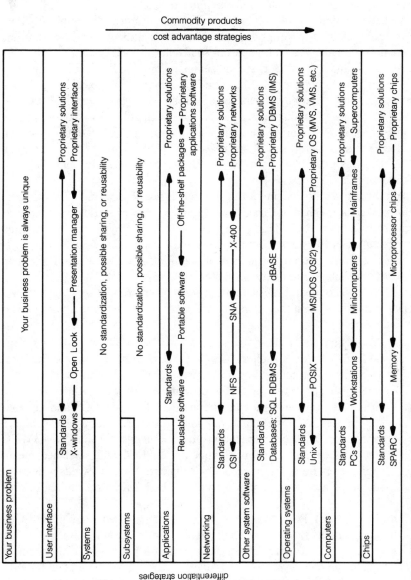

Fig. 2-1. Hierarchy of IS components.

virtue of homogeneous memory structure.) SPARC does not lock its customers, computer vendors, in one company's product and provides potentially easy and unlimited expandability and graceful scalability (transition between generations of semiconductor and computer technologies).

At the computer level, supercomputers, mainframes, and minicomputers have traditionally had proprietary architectures, although IBM mainframe clone makers make this statement not so absolute. Open systems can best be illustrated in the PC and workstation segments of the computer industry.

In the PC segment, Apple Computer's Macintosh is a typical example of a proprietary architecture, while an IBM PC is an open system: an IBM PC customer can choose among a myriad of plug-compatible PC clones, add-on boards, and, most important, a huge portfolio (more than 15,000 application packages and still growing) of application software. With its PS/2 family of PCs, IBM has been trying with some success to "close" an open IBM PC architecture.

In the workstation segment the situation is not so clear-cut. The workstation market is much more fragmented, and open workstation architectures practically do not exist. (One exception is Sun Microsystems' Sparcstation architecture cloned by Soulborne, Inc.) In the workstation segment, open system issues are passed on to the level of operating systems, where Unix is an almost unchallenged candidate for a standard.

At the level of operating systems, there is a spectrum of more or less proprietary solutions, with four points of main interest (listed in increasing order of standardization):

- Proprietary operating systems, such as IBM's MVS and DEC's VMS.
- De facto standards such as MS/DOS, which runs millions of PCs produced by different vendors and tens of thousands of software applications also developed by different vendors. However, there is a big difference between a de facto standard such as MS/DOS and an open system: MS/DOS is still one company's product, and an MS/DOS user cannot port MS/DOS applications to computers other than the IBM PC and plug-compatibles. For the same reason, OS/2 will never become an open system even if millions of OS/2 copies are sold. Obviously, de facto standards are every vendor's dream as both Microsoft and Bill Gates prove.
- IEEE 1003.1 Posix standard, which is actually a toolkit of interface specifications rather than a complete operating system standard.
- Unix, which currently is a de facto standard but has a good chance to become an open system, especially if Open Software Foundation (OSF) and Unix International come to an agreement, which seems unlikely. Unfortunately, the famous line "A good thing about standards is that there are many of them to choose from" still works.

The level of other system software is represented by DBMSs. One can see three levels of standardization:

- Proprietary DBMSs, such as IBM's IMS or Cullinet's IDMS.
- De facto standards, such as dBase III. Note again the difference between a de facto standard and an open system: dBase III is one company's product (although there are dBase III clones), and a dBase III customer can neither port dBase III applications nor move data in dBase III format to other DBMSs.
- SQL-based relational DBMSs. Structured Query Language (SQL) is a standard, and any SQL-based application can theoretically be ported to any SQL-based DBMS. However, the SQL standard is very weak and, as a result, each DBMS vendor has its own SQL "standard." For example, Oracle SQL applications will run on any Oracle DBMS, from a PC-based to a mainframe-based, but will not necessarily run on other vendors' SQL-based DBMSs. Considering the trend, one can argue that an SQL-based relational DBMS will become an open system in a few years.

At the level of networking, there is again a spectrum of available solutions with four points of interest:

- Proprietary networks, such as DECNet.
- Partial standards, such as the standard for file transfer, access, and management (FTAM) or electronic mail (X.400).
- De facto standards, such as IBM's System Network Architecture (SNA) or Sun Microsystems' Network File System (NFS). SNA, which has been installed in more than 30,000 sites all over the world, is a typical de facto standard that every vendor and customer must reckon with. NFS has all chances to become an open system for additional distributed processing capabilities. At the time of this writing, more than 250 vendors and universities worldwide have licensed the NFS protocols.
- OSI, an international standard currently under development. Once completely developed, it will become an open system at the level of networking. However, at the time of this writing, OSI is no more than a set of guidelines and protocols. Two subsets of OSI, each conforming to the OSI standard, may not work together. To avoid this problem, the United States Government has developed GOSIP, a set of guidelines for determining the compatibility of OSI subsets.

At the level of applications, the establishment of a genuine open system is so difficult that it is mostly an unsolved research problem. Currently, we can see four levels of standardization:

- Proprietary application software. Today, almost all application software is of this kind.
- Off-the-shelf application packages. For some widely used applications, such as payroll and accounting, off-the-shelf application packages from several vendors are available; however, some package customization is almost always required.
- Portable software. Establishing an open system at the level of operating systems and DBMSs opens the possibility to port application software from one computer to another. However, software portability does not make an open system because application software would still be one company's product. Some portable software can achieve a status of de facto standard, as the number of its copies sold exceeds a critical mass.
- Reusable software. With the ability to be used across different, usually unforeseen, applications written by different software developers in different languages, and run under different operating systems and on different computers, software will become a genuine open system. Unfortunately, we are still a long way from the time when reusable software is widely available.

Finally, at the level of user interface, we can see three levels of standardization:

- Proprietary interfaces, such as the Apple Macintosh interface.
- De facto standards, such as IBM's Presentation Manager or Microsoft Windows.
- X-Windows, a de facto standard developed by Massachusetts Institute of Technology (MIT) and approved and adopted by scores of computer vendors. X-Windows will become an open system, but in a sense specific for user interfaces. Since the user interface is as unique as a business problem, an open system at the level of user interface is a toolkit that can be used to build an application-specific user interface.

From this brief overview, you can see that an open system is not a well-defined concept. It is an almost religious movement that pursues the following common goal:

> *To standardize increasingly higher-level system components and thus turn them into commodity products.*

This goal may be pursued on a variety of hierarchical levels. Understanding the chart in FIG. 2-1 that represents this hierarchy is strategically important for both vendors and customers of ISs. From both perspectives an open system is the highest hierarchical level in FIG. 2-1 at which the customer is not yet locked into the vendor solution.

Open systems do (or will soon) bring standardization to at least five lowest levels; that is, customers will be able to obtain the same hardware, system software, and networks from many vendors at the lowest possible price because open systems turn them into commodities. If this happens, how will customers be able to differentiate their SISs from the other SISs to gain a competitive advantage?

To answer this question, let us look one more time at FIG. 2-1. Its top hierarchical level states that "your business problem is always unique." You can see that there is a break of continuity somewhere between the top level, where no standardization is possible, and the five lowest levels, at which standardization is not only possible, but has been or will soon be done.

Thus, the trend in IS development has shifted dramatically from purchasing and putting together various pieces of hardware and system software as a major part of the project, then developing proprietary application software, to developing the application software as a major part of the project on top of standardized hardware/system software that is easily obtained and installed at a minimal cost.

The important conclusion is: To gain a competitive advantage through a strategic use of IT, the company has to:

- Secure highly productive application software development staff, whether by hiring and nurturing it in-house or by carefully selecting and closely working with an outside contractor
- Supply the application software development staff with the newest design methodologies and the best possible development tools to reduce the development life cycle and thus retain a sustainable competitive advantage for a longer period of time (see Interlude 1-2).

Without these two components, all your good intentions to gain a competitive advantage through an SIS will likely be futile.

The next two sections discuss the reasons why both IS customers and vendors should support the open system movement.

Why open systems? The customer's viewpoint

Why should you embrace the concept of open systems if you are an IS customer? The short answer is: "Because at any point in the customer IS's life cycle, open systems provide the closest fit with the customer wish list given previously ("IS Customers Against Vendors: An Intrinsic Conflict")." Let us discuss this answer in more detail.

The first major advantage of open systems for customers is that they get more certainty in planning the development of large-scale systems, such as

SISs, and migration among successive generations of technology. This certainty is especially important in the case of SISs because the SIS life cycle may encompass 5 to 15 years (or even more; consider American Airlines' Sabre first developed in 1961) so that protection of an initial investment in hardware and system and application software may be of paramount importance.

The SIS customer may be fairly confident that this investment is protected all the way up to the highest level in the hierarchy of IS components at which the system is still open. This confidence is based on a well-defined path of updates and upgrades of, or additions to, existing hardware and software, including even a complete switch from one vendor to another.

The second major advantage of open systems is that switching costs are greatly reduced so that replacement of one vendor with another will be relatively easy, inexpensive, and certainly not as painful as it is today. In fact, with the advent of open systems, customers will never again be locked into one vendor's proprietary environment.

Two immediate consequences will result when customers are no longer at the mercy of a single vendor:

- The level of customer service by the vendor will certainly go up. The open systems market is permanently a buyer's market, and vendors will fight for the customer.
- The price of hardware and software products at the open system level will inevitably go down as these products gradually turn into commodities and competition among vendors becomes more ferocious. At low hierarchical levels in FIG. 2-1, such as PCs, we will be witnessing price wars a la McDonalds vs. Burger King.

Suppose, however, that for one reason or another, the customer does not want to switch to another vendor. The customer is a winner anyway. The reason is that multivendor environments are a political reality as well as an economically and technically justified necessity rather than a historical mishap. Customers will incrementally enhance their computational resources and software in a cost-effective way without having to marry a single vendor or to be concerned about such things as compatibility, portability, and the like. Customers will also be able to provide better utilization of their IS resources through network computing, that is, execution of application software by the set of dynamically allocated, currently free or underutilized, and most cost-effective computer network nodes.

The third major advantage of open systems for customers is reduction of customized software development costs. The reduction comes from at least two sources:

- Hiring and training expenditures will go down. A major pool of programmers will develop their application programs under a standard operating system, against standard databases, and, in the more distant future, will also take advantage of huge libraries of standard reusable application software. They will learn all of these standards in a college, and the amount of additional education and training required will be insignificant.

- Program development productivity will go up, while quality assurance, support, and maintenance expenditures will go down as a result of standardization of operating systems, other systems software, and especially application software and user interface.

Why open systems? The vendor's viewpoint

Customers seem to be sure winners in the open systems game. Unfortunately for vendors, this statement cannot be said about all of them. Some will win, while others will lose—and lose big. The stakes for vendors are very high. Thus, it comes as no surprise that the game will be highly politicized, and political considerations will often prevail over common sense and logic. Although virtually all vendors claim that they promote open systems for the sake of their customers, that claim may not always be true. Let us look at the current situation in the computer vendor camp and some plausible future alternatives.

Vendors are not created equal, and open systems are a great leveler. In other words, first-tier vendors that have established their position at the top by selling highly proprietary hardware and system software must oppose or at least resist the open systems movement no matter what they publicly say. IBM and DEC fall into this category.

You might think that first-tier vendors should sincerely support open systems because open systems turn hardware and system software into commodity products. Don't giants have a better chance to survive and prosper in the commodity market because of economies of scale and their unique ability to provide low-cost, high-volume manufacturing? If so, they could have blown away their less fortunate competitors because of their cost advantage and hence should have been pleased with open systems.

The catch is that neither IBM nor DEC wants to be in the commodity market. To win it would be a Pyrrhic victory because they should have forgotten their handsome profit margins once and forever. From the profit margin viewpoint, open systems threaten to turn first-tier computer vendors into department stores such as Sears or Kmart.

As a result, first-tier computer vendors have no other choice than to resist or at least delay open systems as much as they can. Unfortunately for them, they can exert only a limited influence on the market. For example, it would be politically suicidal for IBM and DEC to put their proprietary architectures head-on against open systems, as if to say publicly that they want to keep holding their customers the hostages of proprietary hardware and systems software.

The second best alternative for first-tier computer vendors after proprietary hardware and system software is standards based on their products or de facto standards. A huge installed base of products, new architectural initiatives such as IBM's SAA, and such organizations as Open Software Foundation (both IBM and DEC are its founding members) all provide this alternative for IBM and DEC. Speaking of Open Software Foundation, one must clearly understand that if such archrivals as IBM and DEC are doing something together, there must be a very strong reason. In this case the reason is an attempt to control (and perhaps to delay) the open systems process at the level of system software and user interface.

Unlike IBM and DEC, second-tier computer vendors such as Unisys, NCR, Honeywell-Bull, and Olivetti have no other choice than to vehemently support open systems. As mentioned previously, open systems are a great leveler, and the only way these companies can compete with and take some market share back from IBM and DEC is to promote open systems actively.

For the same reason, workstation vendors such as Sun Microsystems and Hewlett-Packard (HP) actively support open systems. Sun Microsystems has even become an initiator of the open system movement at the level of chips, operating systems, networks, and user interfaces.

Of course, second-tier computer and workstation vendors clearly understand that open systems lead to a commodity-like computer market. They also understand that open systems will result in lower prices and profit margins. Thus, their only hope is further penetration of computers in all areas of our life and business and, as a result, higher sales in their respective markets.

It is hard to say if such hope is completely justified. On one hand, Sun Microsystems, one of the most successful and thriving computer companies in history, is at the same time a company with the lowest profit margins in the computer industry. On the other hand, there may not be enough room for another dozen companies, some of them significantly larger than Sun. It is relatively easy to predict a bloody war at the low end of the workstation market, where Sun may be challenged not so much by IBM, DEC, or HP as by Apple and Compaq.

As follows from FIG. 2-1, the only way to preserve today's margins is to go up in IS component hierarchy; that is, get involved in the application software and eventually system development and integration business. That is why IBM, DEC, and AT&T are trying to become major players in the system integration business, while HP, Sun Microsystems, and Apple demonstrate their presence in it.

Having hundreds of dedicated third-party software vendors, as Sun currently has, may no longer be enough. With the advent of open systems, third-party software vendors may also be dedicated to any other open systems vendor. By the nature of an open system, third-party software will run on any hardware that supports open system standards.

Who is pushing open systems?

The open systems movement has several powerful supporters. First, the hardware and system software vendors have a vested interest in open systems. As mentioned in the previous section, such companies as Sun Microsystems, AT&T, Unisys, NCR, and HP actively support open systems.

Second, United States and European governments actively support open systems. The U.S. Government, a $17 billion-a-year IS user, actively promotes Unix and OSI as an open systems solution at the level of operating systems and networks, respectively. The European Commission already requires open system software for all government computer bids.

Third, some very big IS users and system integrators, such as Boeing and General Motors, really want standards and support proliferation of open system standards as well as actively participate in their creation. Strangely enough, many IS users are fairly indifferent to open systems. Unless IS users become active and say what their requirements are and in what direction the open systems movement should go, they will get only a limited edition of open systems: open systems, vendor style. And it may not be the same as open systems, customer style.

Here are the major reasons—some of them well justified—why IS users still play a relatively passive role in the open system movement:

- Many users remain loyal to their vendors, often for a good reason.
- The largest installed base of business are IBM sites, where users are more conservative and pick a "wait-and-see" tactic.
- Open systems are not on the top of their priority list (for example, many users are more concerned about connectivity).
- Immediate conversion from proprietary architectures to open systems is prohibitively expensive and economically unjustified.
- Many users are concerned that standardization implies reducing the level of technology to the least common denominator.
- Some major standards are claimed and talked about a lot, but not really implemented.

Problems with open systems

Two problems with open systems are commonly cited by their opponents:

- Open systems compromise security because they offer greater portability, interoperability, scalability, and information sharing. OSF defines portability, interoperability, and scalability as follows:

  a. Portability: the ability to run application software on computers from different vendors.

    b. Interoperability: the ability for computers from different vendors to work together.

    c. Scalability: the ability to host the same software environment on a wide range of computer platforms, from PCs to supercomputers.

- Open systems bring standardization and thus impede innovation because innovation is always deflection from standards.

Let us briefly discuss these problems.

Open systems and security

Greater portability, interoperability, scalability, and information sharing should be balanced with security requirements. Unfortunately, these elements are not always balanced properly, and security breaches result. The most common violations of security include:

- Porting uncertified software that may turn out to be infected
- Sending private or sensitive information across the computer network without necessary precautions, such as encryption
- Providing weak protection of computers and the network from the spread of viruses
- Allowing too much freedom in accessing privileged information and programs

Historically, security has had a lower priority than other technological developments, especially in Unix environments, a major stronghold of open systems. For example, in a recent survey of Unix users, security was not even mentioned as a problem, although Unix is not known as the least vulnerable operating system.

Indeed, the fact of life is that open systems have increased vulnerability. However, treating security as one of the major IS design considerations can eliminate many problems that should not have occurred in the first place. Developing an open system first and only then providing its security is a common and serious mistake that can be easily avoided.

Another common mistake is to consider security as a component rather than a system problem. The most secure operating system will not help much if security measures are not provided and enforced at the database level; nor will the secure operating system with effective security measures help in a distributed system that has an insecure computer network.

We will discuss security in more detail in chapter 14.

Open systems and innovation

Since open systems pursue standardization, the conflict between open systems and innovation is intrinsic and inevitable. It may be resolved only by looking at open systems as a dynamic rather than static process.

Standards always lag behind an advanced technology and, unfortunately, usually catch up with it at the time it becomes mature, if not obsolete. For SISs that are designed to gain a competitive advantage, the time factor in using the advanced technology is so critical that the existing standards may be completely ignored just because they are still immature. By the time standards become mature, the strategic use of the specific technology is an open secret. Similarly, high-payoff applications are more often ad hoc and proprietary than standardized.

The resolution of this conflict between standardization and innovation comes from understanding that the most innovative and strategically important systems still have to be developed on top of standards in the areas that are well established and not crucial for innovation. Conversely, today's innovation is tomorrow's standard, provided that the innovation has proved itself successful. These two processes must coexist, complement each other, and be well managed if the enterprise is to reap benefits of standardization and innovation at the same time.

Conclusion

From this chapter you may have gotten overoptimistic expectations that open systems are available today, or at least will appear very soon, maybe tomorrow. Such expectations are naive. First, open systems will not happen overnight. Think of open systems as a process of "opening" information systems—a process that is intrinsically gradual, incremental, and in some cases even painful.

Second, this process is highly politicized by its many participants, who may have different vested interests in how it will proceed, what results it will have, and when these results will occur. IS users, major beneficiaries of open systems, must play an active role in this process if they are to gain all the advantages of open systems.

Third, in order for open systems to materialize, standards at different hierarchical levels must be implemented rather than only claimed or discussed. Many standards for open systems should be discussed and agreed upon in meetings of international standards organizations, such as the ISO or Comite Consultatif International de Tèlègraphique et Tèlèphonique (CCITT). This process automatically means years of discussion; thus both the vendor and user communities are doomed forever to working with incomplete or temporary standards.

As a result of these factors, some skeptics do not even expect radical changes in the implementation of open systems until the next century (which is not that distant). My optimistic view is that we will see implemented open systems by 1995. In order to accomplish this goal, however, IS customers have to be prepared today.

3

Downsizing

Executive summary

Downsizing is a process of entire or partial application migration from larger computers to smaller ones. In addition to economical considerations, downsizing is driven by the changing role of users, IS organizations, and mainframes.

End users are getting more autonomy in acquiring or developing and using ISs of their choice while IS organizations should facilitate the transition to such autonomy, simultaneously shifting their power base in the direction of acquiring or designing and managing corporate networks of downsized distributed computational resources. The role of a mainframe is changing in the direction of greater and deeper involvement in information management functions, including not only data but also knowledge, text, and image management.

Downsizing is not without its problems. Three issues must be addressed in any downsizing effort:

- Cost benefit calculations. Direct cost comparisons may be difficult to make because downsizing brings new costs that do not exist in the mainframe or minicomputer environment. These costs have to be identified and accounted for before the downsizing effort starts.
- Technology implementation. Since downsizing lends itself to distributed architecture, it brings new technological problems that are easier to solve in the old mainframe- or minicomputer-based environment. These problems have to be identified and understood. The cost of solving these problems has to be taken into account as well.
- Organization of a downsizing process. Downsizing must be considered as an intrinsic part of the SPPE process described in chapter 1. It implies several critical success factors, such as encouraging end-user autonomy, obtaining commitment for both senior and line management,

implementing the downsizing effort in the larger context of an information infrastructure, and having all necessary human resources.

Downsizing is not a panacea; and there are certainly some cases in which it is not recommended—where a good old mainframe is still king.

General characterization

Downsizing is a process of entire or partial application migration from larger computers to smaller ones. For example, downsizing may be from a mainframe to a minicomputer (such as from IBM 3090 to AS/400—something IBM hates to see) or, more often, from a mainframe or minicomputer to a network of workstations and PCs. A typical downsizing approach is to put together a *client/server architecture*; that is, a LAN connecting user workstations (clients) and a file, database, or computational resource (server) commonly shared by all clients (see chapter 6 for more information on client/server architectures).

Although the original reason for downsizing was purely economical (see next heading, "Economics of Downsizing"), other factors affect the downsizing trend to no lesser degree. With the advent of PCs and, as a result, end-user computing, three major trends encourage corporate downsizing efforts:

- Changing role of the mainframe. Rather than the only choice for IS implementation, the mainframe appears more as a big, fast server. Although at first glance the mainframe seems to have limited use, its role is changing in the direction of greater and deeper involvement in information management functions. These functions include not only data, but also knowledge, text, and image management (see chapters 6 and 10 for more discussion of this topic).
- Changing role of IS organizations. Rather than an IS "czar" running the whole show, the IS organization appears as a technology transfer facilitator and an end-user supporter. Again, at first glance, the IS organization seems to have a diminishing role in the enterprise when, in fact, it is only shifting from running and controlling every computational resource to running and controlling the entire network of multiple distributed and independently operated computational resources. Some IS organizations even go to such extremes (which I by no means recommend) as trying to regain control of distributed computational resources (PCs) through seizing wide area networks (WAN) and LANs.
- Changing role of end users. Rather than being passive customers of IS organizations, end users appear more as agents of change. They become more technologically proficient and eloquent in expressing their needs. Most end users also welcome the opportunity to manage their information and systems as well as their people and projects.

The bottom line is that end users are getting more autonomy in acquiring or developing and using ISs. In turn, IS organizations should facilitate the transition to such autonomy, simultaneously shifting their power base in the direction of acquiring or designing and managing corporate networks of downsized distributed computational resources.

Economics of downsizing

Facts concerning the economics of downsizing include:

- The cost of one million instructions per second (mips) on a PC is 150 to 200 times less than on a mainframe.
- The cost of one megabyte (MB) of memory on a PC is 10 to 15 times less than on a mainframe.
- The cost of 1 MB of disk storage on a PC is two times less than on a mainframe.
- The disk transfer rate on a PC is only three times slower than on a mainframe (although it may be critical for some applications).
- The speed of a LAN is of the same order of magnitude as the mainframe channel speed; and with proliferation of fiberoptic LANs, the current balance will certainly shift in favor of LANs and, consequently, downsizing.
- The cost of one line of developed application code on a PC is 2 to 30 times less than on a mainframe.
- Off-the-shelf PC software is more affordable (in terms of price and availability) than mainframe software.

Although these figures speak for themselves, throwing mainframes away overnight and buying a bunch of workstations and PCs instead would be a big mistake fatal to a downsizing missionary's career. The next section explains why.

Problems and pitfalls

There are at least three classes of problems to be solved or pitfalls to be avoided if the enterprise is to succeed in its downsizing effort.

Cost/benefit calculations

Direct cost comparisons may be difficult to make because downsizing brings new costs that do not exist in the mainframe or minicomputer environment, such as:

- Cost of workstation and PC support
- Cost of LAN installation, support, and maintenance

- Cost of training old or hiring new field service technicians (more technicians are likely required)
- Cost of centralized network management

In addition to new costs, there will certainly be a shift of operating costs from the centralized corporate IS organization to new owners of the downsized systems (divisions and departments). This shift may become not only a cost, but also a psychological factor that should be taken into account.

Before making a final downsizing decision, think through all its consequences, conceptualize new cost factors, establish new support and maintenance policies and procedures, and estimate their impact on total cost benefits.

Technology implementation

Downsizing brings new technological problems that are easier to solve in the old mainframe- or minicomputer-based environment. These problems include:

- Information recovery is harder to implement as the concept of a state of computation becomes more difficult to define in a distributed environment.
- Information integrity and consistency are harder to enforce, especially if the same information may be concurrently updated in several client sites.
- Information security is harder to provide because of more points of potential security violation.
- Workstation- or PC-based operating systems with multitasking capabilities, such as Unix and OS/2, may be required; but necessary applications running under these operating systems may not be available.
- Increased end-user autonomy and resulting multivendor environment demand solving problems such as basic connectivity, LAN internetworking, and network management.

Some solutions to these problems should be found and assessed from the implementation cost viewpoint before a final downsizing decision is made.

Organization of a downsizing process

As I stated earlier in this chapter, downsizing is much more than just replacing larger computers with smaller ones, and the economics of downsizing is only one of the several factors driving it. Downsizing must not be done for its own sake but, rather, should be considered as an intrinsic part of the SPPE process described in chapter 1. This statement implies several critical success factors:

- Encouraging end-user autonomy should be part of the ASP and corresponding action programs.

- Commitment to downsizing should be obtained from both senior management and those who will be in charge of, and accountable for, the resulting downsized systems (typically line managers).
- The downsizing effort should be considered in the context of a corporate information infrastructure (see chapter 5) and by no means in isolation from other infrastructure-related endeavors.
- Human resources necessary and sufficient to accomplish the downsizing effort, including a downsizing project team, should be fully available. The project team should perform these functions:

  a. Maintain the resulting downsized systems
  b. Train end users
  c. Administer information in downsized systems and provide proper information management functions, such as crash recovery, integrity and consistency preservation, and security protection

Downsizing cannot be torn apart from the corporate organizational structure. Downsizing will be a complete success if it becomes the beginning of the larger effort, creating a work group environment that emphasizes information sharing and exchange and then replacing a rigid hierarchical organizational structure with the flexible structure of small, project-oriented work groups. Needless to say, this entire effort may take two to four years to accomplish and must be an intrinsic part of the SPPE process.

One final remark should be made about the tactics of downsizing. It must not be an all-or-nothing proposition. In fact, downsizing should be considered as a sequence of downsizing projects. The first downsizing project must be successful and thus should be selected on the basis of the following criteria:

- It should be relatively small and implementable in no more than four to six months.
- Applications that run on a downsized system should be contained within one department and relatively free of interdepartmental relationships and dependencies.
- The impact of these applications on the overall corporate performance should be relatively insignificant.

As the experience of downsizing grows, subsequent projects may be increasingly difficult in terms of their size and cross-departmental interdependencies and interrelationships.

WAR STORY 3-1. DOWNSIZING AT ECHLIN, INC.

The story of downsizing at Echlin, Inc. has become a classic. Echlin, a $1.3-billion automotive manufacturer, is a decentralized company with approximately 50 divisions across the United States. In the three-year process, "it replaced its mainframe, which performed all data processing tasks at its corporate headquarters with microcomputers on a local area network" (*MIS Week*, June 19, 1989). As a result of this project, end-user applications were enhanced, while the MIS department saved about $800,000 in 1989.

According to Steven Gold, then Echlin's manager of systems development and now a downsizing consultant, most problems he encountered during the downsizing project were political rather than technical. The good news was that the project was approved by the chairman of the board, based "primarily on reductions of MIS department costs" which were estimated at $300,000 a year.

The bad news was the end-user resistance. Gold said that "the push toward end-user computing with the accompanying goal of reducing the size of MIS was being promoted by MIS and opposed by the end user" (*MIS Week*, June 19, 1989).

End users resisted downsizing for two reasons. The first was a sort of "not invented here" syndrome. The idea of downsizing came from MIS and was supposed to reduce its costs. Users were not sure that they would have any benefits. The second reason was just emotional: the mainframe replacement idea seemed to be a little bit crazy.

MIS dealt with this resistance in two ways. First, no step was made without end-user approval. In particular, end users saw and were convinced that the new system performed better than the old one. Second, the MIS downsizing team smoothed the transition by providing either better or "identical, not just equivalent" functionality.

The downsizing effort started according to a somewhat typical scenario. Steven Gold noticed that "a new under-$5,000 80286-based PC/AT being considered for purchase had 1.45 mips, while that of the $500,000 mainframe (IBM 4341, H.E.F.) was no more than 0.6 mips." As a result of a three-year, $750,000 downsizing project, IBM 4341 had been sold for parts, and all applications run on a Novell LAN consisting of:

- Four Novell servers, two 6800 S-NETs, and two 386-based servers with about 1.1 Gbytes of disk storage
- 60 PCs, including 15 Compaq 386s, 25 IBM PC/ATs, and 20 PCs or OS/2 Model 25s

The major cost component was the rewriting of mainframe application programs. The task took about 10 man-years of effort, mostly because it was impossible to find acceptable off-the-shelf software packages. Another, somewhat unexpected, problem was the "nearly total staff turnover since the conversion began" (*MIS Week*, June 19, 1989).

When not to downsize

There are four special situations in which downsizing may not be recommended:

- Storage requirements are huge. For example, more than 1400 of the biggest IBM disk drives used in American Airlines' Sabre, the air ticket reservation system, is the reason for not even dreaming of its downsizing. At the same time, if the required storage is a few gigabytes, downsizing may be recommended. (In the Echlin story, 1 Gbyte was consumed by the IBM 4341 operating system only, so the downsized system provided more efficient use of storage.)

- A large number of users demand simultaneous access to information or an application. The magic number is estimated at 100 or more. At the same time, if a number of users, say 25, utilize the entire mainframe power, downsizing should be recommended because the same performance can be obtained for much less.
- A huge amount of information should be moved at the same time. In the downsized system, this situation could easily bring the network to its knees because of bandwidth limitations, as well as update propagation and encryption/decryption across the network.
- Applications are at the same time stable and strategically important. If the application is not to be changed and critical for the enterprise, the best approach is not to touch it. If the application is not stable, attempt its downsizing at the next change time. If the application is not critical, downsizing can be tried for economical reasons and because of its relatively low risk.

4

System integration

Executive summary

In the context of this book, integration is thought of as a process of synergistically combining human resources and ISs with the goal to attain CSOs. Integration is a multilevel concept encompassing the physical, transaction, information management and processing, user interface, and organizational levels. Integration at the first four levels comprises *system integration*.

System integration is a philosophy of providing turnkey solutions to business problems, such that the business problem requires organizational integration, and a solution to it cuts across all layers in the system integration pyramid introduced in this chapter.

The most critical issue in system integration is the choice of balance between the IS customer's and outside contractor's involvement in IS development. The comprehensive analysis of major factors that affect this choice and the subsequent matching of these factors against a specific enterprise situation are absolutely necessary if the enterprise is to succeed in IS development. This chapter provides guidelines on the following topics:

- Pros and cons of outsourcing
- What to outsource and how
- How to select an outside system integrator
- When to start a system integration project
- How to overcome the burden of an installed base

The chapter also describes two runaway projects and analyzes the reasons for runaways.

Integration is an abused term that means different things to different people. For some, integration is understood as an organizational concept. For others, integration means putting together public and multivendor private networks or various pieces of software. I could come up with several more interpretations of this term but the point is already clear: before discussing integration in a certain context, one has to specify what integration means in this context.

In the context of this book, integration is thought of as a process of synergistically combining ("blending into a whole," according to *Webster's Dictionary*) human resources and ISs with the goal to attain CSOs.

Levels of integration

Integration is inevitably a multilevel concept. More specifically, one can single out five levels at which integration should be done to provide the desired synergy:

- Physical level
- Transaction level
- Information management and processing level
- User interface level
- Organizational level

Physical level

The major integration problem to be solved at the physical level is to make inevitably multivendor environments (hardware, system software, networks, etc.) as homogeneous and user-transparent as possible. By a *user-transparent environment*, I mean an environment in which the user operates knowing what should be done without having to know how it should be done.

Obviously, just connecting pieces of hardware that cannot talk to each other into an environment whose members can is not enough. Figuratively speaking, one has to determine what the users are going to talk about. The transaction level fills the gap.

Transaction level

The major integration problem to be solved at the transaction level is to provide consistent message propagation (updates, modifications, etc.) to all the points of use of message content. For example, if a design engineer modifies a certain part, the modified drawings must be immediately passed on to involved parties (manufacturing, inventory management, procurement, etc.).

At the transaction level, one tries to figure out what should and what should not be sent along the communication lines and across computers established at the physical level. Since the problems of information management and processing cannot be reduced to consistent information propagation, another integration level is needed to address these problems.

Information management and processing level

The major integration problem at the information management and processing level is to store, retrieve, maintain, use, and process information. The result is information sharing, exchange, integrity, and security as well as information processing performance, accuracy, and timeliness. Some of these requirements intrinsically conflict; thus, one of the more subtle integration problems is to find acceptable trade-offs among conflicting requirements for information management and processing.

Integration at levels 1 and 2 and at the information management sublevel of level 3 makes up an *information infrastructure* that will be studied beginning with chapter 5.

One important but often overlooked effect of IS proliferation is that more people will have to redefine their jobs and become permanent IS users rather than casual ones or nonusers. If the enterprise is to succeed in its integration efforts, it has to address the issue of IS acceptance by its users directly and upfront. This issue is addressed by the user interface level.

User interface level

The major integration problem at the user interface level is to provide a unified, easy, and transparent access to information and information processing facilities for users of different backgrounds, qualifications, and computer proficiencies.

Integration at the information processing sublevel of levels 3 and 4 makes up an *IS architecture* that is implemented on top of the information infrastructure. IS architecture is discussed in more detail in subsequent chapters, especially chapter 6.

Organizational level

The major integration problem to be solved at the organizational level is to break through barriers, both within the company and within the virtual enterprise, and to foster teamwork and cooperation.

Three kinds of organizational integration need to be pursued:

- Functional integration, or integration of two or more functional areas within the enterprise (breaking through the functional barriers)
- Geographical integration, or integration of dispersed components within the enterprise or its functional area (breaking through the physical barriers)
- Interorganizational integration, or integration within the virtual enterprise or even the global industrial infrastructure (breaking through the virtual enterprise barriers)

Integration at level 5 makes up a *human infrastructure*. The information and human infrastructures cannot successfully function in mutual isolation. Matching them is one of the most important (and most difficult) problems that has to be solved in the process of attaining the CSOs. One cannot even hope to attain CSOs without fusing together the information and human infrastructures. Organizational integration is discussed in more detail in chapters 15 and 16.

To conclude this section, I must emphasize again that the successful attainment of the CSOs is predicated on addressing integration at all five levels simultaneously and stressing sometimes hidden interlevel relationships.

System integration pyramid (SIP)

Integration at levels 1 through 4 is often referred to as *system integration*. The set of major issues involved in system integration is graphically depicted in FIG. 4-1 as an SIP.

In terms of the previous section and FIG. 4-1, system integration is a philosophy of providing turnkey solutions to business problems, such that the business problem requires organizational integration, and its solution cuts across all layers in the SIP.

One should realize that this definition is an ultimate one. In practice, system integration is often referred to as a small subset of what is covered by the definition. For example, many computer vendors believe that they are in system integration business. Communication companies claim that system integration is nothing more than network planning, design, and maintenance. Many system integrators equate system integration with running computing facilities. This list of misnomers could be continued. In this book all of these activities are considered to be possible components of system integration projects, but not system integration per se.

Let us discuss the SIP in more detail. Figure 4-1 shows a sample of issues pertinent to each layer of the SIP. It should be stressed from the beginning that the SIP shows only how a typical IS should be organized and what issues should be considered at each layer of its organization. In other words, the SIP provides a static picture. It has nothing to do with the process of determining what IS is necessary and sufficient for the business problem in question (which was discussed in chapter 1) or with the process of IS development.

Basic hardware and system software

At the bottom layer, basic hardware and system software, the issues of interest are what components may be selected for a future IS and how these components should be arranged, operated, and maintained. Here are some examples:

- What operating system should be used? For example, is it one of the proprietary operating systems, such as IBM's MVS or DEC's VMS, or is it Unix?

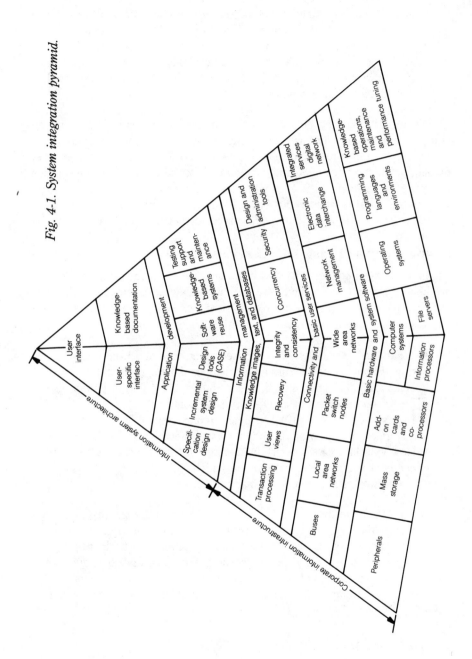

Fig. 4-1. System integration pyramid.

- What mass storage should be used? For example, is it enough to have magnetic disk storage, or should something like optical jukeboxes also be considered? Is there any need for automated tape libraries?
- To what extent is the enterprise willing to go for *"light-out" operation*, that is, running basic hardware in the highly automated fashion, ultimately without operators? What kind of system has to be purchased or developed for this purpose?

These examples by no means exhaust the list of issues that must be addressed at the layer of basic hardware and system software. Moreover, the answers to the same questions may be different for different corporate groups, divisions, functional components, or members of the virtual enterprise. (This is, by the way, one of the reasons why the next layer is needed.)

Strategic issues concerning basic hardware and system software were addressed in chapter 2 and will be discussed further in chapter 6.

Connectivity and basic user services

At the next layer, connectivity and basic user services, the issues of interest are how to connect components selected at the bottom layer with each other and their users in order to lay down a physical foundation for information sharing, exchange, and management. Here are some examples:

- What kind of LAN should be used? For example, Ethernet or token ring? When are private branch exchanges (PBXs) preferable?
- What kind of WAN should be used? Should it be public or private? Is it a proprietary network or an OSI-compliant one?
- How should LANs and WANs be interconnected? What kind of bridges and gateways will be used and when will they be installed?
- How will the entire network be managed? Which part of network management will be decentralized and which will be centralized? How will the network be operated and maintained?

Again, these examples just show the flavor of issues that must be addressed at the layer of connectivity and basic user services rather than present an exhaustive list of such issues. Also, the answers to the same questions may be different for different corporate groups, divisions, functional components, or members of the virtual enterprise.

Issues concerning the layer of connectivity and basic user services are discussed in chapters 7 through 9.

Information management

The next layer is the layer of information management. At this layer the issues of interest are how to manage various kinds of information, such as voice, data, knowledge, images, and text. These issues include information administration, storage, access, sharing, exchange, use, recovery, integrity, and security. Here are some examples:

- How should information be physically allocated to provide on-line transparent access by all involved users? What trade-offs between information integrity, response time, and the costs of information storage and communication bandwidth are acceptable?
- How must information be recovered in the case of soft and hard crashes as well as disasters? What policies of backup and information duplication should be followed?
- What security policies should be adopted and pursued? How can the most vulnerable information assets be protected? How should audit trails be organized and inspected?

Again, the list of information management issues is much longer than the sample presented here. Information management is discussed in detail in chapters 10 through 14.

The three SIP layers discussed thus far make up a *corporate information infrastructure*.

Application development

At the fourth layer, application development, the issues of interest are the approaches to application development that feature high development productivity, short life cycle, capture and preservation of valuable human expertise, incremental growth of IS functionality, and low maintenance costs. Here are some examples:

- How is the requirement and system analysis process going to proceed? How is the problem of incomplete specifications to be handled? Will formal specification languages be used? Which, if any, CASE tools will be incorporated in the requirement and system analysis process?
- How will specifications be translated into an executable code? Which, if any, CASE tools can be applied in this process?
- What policies for encouraging software reuse will be used? How will the libraries of reusable software be organized, accessed, and used?
- What applications will take advantage of knowledge-based systems technology? What are the expected benefits of this technology? What development tools and delivery platforms will be used?
- What support and maintenance policies and procedures will be used? How will change management be organized and carried out?

As in previous sections, the list of application development issues given here is just a small subset of the whole collection of issues that have to be addressed at the stage of application development.

User interface

The top SIP layer is the user interface layer. Two major issues at this layer are how to facilitate the users' learning process and how to let users of various backgrounds, qualifications, and computer proficiencies operate ISs easily and transparently. Here are sample questions to be answered at the user interface level:

- How can an initially generic user interface be customized to different user populations? How can the user interface be modified as user proficiency in operating the IS grows?
- How can IS documentation be organized and structured to provide immediate, highly focused help for the user who experiences a problem operating the IS? How can the IS itself facilitate the problem-solving process?

User interface issues are discussed in chapter 15. The application development and user interface layers of the SIP make up an *information system architecture*.

Discipline of system integration

Viewed as an engineering discipline, system integration is fairly eclectic. In other words, it includes everything that is necessary to develop a turnkey IS satisfying the business need. The discipline of system integration includes:

- Business analysis techniques, such as enterprise modeling or traffic cluster study (see Interlude 5-1)
- IS requirement analysis and specification design methodologies and tools
- IS architecture development methodologies
- Cost estimate and risk assessment methodologies
- IS design and testing methodologies
- Techniques for large-scale project management
- Techniques and tools for ongoing evaluation of project progress and product performance

A system integrator is usually a large organization that adopts and cultivates all of these methodologies, techniques, and tools. Based on its knowledge and experience of previous turnkey IS development, the system integrator traditionally assumes full responsibility for the entire IS project, including:

- Business problem analysis
- Feasibility study

- IS architecture and specifications
- Hardware and packaged software selection and acquisition
- Network hardware and user services selection and acquisition
- Application software and user interfaces
- Integration of all components into a consistent, homogeneous IS and installation of the IS
- Operation, support, and maintenance of the installed and fielded IS

System integration in government and commercial markets

Let us look more carefully at the statement made in the previous section: "the system integrator traditionally assumes full responsibility for the entire IS project." Assuming full responsibility is certainly typical of the government system integration market, where the whole system integration phenomenon came from. However, for the commercial market, the situation may be quite different.

Commercial businesses usually have diverse problems that have to be solved almost immediately and requirements that have to be met jointly. If the problem is really big, the commercial IS customer would be willing to take an evolutionary approach, solving parts of the problem on a step-by-step basis and thus leveraging the later project stages with gains obtained. On the contrary, government customers, especially federal government ones, prefer a longer-term view and a more global approach to solving problems.

As a result, long megadollar contracts awarded to a permanent team of companies, one of them identified as a prime contractor, are commonplace in the government market. On the contrary, commercial IS customers usually do not like the idea of a prime contractor and subcontractors. They also prefer shorter-term, more modular, and less expensive approaches to system integration.

This discussion implies that a typical IS customer should have more technical and project management expertise to be able to assume full responsibility for the entire IS project and split the pieces of the system integration project among many contractors. Obviously, none of these contractors is then closer to being a system integrator than the IS customer.

This brings us to a major paradox of system integration in the commercial market. If the enterprise has all necessary technical and project management expertise, it most likely does not need an outside system integrator. It certainly needs an outside system integrator, however, if it has a shortage of such expertise. For its ignorance or overgullibility, the enterprise may pay dearly in terms of cost overruns and project completion delays.

Simply put, the paradox is: "Outside system integration services will be good for you if you do not need them and not good otherwise." To resolve this paradox, let us take a closer look at the reasons for doing system integration in-house and for outsourcing it.

Outsourcing vs. in-house development

The choice of balance between the IS customer's and outside contractor's involvement in IS development is the most critical issue in system integration. The comprehensive analysis of major factors that affect this choice and the subsequent matching of these factors against a specific enterprise situation are absolutely necessary if the enterprise is to succeed in IS development.

Should system integration be done in-house?

The enterprise can get by without an outside system integrator and develop ISs in-house if it has all necessary technical and project management expertise and capabilities. It can, but should it?

Two factors affect the answer to this question. The first concerns confidentiality. Imagine that you have found an IS application that is a major contributor to a sustainable competitive advantage (see Interlude 1-2). If the project is highly sensitive, you may want absolute control of it. The last thing you want is for an outside system integrator, who has developed the IS that is critically important for your business, to go to your competitor and say: "Look, we have just finished this system for company X (your company) and have acquired a lot of experience in this area. Now we can help you, too." All of a sudden, outsourcing may turn out to be a devastating leveler of the competitive advantage that you have just gained and hope to sustain for some foreseeable future.

The second factor is cost-effectiveness. If you see the sources of cost savings that are unavailable to an outside system integrator, you may want to carry out the IS project in-house. These sources may be quite different, such as already possessed (but wasted) computer or network resources, appropriate reusable software developed in-house for another project, a special deal with a hardware or network vendor, or special project management expertise.

In all cases, having technical and project management expertise is a necessary prerequisite for doing system integration projects in-house. If you do not have this expertise, you should resort to outsourcing.

Why an outside system integrator?

The shortage of adequate system integration expertise is the first reason for outsourcing. The enterprise may not have an IS organization at all, or it may not want to acquire IS expertise. If the enterprise has not had an IS organization, it may not want to hire people for the IS project now because it is a one-time venture. Alternately, the enterprise may have an IS organization but its staff may not have adequate expertise. For example, the IS staff may be too busy handling day-to-day operational and application development responsibilities. As a result, it is unable to stay abreast of new technologies, or it may not have enough practical experience with them or the special skills required for system integration.

The second reason for outsourcing is the enterprise's intent to share IS development risk with an outside system integrator. This situation typically arises in a high-profile, high-risk IS project. Risk sharing is usually built into the contract as an article saying that the IS will be delivered on time and for a certain price, and that it will perform as specified or the customer does not pay.

Needless to say, such arrangements make the contract anything but a formality. Both parties must be very careful to define and include in the contract items such as the following:

- Detailed system specifications
- Mechanism for system specifications update
- Project timetable
- Measurable performance requirements (including a benchmarking methodology)
- Required progress at intermediate checkpoints
- Mechanism for resolving all arising and outstanding conflicts (for instance, using arbitrage rather than the justice system)

One should realize that risk sharing costs money. System integrators going for fixed-price contracts usually put extra premium costs in them (which they deserve): the risk of fixed-price system integration is almost always higher than the monetary reward from it! This statement is especially true when a system integration project includes solving technically complex problems and/or resolving conflicting technical constraints. Ironically, this is exactly the situation of the greatest need for an outside system integrator.

Risk sharing does not necessarily work for the entire project only. Flexible arrangements for partial system integration (for example, only software integration) may work well if the IS customer has enough confidence that the rest of the job can be done in-house.

The third reason for outsourcing is economical. If an outside system integrator can prove to you that it can develop the same system for less money than you would spend in-house, go for it! Here are two basic cases when the outside system integrator can do the project for less:

- The outside system integrator has economies of scale in the acquisition of basic hardware, system software, and networks that are unavailable to the IS customer. For example, the system integrator may also be a major equipment or software vendor, such as IBM, DEC, or AT&T. (Some people believe that this is also the case with Electronic Data Systems (EDS) since they own 20 percent of Hitachi Data Systems.)
- There are severe time constraints for completion of the system integration project and an outside system integrator is committed to meeting the established deadline. The IS customer, on the other hand, would be unable to do the job on time or would do it for more money.

The fourth reason for outsourcing is political. There are two basic situations in which an outside system integrator can help.

First, the IS project cuts across organizational boundaries and threatens entrenched turf holders (a common situation). According to my definition of integration, any full-scale system integration project cuts across organizational boundaries. Students of human nature will agree that people tend to resist changes, especially those depriving them of their turf.

In such a situation, an in-house system integration project may have slim chances for success because the IS staff inevitably will get involved in political fights and eventually take sides instead of doing their jobs. If the enterprise's top management is strongly committed to changes even if surgery is required to accomplish them, inviting an outside system integrator may be the only practical choice.

Second, the internal IS staff may not have enough clout and trust in the corner suites. Statements such as "We made huge investments in MIS, but end users are still complaining" perfectly describe the situation, whether they are true or false.

If the top management perception is that an outside system integrator is more responsible and accountable than an internal IS organization, so be it.

Selecting an outside system integrator

In order to resolve the system integration paradox, one should match the reasons for bringing in an outside system integrator against the company's specific situation. Although each situation is undoubtedly unique, the following questions should always be considered:

- What level of penetration by an outside system integrator is needed?
- What kind of IS-related corporate activity should be outsourced?
- What criteria should be used to select the outside system integrator?

Level of outside penetration

Selection of the proper level of outside penetration is certainly a strategic decision. Figure 4-2 shows some possible options. At one extreme is the area of the greatest outside penetration and the shortest IS development life cycle. This area corresponds to purchasing a complete off-the-shelf system. At the other extreme is the area of the lowest outside penetration and the longest IS development life cycle. This area corresponds to completely in-house IS development, integration, and maintenance.

Both extremes are no more than convenient frames of reference. The first extreme may be attractive but, unfortunately, is practically impossible. As I stated in chapter 2, your business problem is always unique. Even if you were to find an IS that matches your business problem, which is highly unlikely, being able to use it without any customization would be even more unlikely.

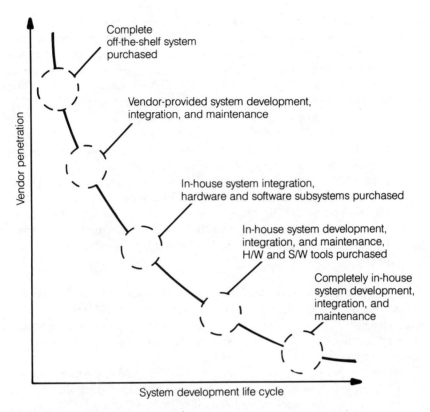

Fig. 4-2. Level of outside penetration.

The second extreme is good only for enterprises and people that suffer from the "not invented here" syndrome. Very few, if any, companies are able to satisfy all their IS needs in-house; and even if they could, they would satisfy at least some of them cost-ineffectively and inefficiently. Examples include the unsuccessful attempts by semiconductor companies to make it big in computers through forward integration and the growing number of strategic alliances between companies that seem to be competitors.

Figure 4-2 shows three intermediate, practically feasible, options:

- The IS customer buys basic hardware, system software, and software development languages and tools but does IS development, integration, and maintenance in-house. The level of outside penetration is relatively low, and the IS development life cycle is relatively long. This approach may be recommended for big companies that:

  a. Have sufficient in-house expertise in all areas of system integration
  b. Can bear the burden of big overhead over a long period of time
  c. Develop highly sensitive ISs and want to keep tight control over their systems

For many mid-size companies, this approach may be unbearable.

- The company buys all hardware and software subsystems from outside system integrators (or should I say "subsystem integrators") but provides system integration and maintenance in-house. The level of outside penetration is moderate, as well as the IS development life cycle. This approach may be recommended for companies that want to minimize in-house development yet control the process of system integration and the functionality of the resulting integrated IS. This approach may be qualified as a sort of "divide-and-keep": divide the job between outside system integrators and keep the entire system to yourself.
- An outside system integrator provides IS development, integration, and maintenance. In this case the level of outside penetration is high, and the IS development life cycle is relatively short. This approach may be recommended if the company has little or no system integration experience, and the resulting IS is not a matter of life or death for the customer.

No matter what level of outside penetration is selected, the IS customer cannot afford to be ignorant in IT or indifferent to what the outside system integrator does. The IS customer has to keep permanent control over what is to be accomplished by the outside system integrator, how it is to be accomplished, for how much, and in what time.

Again, the paradox of system integration in the commercial market is that the less the IS customer does in-house (perhaps because it does not have sufficient expertise), the more experienced it must be in managing the outside system integrator.

The point on the curve (FIG. 4-2) must be chosen by the IS customer based on a clear understanding of its background, strategic objectives, and expertise. Selection of the proper level of outside penetration is a strategic decision because it plays a crucial role in determining the IS customer's future for many years to come.

Outsourceable activities

Another strategic decision concerns the kinds of IS-related corporate activities that may be outsourced. To see the available options, let us first look at major activities of a typical IS organization in a typical enterprise. There are three such activities and, accordingly, three parts of an IS organization:

- Operation management (OM)
- Tools and applications development (TAD)
- Strategic IS planning and design (SISPD)

OM The OM activity includes operating, supporting, and maintaining a corporate information infrastructure and ISs built on its top. The IS staff involved in OM does not generally develop new applications. However, it takes part in new hardware and software acquisitions, checking out its compatibility with the installed base, interoperability, portability, and maintainability. The OM staff may also be in charge of purchasing special software for capacity planning, performance tuning, audit trail processing, etc.

TAD   The TAD staff is involved in developing new, and customizing existing, software development tools, application software, and user interfaces. This activity includes:

- Software design and testing
- Performance evaluation
- Quality assurance
- Assessment of packaged software the enterprise intends to purchase
- Smooth transfer of applications to OM organization

SISPD   The SISPD staff represents the IS organization in strategic planning activities described in chapter 1. These activities include:

- Business problem analysis
- Competitive analysis (business intelligence)
- Technology management, assessment, and transfer
- IS-related strategic planning
- Information infrastructure design
- IS architecture and specification design
- Project prioritization and management

Matrix of outsourcing options   The OM, TAD, and SISPD activities may be carried out in-house or outsourced. Thus, there are eight possible outsourcing options (TABLE 4-1). ("Yes" means that the corresponding activity is carried out in-house; "no" means that it is outsourced.) Each option implies a specific structure of an IS organization, and every enterprise has to choose the IS organization's structure by selecting one of the eight options.

Table 4-1. Matrix of Outsourcing Options.

	OM	**TAD**	**SISPD**
Full-scale IS organization	Yes	Yes	Yes
External SISPD services	Yes	Yes	No
Contract programmers	Yes	No	Yes
External SISPD services	Yes	No	No
External OM services	No	Yes	Yes
External SISPD services	No	Yes	No
External OM services and contract programmers	No	No	Yes
Full-scale outside service (information utility)	No	No	No

In the case of a full-scale IS organization, OM, TAD, and SISPD are all carried out in-house. As discussed previously, the full-scale IS organization must have adequate technical and project management expertise, and can be mostly afforded by big companies. As time goes on, fewer companies—even big companies—will be able to afford a full-scale IS organization for the reasons discussed earlier in this chapter (see "Why an Outside System Integrator?").

Conversely, if all of the three activities are outsourced, the enterprise has no IS organization and makes use of full-scale outside services, which I call an *information utility*. I find the idea of an information utility somewhat utopian and will discuss this concept in Interlude 4-1.

Between the two extremes are six other outsourcing options from which to choose. The logic of option selection might look like this: "There is no way that we will give control over what ISs we are to develop to an outsider. Hence, options 2, 4, and 6 are immediately excluded. On the other hand, we could outsource OM because system integrator X can do the job more cost-effectively than we could. This excludes option 3, so we are left with options 5 and 7. In order to choose from these options, we have to consider the options presented in FIG. 4-2 and discussed in 'Level of Outside Penetration' earlier in this chapter."

Because each enterprise's situation is unique, the decision-making process and the logic of option selection may be quite different. However, the imperative is that each enterprise has to make some decision about balancing the in-house and outsourced OM, TAD, and SISPD.

INTERLUDE 4-1. INFORMATION UTILITY: UTOPIA OR REALITY?

At first glance the idea of an information utility is very attractive. After all, very few companies have their own power plants so why should they have their own computers, networks, application developers, etc.? Is it not better to turn some switch on and get all kinds of information services that the enterprise currently needs?

The idea of an information utility is attractive for both large and small companies. Many large companies want to be freed from technical, organizational, and political complexities of running a full-scale, or close to full-scale, IS organization. Likewise, many small companies cannot afford having a large and always increasing OM, TAD, and SISPD staff.

Unfortunately, the analogy between standard and information utilities is superficial. Standard utilities, such as electric or gas utilities, sell commodities whose price is well determined and regulated, whose supply is measurable and consumed incrementally, and whose consumption scope is local or regional.

On the contrary, information utilities, if created, would sell human expertise and provide value-added services, both of which are diametrically opposite to commodities because their price is ill-defined and negotiable, their supply is immeasurable and consumed as a whole, and their consumption is intrinsically global.

In fact, the concept of an information utility is either no different from that of system integration or just another disguise for selling proprietary architectures and locking the customer into a single vendor's (utility's) hardware and software. Although the information utility is not a monopoly (and not regulated either), switching costs would be exceptionally high; and the more strategic the IS, the higher the cost.

If implemented, information utilities would destroy the very idea of gaining a sustainable competitive advantage through IT. After all, companies that obtain electricity from Pacific Gas & Electric are not superior to those obtaining it from San Diego Gas & Electric.

Conclusion: the information utility is a rather utopian idea, and it may not be as good as one might expect.

Selecting your outside system integrator

Suppose that you have decided to use the services of an outside system integrator. The question is how to select the best one (or ones) from the scores of companies seeking your business.

The first and most important criterion is the system integrator's reputation and experience. Questions that you have to ask and, hopefully, get answers to include:

- What is the candidate's previous system integration experience? Experience in your industry?
- What is the history of problems in previous system integration projects and how were they handled?
- What are the cost estimate and project management methodologies?
- What is the scope of the candidate's IS proficiency?
- Who personally will be in charge of the project? What team is assigned to the project? Have these people worked on the same team before?

The second criterion is loyalty to the customer and its interests. Some of the litmus tests for loyalty include:

- How much does the candidate care about preserving your installed base? What are the candidate's arguments in favor of its replacement?
- How impartial is the candidate? Does the candidate push certain hardware, networking equipment, or software development methodologies? How sensitive is the candidate to your specific requirements?
- Does the candidate agree to adopt a modular approach to system integration with well-defined intermodule interfaces to reduce your switching costs (just in case)?
- Does the candidate agree to train your staff or have it participate in the project? Who will own the source code? What are the support and maintenance arrangements?
- How does the candidate react to your intent to hire and manage several outside contractors? What are the candidate's arguments in favor of being the only one?

In some cases, having multiple contractors, each in charge of a specific functional area, may be a good solution. For example, one contractor could be responsible for putting together workstations and LANs, another for interconnecting multiple LANs, the third for application software, etc. The word of caution is that the IS customer has to have expertise in putting all the pieces together. In other words, the IS customer becomes its own system integrator.

The third criterion for outside integrator selection is geographic proximity to the IS installation site. This criterion may become important if the project includes support and maintenance.

System integration project

Regardless of whether the system integration is outsourced or done in-house, the enterprise has to know when to start the project and how to carry it out.

Starting the project

Perhaps the best time to start a system integration project is when significant changes in corporate strategy have just been made, and these changes are caused, or should be supported, by ISs.

Next is the situation of a major overhaul in the organizational structure, such as a merger or acquisition. This situation is usually accompanied by redefinition of CSOs and consolidation of IS organizations, which may invite the overhaul in ISs.

Another good time for starting the system integration project is when new problems have just been identified, require an immediate solution, and cannot be solved by existing systems. A similar situation arises in the case of undercapacity of computing resources, which causes a major update or overhaul of computing facilities. Another variation on the same theme is hardware and software obsolescence. If the enterprise has made a decision to replace computing facilities, the time for starting the system integration project is opportune.

One situation requires special attention and has to be handled very carefully. If a major hardware/system software overhaul is done with the only purpose to run the same system more efficiently, measure twice and cut once. Check and recheck the price of expected improvements. In many cases, the results may be less impressive than what has been promised by an eager system integrator or vendor of new hardware/system software. The following war story illustrates this situation.

WAR STORY 4-1. BART

For many years the Integrated Control System, used for routing and tracking Bay Area Rapid Transit (BART) trains, ran on old Westinghouse Electric Corporation's computer and could handle only 64 trains. In 1978, the BART board of directors made a decision to replace this system with a new one, based on more advanced technology and the ability to handle more trains.

In 1984, BART purchased a new computer, Data General's MV 10000, and the whole modernization project, including software development, was budgeted at $13 million. According to Jim Steiner, Bart's manager for the project, about $20 million was spent on "early system prototyping and 'unsuccessful starts' " (*Computerworld*, November 20, 1989). Then a new outside system integrator came into the picture.

In the mid-1980s, Logica Data Architects, Inc., won the bid for the software development project and, according to Logica, started working on it in 1987. By late November 1989, Logica was paid $20 million, bringing the entire project cost to $40 million, $27 million over budget.

On November 10, 1989, the system was tested from 1 a.m. to 8 a.m. with 29 trains running. Based on this test, Logica concluded that the Integrated Control System could handle 74 trains using 83 percent of its CPU capacity (*Computerworld*, November 20, 1989). Based on the earlier test in October 1989, BART engineers believed that running 74 trains would require 130 percent of its capacity! At any rate, even if the capacity of 74 trains had been achieved, BART would have paid $4 million for managing each additional train and waited for this "opportunity" for more than 10 years!

Speaking of 74 trains, BART had plans to run extensions to its current lines and schedule 108 trains. Some of the BART board members were "under the impression that the software was supposed to handle the expanded scheduling demand." Logica representatives said that "only the 74 trains were specified on their contract" (*Computerworld*, November 20, 1989).

So is the system a success or a failure? According to Logica, it has been an "unqualified success." According to the BART board of directors, it has been a "complete failure." Now let us see what independent auditors say.

According to LS Transit Systems, Inc., the technical auditor of the project, the system has the following flaws (*Computerworld*, November 27, 1989):

- It does not meet capacity requirements.
- It cannot be transported to a larger computer.
- It has only a single communication path to BART engineers and none to field stations.
- It takes three weeks to change the software to adjust to any physical plant changes.

LF Transit Systems estimated that it would cost another $1.8 million to have Logica complete the project. This was not a very pleasant surprise, especially on top of the news from Peat Marwick, the financial auditor, that Logica overcharged BART by more than $2.6 million.

All this happened in the aftermath of the Bay Area earthquake when BART became the "transportation of necessity around the fallen Bay Bridge" (*Computerworld*, November 20, 1989).

One can see a number of mistakes made by both BART and Logica during the project even from the newspaper article. One of them stands out, however. In the BART project, unlike many other less lucky ones, the requirements are quantifiable in terms of the number of trains to be routed and tracked. It could significantly help both the customer and the contractor to manage the project and plan further extensions. Apparently, it has not.

Burden of an installed base

In addition to deciding when to start a system integration project, an enterprise has to decide how to carry it out. Many companies find themselves in what I call a *bermudian triangle* of installed base (FIG. 4-3).

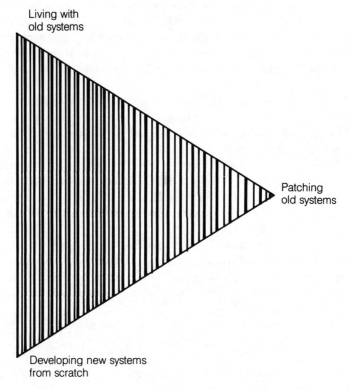

Fig. 4-3. Bermudian triangle of installed base.

Practically every company has old ISs that become more and more inadequate. At best, these systems present a collection of isolated partial solutions that do not work together. At worst, they just do not work.

A natural reaction to such a situation is to develop new ISs that match today's CSOs. However, the enterprise may soon find (and better sooner than later) that developing new systems may take years and tens or even hundreds of millions of dollars. In addition, millions of dollars worth of installed hardware and software, as well as people skills, experience, and know-how, may be thrown away.

Finding themselves between a devil of replacement of old systems and a deep sea of living with them, most companies resort to patching and integrating the old systems. Patching works up to a point, but eventually it creates more problems than it solves. As someone has said, "People who believe it to be the most cost-efficient approach know what they want but don't know what they have."

If the number of old systems to be patched is big, and the systems are heterogeneous, the resulting system may collapse under its own weight. There is always a limit to what one can do in this situation, but, unfortunately, no one knows upfront what this limit is.

I have a rule of thumb that tells when to stop using old systems (or patching them) and start developing a new one:

As soon as the cost of maintaining an old IS exceeds n *percent of the estimated cost of developing a new IS, start a new one and reduce maintenance of the old one to a minimum necessary to run business.*

The value of n depends on the rate of maintenance cost growth and may range from 60 to 90. Needless to say, as soon as the new IS is developed, the old one has to be replaced. The rule can be used as a basis for gradual strategy of installed base upgrade.

Thus, there are four major scenarios for carrying out a system integration project:

- Do nothing. In today's competitive global environment, doing nothing is the easiest way to lose everything.
- Start IS development and integration from scratch—an ideal but not very realistic proposition. The "Think Big—Start Small" strategy described in chapter 1 can be used in all its glory.
- Patch and integrate existing islands of automation. The cost of interfaces is a crucial factor, and feasibility of the entire project is a matter of management intuition.
- Combine the development of new systems with the patching of old ones. Try to preserve the installed base as much as possible and, at the same time, satisfy new needs and requirements. The rule of thumb given previously provides a clue to update the installed base.

Runaways

Unfortunately, not all system integration projects succeed. Some of them result in so-called *runaways*. A runaway is defined as "a system that's millions over budget, years behind schedule, and—if ever completed—less effective than promised" (*Business Week*, November 7, 1988).

Runaways are not an exceptional rarity. According to Peat Marwick's survey of its 600 largest clients, "some 35% currently have major runaways" (*Business Week*, November 7, 1988). The problem is so widespread that Peat Marwick set up a group that provides help for runaway victims. From its inception in 1986 to late 1988, the group earned "$30 million in revenues from nearly 20 clients" (*Computerworld*, November 20, 1989).

In this section, I will give you two real-life runaway illustrations and then discuss some reasons for runaways.

Insurance industry runaways

The following war stories describe two runaway experiences in the insurance industry.

WAR STORY 4-2. NO INSURANCE AGAINST RUNAWAYS?

In 1982 Allstate Insurance Co. decided to build the most sophisticated IS in the insurance industry. The IS was supposed to automate Allstate's office operations and significantly reduce the time span necessary for the introduction of new types of policies (from three years to one month) (*Business Week*, November 7, 1988).

Allstate hired EDS, one of the best known system integrators, to develop and install application software. The completion deadline was December 1987, and the target project cost was $8 million. After $15 million had been spent, and no system had been delivered, Allstate fired EDS, invited Peat Marwick Mitchell & Co. as a consultant, and set a new deadline and cost estimate. These were 1993 and $100 million, respectively.

WAR STORY 4-3. UNHEALTHY SYSTEM FOR A HEALTH INSURER

The planned IS in the previous war story was never developed. In the following war story the IS was developed but it never worked.

In 1983 Blue Cross & Blue Shield United of Wisconsin hired EDS to build an IS that would coordinate all services offered by this health insurer. The system cost $200 million and was completed on time.

During its first year, however, the IS disbursed $60 million in overpayments or duplicate checks. Before the runaway was stopped, Blue Cross lost 35,000 members, which it attributed to IS problems. (EDS challenged this statement and attributed the problems to the multitude of data that had to be converted from the old system to the new (*Business Week*, November 7, 1988).

The Blue Cross experience is interesting because it shows the importance of top management involvement in SIS development projects. According to Tom Hefty, Blue Cross' chief executive officer, "I let it slip, that's the problem. I kept hands off, and it hurt me in the end." Now he is "closely involved with all future system development" (*Business Week*, November 7, 1988).

Reasons for runaways

Runaways happen not because system integrators are villains or absolutely incompetent. (The fact that EDS was involved in both runaways described in the previous section is purely coincidental.) There are several objective reasons for runaways that we will discuss in this section.

First, the IS complexity significantly increases, and the experience acquired in relatively simple IS projects cannot be directly transferred to complex ones. More attention must be given to requirements analysis and specification design; use of CASE tools; project and version management; and the education and training of IS development professionals, which lag behind today's demand.

Second, the nature of system integration projects is rapidly changing. A $100-million project five years ago is different from a $100-million project today. As hardware costs go down, and requirements for IS functionality and scope go up, one can see a significant shift toward spending more on customized software development than on hardware and off-the-shelf software acquisition. Hence, dramatic mistakes in project cost estimates result, as well as failures to meet agreed-upon deadlines.

Furthermore, today's business problems can typically be solved through applying a combination of IS technologies. Understanding the intrinsic interrelationships among these technologies is as important as acquiring skills in using each of them (see War Story 1-1).

Finally, connectivity between IS components has become much more important because IS architectures are more decentralized than in the past. Connectivity is not only a physical communication problem, and system integrators (and companies they serve) pay a dear price for ignoring or underestimating this fact.

As applications become more strategic, breaking through functional and organizational barriers, more hidden interrelationships and interdependencies among previously separated organizations must be explicitly represented in ISs. The process of disclosing these interrelationships and interdependencies is inevitably accompanied by resistance that often turns into "turf wars."

Building an FEM that features intra- and intercorporate product, information, and transaction flows is essential to resolve arising problems and to provide proper connectivity solutions. (The concept of an FEM, first introduced in chapter 1, will be defined in more detail in Interlude 5-1). In turn, the FEM lays down a foundation for the corporate information infrastructure (chapter 5).

The third reason for runaways is almost equally shared by system integrators and the customer's senior management. The latter still looks at ISs as a secondary expenditure and does not pay enough attention to system integration projects. The failure to closely monitor a system integration project may turn into a disastrous runaway earlier than senior managers expect. War Story 4-3 confirms this fact.

5

Introduction to a corporate information infrastructure

Executive summary

A corporate information infrastructure is an organized collection of information sources, storages, processors, and users along with communication systems connecting them. Any enterprise needs the information infrastructure for the following reasons:

- To replace transportation with communications
- To provide effective communications within the virtual enterprise between physically separated individuals and groups
- To provide a unified facility for storing, sharing, and exchanging various kinds of information
- To use information assets and computational resources cost-effectively
- To provide effective protection of information assets and computational resources
- To provide a unified foundation for developing many different applications, both today and in the future.

The corporate information infrastructure provides three functions:

- Basic connectivity and user services
- Effective and efficient management of all kinds of information
- Use of, and interfaces to, information sources, storages, processors, and the corporate network by diverse corporate users

Combined with the concepts of open systems, downsizing, and system integration, the information infrastructure promises to eliminate continuous patching of existing systems until they become unmaintainable and to provide stability of information assets and computational resources as well as smooth transition between generations of technology.

Definition and illustrations

A *corporate information infrastructure* is an organized collection of information sources, storages, processors, and users along with communication systems connecting them (FIG. 5-1). The corporate information infrastructure reflects product, information, and transaction flows within the virtual enterprise that are necessary to run the enterprise's business.

There is an obvious analogy between an information infrastructure and a transportation infrastructure in a country such as the United States. The latter is used for transportation of tangible things (people, mail, furniture, fruit, gas-

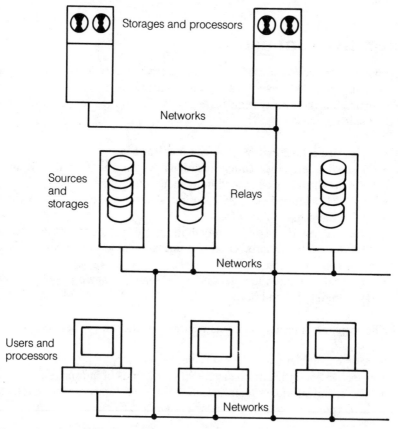

Fig. 5-1. Corporate information infrastructure.

oline, etc.). The former is used for communication, that is, transportation of information.

The transportation infrastructure does not depend on specific features of products to be transported and delivered. For instance, it has nothing to do with product perishability. If the product cannot be delivered fresh on time through the highway and road component of the infrastructure, it should not be transported at all or should be transported by a faster carrier such as the infrastructure's airline or cargo component. Physical and other infrastructure limitations are known in advance, and planners have to take them into account when they transport products. As the transportation infrastructure progresses, its limitations may be reduced or lifted.

Likewise, the information infrastructure should not depend on specific features of information. Information infrastructure limitations are known in advance and have to be taken into account by those planning information transfer and processing. These limitations can be reduced or lifted as a result of advances in computer and telecommunication technology.

As another example, the transportation infrastructure does not depend on the ways in which delivered products will be used or processed. The delivered mail may be read or thrown away, answered or ignored, and the transportation infrastructure has absolutely nothing to do with any of these actions.

Likewise, the information infrastructure should not depend on the ways in which information will be used or processed at the destination. In other words, to be usable and effective for a long time, the information infrastructure has to be application-independent.

A well-developed transportation infrastructure makes its user powerful; a poor transportation infrastructure makes its user weak. The U.S. transportation infrastructure is one of the factors that determines the industrial strength and high level of life of this nation. The Soviet transportation infrastructure is so weak that they cannot deliver the harvest they gather. I was witness to fields of vegetables so desperately needed by urban inhabitants. The harvest was never picked because of a lack of boxes and trucks and the poor road quality.

The same statement can be made about a corporate information infrastructure. All other things being equal, the enterprise with a well-developed corporate information infrastructure will thrive, while the enterprise with a poor one has slim, if any, chances for survival in global competitive battles.

The question is: What makes up a "well-developed" corporate information infrastructure and how can it be developed? We will discuss these issues in subsequent sections.

Corporate information infrastructure: Rationale and requirements

Any enterprise has some information infrastructure, but it may be good or bad, effective or ineffective, sufficient or insufficient, and so forth. If you understand first why the enterprise needs an information infrastructure, you may come closer to determining the requirements for an information infrastructure adequate for your corporate environment.

More communications, more effective communications

The first reason for having an information infrastructure is to replace, wherever possible and worthwhile, transportation with communications. This is one of the major long-term trends in our business and social life.

Such replacement has become necessary to save people's energy, valuable time, and money. For example, a lawyer in the state of Hawaii may have to fly from Oahu to Maui for the sake of a five-minute business transaction, such as filing a motion in court, instead of communicating this motion over the information infrastructure.

Another example that has become a classic one is a commute in the Los Angeles area. I happen to travel 96 miles from home to Los Angeles on Sunday evenings and from Los Angeles back home on Friday afternoons. The first trip takes 1 hour and 35 minutes; the second, 3 hours and 30 minutes! (Some people waste this amount of time every day!)

In many cases proximity between people working together is not necessary, or at least not always necessary, which naturally leads to the idea of a *telecommute*. These cases include people who:

- Work alone for a relatively long time and regularly (but not often) discuss the results of their work with peers (scientists, engineers, programmers)
- Spend most of their time on the road, communicate by phone or via a computer, and need access to information and corporate computational resources (field service technicians, sales people)
- Mostly serve their clients by phone or via a computer and need access to information and corporate computational resources (investment brokers, telemarketeers, hot-line operators)

This list might go on, but the idea is clear. A telecommute is feasible, and many enterprises can capitalize on it by including telecommuters in their information infrastructures. One of the most frequently cited obstacles, the loss of management control, will gradually go away as we shift from highly centralized, control-based to flattened, group work-based organizational structures (see chapter 15 for more information on work groups).

The second reason for having an information infrastructure is to provide effective communications within the virtual enterprise between individuals and groups that are physically separated by necessity (for example, located in different companies and/or countries). The information infrastructure serves as a foundation for information sharing and exchange among such individuals and groups.

Information management

The third reason for having an information infrastructure is that it provides a unified facility for storing, sharing, and exchanging various kinds of information, including voice, data, text, images, and knowledge. (See chapter 10 for more discussion of the five kinds of business information.)

Technological advances in such areas as image processing and artificial intelligence make it possible to take advantage of all kinds of information rather than only data. The shift from corporate databases to information bases managing all kinds of information is inevitable and will lay down a foundation for group work.

Another closely related aspect of information infrastructure is providing easy and transparent access to information in geographically dispersed, multiuser environments. By *transparent access*, I mean a situation in which the user has to know what information he or she wants but not where it resides or how to get it. Instead, the user workstation or other automatically accessible computing resource has knowledge of the information infrastructure sufficient to find requested information and to deliver it to the user's terminal.

The fourth reason for having an information infrastructure is a cost-effective use of information assets and computational resources. As purchasing decisions become more decentralized, the number of computers in the enterprise becomes greater, and the pace of technological changes becomes faster, the information infrastructure comes forward as a facility for:

- Making all hardware, software, and information inexpensively and reliably available to anyone eligible to use them
- Increasing utilization of computational resources and dynamically smoothing the load on them (for example, by using Hong Kong computers at the peak time in Los Angeles)
- Providing incremental growth of computational resources when the need arises

The fifth reason for having an information infrastructure is effective protection of information assets and computational resources. This function of information infrastructures is becoming more important as pressures for managerial and even legal liabilities for information security violations and inconsistency grow in size and scope.

The potential contribution of robust information infrastructures to protection of information assets and computational resources is to provide alternative sources of assets and resources as well as more efficient disaster recovery procedures. However, elaborate distributed information infrastructures can make security enforcement more difficult. Balancing security enforcement against infrastructure robustness may become a challenging, though solvable, problem.

Application independence

The final reason for having an information infrastructure is to provide a unified foundation for developing many different applications, including ones that the enterprise may not even be aware of. The information infrastructure has to be maximally application-independent. Otherwise, orientation toward a specific application or class of applications can make other applications inefficient or hard to develop.

Since users typically want to process the same data but for different purposes, developing an application-independent information infrastructure is feasible but may present a design problem. The game is worth the candle because of the following advantages of application independence:

- Both end users and the IS department will be able to develop a variety of applications for universally structured information.
- Information will keep up with user needs.
- Quicker response to new technologies will be possible.
- New products and services based on the same information will be easier to create.

Summarizing, the information infrastructure may become a major factor in providing IS quality, application development productivity, and painless migration between generations of hardware and software.

Requirements for an information infrastructure

General requirements for a corporate information infrastructure are as follows:

- The information infrastructure must cover the entire scope of, and be derived from, CSOs that support the current state of the company and its vision for the future.
- The information infrastructure must reflect the product, information, and transaction flows within the virtual enterprise. It must also account for all kinds of information rather than only data.
- The information infrastructure must be flexible, incrementally expandable, and easily adaptable to changes in the virtual enterprise.
- The information infrastructure should provide maximum utilization of the installed base of hardware, system software, and applications. (See chapter 4 for the discussion on the gradual replacement of an installed base.)
- The information infrastructure must be implementable using available financial and human resources in accordance with the schedule of its incremental development. Human resources may be in-house, outsourced, or a combination thereof.

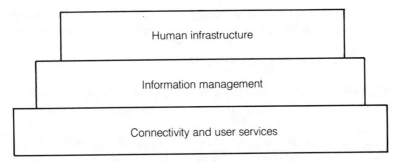

Fig. 5-2. Basic functions of the corporate information infrastructure.

Information infrastructure functions

Figure 5-2 illustrates three basic functions of the corporate information infrastructure:

- Providing basic connectivity and user services. This function implies building a corporate network as a physical substrate for the information infrastructure.
- Providing effective and efficient management of all kinds of information. This function implies building a coordinated collection of possibly distributed data, text, image, and knowledge bases and managing this collection as a corporate asset.
- Providing the use of, and interfaces to, information sources, storages, processors, and the corporate network by diverse corporate users. This function may imply the creation of technological and organizational incentives for bringing the corporate organizational structure and the information infrastructure in accordance and providing synergy between the two.

Factors determining the corporate information infrastructure

Five major factors determine the corporate information infrastructure:

- Kinds of information and their relative importance
- Patterns of information location and exchange
- Requirements for information integrity, consistency, and security
- Problem characteristics and patterns of problem solving
- Application development philosophy

The following paragraphs present each factor as a set of questions that have to be answered in the process of information infrastructure development.

INTERLUDE 5-1. PRODUCT, INFORMATION, AND TRANSACTION FLOWS

Chapter 1 introduced the concept of an FEM that represents all corporate activities and their interrelationships along with intra- and intercorporate product, information, and transaction flows. This interlude defines these flows in more detail.

I proceed from the assumption that each business can be characterized (and hence modeled) by three flows: of its products, of information that accompanies the product flow, and of transactions that accompany the product and information flows. In particular, if the enterprise's product is information, the product and information flows can be merged into a single information flow. However, we still will have to distinguish between two groups of information:

- The information that is the enterprise's product
- The information that describes how the first group of information is produced (information about information)

A *transaction* is any action that changes the state of the enterprise. In this context, acquiring a company, hiring a new person, accomplishing an assembly operation, or shipping a product unit may all be transactions, depending on the level at which the enterprise is represented in its FEM.

Each flow can be characterized by its class (product, information, or transaction), parameters, constraints on its propagation and transformation, and interrelationships with other flows of the same or other class.

Products, information, and transactions flow between entities that are called product processors, information processors, and transaction processors, respectively (FIG. 5-3A). A processor transforms an input flow into an output flow (FIG. 5-3B). Each processor can be characterized by its class, parameters, types of transformations, constraints on its use, and interrelationships with other processors of the same or other class.

Internally, a processor performs three generic functions (FIG. 5-3C):

- Checking input flow and processor constraints. Input flow constraints ensure that the input flow has all necessary prerequisites to be transformed by the processor. Processor constraints ensure that the processor meets the processing demands of the input flow.
- Transforming an input into an output flow. Transformation is allowed if all input flow and processor constraints are satisfied.
- Checking output flow constraints. These constraints ensure that the transformation result satisfies its specifications and has further processing demands attached to it.

In some cases, output flow constraints of the previous processor may coincide or overlap with input flow constraints of the next one. The aggregate conceptual model of product,

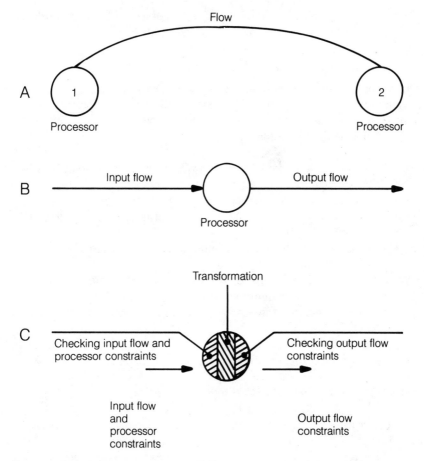

Fig. 5-3. Functional enterprise model: flows, processors, and constraints.

information, and transaction flows and their processors, along with the attached constraints, makes up an FEM.

Product, information, and transaction flows and their processors may be identified, described, and then formally defined by means of object-oriented analysis (Coad 1990).

Kinds of information and their relative importance

This factor is based on a thorough study of information and transaction flows within the virtual enterprise. The questions to be answered include:

- What are the different kinds of information used in each information flow and how are they used (transaction flow) and managed?
- What is the relative importance of each kind of information in each information flow?

- What is the absolute and relative volume of each kind of information and how is it going to grow in the foreseeable future?

Patterns of information location and exchange

This factor is based on clear understanding of corporate geography and information ownership (see chapter 16 for more information on information ownership). The questions for this factor should be answered for each information flow and include the following:

- What are the information sources? Where are they located and why?
- What are potential new sources of information?
- Who owns which information at each information source?
- What regimes of information update are used and how frequently are they updated?
- What are the points of use for information, and how are they related to information sources?
- How is information delivered from its source to its points of use?
- How many users use information at each point of use?
- What is the extent of information sharing, and how often does sharing occur?
- What is the information traffic on each source-to-point-of-use path and how is it likely to increase in the future?

INTERLUDE 5-2. TRAFFIC CLUSTERS

The concept of a traffic cluster complements product, information, and transaction flows and is important for understanding the corporate information geography (Gundon 1989). A *traffic cluster* is a set of users who (1) by virtue of intercommunication and information exchange, create the same type of information traffic and (2) share the same computational resource or accomplish the same set of tasks.

Each user can be a member of several traffic clusters (transaction processing, telephone conversation, videoconferencing, etc.). Traffic clusters may be identified by studying the intra- and interenterprise information and transaction flows.

A traffic cluster may be described by three major parameters:

- Connectivity. Communication-intensive traffic requires high connectivity, while computation-intensive traffic may get by with lower connectivity. Determining the required connectivity is important because high connectivity:

   a. Costs money for installation and management
   b. Requires building and maintaining directories to free users from remembering long addresses
   c. May jeopardize access control and security, especially when combined with using public networks

- Bandwidth. Bandwidth shows how much traffic the communication channel can handle over a period of time and, along with transmission delay, the time required to deliver a message to a destination (response time). Determining required bandwidth may be difficult because bandwidth should be configured to handle traffic at the peak time and to provide sufficient utilization at low load.
- Burstiness. Computer traffic using packet-switching is intrinsically bursty, while telephone traffic using circuit switching is continuous. (See chapter 7 for more information on packet and circuit switching.) From an economic viewpoint (transmission cost), bursty traffic has to be handled separately from continuous traffic. For example, bursty traffic may be multiplexed on fewer channels than transmitting devices and demultiplexed at the receiving end.

Traffic clusters should be classified by combinations of the three parameters. Traffic cluster identification may be done in the following stages:

- Representing the corporate organizational structure as a geographic map of corporate sites with rough distances between them
- Marking the locations of all shared resources (data centers, telephone exchanges, LANs, directories, etc.)
- Drawing major product, information, and transaction flows on a traffic map
- Determining the types of traffic for each information, communication, and transaction flow
- Finding out how many users use each type of traffic and what the patterns of use are
- Estimating a traffic volume for each information, communication, and transaction flow
- Marking possible changes in product, information, communication, and transaction flows
- Observing major traffic clusters on the traffic map

The resulting traffic map shows:

- Opportunities for network integration where traffic clusters overlap and other integration conditions can be met
- Points for gateways and bridges where gaps between traffic clusters occur
- Boundaries between private and public networks as well as international boundaries
- Cost structure for each information, communication, and transaction flow
- Opportunities for multiplexing, route optimization, alternative technologies, and other cost-saving measures
- Gaps in access control and security

Traffic clusters are an indispensable tool for infrastructure planning, design, and management.

Requirements for information integrity, consistency, and security

This factor is based on user-defined assessments of information value and clearly formulated and consistently enforced information management policies (see chapters 5 and 19), including thorough understanding of who owns and who uses each chunk of information. The questions to be addressed and answered include:

- What are current information integrity and consistency preservation policies and procedures and how adequate are they?
- How is information entered in the IS and what are the integrity controls for information entry?
- Are the integrity checks located in the information base or localized in applications? In the latter case, why?
- How are domain-dependent integrity checks made available to all application developers?
- How is information ranked in terms of its value and confidentiality?
- How does each information owner protect information?
- How is information protected at its locations and on its way to points of use?
- How are information users' rights of access to, and update of, information granted and revoked?
- How are logs and audit trails recorded, maintained, and checked?

Problem characteristics and patterns of problem solving

This factor is based on the study of current applications, the backlog of applications to be developed, and the ASP and corresponding action programs that describe future business needs and ISs responding to these needs. The following questions should be answered:

- What are the problems that should be solved regularly and how often should they be solved?
- How are they solved currently?
- Where are they solved currently?
- What is the required response time for each problem?
- Who are the people in charge of solving these problems, how many of them should solve each problem, and where are they located?
- What is the breakdown of these people by corporate components, geographic location, etc.?
- Who are the customers of problem solutions, where are they located, and what is their status within the company?

Application development philosophy

This factor is based on the enterprise's culture, CSOs, and available resource of in-house application development expertise. Questions that should be answered include:

- Are applications typically developed in-house or outsourced? Why?

- What sensitive application development projects should be developed to attain CSOs?
- What is their estimated complexity relative to the available application development resource?
- Is the available application development resource centralized or decentralized?
- How much are the same applications shared by different corporate components?
- How many off-the-shelf application packages are used in the enterprise, and what is the history of their installation and customization?
- What are their visible limitations?
- What is the current application backlog, and what is the average rate of its unload?
- What development tools are used or will be used? Why?

Impact of IM/SD policy

The answers to many of the previous questions are a matter of corporate policy more than anything else. In fact, all of the factors that determine the corporate information infrastructure are to a degree a matter of corporate policy. This emphasis on policy is important: each enterprise has to have a comprehensive and explicitly formulated policy.

A part of the corporate policy pertaining to information management and information systems is referred to throughout this book as an IM/SD policy. Chapter 16 discusses this policy in detail in connection with other human aspects of SISs. The following paragraphs provide a short overview of two components of the IM/SD policy that have the greatest impact on the corporate information infrastructure.

Information ownership and management

The first component is a set of policies, procedures, and guidelines concerning information ownership and management. People like to own information but do not like responsibilities naturally stemming from information ownership. Thus, it is important to identify the owner of the information and the owner's information management responsibilities.

The information ownership guidelines dictated by the technology itself are simple:

- Information can be accessed only by people who are explicitly authorized to do so by its owner.
- Information can be updated only by its owner or by people who are explicitly authorized to do so by its owner.

Additional guidelines are fairly arbitrary and hence a matter of the corporate IM/SD policy. Issues that have to be addressed by this policy include:

- Information owner's rights and liabilities

  a. What are general ownership rights?
  b. How can the rights of access be granted to, or revoked from, those leasing information?
  c. What are the information lease conditions and terms?
  d. What are the lessee liabilities for violating these conditions and terms?
  e. What are the limits of information owner liabilities?

- Management of geographically dispersed information

  a. Who makes a decision to duplicate information at different sites?
  b. May the information owner's decision not to duplicate information be overridden and by whom?
  c. Who is liable for information management at remote sites where information duplicates reside?

- Integrity and consistency preservation measures

  a. What are the basic integrity/consistency checks and controls available to the information owner?
  b. How can these checks and controls be certified?
  c. If these checks and controls are put into an application rather than into a database engine, who is responsible for information integrity and consistency?

- Security measures

  a. What are the basic security controls available to the information owner?
  b. How can these controls be certified?
  c. What are admissible trade-offs between information security and flexibility of information sharing and exchange?

- Conflict resolution

  a. How are potential conflicts between information owners and users, or between information owners and centralized information administrators and security enforcers, to be resolved?
  b. What are the qualifications of a reasonable conflict arbiter?
  c. What are the normal arbitrage procedures?

Unfortunately, some of these issues are completely or partially ignored by corporations with a centralized or simplistic information infrastructure. However, with proliferation of end-user computing, downsizing, and work groups, neglecting the IM/SD policy can cost dearly.

Information value assessment

Another component of the IM/SD policy that may have a great impact on the corporate information infrastructure is a set of principles and guidelines for *information value assessment*. If one says that information is a major corporate asset, this asset must be properly managed. In an oversimplistic way, "proper" implies not spending for information management more than the managed information is worth; that is, one has to know what the information is worth and how to assess its value (probably as a function of time). This assessment is mostly a matter of the corporate IM/SD policy. The policy issues include:

- How the information value is defined (a commonly accepted methodology of information value definition)
- How the corporate information is ranked in terms of its value
- How the value of corporate information changes in time
- Ways of increasing the information value
- Impact of the information value on information protection procedures (for example, classes of information protection)

The issue of information value is often ignored because of its subjectivity. However, subjective information value assessments are better than none, and both the quality and cost of the corporate information infrastructure may be significantly affected by these assessments.

In the absence of such assessments, the enterprise will either (1) ignore the information protection problem, (2) equally protect all the information across the board, or (3) provide partial information protection across the board. All three propositions are deficient:

- The first one may jeopardize security of valuable information.
- The second one will certainly be cost-ineffective.
- The third one will overprotect information of relatively low value and underprotect valuable information.

Blueprint for information infrastructure development

Based on the discussion in this chapter, we can now formulate a blueprint for information infrastructure development.

Stage 1: Determine total business needs and requirements

First of all, business needs and requirements should be determined. These include:

- What users demand and have today, that is, their current operational requirements

- What users demand but do not yet have, that is, their short-term operational requirements
- What is derived from CSOs and action programs supporting them, that is, the virtual enterprise's strategic and corresponding long-term operational requirements

The total of current, short-term, and long-term operational requirements forms the basis for information infrastructure development.

Stage 2: Draw the virtual enterprise's infrastructure map

With this basis at hand, one can start developing an underlying architecture and topology. This stage of infrastructure development includes developing a "grand" architecture first and then specifying it through answering the questions given in "Factors Determining the Corporate Information Infrastructure" earlier in this chapter. The result may be presented as the virtual enterprise's *infrastructure map*, which plots all the information sources, points of use, information processing centers, and communications among them. This map is the skeleton of the corporate information infrastructure in its most hardware- and application-independent form.

Stage 3: Select specific hardware and software

The next stage of information infrastructure development is to add flesh to the information infrastructure skeleton—specific computers, voice and data communication facilities, networks, interfaces, bridges, routers, gateways, databases, textual and image bases, knowledge bases, etc. Two of the most demanding and difficult problems at this state are as follows:

- To provide maximum utilization of the existing installed base of hardware, system software, and applications
- To select new hardware and software that will satisfy total business needs and requirements (stage 1) and provide the easiest possible interfaces between new selections and the installed base.

These two problems are by no means the only ones that have to be solved at this stage. Recall integration, flexibility, and information management (the three critical factors introduced in chapter 1) and the set of design philosophies and guidelines that support them. Critical success factors must be taken into account when selecting hardware and software for the information infrastructure.

Generic issues of open systems, interoperability, system integration, and connectivity must be interpreted in the virtual enterprise context before making final purchasing decisions. Also, the following trade-offs, which are typical of distributed information architecture, need to be carefully analyzed:

- Between architecture robustness (duplication of information at several sites) and consistency (synchronous updates of information at all sites having this information)
- Between the cost of information storage at several sites and the cost of network bandwidth necessary to pass this information around
- Between immediate information availability (including low response time) and potentially compromised information security

Stage 4: Determine necessary information infrastructure management functions

By the end of stage 3, few SIS architecture alternatives should be selected. However, no purchasing decisions should be made yet. One more aspect of information infrastructure development should be carefully investigated before making any hardware and software commitments: its management.

Information infrastructure management comprises three areas:

- Capacity management
- Network management
- Information management

Capacity management   Capacity management is aimed at providing maximum utilization of computational, network, and human resources. It should provide dynamic allocation of all these resources, based on business priorities and understanding of information traffic patterns. The predictive function of capacity management is to request proactive, incremental growth of the information infrastructure, based on forecasting the future volume of information traffic.

Network management   Network management includes functions such as network design and planning, network troubleshooting and fault isolation, network performance management, accounting management, and security management. There is an intrinsic conflict between the distributed nature of corporate networks and increasing demands for centralized network management; and each selection of basic networks, hardware, and software presents different trade-offs at different costs. Network management is discussed in chapter 9.

Information management   Information management includes management of different kinds of information, such as data, text, images, and knowledge, as well as management functions common to all kinds of information. These functions include recovery, concurrency control, integrity, and security. Specifics of data, knowledge, text, and image management are discussed in chapters 11 and 13. Common information management functions are discussed in chapters 12 and 14.

Stage 5: Estimate life cycle costs of selected alternatives

With an understanding of the information infrastructure management functions required and the functions provided by selections made at stage 3, one can estimate more precisely the full infrastructure cost. This estimate includes the purchasing price plus the cost of infrastructure support and maintenance.

At this stage another comparative estimate of in-house and outsourced information infrastructure support and maintenance (operation management) should be made. In some cases this estimate may affect the final purchasing decision.

Stage 6: Purchase and install
information infrastructure components

At this stage information infrastructure components that belong to the selected alternative are purchased and installed. Support and maintenance policies and procedures should immediately be put into action.

Conclusion

With increasing IS complexity and diversity, it is going to be more difficult to develop ISs—especially SISs—on the ad hoc, one-by-one basis and then to make them work together. A recommended approach instead is to plan and design a relatively general-purpose, application-independent, incrementally enhanceable platform on whose top one can then develop diverse applications. This platform is the corporate information infrastructure.

Combined with the concepts of open systems, downsizing, and system integration, an information infrastructure promises to eliminate continuous patching of existing systems until they become unmaintainable and to provide stability of information assets and computational resources as well as smooth transition between generations of technology.

An important advantage of the information infrastructure is that it does away with the IS department vs. end users controversy, putting this controversy in the right perspective. End users will be in charge of developing, testing, and maintaining their applications, while the IS department will retain responsibility for developing, supporting, and maintaining the information infrastructure.

6

Information infrastructure components

Executive summary

The lowest level of the SIP introduced in chapter 4 concerns the information infrastructure's basic components. The computer hardware market is traditionally divided into several relatively independent segments, with mainframes, minicomputers, PCs, and workstations being four major ones.

An analysis of major trends in each segment shows the shift of information processing to microcomputers (PCs and workstations) and, simultaneously, the shift of information storage and management to mainframes and other centralized computing resources.

An analysis of major trends in system software shows two main possibilities that should be carefully studied and compared by IS customers before making serious commitments to hardware and software purchases:

- Proprietary architectures, such as the combination of OS/2 and MVS within the general framework of IBM's SAA
- Open architectures, such as Unix-based components, throughout the entire information infrastructure

Making a commitment to either of these or to any intermediate architectures would be much easier if the IS user could consider and select not isolated infrastructure components and their connections, but basic configurations from which the information infrastructure could be assembled. Basic configurations consist of components such as basic hardware that should be interconnected. Connections within a basic configuration are mostly provided by

LANs. Ethernet, a token bus, and a token ring are three major LAN standards products.

Comparison of these standards shows that there is no such thing as the "best" LAN. By matching specific business conditions and requirements against LAN features and parameters, one can find the LAN adequate for these conditions and requirements.

Four factors influence the variety of basic configurations:

- Where information resides
- Where applications run
- How information is used and distributed
- How information is updated

This chapter shows how different combinations of these factors result in a variety of basic configurations and discusses the ways these configurations are used. The chapter also defines information update regimes and describes a basic client/server model encompassing some of the basic configurations.

System integration pyramid revisited

Look at the SIP again (FIG. 6-1). Its three lowest layers make up a corporate information infrastructure, and its lowest level (basic hardware and system software) contains the information infrastructure's basic components.

The statement that a computer—for example, a mainframe—is just a component of anything rather than a system in its own right would be heretic only a few years ago. Today it is almost an accepted fact. This situation reflects two continuing long-term trends:

- IS users care more about turnkey solutions to their problems and less about purchasing hardware and software and then wondering how to use it.
- Responding to IS user needs, IS vendors are trying to supply them with more integrated solutions.

In other words, a computer is not an answer; a system is. But what is the system of the 1990s and beyond? It is a flexible and incrementally enhanceable corporate information infrastructure with a variety of applications running across its functional subsystems and their components.

Even for a midsize enterprise, the information infrastructure may be a very big system; thus, the capability to assemble it from a variety of relatively large building blocks would be advantageous. This idea is indeed not new in IT. Technology has gone a long way from discrete components, such as transistors and resistors, to integrated circuits of increasing scale of integration, and then to single-chip microprocessors of increasing complexity (from 8 bits to 32

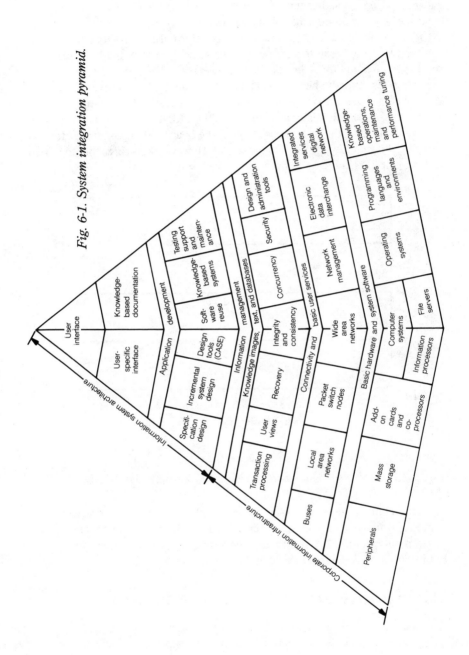

Fig. 6-1. System integration pyramid.

bits on a chip). It is only natural that a computer has become the next step in the integration crusade, and one needs even larger basic configurations to build the large-scale information infrastructure.

Identifying basic configurations of the information infrastructure is not easy, and we only begin to address this issue. In spite of difficulties, the solution has to be found for at least two simple reasons: the user needs it, and the technology is already here. For example, using a 0.8 micron technology, Motorola developed its first four-million-transistor chip, and a 0.5-micron technology will be commercially available in 1993 (FIG. 6-2). According to Gordon Moore, Intel's co-founder and chairman of the board, 50 million transistors on a chip by the year 2000 is not a big problem. However, knowing what to put on such an incredible chip and how to do it is a big one.

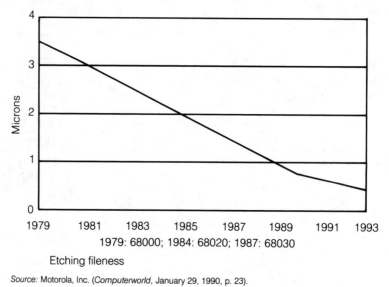

1979: 68000; 1984: 68020; 1987: 68030

Etching fileness

Source: Motorola, Inc. (*Computerworld*, January 29, 1990, p. 23).

Fig. 6-2. The 68040 is a 1.2-million-transistor, 0.8-micron microprocessor.

This chapter looks at major trends in the information infrastructure's component market, that is, the layer of basic computer hardware and system software shown in FIG. 6-1. It then gives a rationale for, and presents a set of, the information infrastructure's basic configurations.

Basic hardware and system software

The computer hardware market is traditionally divided into several relatively independent segments. Here are four major segments:

- Mainframes
- Minicomputers

- PCs
- Workstations

Let us look at major trends in each segment and then summarize the general state of the computer hardware market.

Mainframes

The slowdown in demand for mainframes is commonly recognized. The mainframe sales growth rate is low, if not practically nonexistent, and almost 100 percent of mainframe revenues come from *replacement* business, i.e., from customers who upgrade their existing mainframes, rather than from first-time buyers. Figure 6-3 shows one of the many, almost identical forecasts for mainframe shipments until 1992.

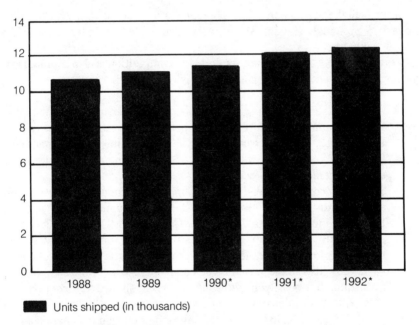

■ Units shipped (in thousands)

Source: Computer and Business Equipment Manufacturers Association (CBEMA), Washington, D.C. (*Computerworld*, December 25, 1989, p. 88).
*Estimated

Fig. 6-3. Mainframe shipments.

The slowdown has caused an unusually heated competition in the mainframe market. No longer is the competition only between IBM and Unisys; nor is it only between IBM and plug-compatible mainframe (PCM) vendors. Although this competition has become more intense than ever before (FIG. 6-4),

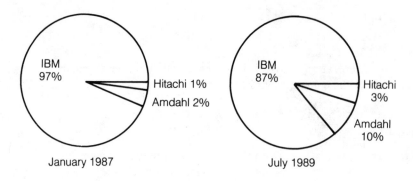

Source: Computer Intelligence Market Research Co.

Fig. 6-4. Erosion of IBM dominance.

it likely will be even fiercer as Hitachi Data Systems (formly National Advanced Systems) establishes itself as a formidable contender in the PCM market segment.

To the surprise of mainframe vendors, the competition is also coming from microcomputer vendors. This competition is two-fold:

- As part of the downsizing trend, some mainframe customers switch to minicomputers having a better price/performance ratio (*Computerworld*, February 12, 1990). In particular, IBM's mainframe business suddenly found itself competing with IBM's AS/400 business (a situation IBM top management hates to see).
- Some minicomputer vendors get into a mainframe business in their attempts to leave the even more depressed minicomputer market. Examples include Digital Equipment Corporation (DEC) with its about 30-mips DEC VAX 9000; Data General with its 50-mips MV/40000 (in four-processor configuration); and Prime with its 120-mips, 1,000-user EXL 1200. It is unlikely that these companies, as new entrants into the mainframe business, will take a major market share away from IBM or Unisys. Rather, minicomputer vendors are playing a "hold the installed base" game, trying to sell mainframes to their current customers to prevent them from switching to another vendor with a broader or more cost-effective product line.

There are several reasons for the uneasy situation in the mainframe market:

- In more advanced mainframes, more mips and megabits are consumed by system functions, such as an operating system and networking (gateways, network management), which means that users pay more for the same or worse cost-effectiveness and memory efficiency, while mainframes lose more to PCs and workstations in terms of cost per mips or megabit (see "Economics of Downsizing" in chapter 3).

- First positive results of downsizing efforts divert prospective first-time buyers from mainframes.
- Mainframes with their proprietary architectures go against a very strong open system tide, which reduces the number of customers loyal to mainframe-based architectures.
- Significant growth in the PC market continues to reduce the number of users accessing the mainframe from dumb terminals and to increase the number of PC users who access a mainframe only occasionally and mostly for data.
- Many applications have been successfully developed on, or ported to, PCs and workstations, which gradually reduces mainframes to mostly information repositories or servers in the networked information infrastructure (which is where mainframes really belong).

What mainframe market changes can be expected in the near future? First, a mainframe will become an information management rather than an information processing tool as information processing shifts more to end-user workstations and PCs, while the requirements for larger databases with faster response time, very large image bases, centralized network management, and tighter security continue to grow. Two recent indications of this trend are (1) the introduction of MVS/ESA, IBM's new operating system, which was mainly caused by relatively poor DB2 performance; and (2) large-scale imaging applications, some of the most successful applications ever on mainframes.

Second, a mainframe will be used more widely as a big, fast server. The attractive feature of this mainframe use is centralized network management and host-based security. One recent indication of this trend is Microsoft's LAN Manager/MVS, a mainframe server supporting DOS, OS/2, and Microsoft Windows clients. LAN Manager/MVS is expected to turn a mainframe into a "massive server and a gateway through which administrators could manage local area networks" (*Computerworld*, February 12, 1990).

Third, a major split in mainframe business can be expected. IBM will be trying to make its mainframe architecture more proprietary through two separate undertakings:

- Implementing its System Application Architecture (SAA) strategy.
- Developing more specialized architectures that cannot be copied by the PCM vendors. For example, these architectures might be oriented toward faster database implementation and hardware-based system security.

At the same time, Unisys and NCR will likely move toward an *open mainframe*, the concept that currently seems to be, but actually is not, a contradiction in terms. An open mainframe will be a higher level of a two-tier Unix-based system architecture compatible with its lower-level counterpart, a workstation.

Minicomputers

The future for minicomputers is uncertain. They are getting dangerously squeezed by mainframes and workstations, especially since many companies are switching to a two-tier strategy (networks of PCs connected to corporate mainframes), with midrange computers playing no role (or a minimal role) in their future. Problems experienced by Data General, Wang, Prime, and even DEC and IBM are indications of this trend.

It is not unlikely that in five to seven years minicomputers will fade away, except for special niche markets. Not surprisingly, forecasts for future revenues in the minicomputer segment are not rosy (FIG. 6-5).

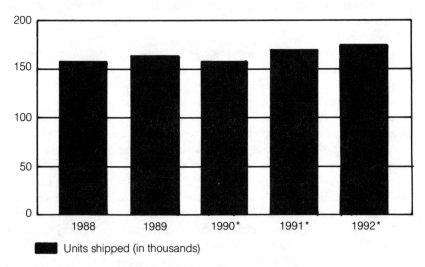

■ Units shipped (in thousands)

Source: CBEMA (*Computerworld*, December 25, 1989, p. 88).
*Estimated

Fig. 6-5. Minicomputer shipments.

As discussed in the previous section, the only good news for minicomputer vendors is that, as a result of downsizing, minicomputers begin to play the role of mainframes, especially in small to midsize enterprises.

The only healthy segment of the minicomputer market is fault-tolerant computers. This segment has experienced a steady growth (FIG. 6-6) which is expected to remain at about the same pace.

Microcomputers

Under an umbrella of microcomputers, we include both PCs and workstations. This segment of the computer hardware market is the fastest growing and so

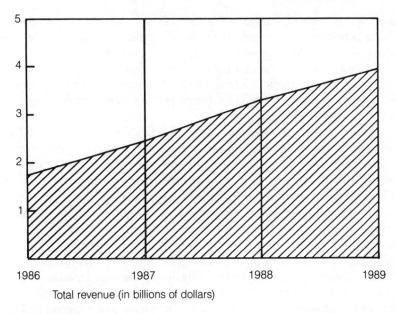

Total revenue (in billions of dollars)

Source: Frost & Sullivan
(*Computerworld*, February 5, 1990, p. 1).

Fig. 6-6. Fault-tolerant system sales.

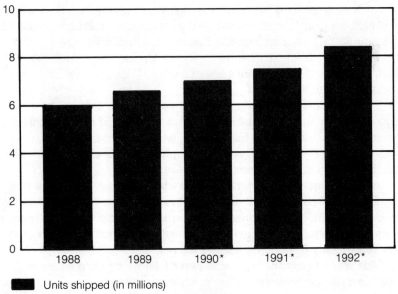

Units shipped (in millions)

Source: CBEMA (*Computerworld*, December 25, 1990, p. 88).
*Estimated

Fig. 6-7. Microcomputer shipments.

far shows no signs of slowdown (FIG. 6-7). The growth rate is even more surprising considering an already deep market penetration of microcomputers: there are close to 200 PCs per 1000 population in the United States.

There are many reasons for the popularity of microcomputers. Suffice it to say that no serious IS can be built today without microcomputers, and there are serious reasons to believe that future ISs will include microcomputers as their main and dominating component.

In the context of this section, it seems worthwhile to address the following question: What is the real difference between a PC and a workstation? Answering this question was easy four years ago but is becoming increasingly difficult. Three years ago, one could point at the difference in applications. PCs were said to be used for "business applications," workstations for "engineering applications." Today, workstations so deeply penetrate the financial services industry that this difference has vanished. Two years ago, the difference was a graphic interface. Today, with such interfaces as Microsoft Windows 3.0, this difference practically does not exist (with the exception of graphic supercomputers that still provide the incomparable quality of graphics but at a much higher price). One year ago, the difference was price. Today, PCs and workstations have very little, if any, difference in price in comparable configurations, and this difference will soon disappear. So what, then, is the difference between a PC and a workstation?

At first glance, the answer is somewhat strange. PCs are based on Intel's 80000 series of microprocessors and run mostly under DOS and its successor, OS/2. (One exception is Microsoft's Xenix, which currently is sold under the label of Santa Cruz Operation Inc.) On the contrary, workstations are based on Motorola 68000 and, more recently, Reduced Instruction Set Computer (RISC) microprocessors from multiple vendors. (Sun Microsystems, Motorola, MIPS, IBM, and Hewlett-Packard are a few examples.) With very few exceptions, all workstations run under Unix.

This real difference between PCs and workstations does not seem to have any significance for an IS customer. Indeed, why should it bother the IS customer what chips are inside the box used or what operating systems run this box? Theoretically, the answer is self-implying: it should not. However, in practice, the situation is somewhat complicated.

As we discussed in chapter 2, there is a big difference between a standard and a de facto standard. Following the standard brings the user closer to an open system with all its advantages. Following a de facto standard always carries a risk of getting locked into a single vendor's solution. The more powerful a de facto standard setter, the greater the risk.

This is not to say that one must never follow a de facto standard. Sometimes de facto standards are available, while standards are not. The enterprise may have no time to wait for them to become available, and thus it has no choice except to go for products complying with the de facto standard. IBM's SNA is one such example: it may take years for the OSI Reference Model to reach the state that SNA is in today.

In this and similar situations, IS users have to understand the dynamics of standard development and follow the market to determine the switching costs for moving from a de facto standard to a standard. From this viewpoint let us look at what currently distinguishes a PC from a workstation—the operating system.

DOS vs. OS/2 vs. Unix

Although OS/2 is a DOS successor, its target market is very different from the DOS market. It is not even clear why anybody who does not need true multitasking and connectivity with an IBM mainframe would want to switch from DOS to OS/2. Figure 6-8 demonstrates one result of Dataquest's market research on, and forecast for, DOS and OS/2 sales. It clearly shows the poor acceptance of OS/2. Another unrelated market survey was aimed at pinning down the factors influencing OS/2 acceptance. The result is as follows:

- 65 percent of respondents point at a too small number of new OS/2 applications (to compare, there are more than 15,000 estimated DOS applications on the market).
- 60 percent of respondents are waiting for reduced memory prices (it takes 4M to 5M bytes of memory only to run OS/2).
- 60 percent of respondents complain about porting of existing DOS applications (OS/2 runs only those DOS applications that require less than 520K bytes of memory).

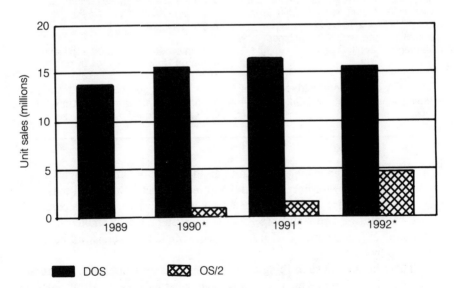

Source: Dataquest (*Computerworld*, December 25, 1990, p. 36). *Estimated

Fig. 6-8. DOS vs. OS/2 Sales.

This market research does not necessarily mean that OS/2 compares unfavorably with DOS. OS/2 is a much more powerful and complex system, potentially with excellent graphics and database capabilities. The point is that OS/2 should not be compared with DOS at all. OS/2 and DOS are completely different products, and their markets are almost disjoint. (The only thing common for them is that they run on the same class of microcomputers, based on Intel 80286, 80386, and 80486 chips.) The real competition for OS/2 comes from another side—Unix.

OS/2 vs. Unix   TABLE 6-1 provides a comparison of OS/2 and Unix, showing advantages and disadvantages of both operating systems. The major advantage of OS/2 is its homogeneity resulting from the fact that OS/2 is a proprietary system, or "packaged product" (using the euphemism of Bill Gates, Microsoft's Chairman). It is not even a de facto standard because, in order to become one, it must have been sold in many more copies. The result of OS/2 homogeneity is that OS/2 is a single operating system, with a single graphic user interface, Presentation Manager.

Table 6-1. OS/2 vs. Unix.

OS/2	Unix
Proprietary system ("packaged product")	Open architecture
Single homogenous system	Variety of dialects.
Single user interface (Presentation Manager) incompatible with DOS Windows	Variety of user interfaces (Motif, Next-Step, OpenLook, Open Desk)
Developed for a 16-bit 286 chip but should be used on 32-bit machines	A 32-bit system
Shortage of applications	Unix International: 15,000 applications to run on Unix System V.4 by end of 1990
Runs DOS applications with restrictions	Runs all DOS applications as tasks
Provides multitasking for OS/2 applications	Provides full multitasking for Unix and DOS applications

The lack of homogeneity is a major disadvantage of Unix. In fact, Unix is a variety of slightly (or not so slightly) different dialects. Even if all these dialects get standardized (what all IS users would like to see as soon as possible), there will still be two standards: one, Unix System V.4, promoted by Unix International; and another based on Carnegie-Mellon University's Mach OS, promoted by OSF.

There is also no such thing as a standardized user interface. There are four "standards" from which to choose (in alphabetical order): Motif, selected and promoted by OSF; NextStep, developed and promoted by Next, Inc., and licensed by IBM; Open Desk, developed and promoted by Santa Cruz Operation, Inc.; and OpenLook, developed by Sun Microsystems and promoted by Unix International.

In principle, Unix is a genuinely open system but it does not necessarily have a lot of dialects and user interface standards. Hopefully, this deficiency of Unix will be straightened out in the next couple of years.

Conflicting Unix standards do not seem to impede IS users' acceptance of Unix as an open operating system of choice. Neither do current shortcomings of Unix, such as insufficient transaction processing performance and security leaks. The market survey of 129 commercial sites, conducted by International Data Corporation (IDC) and described in its White Paper, confirms these observations (FIGS. 6-9 and 6-10).

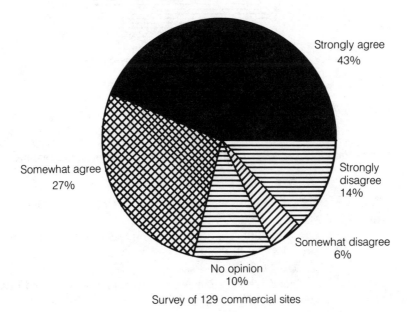

Survey of 129 commercial sites

Source: "Unix—opening the door to business solutions," IDC White Paper, 1990, p. 5.

Fig. 6-9. Unix is the preferred OS for business addressing problems in the 1990s.

One major shortcoming of OS/2 is shortage of applications—a situation that, unfortunately, does not seem to be temporary. On the contrary, the number of Unix applications is large and growing. (Unix International predicted that more than 15,000 applications would be run on Unix System V.4 by the end of 1990.)

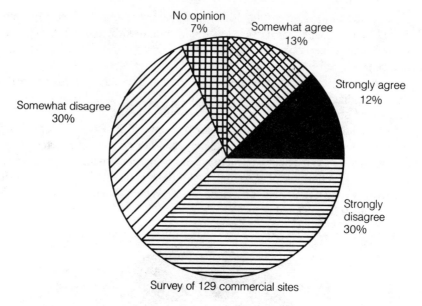

Survey of 129 commercial sites

Source: "Unix—opening the door to business solutions," IDC White Paper, 1990, p. 8.

Fig. 6-10. Conflicting Unix standards are delaying Unix purchases.

Two of the Unix surprises (and OS/2 creators' strategic mistakes) are as follows:

- Unix runs all DOS applications as tasks, that is, slower, but it does run them, while OS/2 runs them with restrictions.
- Unix provides full multitasking for both Unix and DOS applications, while OS/2 provides multitasking for OS/2 applications only.

Finally, OS/2 was conceived as an operating system for 80286-based PCs, but to run it requires a top-end 80386- or 80486-based PC. In other words, OS/2 does not use all features of the advanced microcomputers available today. In fact, the user pays for an 80386- or 80486-based PC in order to be able to run OS/2 rather than to use the features of the PC. This irony is one of the side effects of going for a proprietary system.

Areas of OS/2 use All this does not mean that OS/2 is unusable. What it does mean is that the scope of its usability is much narrower than its creators expected and would like to see. A typical OS/2 user is a heavy IBM mainframe-oriented enterprise that uses an advanced PC rather than a workstation as its information infrastructure's basic component, has a lot of PCs, and seeks for connectivity between them and IBM mainframes. An OS/2 user most likely does not care about open systems and follows IBM directions, including SAA.

This profile of a typical OS/2 user seems to be confirmed by some of the latest market surveys. Figure 6-11 shows the result of a survey conducted by Computer Intelligence Market Research Co. Only among users with more than 250 installed PCs, did more than 40 percent of them plan to migrate to OS/2. Bears Stearns & Co./Goldstein Golup Kessler Co. conducted a survey exploring the migration to OS/2 by industry (FIG. 6-12). Only in the banking and financial industry, a heavy mainframe user, did more than 50 percent of respondents plan to move to OS/2 within the next 24 months. For contrast, in the government, a major Unix supporter, less than 7 percent of respondents plan this step.

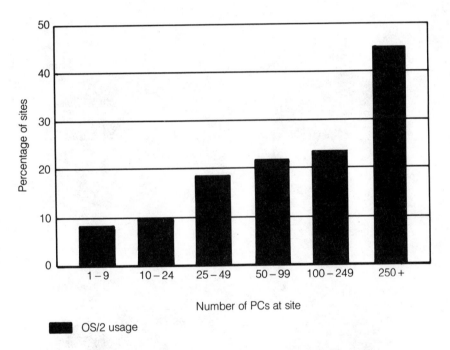

OS/2 usage

Source: Computer Intelligence Market Research Co. (*Computerworld*, February 12, 1990, p. 122).

Fig. 6-11. Planned use of OS/2 by number of PCs installed.

Many users postpone their decisions concerning OS/2 waiting for (1) a significantly larger number of OS/2 applications or (2) a 32-bit OS/2 version (should we call it OS/3?) featuring full use of 80386- and 80486-based PCs, full coexistence of this version and DOS, and better network management.

General state of basic hardware and system software

The advent of very large-scale integrated circuits (VLSI) and PCs has caused dramatic changes in our business and personal life. Through unprecedented

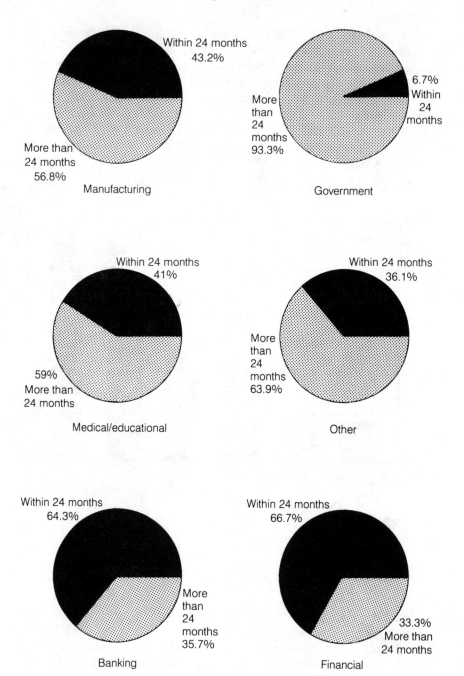

Source: Bears Starns & Co./Goldstein Golup Kessler Co. (*Computerworld*, February 12, 1990, p. 122).

Fig. 6-12. Moving to OS/2 by industry.

economies of scale, PCs have been relentlessly driving the price of computing power down, taking this power away from the "glass-wall rooms" and bringing it to the end user's desk.

Through a number of popular applications, such as word processing, file and database management, spreadsheets, desktop publishing, and project management, PCs have also freed the end user from IS department domination. However, that was not the end of a story.

The real revolution occurred in a literally personal, stand-alone use of the computing power. As a side effect, PCs also led to greater people isolation in the workplace and, in some cases, became an impediment to information sharing and group work. To change this unfortunate situation, many corporations have begun to look for ways to combine the power of PCs with that of existing computers, first of all mainframes.

First attempts of linking PCs to centralized computing resources revealed a number of technical and organizational problems. The following problems have been cited most commonly:

- PC costs turn out to be just a tip of the iceberg, compared with the cost of links and interfaces.
- Central files and databases as well as applications written against them on mainframes turn out to be inappropriate for work with PCs and workstations.
- Information sharing turns out to be much more than just linking a mainframe with PCs and file transfer between them.
- Connecting PCs with LANs does not solve the problem either because the enterprise winds up with dozens or even hundreds of LANs that are installed by different departments and do not talk to each other.
- Information stored on PCs is vulnerable to both external and internal attacks.

These problems cannot be solved apart from system software, specifically operating systems and environments on top of them. An analysis of major trends in system software shows two main scenarios that should be carefully studied and compared by IS customers before making serious commitments to hardware and software purchases:

- Proprietary architectures, such as the combination of OS/2 and MVS within the general framework of IBM's SAA. DEC's Enterprise System Architecture (ESA) is another example. Two problems with this scenario are locking in a single vendor and major doubts that these architectures are feasible and will ever be delivered.
- Open architectures, such as Unix-based components throughout the entire information infrastructure. The major problem with this scenario is the lack of implemented standards and packaged solutions for interfacing Unix-based systems with the installed base.

In either case, the well-planned and implemented corporate information infrastructure is necessary if the enterprise is to succeed in a strategic use of IT.

LANs

At this point, let me remind you that we defined a corporate information infrastructure as an organized collection of information sources, storages, processors, and users along with communication systems connecting them. Basic hardware and software covers one part of this definition, namely, information sources, storages, processors, and (partially) users. Another part of this definition, communication systems, is represented by LANs and WANs.

LANs and WANs are components of the information infrastructure. It is intuitively evident that LANs are used almost exclusively as intraconnections for the basic configurations discussed later in this chapter. In other words, an LAN's role is mostly limited to being a component of basic configurations of the information infrastructure. WANs, on the other hand, play a broader role, providing a skeleton for the information infrastructure that is "fleshed out" by multiple diverse basic configurations.

At the less intuitive level, TABLE 6-2 shows the differences between LANs and WANs. LANs differ from WANs in both technical (range, data rate, and reliability) and organizational (ownership, design strategy, and bandwidth importance) parameters. The cost comparisons apart from a particular corporate information infrastructure are somewhat irrelevant because of the very different roles LANs and WANs play and the diversity of possible LAN/WAN configurations across various information infrastructures.

An additional kind of network intermediate between an LAN and a WAN is the metropolitan area network (MAN). The MAN network uses LAN tech-

Table 6-2. LAN vs. WAN.

Feature	LAN	WAN
Range	No more than a few miles	Thousands of miles
Data rate	Several Mbps (to hundreds or thousands with fiberoptics)	Typically below 1 MBps
Ownership	By a single organization	By multiple organizations (carriers and clients)
Design strategy	May be designed from scratch using own high-bandwidth cables.	Almost always uses existing telephone network.
Bandwidth importance	Insignificant	All-important
Reliability	High (1000 times lower error rate vs. WAN). Error handling may be done only in higher layers.	Relatively low. Error handling must be done in each layer.

nology but covers a very big corporate or college campus or a whole city. Most of the discussions of LANs also pertains to MANs.

Subsequent sections discuss LANs as a component of basic configurations and compare three existing LAN standards. The current LAN market and future trends are also presented. The joint discussion of WANs and LANs as a skeleton of the information infrastructure is postponed until Part II, in which chapters 7, 8, and 9 are dedicated to these issues.

LAN standards

The Institute of Electrical and Electronic Engineers (IEEE) has developed three LAN standards:

- IEEE 802.3 for 1-persistent carrier sense multiple access with collision detection (CSMA/CD)
- IEEE 802.4 for token bus
- IEEE 802.5 for token ring

Let us briefly describe each standard.

IEEE 802.3 and Ethernet To understand the meaning of the "1-persistent CSMA/CD" gibberish, look at FIG. 6-13. Imagine an LAN as a collection of stations (computers) connected with each other through some kind of communication channel. Stations can independently transmit messages through the same channel. In order to avoid collision, the station listens to the channel before transmitting the message.

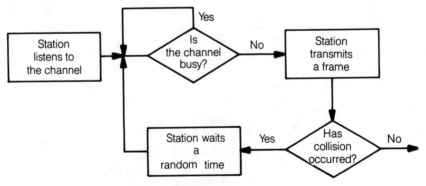

Fig. 6-13. 1-persistent CSMA algorithm.

If the channel is already busy, the station waits until the channel becomes idle. If the channel is idle, the station transmits a frame. This frame can collide with another frame just transmitted by another station. If a collision does not happen, everything is fine. If it does happen, the station waits for a random amount of time and starts over again.

Figure 6-13 describes a basic *1-persistent CSMA algorithm* because, when the channel is idle, this algorithm transmits a frame with the probability equal to 1. (It is a particular case of the p-persistent CSMA algorithm which instructs the station to transmit a frame with the probability p and to wait for another slot of time with the probability $q = 1 - p$.)

The basic 1-persistent CSMA algorithm may be complemented with *collision detection*, thus forming the CSMA/CD algorithm. If two or more stations transmit simultaneously and detect collision, they stop transmitting immediately, thus saving time and bandwidth. The stations all wait for a random time before trying frame transmission again. Indeed, any station must be equipped with the corresponding analog circuitry to detect collisions.

The IEEE 802.3 standard describes a family of CSMA/CD systems with a transmission rate ranging from 1 megabit per second (Mbps) to 10 Mbps, depending on the specific physical medium. The most popular member of this family is Ethernet, a 10-Mbps, baseband coaxial cable-based implementation of the 802.3 standard (see chapter 7 for more information about baseband cables).

A typical Ethernet configuration is shown in FIG. 6-14. A station is connected with a coaxial cable through a transceiver, a transceiver cable, and an interface board. The *transceiver* is tightly held to the cable to provide a reliable contact with the inner core of the cable. The transceiver contains analog circuitry to provide carrier sensing (listening to other stations' transmission) and collision detection. It also lets other transceivers know when collision is detected. One transceiver may be connected to as many as eight stations.

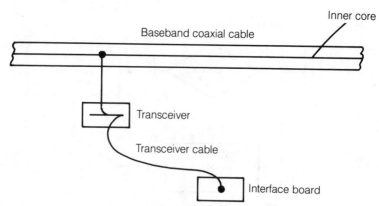

Fig. 6-14. Typical Ethernet configuration.

The *transceiver cable* connects the transceiver with the interface board. It carries data and control signals to and from the station. The *interface board* contains a controller chip that transmits frames to and receives frames from the transceiver and provides frame assembly, buffer management, and checksum computation and verification.

The maximum length of the coaxial cable is 500 meters. However, using two-way amplifiers called repeaters (see "Kinds of Relays" in chapter 8), this limit can be increased. The two restrictions are that no path between two transceivers may be longer than 2.5 km, and no more than four repeaters may be on that path.

There are four basic cable topologies:

- Single cable. The LAN consists of a single cable, with stations (computers) connected at the most convenient point.
- Backbone. Multiple single cables with stations are merged to another cable called a backbone whose function is to transfer frames between single cables. For example, the single cable can connect stations located on the same floor, while the backbone provides frame transfer between floors.
- Tree. Since there is only one path between any two nodes of a tree, this topology is interference-free and hence popular.
- Segments connected by bridges (see chapter 8). Bridges forward only signals going to other segments, reducing the number of signals simultaneously traveling through the LAN. Bridges must know the LAN topology and location of all stations.

IEEE 802.4: A token bus   The IEEE 802.4 standard is called a *token bus*. As shown in FIG. 6-15, the token bus is physically a linear or treelike broadband coaxial cable (see chapter 7) with attached stations (computers). The token bus allows three speeds of 1, 5, and 10 Mbps. The 802.4 standard is physically incompatible with the 802.3.

Logically, a token bus is a *ring*, with each station knowing the address of its logically left and right neighbors. Since the token bus, like any LAN, is a broadcasting subnet (see chapter 7), the physical order of stations is irrelevant.

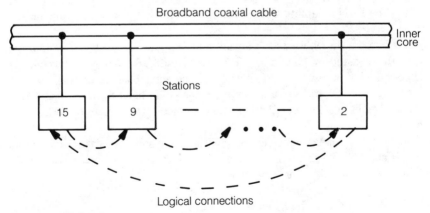

Fig. 6-15. Token bus.

Since the ring is logical, the addition of stations to, or the deletion of stations from, the token bus is easy.

After successful transmission the station sends a special control frame, called a *token*, to its right neighbor. Only the token holder is allowed to transmit a frame (or a series of short frames); thus, collisions in the token bus never occur.

Unlike Ethernet frames, token bus frames may have priorities. Each station is conceptually divided into four substations, each handling frames of one out of four possible priorities. The token is passed to substations in the order of their priorities and is kept there within some time limits. The highest-priority substation always has a guaranteed fraction of the LAN bandwidth.

Some of the 802.4 features were dictated by the manufacturing environment, specifically, real-time requirements. However, the 802.4 standard is very complex, and token buses have proved to be difficult in maintenance.

IEEE 802.5: A token ring The IEEE 802.5 standard is called a *token ring*. It is somewhat ironic that while the token bus is logically a ring, the token ring is logically not a ring. It is actually a collection of individual point-to-point links that form a ring. The token ring uses shielded twisted pairs that normally run at 4 Mbps (there is also a 16-Mbps version).

A special 3-byte control frame, called a *token*, circulates around the ring whenever stations are idle. In this regime the ring must have a sufficient delay to contain a complete token. Normally, this delay consists of the signal propagation delay and one bit delay at each station. If the natural delay is insufficient, a special station called a *monitor* must introduce an additional delay to keep the token alive. (One bit on a 4-Mbps token ring takes about 50 meters. For a 3-byte token, the ring must be about 1200 meters long.)

Each station has a ring interface that has two operational modes:

- LISTEN: the station copies input bits to output with a 1-bit delay.
- TRANSMIT: the station enters its data on the ring and drains "old" data from the ring. Removed data may be discarded or saved to check the LAN reliability by comparing it with what previously transmitted.

When the station wants to transmit a frame, it seizes the token, removing it from the ring, and switches to the TRANSMIT mode. Since only the token holder is permitted to transmit, the token ring, like the token bus, has no collisions.

After the last transmitted frame bit has come back to the transmitter, it must regenerate the token, let it go, and immediately switch to the LISTEN mode.

Token ring maintenance is provided by a specially dedicated monitor station. Each station can become a monitor if the current one goes down. Here is a sample of monitor station functions:

- Watching that the token is not lost
- Taking an action when the ring breaks

- Cleaning up the ring
- Removing orphan frames
- Entering artificial delays to hold the token on the ring

LAN comparison

TABLE 6-3 compares the technical and operational parameters of the three IEEE LAN standards and clearly shows that there is no such thing as the "best" LAN. By matching specific business conditions and requirements against LAN features and parameters, one can find the LAN adequate for the desired application.

Some general conclusions, however, can be drawn. Ethernet is still the most popular kind of LAN because of its fair speed, relatively easy maintenance, and low cost. Nevertheless, as fiberoptics-based LANs (see chapter 7) become affordable, while the load on an LAN and, accordingly, the demand for its higher speed increases, Ethernet LANs will lose their turf.

The major drawback of the token bus is its complexity: hence, high cost, relatively low reliability, and maintenance problems. Except for special-purpose applications, such as a combination of real-time requirements with high load on the LAN, the future of token bus LANs is unclear if not bleak.

Token ring LANs have a bright future. In addition to the advantages shown in TABLE 6-3, the token ring is the only configuration suited for fiberoptics (see chapter 7).

Market trends

As a direct consequence of downsizing and the shift of information processing toward PCs and workstations, the demand for LANs will continue to grow. Figure 6-16 representing the results of market research by Eastern Management shows this trend. IDC predicts a 78 percent compound annual growth in the number of LAN-based integrated office systems (FIG. 6-17).

An interesting problem with LANs that we currently are witnessing is that an average company already has or may have in the future too many of them. The good news is that LANs encourage and promote information sharing and exchange within a basic configuration, providing serious advantages over centralized mainframe-based systems. The bad news is that they do not promote information sharing and exchange between basic configurations that can use different LAN standards and thus make inter-LAN communications more difficult. (Refer to "Internetworking," chapter 8.)

Another negative aspect is that proliferation of LANs creates new problems in network management. There is an intrinsic conflict between decentralization brought by LANs and increasing demands for centralized network management. (Refer to chapter 9 for a discussion of network management.)

Table 6-3. LAN Comparison.

Feature	Ethernet 802.3	Token Bus 802.4	Token Ring 802.5
Frame size	64 to 1500 bytes; significant overhead for short messages	Up to 8182 bytes; can handle short frames	No upper limit except for token holding time (10 ms); handles short frames
Cable type	Passive, baseband, not good for higher bandwidth cables such as fiberoptics	Broadband, standard cable TV equipment; poorly suited for fiber-optics implementation	Any transmission media, point-to-point connection
Cable length	No longer than 2.5 km (even with repeaters); degradation of performance for long cables	No limits	No upper limits; for short cables, artificial delays may be necessary
Engineering	Critical analog component for collision detection	Needs modems and analog amplifiers, special cable, and dual cable topologies	Easy and fully digital
Topology	Multiple topologies are feasible, including backbone, tree, and segments	Linear or tree; fits in linear topology infrastructures such as assembly lines	Ring; fits in circle topology infrastructures such as tall, narrow buildings
Protocol	Simple	Extremely complex with complex maintenance	Moderately complex
Dynamic station installation	Simple and straight-forward	Simple automated procedure	Requires taking LAN down
Behavior at low load	Delay is practically zero	Substantial delay	Moderate delay
Behavior at high load	Collisions present a major problem; efficiency is low (may collapse)	Excellent throughput and efficiency; cable supports multiple channels	Excellent throughput and efficiency
Worst-case performance (delay)	Delay is potentially infinite	Finite; known in advance	Finite; known in advance
Control functions	Decentralized	Decentralized	Central monitor station is a critical component
Reliability	High	Repeated losses of a token at critical moments may present a serious problem; cable supports multiple channels	Break in ring cable brings whole network down, or wire centers are required (provide automatic elimination of failed cables)
Frame priorities	No priorities	Multiple; fair for all stations	Multiple; stations with low priorities may wait a long time

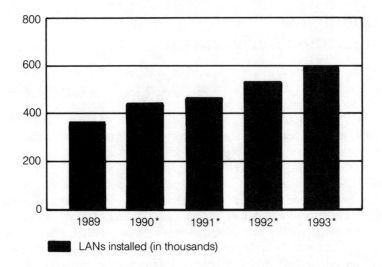

Source: The Eastern Management Group (*Computerworld*, February 5, 1990, p. 90).   *Estimated

Fig. 6-16. Number of LAN installations.

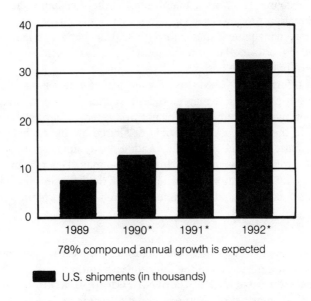

Source: IDC (*Computerworld*, March 5, 1990, p. 88).   *Estimated

Fig. 6-17. Growth of LAN-based integrated office systems.

Basic configurations of an information infrastructure

Basic hardware and system software should be incorporated in bigger entities, referred to earlier as basic configurations. We assume that a corporate information infrastructure consists of a set of these configurations and their interconnections. We only start seeing possible approaches to addressing the issue of basic configurations. Success in this endeavor is predicated on our ability to single out typical patterns of information location and exchange as well as application development philosophy (chapter 5).

Chapter 5 listed questions that should be asked to understand patterns of information location and exchange and then determine the topology of an information infrastructure. Chapter 5 also listed questions that should be answered to develop, share, and maintain applications. Now, I will answer some of these questions by defining four basic architectural building blocks (BABB) of an information infrastructure and four basic infrastructure patterns.

Four factors influence the variety of basic configurations:

- Where information resides. Information may be stored in a central storage or be distributed across several information management sites. The mixture of both is also possible.
- Where applications run. Applications may run in a centralized information resource (such as a mainframe) or be distributed across several information processing sites. (Note that, generally speaking, an information management and information processing site may not be the same site or even the same computer at the same site.) Again, the mixture of both is also possible.
- How information is used and transferred. Information may be used only where it resides, or it may be transferred for storage at a remote information management site or for use at a remote information processing site. In the latter case it may only be shared by, and exchanged among, information management sites or additionally updated at such sites.
- How information is updated. Information may (1) not be updated at all (read-only information), (2) be updated periodically (off-line information update), or (3) be updated immediately (on-line information update).

Four BABBs

The first two factors influencing basic configurations give rise to four BABBs. These BABBs are described in the following paragraphs.

Centralized information/centralized applications (CICA) In a CICA BABB all information is stored, and all processing is done, in a centralized computational resource such as a mainframe. "Dumb" user terminals are usually sufficient. A schematic of the CICA BABB is shown in FIG. 6-18.

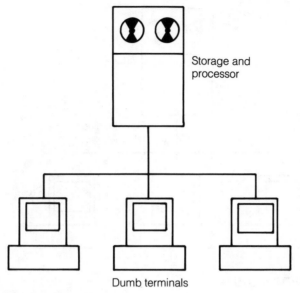

Storage and
processor

Dumb terminals

Fig. 6-18. CICA BABB.

Centralized information/distributed applications (CIDA)   In a
CIDA BABB all information is stored in a centralized computational resource,
while all application-related processing is done on end-user workstations. The
CIDA BABB implies that information should be downloaded from a centralized resource to an end-user workstation. Depending on the user's update
rights, the results of processing may be left in the workstation or uploaded
back to a centralized resource. A schematic of the CIDA BABB is shown in
FIG. 6-19.

Distributed information/centralized applications (DICA)   In a
DICA BABB information is stored on end-user workstations, while all process-
ing is done on a centralized computational resource. A schematic of the DICA
BABB is shown in FIG. 6-20.

The DICA BABB implies that information stored in a certain workstation
should be uploaded to a centralized computational resource for processing.
The results of processing should be downloaded back to the workstation that
stores this information or other workstation identified by the user. The DICA
may require high bandwidth to provide many uploads.

Generally speaking, DICA is a peculiar architecture that contradicts the
trend toward decentralization of information processing (see chapter 10 for
more discussion of information centralization and decentralization of information processing). However, it may serve some special situations: for example,
real-time data acquisition, its consolidation at the central site, and consequent
processing of consolidated information.

Distributed information/distributed applications (DIDA)   In a

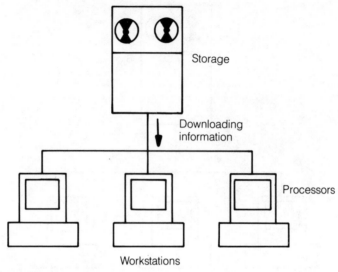

Fig. 6-19. CIDA BABB.

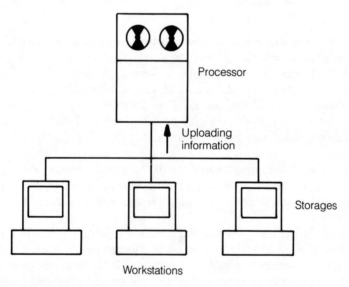

Fig. 6-20. DICA BABB.

DIDA BABB all information is stored in, and all processing is done on, end-user workstations. A schematic of the DIDA BABB is shown in FIG. 6-21.

To implement the DIDA BABB, an LAN of workstations is generally sufficient. The LAN may include a dedicated server that stores all the information, or, alternatively, each user workstation may store some part of the total information. Parts are not necessarily mutually disjoint; that is, information can be

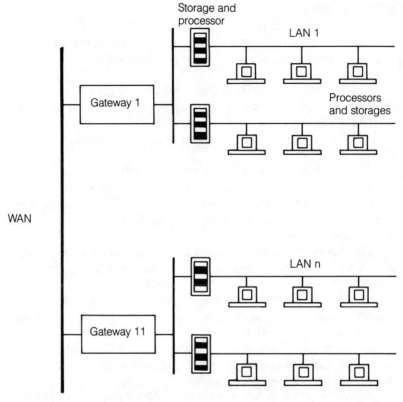

Fig. 6-21. DIDA BABB.

duplicated at several workstations. The bandwidth required to pass information around the DIDA is determined by the degree of information and application sharing.

Basic infrastructure patterns

Within each BABB, four basic infrastructure patterns can be identified, depending on whether information and applications are possessed by and used at only one site or shared among many sites. These patterns are as follows:

- Shared information/protected applications (SIPA)
- Shared information/shared applications (SISA)
- Protected information/protected applications (PIPA)
- Protected information/shared applications (PISA)

Basic configurations   Thus, there are 16 possible combinations of BABBs and infrastructure patterns that represent basic configurations of the information infrastructure. These combinations are as follows:

CICA/SIPA: A mainframe environment with a common database and applications that run against this database. The applications are used by individuals or small groups and are not shared with other individuals or small groups.

CICA/SISA: A mainframe environment with a common database and standard transaction processing applications that run against this database.

CICA/PIPA: A mainframe environment with protected applications (see CICA/SIPA) that run against individual data sets (or, hopefully, mutually disjoint databases).

CICA/PISA: A mainframe environment with shared applications that run against individual data sets (or, hopefully, mutually disjoint databases).

CIDA/SIPA: A client/file server architecture with all information stored in a server; each client runs its specific applications against a commonly shared server database.

CIDA/SISA: A client/file server architecture with all information stored in a server; each client runs the same applications against a commonly shared server database.

CIDA/PIPA: A client/file server architecture with all information stored in a server; each client runs its specific applications against individually used databases stored in the server.

CIDA/PISA: A client/file server architecture with all information stored in a server; each client runs the same applications against individually used databases stored in the server.

DICA/SIPA: A compute server/local data collection environment with local microprocessors that collect and store information and upload it for processing in the compute server. Information stored in microprocessors is shareable (perhaps with other building blocks), while applications are specific to each local microprocessor. This is one of the strangest architectures, but it may be used in some peculiar cases.

DICA/SISA: A compute server/local data collection environment with local microprocessors that collect and store information and upload it for processing in the compute server. Information stored in microprocessors is shareable (perhaps with other building blocks), and applications are common for all local microprocessors.

DICA/PIPA: A compute server/local data collection environment with local microprocessors that collect and store information and upload it for processing in the compute server. Information stored in each local microprocessor is special, and applications running on a compute server are specific to each local microprocessor. This and the next architecture are two of the more natural (among peculiar) DICA BABBs.

DICA/PISA: A compute server/local data collection environment with local microprocessors that collect and store information and upload it for processing in the compute server. Information stored in each local microprocessor is special, while applications running on a computer server are common for all local microprocessors.

DIDA/SIPA: A client/server architecture, with each client running its specific applications against shared data that may be stored in any client and/ or the server.

DIDA/SISA: A client/server architecture, with each client running the same applications against shared data that may be stored in any client and/or the server.

DIDA/PIPA: A client/server architecture, with each client running its specific applications against its specific data that may be stored in it and the server.

DIDA/PISA: A client/server architecture, with each client running the same applications against its specific data that may be stored in it and the server.

Selection of infrastructure patterns   Selection of an infrastructure pattern is determined by factors such as the following:

- Actual need for sharing information and applications
- A site's procedures and policies
- How decisions for purchasing hardware and software are made
- How IS personnel are distributed across sites

TABLE 6-4 shows areas of advantageous use of each infrastructure pattern. The first decision that should be made in the selection process is whether there is an actual need to share information for each relatively independent information chunk (for example, a relational data table). This decision should be based on the analysis of business requirements and adopted policies of information ownership (see "Impact of IM/SD Policy," chapter 5; and chapter 16). As a helpful side effect, the information-sharing decision provides guidelines for physical location and proper groupings of information.

If information at the sites is mutually independent, the PIPA or PISA pattern should be selected. If information must be shared, the SIPA or SISA pattern is a good choice. Since, in most practical cases, some information at each site must be shared and some must not, one can expect a combination of several infrastructure patterns at each site. This fact is just one more hint that the information infrastructure is a complex web of many different BABBs having different infrastructure patterns.

The second decision that should be made in the selection process is whether there is an actual need for application sharing. If various sites have different or ad hoc or proprietary procedures and processes, applications run at one site will likely have little commonality with those run at another site. Conversely, if various sites have standardized procedures and processes, applications may have to be shared.

Table 6-4. Basic Infrastructure Patterns: When to Use Which.

SIPA	SISA
Advantages if: Information must be shared Sites have different or ad hoc procedures and policies Variety of applications against same information Many users of information; only local users of applications Hardware/software purchasing decisions are local (site-based) Qualified personnel at all sites	*Advantages if:* Information must be shared Sites have standard procedures and processes Many users of both information and applications Central hardware/software purchasing decisions Centralized IS personnel
PIPA	**PISA**
Advantages if: Independent information at sites Sites have different or ad hoc procedures and processes Only local users of both information and applications Hardware/software purchasing decisions are local (site-based) Qualified personnel at all sites	*Advantages if:* Independent information at sites Sites have standard procedures and processes Local users of information; many users of applications Central purchasing decisions Centralized IS personnel and on-site information management

Thus, the application-sharing decision, like the information-sharing decision, should be based on the analysis of business requirements, policies, procedures, and processes. If applications at the sites are different or proprietary, the SIPA or PIPA pattern should be selected. If applications are shared, the SISA or PISA pattern is a good selection.

Selection of an infrastructure pattern should be done in the context of existing personnel and purchasing policies, or these policies should be changed according to the preferred infrastructure pattern and prior to its selection.

Protected applications should be supported by qualified personnel at all sites where these applications run, while shared applications must be supported by centralized IS personnel to provide proper version management, that is, to avoid running different versions of the same application at different sites. Protected information may require site-based information management, while shared information must be managed centrally to provide its consistency at different sites.

Central or local hardware/software purchase decisions also affect the selection of an infrastructure process. Local purchasing decisions almost inevitably lead to a greater variety of hardware and software and, as a result, to more difficulties in information and application sharing. Indeed, difficulties of information and application sharing are different. In heterogeneous infrastructures, information sharing is technologically easier to achieve than application sharing.

Central purchasing decisions more likely result in system homogeneity and, consequently, easier information and application sharing. Since a completely centralized hardware/software purchase decision-making process is hardly realistic to expect, some interoperability guidelines should be considered as the second best choice.

Thus, centralized purchasing decisions lend themselves to application sharing—that is, to the SISA and PISA infrastructure patterns—while local ones fit in better with protected applications—the SIPA and PIPA infrastructure patterns.

Shared information and applications: Some problems

Theoretically, shared information may be stored everywhere and shared by everyone. In practice, however, many restrictions are imposed by specifics of a business, information management, and infrastructure implementation.

Shared but unchangeable information causes very few problems. Perhaps the only problem is access control. On the contrary, shared and changeable information may cause multiple problems, such as concurrency control, crash recovery, integrity and consistency preservation, and security protection (see chapters 12 and 14). These problems may be quite different for each of the 16 basic configurations.

Information update regimes   For shared information it is important to define and enforce information update regimes. These regimes may differ, depending on whether information updates should be done immediately or off-line. The following paragraphs describe three possible update regimes. Keep in mind that other regimes may be proposed and enforced, and that many update regimes may be used at the same time for information of different value and timeliness. (Refer to chapter 10 for a discussion of these and other parameters of information.)

Master copy update   A master copy of the full database (or, more generally, information base) is kept in a centralized information resource such as a mainframe or other file server. Periodically (for example, every workday morning), subsets of the database are downloaded to end-user workstations, where transactions are carried out and, consequently, information updates occur. Also periodically (for example, by the end of every workday), updated database subsets are uploaded back to the centralized information resource.

Three fundamental limitations of this update regime are as follows:

- The master copy update is essentially off-line.
- The update works only for CIxx/PIyy basic configurations, where xx stands for CA or DA, and yy stands for PA or SA. The reason is that information must be stored centrally and must not be shared. Even more important, database subsets must be mutually disjoint.

- The state of the database's master copy is inconsistent during the whole period between the first download and the last upload. In other words, from the database viewpoint, the whole workday (or whatever other period is taken) is one eight-hour-long transaction (see chapter 12 for the definition of *transaction*). After a certain database subset has been downloaded, no other workstation (client) can download the same subset until the end of this huge transaction. (With more transaction granularity, the workstation must wait until this subset has been uploaded back to the information resource.)

Clearing house update   In this regime all information updated in workstations is sent to a specially dedicated information resource (such as a file server) periodically, immediately, or by its request. The dedicated information resource plays the role of clearing house because each workstation may request this information from it and be sure that information is consistent. The requested information will be provided or locked until the update of the previously downloaded information comes back to the clearing house.

The information administrator can select an update period and an information transfer carrier. For example, if updates are sent once in a day, the carrier could be a van with magnetic tapes. If updates are sent immediately, information must be transferred via the network along the fastest possible route. The clearing house update may be both off- and on-line.

The clearing house regime can be used for $zzxx$/PIyy, where zz stands for CI or DI, and, in more restricted fashion, for DIxx/SIyy. The restriction is that information may be shared only by the workstation that initiated the information update and by the clearing house.

There are two major drawbacks of the clearing house update regime, both of them associated with IS availability:

- The clearing house's failure paralyzes the whole basic configuration and perhaps its neighbors, too. For DIxx BABBs, it kills one of the main rationales for distributed information: high IS availability.
- During the period between the information update and the transfer of the updated information to the clearing house, this information is not available. The user query will be locked until the clearing house receives the update.

Unlimited immediate update   In this regime each information update propagates automatically to all locations where duplicates of the updated information reside. If properly implemented, this regime works for all DIxx BABBs with virtually no limitations. Proper implementation may present some problems, though.

The propagation process is controlled by an information directory (data dictionary and repository are other synonyms) that "knows" locations of all IS information. Like information, the information directory can be distributed, at least partially. With such a directory, physical location of information and the fact that information is duplicated are completely invisible (transparent) to the users.

Technical problems with the unlimited immediate update regime include:

- Recovering from system failures. If the failure occurs after the information update but before this update propagates to the duplicating sites, one must bring the system back to its previous state. The problem is how to define a "previous state" and how to implement return to it in a distributed environment.
- Finding a reasonable trade-off among the following requirements:
  a. System robustness and availability (which needs information duplication)
  b. Information consistency (which may suffer or become more expensive to sustain because of information duplication)
  c. Response time to user queries (which may degrade if information is not duplicated)
  d. Network bandwidth (which may grow because of immediate updates if information is duplicated)
- Providing adequate security protection, especially access control, which may be compromised in a distributed environment. If valuable information is transferred across the network, it may have to be encrypted/ decrypted. This process may lead to additional performance degradation.

Shared applications Shared applications in *zz*DA BABBs (*zz* again stands for CI or DI) or, more precisely, in *zz*DA/*ww*SA basic configurations (*ww* stands for SI or PI), imply a high level of application standardization and management, including well-defined and properly enforced coordination of new application versions and updates during application maintenance.

With proliferation of an object-oriented approach to application development, the differences between information management and application management will become blurred. Thus, we can expect that shared and changeable applications will cause about the same problems as shared and exchangeable information.

Shared applications in *zz*CA BABBs, or *zz*CA/*ww*SA basic configurations, will cause fewer management problems, allowing a higher level of control over the application maintenance process. A client/server architecture is a currently popular example of such a basic configuration. In the client/server architecture, all applications reside in a server and are accessed by the clients through remote procedure calls.

Client/server architecture

A *client/server architecture* is a set of usually diskless PCs or workstations, called *clients*, connected through a network, usually an LAN, with another computer, called a *server*, that stores all client files in its disk storage and satisfies requests sent by clients.

If a client wants to access its data or to run an application against that data, all it has to do is send a request to a server. The server will carry out all necessary work and return the response to the client. All communications between clients and the server are done in the form of *request/response pairs*.

The analogy between a client and a program, a server and a procedure called by a program, and a request/reply pair and a procedure call/effect return pair suggests itself. Like a program, a client calls a server to carry out some work and then waits for the server's response.

The only difference between the ordinary procedure call/effect return and the request/reply pair is that the procedure runs on the same computer as the calling program, while the client and the server are two physically separate computers. For this reason a request/reply pair is said to be implemented through a *remote procedure call* (RPC). The RPC should be designed so that:

- Its implementation will be *user-transparent*, i.e., indiscernible from an ordinary (local) procedure call.
- All details of LAN operation will be hidden from an application program by defining special local procedures called *stubs*.
- Stubs can invoke an arbitrary action in a server (file transfer or manipulations, computations, etc.).

For example, if the client wants to update a file (and is eligible to do so), it issues a local procedure call to the stub in charge of update operations. The stub sends the corresponding message to the server and waits for the response. However, all stub and server manipulations are invisible to the application program. From its viewpoint, the call is just an ordinary local procedure call.

Figure 6-22 shows 10 steps necessary to implement the RPC (Tanenbaum 1988). At step 1 a client program calls the stub that resides in the client. At step 2 the stub collects the message and passes it to a transport entity for transmission to its peer on the server (step 3). The peer transport entity on the server passes the message to the server stub (step 4). At step 5 the server stub calls the server procedure and waits for it to return the result (step 6). At step 7 the server stub collects the response message and passes it to the transport entity for transmission to its peer on the requesting client (step 8). At step 9 the RPC result is passed to the client stub, which returns the result to its caller, i.e., to the client procedure.

RPC is not without its implementation problems. Without going into technical details, I will just raise red flags listing some of the problems. Refer to

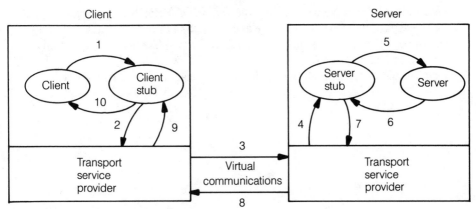

Fig. 6-22. RPC implementation.

Birrell and Nelson's classic article, "Implementing Remote Procedure Calls" (1984), for more detail.

- How to provide full transparency. Since clients and the server are different computers, RPC may have a problem where a local one does not. As soon as implementation of the local and remote procedure calls differs, transparency is lost because the user sees a difference between the two.
- How to let the client stub know where the server stub it is looking for is located. One solution proposed by Birrell and Nelson (1984) is to provide a database that all server stubs must check in with for later identification by client stubs.
- How to handle exceptions, such as server crash, message loss, and client crashes. A special *exception handler* is needed to hide these exceptions from the user and the clients calling program.
- How to cope with *orphans*, that is, running servers with no clients waiting for the response. Several ways for dealing with orphans were proposed by B.J. Nelson in his doctoral dissertation (1981).

Conclusion

I have defined and briefly described main components of an information infrastructure based on the SIP introduced in chapter 4. The main idea of this chapter was to formulate the factors that determine a variety of basic configurations and then to define them.

I believe that in the very near future, IS organizations will buy a set of basic configurations and standard protocols connecting them to assemble a customized information infrastructure in the same manner as today's microcomputer vendors buy component kits and assemble PCs and workstations.

In oversimplified form, the order for the information infrastructure's component kit will go like this: "I'll have one CICA/SISA basic configuration for my headquarters in New York City and five DIDA/SIPA basic configurations for the departments located in Cleveland, Ohio; San Francisco, California; Peoria, Illinois; Paris, France; and Tokyo, Japan. I would like to interconnect all of these locations via a WAN according to the following set of protocols." The result would be a corporate information infrastructure that satisfies CSOs.

Part II

Computer networks:
A foundation for the
information infrastructure

7

Networking

Executive summary

As stated in chapter 5, the first function of a corporate information infrastructure is to provide basic connectivity and user services. This function implies building a corporate network as a physical substrate for the corporate information infrastructure.

From the network user's viewpoint, a *network architecture* is the set of layers and services that each layer provides for the layer above it. The service defines what the service provider can do for a service user, but not how to do it.

Layers can provide two types of services: *connection-oriented* and *connectionless*. The connection-oriented service user must first establish a connection between itself and the receiver; then it transmits a message along this connection and releases the connection after it has been used. The connectionless service user specifies the receiver address and then issues a message to be sent to this address. The network delivers the message to the destination. Both services may be reliable (acknowledged) or unreliable (unacknowledged).

One of the best known and most comprehensive conceptual implementations of a layered network architecture is the ISO's OSI Reference Model, which consists of seven layers:

- Physical layer transmitting raw bits of information
- Data link layer providing reliable communication between two adjacent packet switch nodes (PSNs)
- Network layer providing end-to-end transmission, or transmitting packets from the source PSN to the final destination
- Transport layer providing end-to-end communication between hosts rather than PSNs

- Session layer providing user-oriented services, such as remote login, file transfer, and data transfer with a graceful release
- Presentation layer providing data management functions, such as its representation, conversion, compression, and encryption/decryption
- Application layer providing general user services, such as file transfer, access, and management, electronic mail, virtual terminals, directory services, and job transfer and management

Although OSI is more a promise than a reality, it may at least serve as an excellent set of conceptual guidelines for planning and design of the corporate information infrastructure.

Introduction to network architectures

This section introduces basic networking definitions and concepts necessary to speak the networking jargon and understand the network architecture.

What is a network?

A typical computer network (FIG. 7-1) consists of the following:

- Computers that should be connected (networked). In the networking jargon, computers are alternatively referred to as *end systems, stations* (see "LANs," chapter 6), or *hosts.*
- Transmission lines that carry messages, often called *packets* or, in OSI jargon, network protocol data units (NPDU), between hosts. In the networking jargon, these lines are called *channels, circuits,* or *trunks.*
- Switching elements, specialized computers whose function is to connect hosts with transmission lines. In the networking jargon, switching elements are called PSNs or *data switching exchanges, intermediate systems,* or *interface message processors.* A single PSN may serve one or more hosts. All traffic to or from a host goes through the PSN.

The last two network components are often referred to generically as a *subnet.* There are two classes of subnets:

- Packet-switched subnets, also called *point-to-point* or *store-and-forward* subnets
- Broadcasting subnets

In packet-switched subnets, two PSNs that need to communicate but do not have a direct connection may do so through intermediate PSNs. An intermediate PSN receives a packet, waits until an output channel to the destination or the next intermediate PSN is free, and transmits the packet via this

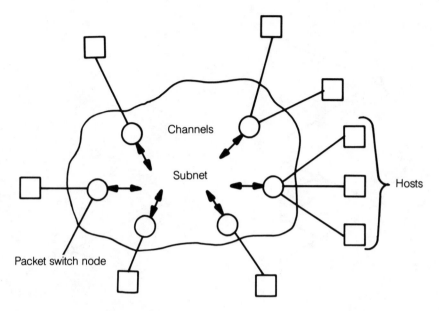

Fig. 7-1. Computer network.

channel. Almost all WANs (satellite WANs are one notable exception) use packet-switched subnets.

Broadcasting subnets have a single communication channel common for all hosts. When a host issues a packet, it is received by all hosts it is addressed to and ignored by those it is not. Almost all LANs use broadcasting subnets. Token rings are a partial exception since they have some packet-switching flavor (see "IEEE 802.5: A Token Ring" in chapter 6).

The common channel causes the problem of deciding at any moment which host is allowed to transmit and which is not. Chapter 6 shows how this problem is solved in three different LAN standards.

Both packet-switched and broadcasting subnets may have various *interconnection topologies*. Figures 7-2 and 7-3 provide examples of widely used topologies. Almost all WANs have irregular topology, while the token ring LAN has a ring topology (FIG. 7-2). The token bus has a bus topology (FIG. 7-3). As described in chapter 6, Ethernet may have four different topologies (some of them not shown in FIG. 7-3).

Layers, services, and protocols

Most networks are organized as a set of *layers* (FIG. 7-4). Although the number of layers may vary from one network to another, the common function of any layer in any network is to provide certain services for the layer above it. The lower layer is said to be a *service provider*, while the layer above it is called a *service user*.

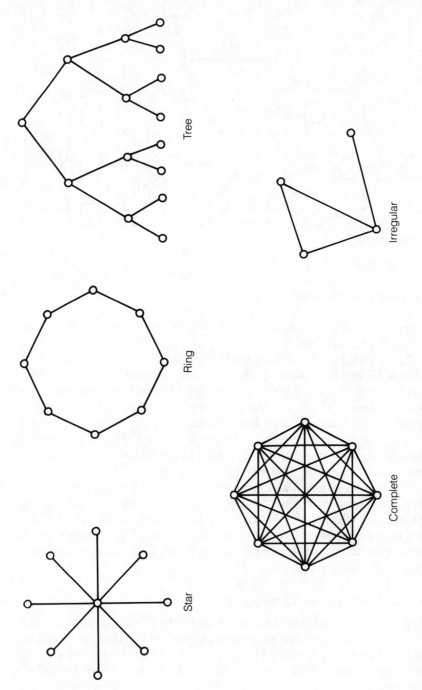

Fig. 7-2. Interconnection topologies: a point-to-point subnet.

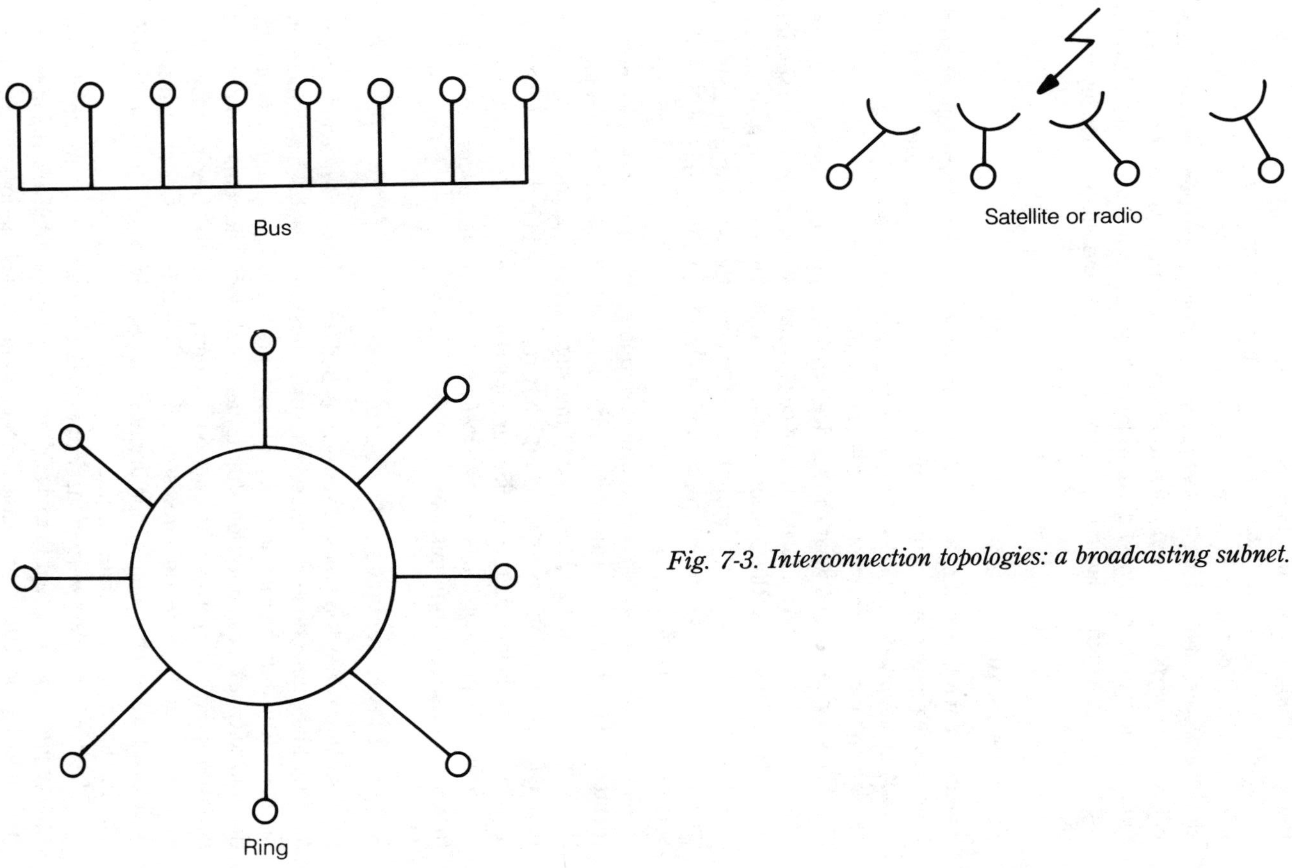

Fig. 7-3. Interconnection topologies: a broadcasting subnet.

Communications between *peers*, that is, equally numbered layers on the transmitter and receiver sides, are governed by the set of rules and conventions commonly known as *protocols*.

In FIG. 7-4, layer i provides services for layer $i+1$, and layer i on the transmitter side (left computer) communicates with its peer (layer i) on the receiver side (right computer) through a *layer i protocol*. Communication between peers is known as *virtual communication* to distinguish it from *physical communication*, which goes from layer i down to layer 1 on the transmitter side, through the physical medium to layer 1 on the receiver side, and finally up to layer i on the receiver side.

Services vs. protocols

The difference between a service and a protocol must be clearly understood from the beginning. A *service* describes the set of a service provider's capabilities. It is usually described as the set of primitive operations (*primitives*) the service provider can carry out for the service user.

The service defines what the service provider can do for the service user but not how to do it. As a result, a service is completely transparent to service users. In other words, the service user (a network layer or a human) has no idea how the service is carried out. Furthermore, the service user may not even know that the way a service is provided has been changed as long as the service itself stays intact.

On the contrary, a *protocol* is a description of how the service is implemented. The protocol is usually described as a set of rules and conventions that govern the format and meaning of messages exchanged by peer layers. A protocol can be modified or even completely replaced, and it does not concern a service user as long as the service remains the same.

Beware of protocols that are in any way visible to service users. These protocols are a major design mistake.

Types of layer services

Layers can provide two types of services called *connection-oriented* and *connectionless*. The connection-oriented service user must first establish a connection between itself and the receiver; then it transmits a message along this connection and releases the connection after it has been used. The connection cannot be interrupted during the entire period of connection use. Several messages sent to the same destination are essentially FSFA (first sent, first arrived). A typical example of a connection-oriented service is a telephone network. Another example is a remote login.

The connectionless service user specifies the receiver address and then issues a message to be sent to this address. The network delivers the message to the destination, but the message must contain the destination address for its entire life cycle. There is no guarantee that several messages sent to the same destination are FSFA. A typical example of a connectionless service is a postal

Fig. 7-4. General network architecture.

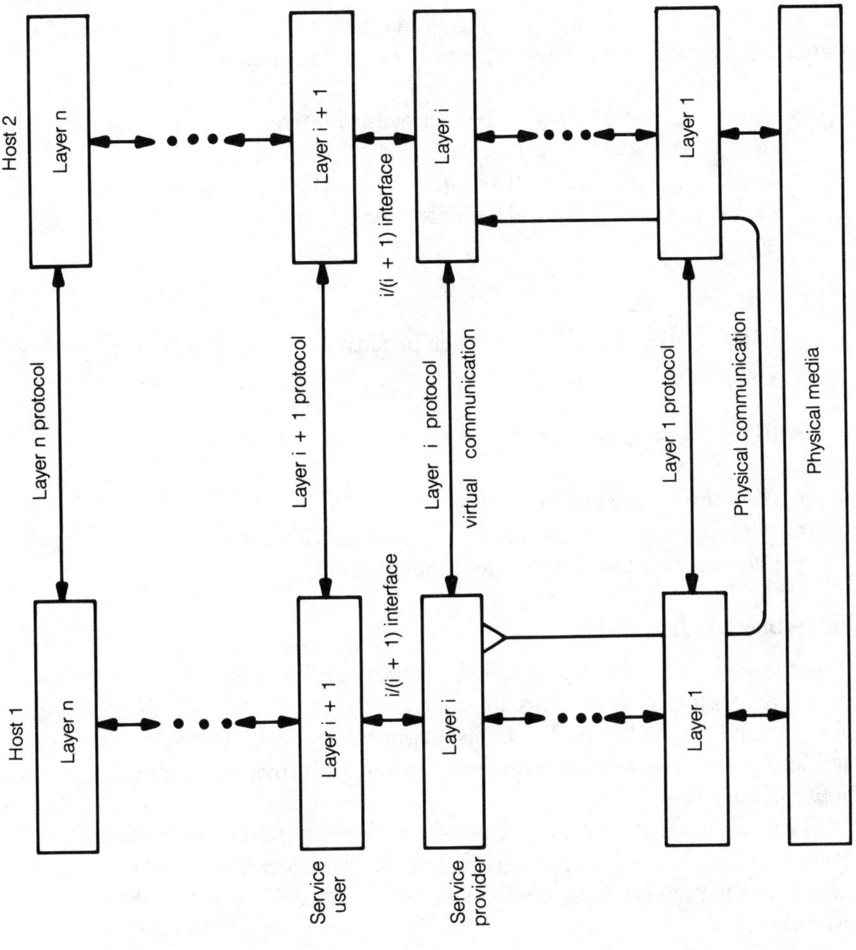

system. Another example is a request/response service as in the client/server architecture or a database query.

Both services may be reliable (*acknowledged*) or unreliable (*unacknowledged*). The acknowledged service implies additional overhead and time and thus costs more.

Protocols vs. interfaces

Services are provided through *interfaces*. An interface is to a physical communication what a protocol is to a virtual one. In other words, the concept of a protocol is an abstraction describing how peer layers can communicate. Actually, the transmitting layer communicates with its peer through a sequence of interfaces that pass the message all the way down to a physical medium and then all the way up to the receiving peer layer.

In FIG. 7-4, layer i provides services for layer $i + 1$ through interface $i/(i + 1)$. The implementation of a layer i protocol is, in fact, a recursive structure of layer protocols and interface primitives that can be expanded as follows ("+" denotes a connection between layer protocol constituents):

- Layer i protocol = $i/(i - 1)$ interface primitives + layer $i - 1$ protocol + $(i - 1)/i$ interface primitives
- Layer $i - 1$ protocol = $(i - 1/(i - 2)$ interface primitives + layer $i - 2$ protocol + $(i - 2)/(i - 1)$ interface primitives

    .
    .
    .

- Layer 2 protocol = 2/1 interface primitives + physical transmission + 1/2 interface primitives

Attributes of a good interface are as follows:

- Well-defined service primitives
- Minimum information passed between service provider and user
- Ease of layer modification and replacement

Network architecture

There are two views of what is called a *network architecture*. From the network user's viewpoint, a network architecture is the set of layers and services provided by and for the layers. From the network designer's viewpoint, a network architecture is the set of layers and protocols providing communications between peer layers.

In either case the network architecture does not concern itself with the specifics of service implementation details, such as low-level interface specifications in the network designer view or protocol specifications in the network user view.

In this chapter we will discuss network architectures from the network user viewpoint. In other words, we will concern ourselves with layers and services rather than layers and protocols.

OSI Reference Model

One of the best known and most comprehensive conceptual implementations of a layered network architecture is the ISO's OSI Reference Model. The network architecture based on the OSI Reference Model consists of seven layers (FIG. 7-5):

- Layer 1: physical layer
- Layer 2: data link layer
- Layer 3: network layer
- Layer 4: transport layer
- Layer 5: session layer
- Layer 6: presentation layer
- Layer 7: application layer

The first (lowest) three layers are concerned with information transmission in the subnet. Most of their services and protocols are implemented in the PSN. The transport layer provides end-to-end communication between hosts. The three highest layers provide various user-oriented services. Services and protocols of layers 4 to 7 are usually implemented in hosts. OSI layers are discussed in subsequent paragraphs.

Physical layer

The physical layer transmits raw bits of information. The physical layer is concerned with physical parameters of signals sent over the physical transmission media that serves it. In turn, the physical layer serves the data link layer. The following paragraphs outline some approaches to physical transmission and the most popular physical transmission media.

Physical transmission

Information may be transmitted in analog or digital form. Analog transmission has been the only choice for many years; until recently, the entire telephone network worldwide was based on analog transmission. In analog transmission, a signal (voice or data) is represented by voltage or current changing as a function of time. In digital transmission, a signal is represented by a sequence of impulses rather than continuing voltage or current. Each impulse may be interpreted as 0 or 1.

Digital transmission has a number of unquestionable advantages over analog transmission. It provides a higher data transmission rate using the same

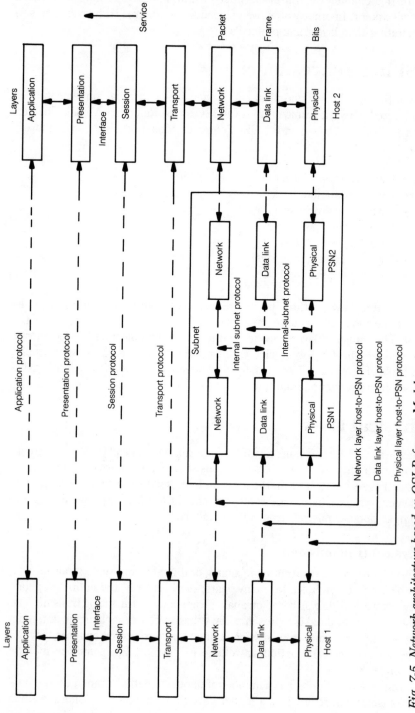

Fig. 7-5. Network architecture based on OSI Reference Model.

equipment and a significantly lower error rate. With hardware price reduction as a major trend (see chapter 6) and potentially lower maintenance costs, digital transmission will soon also become a less expensive technology.

One major advantage of ditigal transmission from the user viewpoint is that it allows diverse kinds of information, such as voice, data, hi-fi sound, still images, video, and facsimile, to mix and transmit in one channel. Not only does it provide more efficient utilization of a channel; it also opens new horizons for information exchange, remote group work, and completely new applications such as multimedia.

Because of all these advantages, the strong tendency to replace analog transmission with digital transmission comes as no surprise. The process started several years ago and is well underway; however, many years will go by before the entire world speaks and sends information in completely digital form.

Several mixed analog/digital transmission standards are now in effect. One of the most widely used standards is Bell System's T1 carrier. The analog part of it is indeed a customer's telephone. The analog signal from the telephone is converted into digital form by using a technique called *pulse code modulation*.

The T1 carrier can handle 24 multiplexed voice channels, each having a 64-kilobit-per-second (kbps) bandwidth (56 kbps for data and 8 kbps for signaling (control) information). Customers can lease both the entire circuit, which gives them 1.544 Mbps of gross bandwidth (64 kbps × 24 + 8 kbps for synchronization), or any part of it. In the latter case, the carrier is referred to as a *fractional T1*.

For higher-bandwidth carriers, there are three additional Bell System standards: T2 at 6.312 Mbps, T3 at 44.736 Mbps, and T4 at 274.176 Mbps.

Bell System's standards are mostly used in North America and Japan. In Europe, a CCITT 2.048-Mbps standard that handles 32 channels (30 for data and two for signaling), each having a 64-kbps bandwidth, is widely used.

Circuit switching vs. packet switching

There are two distinct ways of information delivery to a receiver: *circuit switching* and *packet switching*. With circuit switching, the complete physical path (connection) from a transmitter to a receiver must be established by the former's request before any communication starts and is released only after the session between the transmitter and the receiver is over.

Connection establishment includes request propagation to the receiver and acknowledgment propagation all the way back to the transmitter, causing some delays. However, once started, communication is uninterruptible (except for a connection crash), and the delay in information delivery is just a delay of propagation through the transmission media.

With packet switching, no connection must be established beforehand. The transmitter sends the *packet*, a message of a certain limited size, to the first intermediate PSN. The packet may be stored in the PSN, then forwarded to the next PSN, and so forth until it reaches the intended receiver. As we discussed previously, networks using this approach are called *packet switch* or *store-and-forward* networks. Packet switching does not allow any transmitter to monopolize the transmission channel for a long time and thus is better suited for interactive and bursty traffic.

The first difference between circuit switching and packet switching is that the latter acquires bandwidth on demand, while the former reserves it statically. Packet switching also provides better channel utilization because unused capacity is always available to other packets coming from different transmitters and going to different destinations. Circuit switching loses unused capacity. For the same reason, circuit-switching networks never experience congestion. In packet-switching networks, congestion may become a major problem (see "Congestion Control" later in this chapter).

Another advantage of circuit switching is that it always delivers information in the same order it was sent, while packet switching does not guarantee the order. (Packet switching in combination with connection-oriented service, however, does; see "Layer Services" earlier in this chapter.)

Finally, carriers of packet-switching and circuit-switching networks charge differently. A customer of packet switching is charged for information volume and connection time, but not for distance. A customer of circuit switching is charged for connection time and distance, but not for information volume.

Physical transmission media

This section provides a brief overview of six main types of physical transmission media:

- Twisted pairs
- Baseband coaxial cable
- Broadband coaxial cable
- Fiberoptics
- Line-of-sight transmission
- Communication satellites

Twisted pairs The most widely used transmission medium is a *twisted pair*, which is a pair of twisted copper wires usually used in the telephone system. A twisted pair has a fairly high bandwidth of several megabits per second for a few miles of distance and can run several miles without special amplifiers, called *repeaters* (see "Kinds of Relays" in chapter 8). Twisted pairs can support both analog and digital transmission.

In spite of recent technological advances, such as fiberoptics, twisted pairs will be used for many years for at least two reasons:

- The technology is well tested and inexpensive.
- The United States has an installed base of twisted pairs worth about $130 billion.

Baseband coaxial cable A *baseband coaxial cable* is used for digital transmission, specifically for LANs and long-distance telephone communications. It has a high bandwidth, with 10 Mbps feasible for a 1 km cable, higher for shorter cables and lower for longer ones. It also provides a low propagation delay (8 μs per mile).

A baseband coaxial cable has excellent noise immunity. Also, it is inexpensive and easy to install and maintain. Baseband coaxial cables are widely used in Ethernet LANs (see "IEEE 802.3 and Ethernet" in chapter 6).

Broadband coaxial cable Unlike a baseband coaxial cable, a *broadband* coaxial cable is used for analog transmission, especially for cable television and high-quality audio. It can also be used for digital transmission, but digital-to-analog and analog-to-digital conversions are necessary.

The broadband coaxial cable has an exceptionally high bandwidth at long distance (150 Mbps at distances up to 70 miles is feasible). The available bandwidth can be split into multiple independent channels, each 3 Mbps; and television and data may be mixed on the same cable.

On the negative side, the broadband coaxial cable is expensive and its maintenance is complex. It needs analog amplifiers to support the signal amplitude. These amplifiers are one-way, requiring special treelike cable architectures with a head end at the tree root to provide two-way communication between tree nodes. The cost of installation, including cable routing and amplifier layout, is high.

Fiberoptics *Fiberoptics* provides transmission by light pulses propagating through a thin fiber of glass or fused silica. Light-emitting diodes (LEDs) or lasers are used as light sources, and photodiodes are used as light detectors.

Fiberoptics has a potentially enormous bandwidth, with up to 1000 Mbps feasible today at a distance of 1 km. With powerful lasers, the signal can propagate for up to 100 km without repeaters (but at lower speed). With active repeaters, there is no practical limit on the distance or size of a token ring LAN, which is seen as one of the main fiberoptics applications today.

Other possible applications include:

- Long-distance telephone communication, where fiberoptics replaces coaxial cables
- High-capacity backbone LAN connecting a number of smaller LANs to a T1 line through a bridge or router (see chapter 8)
- Fault-tolerant networks (converting high bandwidth into redundancy)

Some advantages of fiberoptics that put other transmission media out of the competition include:

- Fiberoptics is good for factory floor applications because it is not affected by power surges, electromagnetic interference, or corrosive chemicals.

- Fiberoptics has high noise immunity.
- Security protection is good because it is difficult to splice and tap into a fiber.
- The fiber is very thin; thus, one can avoid bulging cable ducts even with thousands of communication links.

A major disadvantage of fiberoptics at this time is its high cost. However, all trends are on the fiberoptics side; and as soon as it breaks through the economies of scale barrier, we can expect that fiberoptics will come closer in price to other, more conventional, physical transmission media. Major factors that encourage further proliferation of fiberoptics include:

- Trend to internetworking causes increased demand for a high-speed backbone connecting LANs.
- Interexchange T3 traffic at 45 Mbps creates demand for higher-speed communication links.
- Vendors and users of high-performance workstations demand higher-speed LANs to connect them.
- Defense and intelligence communities demand high reliability and security protection.
- Major vendors, such as IBM and DEC, have announced that they will support fiberoptics LANs for connecting their products.

Most commercial activity in fiberoptics develops around the fiber distributed data interface (FDDI). The FDDI is a token ring LAN running at 100 Mbps at a distance of up to 150 miles. Up to 1000 stations can be connected to the FDDI.

Topologically, the FDDI is a combination of two fiber rings, one transmitting clockwise and the other counterclockwise (FIG 7-6A). Stations can connect to one ring (class B) or to both rings (class A). Class A stations provide fault

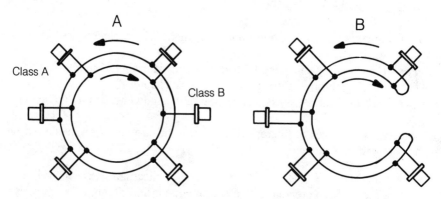

Fig. 7-6. FDDI topology.

tolerance but are more expensive. If one ring goes down, another can be used as a backup. If both rings go down simultaneously, the two rings can be turned into one (FIG. 7-6B).

FDDI permits both packet switching and circuit switching. Circuit-switched data can be connected to both T1 and CCITT channels. Thus, FDDI can be used anywhere in the world (see "Physical Transmission" earlier in this chapter).

Line-of-sight transmission *Line-of-sight transmission* is a generic term that refers to any kind of highly directional transmission through the air rather than a physical medium. Examples of line-of-sight transmission are microwave, infrared, lasers, and radio communications.

Typical examples of line-of-sight transmission applications include:

- Use of microwave radio transmission for television or long-distance telephone communication. When a tall transmission tower (about 300 feet) with a parabolic antenna on top of it is used, distances up to 60 miles are feasible.
- Use of infrared and laser transmission for interfacility LANs. The infrared or laser link is fully digital and highly directional; thus, it is immune to jamming or tapping.

The major advantage of line-of-sight transmission is that it is less expensive than wire-based communication media involving digging and closing trenches, laying out cables, and overcoming various legal and political barriers. Another advantage is low propagation delay (about 5 μs per mile).

The major drawback of line-of-sight transmission is its sensitivity to out-of-phase signals and adverse weather conditions (thunderstorms, rain, etc.).

Communication satellites *Communication satellites* provide transmission through multiple microwave repeaters, or transponders, that listen to some fraction of the spectrum, amplify the incoming signal, and rebroadcast it in another frequency to avoid interference.

Communication satellites can be used for data transmission as well as telephone and television communication. A typical satellite splits its 500-MHz bandwidth over a dozen transponders, each having 36-MHz bandwidth, which corresponds to a single 50-Mbps data stream, or 800 ditigal voice channels, each having a 64-kb bandwidth.

Unlike other physical transmission media, communication satellites provide a single user with an extremely high bandwidth for a short time. For comparison, fiberoptics has a greater bandwidth but provides it for many users simultaneously. This feature of communication satellites makes them attractive for bursty traffic. The cost of transmission over the communication satellite does not depend on the distance.

The propagation delay in communication satellites is longer than in any other physical transmission media (250 to 300 ms independent of the distance). However, a lower error rate can partially compensate for the delay since messages should not have to be retransmitted. Also, for very long messages, satellite communication is faster than telephone or fractional T1 because of its higher bandwidth.

Finally, communication satellites are intrinsically broadcasting media. To provide a necessary level of security, information encryption may have to be required.

Data link layer

The data link layer provides reliable communication between two adjacent PSNs. It carries out five basic functions:

- Services for the network layer
- Framing, i.e. grouping the physical layer's bits into so-called frames
- Transmission error control
- Flow control
- Link management

Services for the network layer

The main data link layer function is to pass a message (usually called a *packet*) from the transmitter's network layer to the receiver's network layer. Three services are commonly performed:

- Unacknowledged connectionless service
- Acknowledged connectionless service
- Connection-oriented service

Unacknowledged connectionless service has by definition no connections, establishment or release. Instead, it sends independent frames to the destination. The frame arrival is not acknowledged, and no attempt is made to recover lost frames. This service is appropriate if the physical medium is very reliable (low error rate) or if the traffic is real-time and does not allow for delays caused by acknowledgments.

Acknowledged connectionless service does not establish or release connections, but it provides acknowledgment for each individual frame sent. The lost frame can be retransmitted. This service is more reliable than the unacknowledged connectionless service. However, its major problem is handling lost acknowledgments. If no special measures are taken, the lost acknowledgment can result in multiple transmissions of the same frame. The transmission error control function may take care of this problem.

Connection-oriented service is the most sophisticated and, nor surprisingly, the most expensive service. It is usually provided in three stages:

1. The transmitter and the receiver establish a connection.

2. One or more frames are transmitted.
3. The connection is released, freeing all resources involved in it.

The data link layer guarantees that each transmitted frame is received, each frame is received only once, and all frames are received in the order of their transmission.

Framing

The bit stream transmitted by the physical layer is not guaranteed to be error-free. Some bits may be lost, some added, and others may change their value. The approach used by the data link layer to provide an error-free communication channel is to break the bit stream down to discrete *frames*, each having a verifiable checksum. If at the receiving end, the checksum is different from that at the transmitting end, some measures must be taken; for example, the frame must be retransmitted.

Several approaches have been proposed to provide proper framing. All of them combine the following methods:

- Counting the number of characters in a frame and storing it in a special frame header field
- Special start and end characters or bit patterns
- Character or bit stuffing

Such popular data link protocols as IBM's Synchronous Data Link Control (SDLC) and ISO's High-level Data Link Control (HDLC) use bit patterns and stuffing.

Transmission error control

Framing makes sure that each frame has the recognizable start and end. *Transmission error control* makes sure that transmitted frames arrive at the receiving end in the right order. Indeed, having frames arrive in the right order is not a problem for the unacknowledged connectionless service; but for reliable services, such as acknowledged connectionless or connection-oriented services, it certainly is.

Transmission error control is based on the feedback from the receiver about frame delivery. In the simplest case the receiver sends a positive (the frame arrived) or negative (something is wrong) acknowledgment to the transmitter. However, this approach does not solve the problem of completely destroyed frames because the receiver does not even know that the frame has been sent.

A more comprehensive approach is to supply the data link layer with timers. Each frame transmission starts a timer. The timer will go off after the timeout long enough to allow for frame transmission, processing at the receiving end, and acknowledgment delivery at the transmitting end. The timer that has gone off triggers frame retransmission, indicating that something was wrong. This approach is usually complemented by the assignment of unique IDs (called *sequence numbers*) to each frame to avoid receiving the duplicates of an already delivered frame.

Implementation of transmission error control requires fairly complex protocols whose description goes far beyond the scope of this book. For more details concerning transmission error control protocols, refer to Andrew Tanenbaum's excellent book, *Computer Networks* (1988).

Flow control

One more function of the data link layer is to handle peer entity pairs with the transmitter faster than the receiver. In such a situation, the transmitter may flood the receiver with information, causing the receiver to lose frames even if everything else is perfect. To avoid this situation, the data link layer provides *flow control*.

Flow control is based on the feedback from the receiver letting the transmitter know if the receiver is keeping up with the frame stream from the transmitter. This feedback may include the set of instructions and rules telling the transmitter if it can send the next frame(s) and under which conditions.

Link management

The last function of the data link layer is *link management*. Link management is fairly simple for connectionless service. For connection-oriented service, however, connections must be established and released; and sequence numbers must be initialized and, if errors occur, reinitialized. In addition, links may have to be established between peers (such as LAN stations) or between the master and slaves (such as a central computer and dumb terminals). Link management is essentially different for these two cases.

Network layer

Unlike the data link layer, which passes frames from one PSN to another, the network layer transmits *packets* from the transmitting PSN to the final destination, or, in network jargon, provides *end-to-end transmission*. In order to do this, the network layer must have knowledge about network topology and current loads on communication channels.

The network layer carries out four basic functions:

- Serving the transport layer
- Routing packets through the subnet
- Controlling congestion
- Internetworking, i.e., connecting multiple heterogeneous networks

This chapter discusses the first three functions of the network layer. Internetworking is discussed in chapter 8.

Services to the transport layer

For many networks the network layer is the highest *subnet* layer, and the transport layer is the lowest *host* layer. Not only may these layers reside in different computers (a PSN and a host, respectively); they also may be run by different organizations, such as a carrier and a network customer, respectively. Thus, the network layer's services are especially important, representing, from the transport and all higher OSI layers' viewpoint, the subnet service.

From the transport layer's viewpoint, there are three types of network services (TABLE 7-1). Type A provides the best services for the transport layer, and there is very little if anything that the transport layer has to do to improve services for the higher OSI layers. Unfortunately, practically no WAN is type A.

Table 7-1. Network Types.

Network Type	Description
A	Ideally reliable network service with no network resets. Some LANs come close to type A but WANs of type A are practically nonexistent.
B	Ideally reliable packet directory, but network resets are possible (due to network congestion, hardware problems, or software bugs). Most public networks are type B.
C	Not reliable. Packets may be lost, duplicated, or garbled. Possible network resets. Connectionless WANs and many internetworks are type C.

Type B permits network resets that require the transport layer's interference to create an illusion for the higher OSI layers that the network is error-free and permanently on (see "Services to the Session Layer" later in this chapter). Most public networks are type B.

Type C networks are unreliable; thus, most services for the higher OSI layers are provided by the transport layer in the host. Connectionless WANs and many internetworks are type C.

In any case the transport and higher OSI layers must be isolated from a particular subnet topology, technology, and implementation. For example, replacement of the public telephone with private satellite communications would in no way affect these layers. The service should also create an illusion of network uniformity, including addressing.

The network layer's services to the transport layer may be connection-oriented or connectionless. In addition to the differences between these two services, discussed previously in "Types of Layer Services," the following aspects are specific to the network layer:

- In connection-oriented service, error and flow control is taken care of by the network layer, that is, by the subnet. On the contrary, in connectionless service, these services are provided in the transport layer, that is, often by the user organization itself.
- In connection-oriented service, the service provider and user can negotiate optional services, such as acknowledgments, expedited (high-priority) data, and quality of service. In connectionless service, these services are unavailable.

The issue of connection-oriented vs. connectionless service has been a subject of hot debates, with carriers being the proponents of the first service and the Defense Advance Research Agency (DARPA) Internet community being the proponents of the second service. Although the OSI Reference Model includes both services, some networks, including SNA, provide only connection-oriented service.

Routing

Routing packets between the transmitting and receiving hosts is a major function of the network layer and is reflected in a very large number of routing algorithms. A *routing algorithm* selects which output channel to assign to the packet that has just arrived at the PSN in question.

Routing decisions are different for the connection-oriented and connectionless services. For the first service, the routing decision has to be made once for the whole connection life cycle. For the second service, this decision has to be made each time for every packet arriving at any PSN.

Routing decisions made by routing algorithms should satisfy the following requirements:

- *Robustness*, which implies the algorithm's insensitivity to network topology and traffic changes as well as failures of various network components at various times.
- *Optimality*, which implies maximizing the global network efficiency. Two main difficulties are (1) figuring out what network parameter to optimize to achieve such an elusive thing as the "global efficiency" and (2) balancing the global efficiency with fairness in satisfying individual service requirements. These two parameters are often mutually conflicting.

There is a great deal of literature on routing algorithms, their assessment, and comparison. (Refer to Andrew Tanenbaum's textbook (1988) for an excellent introduction to the subject.) The description and analysis of routing algorithms go beyond the scope of this book. However, you should be aware that the way the network layer resolves conflicts between fairness and optimality can seriously affect the quality of its services and, eventually, the customer's pocket.

Congestion control

Congestion is a situation in the subnet when it is overloaded with packets. Congestion is like an avalanche. When the number of packets simultaneously in the subnet challenges its global capacity, the subnet starts losing packets, for example, because of the receiving PSN's insufficient buffer capacity. The source PSN retransmits the lost packet, sometimes many times, and thus makes things even worse. If no special measures are taken, congestion inevitably leads to *deadlock*, an ultimate form of congestion, or to network collapse. Corrective measures are generically referred to as *congestion control*.

Two major reasons for congestion are insufficient buffer capacity in the receiving PSNs and poor routing decisions. Insufficient buffer capacity can be seen when the PSNs receive the packets too slowly or when the input traffic rate exceeds the output capacity. These problems could be handled if PSNs had an infinite buffer capacity but, alas, they do not.

The impact of poor routing decisions on congestion is fairly evident. If the routing algorithm holds packets in the subnet for too long or if it sends most packets along few channels, the congestion results.

There are four major strategies for congestion control:

- Permanent buffer allocation for each possible connection in each PSN. Although expensive, this approach completely eliminates congestion which may be obligatory for applications requiring low delay and high bandwidth simultaneously (for example, digitized speech). One possible relaxation of this approach is to assign buffers for some prespecified time rather than permanently.
- Packet discarding. No buffers are reserved in advance. When there is no place for the incoming packet, it is discarded. This strategy requires the formulation of a set of rules, some of them heuristic, telling when to discard and when to keep the packet. In particular, the minimum and maximum number of buffers that any output channel can seize must be defined. Since packets are discarded on a regular basis (an intrinsic part of the strategy), duplicate retransmission and management is a problem that has to be addressed and solved.
- Restricting the number of packets. The number of packets in the subnet is limited through issuing special *permits* that must be captured by a new packet to travel and be regenerated by the receiving PSN when the packet arrives. This strategy suffers from several drawbacks, mainly permit distribution and management. For example, if a permit is lost for whatever reason, a fraction of network capacity becomes unusable and hard to recover.

- Choke packets. Unlike previous strategies, this one reacts to actual network congestion, rather than controlling it upfront, on the basis of static information. Using channel utilization or queue length at the receiving PSN as a trigger, this strategy sends choke packets back to the transmitting PSN whenever either or both parameters exceed some predetermined and changeable norm. The PSN reduces its traffic to the receiving PSN for a prespecified timeout and keeps waiting for more choke packets to see if it still should restrict its traffic to the receiving PSN after the timeout. Better yet, congestion information can propagate along with routing information, making choke packet sending decisions based on more global information than channel utilization or queue length at one PSN.

Some early networks, such as ARPANET, have tried to use flow control rules to reduce congestion. The problems of such a strategy just emphasize a big difference between flow and congestion control. While flow control deals with local traffic between a transmitter and a receiver, congestion control is concerned with the global network capacity. Thus, the violation of flow control rules may not mean that the network is congested.

The traffic between two adjacent PSNs is usually bursty, and heavy transmission at the peak does not necessarily mean that the entire network is congested. It is just business as usual.

Transport layer

Unlike the network layer, which provides end-to-end communication between PSNs, the transport layer provides end-to-end communication between hosts. Its services to the session layer bridge the gap between what transport service users need and what the network layer can provide.

Services to the session layer

The transport layer is the lowest OSI layer in which the network user is able to control the subnet. (Recall that the user has no direct control over the subnet.) This ability has three important consequences:

- The transport layer insulates the upper OSI layers from specifics of subnet technology, topology, and design.
- Transport service can be made more reliable than the underlying network, taking care of lost packets, network resets, etc. Thus, it is possible to write applications that are insensitive to unreliable transmission.
- Transport service operations can be made independent of network service ones. While network service operations may vary widely from one network to another, it is possible to write applications that will run across various networks.

Summarizing, transport layer services can make the network user virtually independent of the network carrier. This situation may be especially attractive or even necessary for users of type B and C networks (see "Services to the Transport Layer" earlier in this chapter). Like the network layer service, the transport layer service may be both connection-oriented and connectionless.

Quality of service

In the transport layer the network user can request a certain quality of service. The parameters that determine quality of service include:

- Connection establishment (release) delay: the elapsed time between the request for a transport connection (connection release) and actual connection establishment (release).
- Connection establishment (release) failure probability: the likelihood of not establishing (releasing) a transport connection during the maximum establishment (release) delay time.
- Throughput: the number of user data bytes transferred per second and measured over some recent time interval and separately for each direction.
- Transit delay: the full time of peer-to-peer transport communication measured separately for each direction.
- Residual error rate: the number of lost messages relative to the total number transmitted.
- Transfer failure probability: the fraction of times that agreed-upon throughput, transit delay, and residual error rate were not provided during some time interval.
- Protection: the extent to which user data are protected against unauthorized access or update.
- Priority: the ranking of transport user connections according to their importance (to be taken into account in the case of congestion).
- Resilience: the probability of service termination by the transport layer.

At the time of a connection setup, the transport layer service user may specify preferred, acceptable, and unacceptable values for each parameter. The transport layer then determines if it can provide the requested services. If it cannot, the failure report is issued, with failure reason explanations.

Alternatively, the discrepancy between the requested and available quality of service may initiate an *option negotiation process*. If this process succeeds, the negotiated parameter values stay intact for the entire connection life cycle.

Some of the parameters listed are also relevant for connectionless transport service.

Connection management

At first glance, transport layer services seem to be similar to data link ones. However, there is a significant difference in how these connections are managed. Let us compare the transport and data link layer services from the management viewpoint.

There are three major elements of connection management:

- Addressing scheme
- Connection establishment and release
- Connection use

Addressing scheme In the data link layer, no explicit destination address is necessary because each output channel uniquely specifies the destination. In the transport layer, an explicit destination address is necessary, and at least two problems have to be solved:

- Letting the transmitting host know the address—called *transport service access point* (or TSAP in OSI jargon)—of the destination process in the receiving host. A usual solution is to arrange in each receiving host a special server, sometimes called a *directory server*, which has access to the database of TSAPs for all processes (compare with the database of server stubs in "Client/Server Architecture," chapter 6). In this case, the transmitting host will always communicate first with the directory server to find out the TSAP of the destination process.
- Determining which host the destination TSAP belongs to. A solution to this problem is to organize a *global addressing scheme*, which, in most cases, is a hierarchical scheme consisting of the address of the network, then the host, and finally a port on that host (compare with global telephone numbers, such as 1-619-723-2806).

Connection establishment and release In the data link, connection establishment and release are straightforward: unless the receiving end is down, the packet is already there. In the transport layer, however, the situation is different because the network can lose, store, and duplicate packets.

The basic problem of connection establishment is how to manage delayed packets that are wandering around in the network. One solution is to kill such packets after their lifetime is over. This solution, however, is not easily accomplished, especially for type C networks.

The basic problem of connection release is how to avoid data loss when both a transmitter and a receiver try to release a connection asynchronously at about the same time. (This type of release is called an *abrupt release*.) For example, one host may send a packet while, at the same time, another one disconnects. In the OSI Reference Model the transport layer ignores this problem, and its solution is left for the session layer.

Theoretically, this problem has no solution. In ARPANET a *three-way handshake algorithm* in the transport layer (called TCP in ARPANET jargon) represents an adequate solution. The idea is that transmitter T informs receiver R that it is going to release the connection. R sends back a message saying: "I don't mind," and T sends the third message saying: "I got your message so I go ahead."

Connection use   In the data link protocol, connection management is limited to flow control and buffering. The transport protocol provides the same services but with three significant differences:

- PSNs have fewer connections than hosts; thus, the buffer assignment strategy in the transport layer is more complex and allows for more options.
- Available buffer space is not the only bottleneck; another one is the network's carrying capacity. To provide effective flow control, flow control mechanisms based on the network's carrying capacity must be used at the transmitting end (to avoid too many outstanding, yet unacknowledged packets) rather than those based on the receiver's buffering capacity at the receiving end.
- The transport layer has additional functions, such as multiplexing and crash recovery management. *Upward multiplexing* uses several transport connections on the same network connection to avoid paying for idle connections. *Downward multiplexing* uses many network connections for one transport connection to increase the effective network bandwidth. Crash recovery management is necessary to find out which packets must be retransmitted after the crash.

Session layer

The session layer is the lowest of three layers that provide user-oriented services on top of the four lower layers that provide reliable end-to-end communications. The session layer performs five major functions:

- Services to the presentation layer
- Dialog management
- Synchronization
- Activity management
- Exception reporting

Services to the presentation layer

The session layer establishes sessions for functions such as remote login or file transfer and provides data transfer with a *graceful* rather than abrupt release. (Recall that the OSI transport layer does not provide a graceful release.)

The graceful release is one of the few differences between the session and transport layer services. Unlike the abrupt release in the transport layer, the graceful release guarantees that no data will ever be lost during the connection release.

Another difference is that one-to-one mapping between a session and a transport connection is not obligatory. Two or more sessions may be carried out by one transport connection if sessions are regular and frequent. Conversely, one session can be carried out by two or more transport connections if the transport service provider that resides outside the host fails.

Finally, unlike the transport layer, the session layer makes only connection-oriented service meaningful.

Dialog management

When the user accesses a remote database, it is only natural to alternate the user's queries and the database's responses. In this case the function of *dialog management* is to keep track of whose turn it is to talk—the user's or the database's.

This function is implemented by means of a *data token*, which is initially issued to start the dialog and then is passed back and forth between the communicating peers. Only the token holder is allowed to transmit data. Tokens can be requested from the token holder by its peer, and the token holder can grant the token or turn down the request.

Synchronization

Synchronization provides recovery from noncommunication errors by moving the session service provider to the previous state known to be correct. This action can be done by breaking down the entire message into so-called *dialog units* separated by *major synchronization points*.

Major synchronization points inserted into the message are always acknowledged, and setting a synchronization point requires possession of a token. When a noncommunication error occurs, the state of the session is reset to the previous major synchronization point. Resetting to the previous major synchronization point guarantees that the message has been recovered. A major synchronization point also guarantees that the transmitter may erase all data that were sent before it.

The idea of synchronization points is similar to that of *checkpoints* in recovery subsystems of database management systems (DBMSs). We will discuss data recovery in databases in chapter 12.

Activity management

The message stream in the session layer can be broken down into independent logical entities called *activities*. The user has complete freedom in defining what an activity is, where its start and end should be, or how the receiving host should handle it. The function of the session layer is to manage the activity once the request for it has been issued by the user.

Using activities, one can structure sessions and determine when a peer can start an activity. To start an activity, the peer has to hold a token similar to that used for major synchronization points. Events are not just coincidental.

Each activity always starts with the major synchronization point, thus building a wall between itself and the previous activity. One cannot return to the previous activity after the next activity has started.

Activities can be interrupted and then resumed. For example, if an urgent query requiring an immediate response comes during the transfer of a very big file, the user may interrupt the file transfer, respond to the query, and then resume the transfer.

Two good examples of activity management are as follows:

- Quarantining, that is, collecting at the receiving end all the messages comprising a single transaction before starting to process any one of them. These messages are organized as an activity. In this example, the activity supports transaction atomicity, allowing the receiving host to process the transaction independently of anything that could happen in the transmitter between messages.
- Separating consecutively transferred files. The transfer of each file is organized as an activity eliminating the chance of confusing other file separators with data.

Exception reporting

The session layer provides a general-purpose exception-handling mechanism that can be used in different applications. Abnormal situations can be reported to the session peer, possibly with some explanations of what is happening. Any internal problems in the session or lower layers can also cause the exception report that describes a particular problem.

Presentation layer

The presentation layer is the lowest layer concerned with the meaning of information. In addition to providing basic services for the application layer, it handles all data management functions, including its representation, conversion, compression, and encryption/decryption.

Contexts

The presentation layer provides most of its services to the application layer by passing a request for services on to the session layer. A notable exception is that users are allowed to include data structures necessary for applications. These data structures may be combined into groups called *contexts*.

The presentation layer can maintain multiple contexts to make it easier to switch contexts in the course of a session. Context switching can be coordinated with the activity resumption or the return to the previous major synchronization point. The decision as to what particular data structures become context members is negotiable between the communicating peers.

Data management

The presentation layer carries out the data management functions described in the following paragraphs.

Data representation and conversion   Since different computers represent data differently, some meaning-preserving data conversions are necessary. The data conversion can be done by a transmitter or by a receiver, or the *universal data representation* should be adopted so that both the transmitter and the receiver do the data conversion. The transmitter converts its data format to universal data representation, and the receiver converts universal data representation to its data format. Abstract Syntax Notation 1 (ASN.1) is (and its subsequent versions will be) adopted as an international standard for the universal data representation.

Data compression   Data compression reduces the amount of data that should be transmitted to deliver the same meaning and, consequently, saves money. Three widely used approaches to data compression are as follows:

- Coding a finite set of equally plausible symbols by converting them to sequential numbers
- Frequency-dependent coding based on assigning shorter codes to more frequently used symbols
- Context-dependent coding using application-specific properties of information to be transmitted (such as a number of consecutive zeros or relative changes in two consecutive snapshots of the same data)

Data security   Data security is currently one of the weakest OSI Reference Model points. OSI security will ensure that transmitted data are not modified, disclosed, replayed, or lost in the network; that a message transmitter's authenticity is verified; and that messages themselves are not repudiated. The following security standards are currently under examination:

- Access control
- Integrity
- Confidentiality
- Authentication
- Nonrepudiation
- Audit trails

Placing some of the security features, such as user authentication and nonrepudiation in the presentation layer seems somewhat strange (see also "OSI Service Elements" later in this chapter). Chapter 14 discusses security in more detail.

Application layer

The application layer, the highest layer of the OSI Reference Model, provides six general user services. General user services are those that can be used by many applications and thus factored out in the application layer.

User services

User services provided by the application layer are described in the following paragraphs.

File transfer, access, and management (FTAM)   FTAM is used to provide information sharing within work groups through centralizing file storage in file servers and making files available to their points of use. The idea behind FTAM is to define a *virtual filestore*, an abstract file server that represents a standard interface to its clients and serves them by providing a standardized operation set.

Electronic mail (EM)   EM is a faster and more convenient alternative to a postal service. EM also has some obvious advantages over telephone service:

- It does not require all parties to be available at the communication time.
- The written copy of an EM message can be filed away or forwarded.
- Messages can be sent to several parties at once, an analog of the telephone conference call.

EM is different from file transfer in two important aspects:

- Both the transmitter and the receiver are humans; thus, the message transfer must be augmented by a *user interface* for creating, editing, and reading EM messages.
- EM messages are much more structured than file records, including many fields concerned with how the message must be sent and handled at the destination.

Virtual terminals   Virtual terminals were introduced as perhaps the only practical solution to severe terminal incompatibility problems. A *virtual terminal* is an abstract data structure that represents the state of a physical terminal, can be manipulated by both a keyboard and a computer, and can be easily converted into any physical terminal's format.

Directory services   Directory services are used to find the network address of users and available network services. The idea behind directory services is to structure network addresses as a collection of *attributes* and to provide access to these addresses through a (perhaps incomplete) set of network address attributes. An entry in the directory consists of the entire attribute collection and an *access control list* that determines who can access or modify it.

Job transfer and management (JTM)   JTM allows the user to submit a remote job entry and direct an output to some destination. Typically, the user would like to specify what has to be done, where it should be done, where the input should be taken from, where the output should go, and what progress reports are desired and when. JTM is supposed to carry out the job specified, solving in the process such problems as user authentication, worldwide addressing, and subjob transfer and management.

Telematics   Telematics is a generic term for such services as *teletext* and *videotext*. Teletext is a one-way service that broadcasts information from a database on a television channel. Teletext may broadcast such information as weather and stock market reports, commercials, and product information.

Videotext is an interactive telephone service for accessing large public or corporate databases and performing transactions against them. Videotext may be used for making air ticket, hotel, restaurant, game, or movie reservations; catalog shopping; accessing library catalogs; distributing information to a selected group of people, etc. Subsequent paragraphs discuss the virtual filestore and EM in more detail.

Virtual filestore

A virtual filestore can be characterized by three properties:

- File structure
- File attributes
- File operations

There are three conceptual models of file structure:

- An *unstructured file* is an indivisible piece of data having no internal structure. The only available operations on unstructured files are reading and writing an entire file.
- A *flat file* is an ordered sequence of records, perhaps of different sizes and types. The virtual filestore's clients can access records by their relative position in the file or by labels attached to them. For flat files the filestore supports a variety of operations over records, including creation, deletion, replacement, and modification.
- A *hierarchical file* is a treelike structure, each node of which may be interpreted as a labeled or unlabeled data record. Data records may also be enumerated by means of one of the standard tree enumeration methods (for example, *depth-first search*, which gives the next number to the leftmost, yet unvisited, node; see FIG. 7-7).

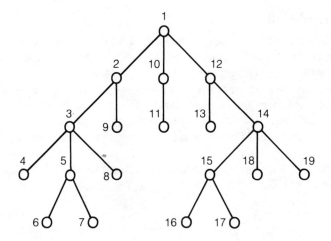

Fig. 7-7. Depth-first search.

Each file has a collection of attributes. The OSI virtual filestore allows up to 19 file attributes. The following sample includes the most frequently used attributes:

- Name
- Current and maximum future file size
- Allowed file operations
- Access control (who may access the file and how)
- Date and time of file creation and last modification or access
- Identification of last file reader or modifier
- File owner

Each file attribute may be created when the file is created and held unchanged thereafter, changed by a client (for example, its owner), or automatically maintained by the virtual filestore.

For all files except unstructured ones, file operations may be applied to both the entire file and individual records. The OSI virtual filestore supports up to 14 file operations. Possible file operations include:

- Create or delete a file
- Open a file for reading or modification or close it
- Overwrite existing data in a file
- Select a file for attribute management
- Read or modify a file attribute
- Locate, insert, or delete a file record
- Append data to a file record

Multithreaded file servers

The OSI Reference Model does not prescribe how the virtual filestore must be implemented. In this and the next sections, we describe two important practical extensions of the abstract virtual filestore concept.

The simplest file server implementation is a *single-task server*. While working on the current client request (task), the single-task server queues all incoming tasks and serves the next one only when the previous task's disk accesses are completed. The result is a low central processing unit (CPU) utilization.

In a multitask server each task forms a separate thread of control that shares the global data with other tasks (FIG 7-8). These file servers are also called *multithreaded*.

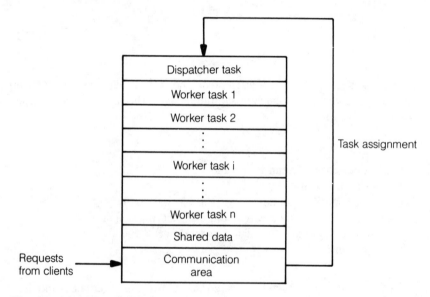

Fig. 7-8. Multithreaded server.

In the multithreaded server, the next incoming task is passed on to a special *dispatcher task* whose role is to find an idle thread (called a *worker task*) and to assign the task to it. When the worker task completes its job, it reports to a dispatcher task that it is available for future assignments.

The next extension, a multiple client/multiple server architecture, goes one step beyond a multithreaded server, replacing multitasking with multiprocessing, that is, using multiple, physically separate file servers.

Multiple client/multiple server architecture

In "Client/Server Architecture," chapter 6, we described an architecture consisting of multiple clients connected with a single server. A *multiple client/mul-*

tiple server architecture extends this model, allowing many servers to be connected to many clients. The rationale behind this extension is fairly obvious:

- System performance can be improved through splitting the workload among multiple servers.
- System availability increases. When one server crashes, the rest of them may proceed with only graceful performance degradation.
- System reliability increases because of *file replication* on multiple servers and independent file backups.

However, it is exactly file replication that becomes a problem. Maintenance of multiple file copies on multiple servers is easy only if files are never modified; in most cases, this never happens. Files are modified, and this action causes a so-called update propagation problem (see "Regimes of Information Update," chapter 6; and "Distributed Databases," chapter 11).

File replication in multiple client/multiple server architectures represents further expansion of the regime of *unlimited immediate update*, described in chapter 6. Recall that in this regime each information update propagates automatically to all the locations where duplicates of the updated information reside.

Automatic propagation of information updates in the multiple client/multiple server architecture, however, may not always be possible because some servers could be busy at the time of update propagation. As a result, the file will be updated in some servers, and in others it will not. In order to provide unlimited immediate update, two additional features are required:

- File version management. As a bare minimum, file version management involves assigning sequential numbers to consecutive file versions and maintaining the last version number as a file attribute.
- Multiple file access. When a client tries to access the file, the file's version number should be checked at several servers to see which version is the most recent and which server stores it.

Indeed, these features must be completely transparent for the client.

Electronic mail

OSI Message-Oriented Text Interchange System (MOTIS) is concerned with all aspects of EM. Its six basic services are as follows:

- Composition: creating messages and answers. Composition provides assistance with addressing and filling in header fields.
- Transfer: moving messages from the sender to the recipient. Transfer provides connection establishment and release by requesting services of the presentation layer. It also outputs the message.

- Reporting: telling the sender what happened to the message. Reporting provides confirmation of message delivery, rejection, or loss.
- Conversion: displaying the message. Conversion may involve various message format conversions that depend on the nature and specifics of the sending and receiving equipment.
- Formatting: defining the form in which the message should be displayed. A particular form depends upon the format of the original message and the message recipient's requirements.
- Disposition: dealing with the message after its reception. Possible options include throwing the message away immediately (junk electronic mail!); filing it; or reading the message and then forwarding it for further action.

Many more advanced features may be additionally provided by EM systems (and are provided by some of them). These features include:

- Time-dependent automatic mail forwarding
- Sending mail to alternative recipients
- Sending mail to a distribution list
- Sending boilerplate messages and keeping track of their recipients
- Creating and managing mailboxes for mail storage

Each message consists of an *envelope* and *message contents*. The envelope contains the message and parameters that help to interpret and transport the message. These parameters may include the destination address, message priority, IT security level, etc.

OSI service elements

Among many functions carried out at the application layer by its different services described in the previous sections, two stand out as most generic and used by most services. These two services, *connection management* and *transaction management*, are singled out by ISO as OSI *service elements*. Connection management is done by the Association Control Service Element (ACSE). Activity coordination is provided by the Commitment, Concurrency, and Recovery (CCR) service element.

There is very little that the ACSE does today. In fact, its only function is to translate one-to-one the application layer's *association* (the name for connections in this layer) primitives into the presentation layer's *connection* primitives. There is hope, however, that connection management will have independent functions in the future. User authentication, nonrepudiation, and some access control functions seem to be the first candidates for connection management in the application rather than the presentation layer.

The CCR service element provides transaction management in multiparty interactions. It guarantees that the intended multiparty interaction either completely succeeds or completely fails, with nothing in between. The CCR service element makes each such interaction an indivisible, or atomic, action: hence a *transaction* (see chapter 12).

The main transaction management mechanism used in CCR is called a *two-phase commit*. In the first phase, the *transaction initiator* lets each involved party know what this party is supposed to do. Each party examines its state of affairs to see if it is capable of performing the transaction and, if it is, records the request and its current state, locks its data to preclude interference from other transactions, and reports success back to the transaction initiator. If the party is unable or does not want to do its job, it reports failure.

In the second phase, the transaction initiator sees if all parties reported success. If at least one of them reported failure, the whole transaction falls through, and the transaction initiator broadcasts the failure, letting each party know that it must unlock its data and return to the recorded state. If all parties report success, the transaction initiator sends each of them a *commit message* meaning that they have to do their job.

During the second phase the only possible source of failure is a crash of one of the parties. However, if a crash happens, the party may restore its previous state and the request description, and then redo its job (see "Data Recovery," chapter 12, for further details).

Conclusion: Some problems with OSI

Fully recognizing the significance of OSI for building corporate information infrastructures satisfying the set of requirements in chapter 5, we still have to admit that at this point OSI is more a promise than a reality. It may become a reality only after OSI standards have been implemented, that is, when (1) a reasonably sufficient number of different OSI-compliant products from different vendors become commercially available and (2) users become convinced that these products can work together.

Unfortunately, these conditions have not happened yet. In a recent market survey by Business Research Group, 82 percent of IS executives agreed that OSI is still in the development stage and not widely available (FIG. 7-9). As a result the acceptance of OSI by users is low.

The situation is skillfully used by vendors of proprietary network solutions to lock their customers into such solutions before OSI comes. For example, at the Communication Network '89 show, Ellen Hancock, IBM vice president in charge of networking business, said that she no longer takes seriously the idea that OSI will catch up with SNA. "It will be years and years before OSI will have the equivalent of what SNA how has," she said.

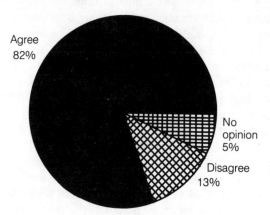

OSI not widely available; has little impact on IS executives

Source: Business research group (*Computerworld*, January 29, 1990, p 16).

Fig. 7-9. OSI is still in development.

On top of the shortage of OSI products and low user acceptance, there are still deficiencies in the OSI Reference Model itself. Some of the weakest points in the OSI Reference Model are the following:

- Data security
- LANs
- Internetworking
- Network management

With all the drawbacks of OSI, we still look optimistically into its future. The powerful user-driven movement for standardization has just begun (see chapter 2), and it is up to users to determine by the level of their involvement whether the advent of OSI will be significantly sped up or they will remain at the mercy of proprietary solution vendors.

8

Internetworking

Executive summary

There are several reasons why using multivendor heterogeneous networks is inevitable for years to come:

- There is already a big installed base of proprietary networks.
- Organizations running private proprietary networks may experience difficulties communicating with the rest of the world.
- Network acquisition decisions are often made at a relatively low corporate level, at which the importance of an all-corporate information infrastructure may not be completely understood.
- Network technology is still developing and changing rapidly, and innovative solutions may conflict with standard solutions.
- The number of LANs in corporations grow rapidly, and their standardization is hard to attain.

Internetworking can be done in virtually any OSI layer:

- Repeaters, physical layer relays, copy bits between cable segments, thus extending the network reach.
- Bridges, data link layer relays, are used to interconnect LANs of the same type.
- Routers, network layer relays, are used for LAN interconnections more sophisticated than those provided by bridges (for example, LANs with incompatible addressing schemes).
- Gateways, relays of the transport and higher layers, are capable of translating all protocols on one network into the protocols on another.

The important lesson from the past is that the corporate information infrastructure should not necessarily be homogeneous, but it must be flexible. Internetworking is a powerful technological solution that may provide a valuable combination of end-user freedom, overall infrastructure flexibility, and transparent information sharing and exchange.

Case for internetworking

As I stated in the conclusion of chapter 7, OSI at this point is more a promise and a framework for the future than today's reality. In other words, for many years to come, designers of corporate information infrastructures will have to cope with odd blends of proprietary and private network architectures (sometimes not even capable of talking to each other) and make them work together.

Information architecture designers who ignore the OSI Reference Model are so shortsighted that they eventually will create a monster that they cannot cope with. However, information infrastructure designers who take OSI at face value are naive and will jeopardize the future of their enterprises waiting for the Shangri-La of commonly accepted standards and products implementing them.

For some time, IS executives and managers believed that, through a mixture of technical and administrative measures, they would be able to enforce homogeneous networks. This dream has never come true. Several factors explain why network homogeneity is just a dream.

First, there is already a large installed base of proprietary networks. Here are some facts:

- There are about 30,000 IBM SNA networks. In the networking world, SNA is a virtually uncontested de facto standard. SNA is a solid product that has been around for many years and today offers many of the OSI features, but in a proprietary environment.
- There are about 3000 DEC DECNets, and DEC's own corporate network is one of the largest and best in the world.
- There are hundreds of thousands of LANs. A typical large company may have a few hundred LANs, usually of more than one type. (Some convincing reasons for having multiple LANs are given in this chapter.)
- As Unix becomes more popular, the number of Transmission Control Protocol/Internet Protocol (TCP/IP) networks grows rapidly. Some claim that a TCP/IP network is the best intermediate step on the way to OSI.

Many vendors and even some users, however, are not so eager to standardize. The vendor behavior is easy to explain (see chapter 2). Users, especially in the service industry, want networks that allow them to communicate with their customers in an easy and transparent way. If the customers that belong to their virtual enterprise have networks, they will have them, too.

Second, some organizations do not want to give up control of their networks to vendors or public network carriers. Their private proprietary networks may experience difficulties communicating with the rest of the world.

Third, network acquisition decisions are often made at a relatively low corporate level; and as hardware costs go down, the decision-making level may go further down. At this level people may not completely understand the importance of the information infrastructure. Instead, they are trying to solve their specific problems, creating, as a side effect, "islands of networking."

Fourth, network technology is still developing and changing rapidly. Thus, innovative solutions may conflict with standard solutions (see "Open Systems and Innovation" in chapter 2). Hence, the enterprise that incorporates an innovative technology for the sake of gaining a competitive advantage may end up being at the disadvantage of not following the standards prevailing at that time. This statement reinforces the point I made in chapter 2: open systems and standardization should be looked at as a dynamic rather than static process.

Finally, even if all WANs miraculously became OSI-standardized, LANs would hardly be touched. LANs are one of the weakest parts of the OSI Reference Model. At the same time, the number of LANs in corporations rapidly increases (see FIGS. 6-16 and 6-17), and their standardization is the hardest to attain. Factors that explain the expected growth of multiple LANs in a typical enterprise include:

- As the end-user autonomy grows, different divisions, departments, and other functional units will choose different LANs that are best suited to their local needs.
- Geographic spread of end-user workstations over several buildings or large physical distance between the most remote workstations may have to result in LAN partitioning and subsequent interconnection.
- Heavy total traffic load may have to be divided among many separate LANs forming client/server clusters that have to be interconnected through high-speed backbones also using LAN technology.
- LAN reliability may be increased by isolating separate LANs and then connecting them with bridges (see "Kinds of Relays" later in this chapter).
- LAN security may be improved by isolating separate LANs and then screening all the information at separating bridges, especially in a promiscuous mode (see "Transparent Bridges" later in this chapter).

These factors do not seem to go away overnight. The enterprise has to learn to live with heterogeneous networks as a fact of life and an intrinsic part of the real world. It may cope with heterogeneous networks through connecting, or *internetworking*, two or more networks into a single user-transparent network called an *internetwork*. Internetworking is done by special devices whose major function is to convert a packet from one network's format to another's. These devices are generically referred to as *relays*. Four major kinds of relays and their possible modifications are discussed in this chapter.

OSI view of internetworking

In chapter 7 internetworking was introduced as one function of the network layer. For purposes of internetworking, the network layer can be divided into three sublayers (FIG. 8-1):

- Subnet access sublayer
- Subnet enhancement sublayer
- Internetwork sublayer

A *subnet access sublayer* performs ordinary network layer functions—in particular, data and control packet transmission and reception. It performs its function for a certain subnet, and there is no guarantee that it would be adequate for other subnets.

An *internetwork sublayer* performs end-to-end routing between two or more subnets. In the first case, the corresponding relay is called *bilateral*; in the second case, it is called *multilateral*. The internetwork sublayer assumes that both subnets it is to connect comply with OSI even if they do not.

It is the function of the *subnet enhancement sublayer* to reconcile the differences between heterogeneous subnets and thus make internetworking possible. Two typical subnet enhancement sublayer functions are (1) reconciliation of the subnets' addressing schemes and (2) reconciliation of connection-oriented and connectionless services.

Internetworking can be done not only in the network layer but also in virtually any layer. In the next section, we will discuss four major kinds of relays that connect subnets in different layers.

Kinds of relays

There are four major kinds of relays: repeaters, bridges, routers, and gateways. In addition, there are two mixed relays. Relays are described in the following paragraphs.

Repeaters

Repeaters are physical layer relays. Repeaters copy bits between cable segments, thus extending the network reach (cable length). They repeat all signals, and the result is useless traffic. They also cannot connect different subnets, such as Ethernet and token ring, or baseband and broadband cables. Because of their simplicity, repeaters are relatively fast and inexpensive. Examples of repeater use include Ethernet (chapter 6), twisted pairs (chapter 7), and fiberoptics (chapter 7).

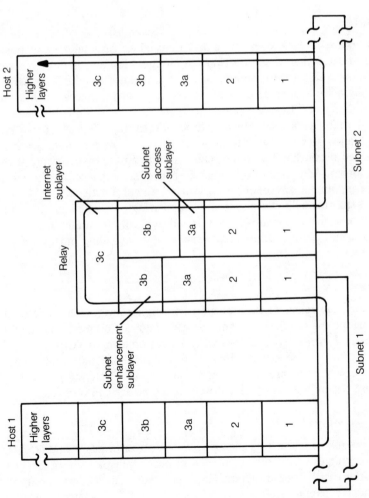

Fig. 8-1. OSI view of internetworking.

Bridges

Bridges are data link layer relays used for LAN interconnection. A typical bridge stores and forwards frames between LANs of the same type. (For example, a bridge cannot connect different LANs, such as Ethernet and token ring.) The bridge includes software for frame format conversion and checksum verification and does not pass (filter) frames that are already on the right destination LAN.

The bridge can provide network statistics but only for the network they sit on. It cannot forward frames to nodes that are not on a directly attached LAN. Since a bridge represents a hardware/software mixture, it is slower than a repeater. The bridge can transmit from 1.5K to 12K frames per second depending on the software complexity. Bridges are also more expensive than repeaters.

Routers

Routers are network layer relays that are used for LAN interconnections more sophisticated than those provided by bridges. Routing is mostly a software function, with software running on a server or a dedicated PC. Its hardware is usually a LAN adapter card connected to other interfaces, such as another LAN, X.25, or T1 cards.

A router can handle incompatible addressing schemes. It can typically store and interpret an internetwork map and routes even for indirectly attached networks. The router can also find an alternative route if the link goes down. Additionally, a router can collect statistics across the whole network and implement other network management functions.

Some router limitations include supporting only a predefined set of network protocols and relatively low speed (typically from 500 to 1000 packets per second). Router prices may vary widely depending mostly on software functionality and complexity.

Gateways

Gateways are relays of the transport and higher layers. They are capable of translating all protocols on one network into the protocols on another (for example, Vines-to-SNA or the OSI transport protocol to TCP).

A gateway is mostly a software function, with software running on top of the gateway hardware. It is slower than routers. Gateway prices may vary widely, depending mostly on software functionality and complexity.

Mixed relays

The two mixed relays are called *routing bridges*, or brouters, and *bridging routers*, or rridges. A *brouter* combines protocol transparency of bridges with rerouting capabilities of routers. However, brouters do not have a router's management capabilities. A *rridge* routes one or a few selected protocols and bridges some others. For example, a rridge could serve as a router for TCP/IP and, at the same time, as a bridge for Novell's Netware.

Transparent and source routing bridges

There are two major classes of bridges: *transparent* and *source routing*. As we will see later in this section, a source routing bridge is actually a router (Perlman, Harvey, and Varghese 1988). While a transparent bridge works completely within the data link layer, a source routing bridge needs information that is usually available only in the network layer.

Transparent bridges

The goal of a transparent bridge, as its name implies, is complete user transparency. The user buys a bridge, plugs it into the network, and it works without any interference from the user. In particular, no hardware or software changes are necessary; and no address switch settings or a prior information, such as static tables maintained by humans, are required.

After the set of transparent bridges has been installed, it initially works in a so-called *promiscuous mode* with learning as follows:

1. Each transparent bridge accepts every frame transmitted on all LANs it is attached to and first decides whether to forward or discard the frame. The general rules (FIG. 8-2) are as follows:

   - If the source and destination LANs are the same (intra-LAN communication), discard the frame.
   - If the source and destination LANs are different, forward the frame.
   - If the destination LAN is unknown, learn where it is.

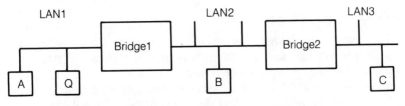

- Frame sent from A to Q is discarded by bridge1
- Frame sent from A to B is forwarded by bridge2

Fig. 8-2. Forwarding frames by a transparent bridge.

2. The transparent bridge forwards the frame to all LANs it is attached to (except for the one the frame arrived from) using a so-called *flooding*

algorithm (Tanenbaum 1988). The flooding algorithm is used because at this point no destinations are known yet.

3. By using the *backward learning* algorithm (Baran 1964), transparent bridges learn the network topology by looking at the source address of all incoming frames. After a while the transparent bridge starts receiving frames with the destination it knows. At this point it stops flooding and forwards the frame along the correct LAN.

Starting with this point, the transparent bridge supports the *dynamic network topology* by periodically repeated flooding to learn if anything has changed in the network topology. If a change has occurred, the transparent bridge updates its destination tables. For example, stations and bridges could be down or relocated. If the station has been relocated within the building, it will return to normal operation in a few minutes, after the transparent bridge learns its new address.

To increase communication reliability, two or more parallel transparent bridges may be used to connect the same pair of LANs. However, such a network topology may have loops that result in infinite frame forwarding.

To avoid loops, the topology is covered by a *spanning tree* (FIG. 8-3). The spanning tree eliminates loops because there is only one path between any pair of LANs. Since the same network can be covered with many spanning trees, it is selected by all transparent bridges by consensus. After the spanning tree is agreed upon, each transparent bridge forwards all frames only along this tree. Note that some bridges may be excluded from certain spanning trees, even though all LANs will be covered by each spanning tree. (The goal is to reach each LAN in a unique way, not each bridge.) The spanning tree is permanently updated as the network topology changes.

Transparent bridges can be used to connect remote LANs. Part of the communication paths between two LANs may go through one or more WANs, and the WAN traffic should be optimized for some obvious reasons: WANs are slower, less reliable, and more expensive.

Source routing bridges

Unlike a transparent bridge, a *source routing bridge* assumes that the frame transmitter knows the exact path to every possible destination. A route from a source to a destination is presented as a Bridge1, LAN1, . . . Bridgen, LANn sequence. All inter-LAN frames are marked to be inspected by a source routing bridge, and the bridge forwards the frame to the LAN following its own identifier on the route. The inspection function can be implemented in hardware, software, or a mixture of both, with an obvious trade-off between speed and complexity: hence price.

What happens if the frame transmitter does not know the destination? In this case, it issues a broadcast *discovery frame*. The discovery frame is forwarded by every bridge and reaches every LAN on the internetwork, using

A. Initial Network

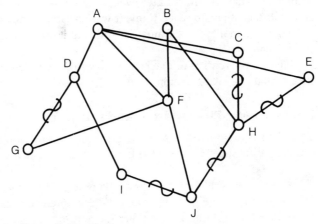

B. Spanning Tree with Root in F

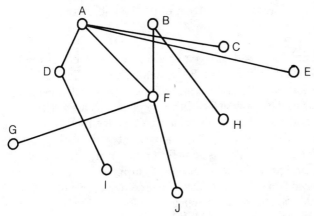

C. Another representation of same spanning tree

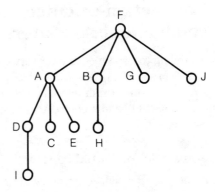

∿ denotes communication link lost because of transmission through a spanning tree.

H can communicate with I only through root F of a spanning tree.

Fig. 8-3. Spanning tree.

some sort of flooding. All bridges and LANs record their identity (unique address) so that the transmitter eventually knows all possible routes and can choose the best one for each frame it will transmit. The overhead of exponential explosion of discovery frames is large, but it occurs only until the transmitter finds all routes.

The source routing bridge has nothing to do with internetwork administration, which is a host function.

Comparison of transparent and source routing bridges

TABLE 8-1 compares transparent and source routing bridges. The core philosophical differences between the two types of bridges are as follows:

- A transparent bridge provides connectionless service, while a source routing bridge provides connection-oriented service.
- A source routing bridge relies on centralized and given upfront knowledge of the total network topology, while a transparent bridge relies on distributed knowledge of the bridge's direct neighbors that it has to acquire itself.

All other advantages or disadvantages of either class of bridges result from these two philosophical differences. For example, one implication is that all source routing bridge functionality is in the host, while all transparent bridge functionality is in the bridge itself. Other implications are better flexibility of transparent bridges or better performance of source routing ones.

One final point in the comparison of transparent and source routing bridges is that a source routing bridge is actually a router rather than a bridge. While a transparent bridge can work with only local information concerned with a data link between two separate LANs, a source routing bridge requires total information about the internetwork topology to forward the frame (actually a packet because it has an additional header to state a route explicitly).

Connection-oriented and connectionless routers

According to two types of layer services discussed in chapter 7, there are two classes of routers: *connection-oriented* and *connectionless*. Recall that the goal of a router is to establish interconnection in the network layer. In other words, routers should handle both LAN-to-LAN and LAN-to-WAN or WAN-to-WAN internetworking.

Connection-oriented routers

In the case of a connection-oriented router, the sequence of data links connecting the source and the destination, possibly through a number of routers, must

Table 8-1. Comparison of Transparent vs. Source Routing Bridges.

Feature	Transparent Bridge	Source Routing Bridge
Service	Connectionless; each frame is sent independently.	Connection-oriented (routes are determined in advance by discovery frames, then established and used).
Transparency	Completely transparent to hosts and compatible with all 802 products.	Neither transparent nor compatible. Hosts must know the topology and provide administration.
Installation and management	Installation is easy and straightforward. No configuration management is required.	Manual installation of LAN and bridge numbers; critical to installation mistakes. Connecting two existing networks may involve major overhaul of numbers.
Routing	Spanning tree-based. Does not use bandwidth optimally (some links are always ignored).	Optimal routing is possible. Parallel bridges can be used to split load.
Locating destinations	Backward learning. Frames from all sources are required to determine destinations.	Discovery frames. Exponential explosion with parallel bridges.
Flexibility	Dynamic topology. Loss of bandwidth due to periodic flooding, especially with bursty traffic. Easy to install new machines and bridges or move them around.	Routes are preestablished. Discovery frames are a one-time effort. Installation of new machines and bridges is complex and not fully automatic.
Failure handling	Monitoring control frames. Provides quick, fully automatic failure detection. Hosts are not involved	Repeated retransmission and sending of discovery frames. Loss of many frames even though alternative routes are available. Hosts are involved.
Complexity	In the bridges.	In all hosts (store routes, send discovery frames, copy route information in each frame sent). Typical IBM approach.
Performance	Inefficiencies of flooding. More expensive bridges	With hardware-based solutions, better performance for a given investment. Costs of hosts are hidden but significant.

be established from the beginning. All packets belonging to the established connection will go along the same path, including all connection-oriented routers on this path.

If two networks that should be interconnected through a router are owned by different organizations or even by different countries, ownership problems may result. To avoid these problems, the router can be divided into two parts belonging to two network operators that are to be connected through the router. Each part is called a *half-router*. The only necessary agreement between network operators is a common protocol for a wire connecting the two halves of the router. CCITT's X.75 provides such a protocol (FIG. 8-4).

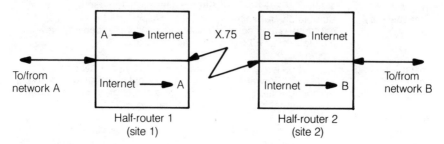

Fig. 8-4. Half-router.

Connectionless routers

In the case of a connectionless router, no connections must be established in advance. As a result there is no requirement for all packets belonging to the same connection to go through the same sequence of routers. Accordingly, there is no guarantee that packets arrive in the same order as they were sent, or that they arrive at all.

As messages travel through the internetwork, they may go through various transformations caused by the diversity of network data formats and protocols. For example, if the message is longer than the maximum packet size allowed by the network, it will be divided into several fragments. *Fragment reassembly* may then be provided at each router (*transparent fragmentation*) or only at the destination (*nontransparent fragmentation*).

Comparison of connection-oriented and connectionless routers

TABLE 8-2 compares connection-oriented and connectionless routers. Their advantages and disadvantages are typical for connection-oriented and connectionless services in general.

In the case of connection-oriented routers, the order of packet arrival is guaranteed, buffers may be reserved in advance to alleviate congestion problems, and shorter headers can be used because the connection has been established in advance.

Unlike connection-oriented routers, connectionless routers can work over diverse networks including connectionless ones, such as LANs and broadcasting WANs. They are also more robust and flexible.

Table 8-2. Comparison of Connection-Oriented and Connectionless Routers.

Feature	Connection-Oriented Routers	Connectionless Routers
Handling heterogenous networks	Serious problems if internetwork includes connectionless networks such as LANs, mobile networks, and satellite WANs	Can be used over connectionless networks
Reliability	Vulnerable to router failures	Alternative routes can be found and used
Sequencing	Guaranteed	Is not guaranteed
Handling congestion	Can be provided (reduced) through buffer reservation in advance	More potential for congestion, but also more potential for adapting to it
Packet overhead	Small: short headers can be used	Big: longer headers are needed

When to use which relay

It is easy to say when to use a repeater or a gateway. A repeater must be used for extension of a physical cable. A gateway must be used to provide remote connection between systems with different network layer (including routing) protocols.

The decision of when to use a bridge and when to use a router may not be so trivial. Generally speaking, a bridge should be used to provide fast and effective interconnection between LANs of the same type. If LANs to be interconnected are of different types, a router should be used. A router should also be used if additional management capabilities, such as dynamic reconfiguration in the presence of failed links, are available. For a combination of transparency, flexibility, and management capabilities, a choice between a brouter and a rridge may have to be made.

However, general considerations of this kind may be insufficient for practical selection of the most appropriate class of relay for the problem at hand. TABLE 8-3 presents some of the problems that may arise when various IEEE 802 LANs are interconnected. Even internetworking of the same kinds of LANs, such as Ethernet-to-Ethernet, may present problems if the two Ethernets have different error rates or loads. If they do, a router may be necessary even in this relatively simple case.

Here are some additional statements or recommendations concerning bridge/router selection:

- If stations that have to be interconnected do not comply with a common network protocol, a bridge should be used.

Table 8-3. 802-to-802 Internetworking.

Standard	Ethernet	Token Bus	Token Ring

Ethernet	Possibly different data rate
	  Collisions reduce data rate
	  Lightly to heavily loaded LAN transmission may cause flow control problem or require more buffers
		Different frame formats
		  Reformatting takes time, reduces reliability
		Priority assignment problem
			Different frame formats
			  Reformatting takes time, reduces reliability
			Different data rate
			  Flow control problem (for 4 Mbps); timer can go off too early
			Priority assignment problem

Token bus	Different frame formats
	  Reformatting takes time, reduces reliability
	Different data rate
	  Flow control problem
	Different frame length
	Priority information lost
		Acknowledgment hard to verify	Different frame formats
			  Reformatting takes time, reduces reliability
			Different data rate
			  Flow control problem (for 4 Mbps); timer can go off too early
			Different frame length
			Acknowledgment hard to verify

Token ring	Different frame formats
	  Reformatting takes time, reduces reliaity
	Different data rate
	  Flow control problem (for 16 Mbps)
	Different frame length
	Priority information lost
	Acknowledgment hard to verify
		Different frame formats
		  Reformatting takes time, reduces reliability (if token holding time > 18 ms)
		Different frame length
		Acknowledgment hard to verify
		Priority assignment problem
		  Different defintions of priority although same number of bits
			Acknowledgment hard to verify

Assumptions:

802.3: 1518-byte frame, 10 Mbps (minus collisions)
802.4: 8191-byte frame, 10 Mbps
802.5: 5000-byte frame (if token holding time is 10 ms), 4 or 16 Mbps

- If interconnected links have similar bandwidths, error rates, and addressing systems, bridges will do well.
- Because of their simplicity, bridges have better cost/performance characteristics than routers; thus, routers should be used only if there is a special need for their unique features.
- Bridges may use network bandwidth more efficiently because they have relatively low overhead compared with routers. However, bridges waste bandwidth because of periodic flooding and using a spanning tree rather than the entire network.
- In the case of a broad range of packet sizes or links with a small maximum packet size, the use of routers is almost necessary because bridges cannot do fragmentation and packet reassembly.
- In the case of nonuniform network bandwidth, there is a real danger of congestion, which dictates the use of routers since bridges can control flow but not congestion (see "Congestion Control," chapter 7). For example, bridges cannot inform stations to reduce their transmitted traffic.
- From the viewpoint of congestion, big variations of network error rates have the same effect as bandwidth variations. Thus, if such variations take place, the use of routers is as necessary as in the case of nonuniform network bandwidth.
- In the case of very large internetworks, the use of routers may be preferable because a hierarchical addressing scheme (see "Connection Management," chapter 7) significantly raises the number of stations addressable in the internetwork (Perlman, Harvey, and Varghese 1988).
- To fulfill increased requirements for internetwork availability and bandwidth, parallel routers may be used, resulting in multiple paths to the same destination, hence, spreading the load among multiple links and rerouting in the case of link failure.

Conclusion

Even with proliferation of OSI standards, the demand for internetworking will certainly grow over the next decade and beyond. The trend to internetwork growth is highlighted by recent market research. Eastern Management estimates that the number of interconnected LANs as a percentage of the total number will grow to almost 40 percent in 1993 (FIG. 8-5). IDC predicts a significant growth in U.S. bridge/router shipments over the next few years (FIG. 8-6).

The important lesson from the past is that the corporate information infrastructure should not necessarily be homogeneous, but it must be flexible. Internetworking is a powerful technological solution that may provide a valuable combination of end-user freedom, overall infrastructure flexibility, and transparent information sharing and exchange. In order to take advantage of internetworking opportunities, one must understand why internetworking is needed in a specific business environment and how it should be implemented.

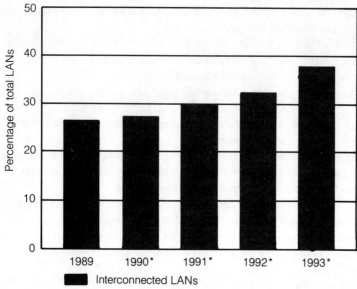

Source: The Eastern Management Group (*Computerworld*, February 5, 1990, p 90).

Fig. 8-5. Interconnected LANs.

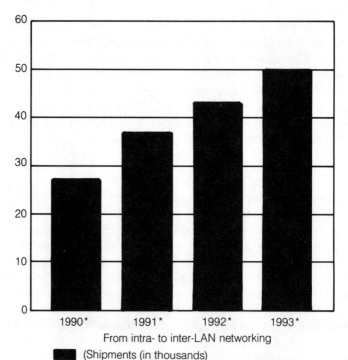

Source: IDC (*Computerworld*, February 5, 1990, p. 145). *Estimated

Fig. 8-6. U.S. bridge/router shipments (excluding FDDI).

9

Network management

Executive summary

Network management is necessary to provide an adequate quality of network service in terms of bandwidth, transmission delay, error rate, user transparency, and reliability, as well as network adaptability to everchanging technology and user needs without service disruption.

There are three facets of network management: organizational, technical, and functional. The main issue of the organizational facet is how to organize a network management process. The main issue of the technical facet is how to cope with difficulties of managing extremely complex, heterogeneous, multivendor internetworks. From the functional standpoint, network management is a set of operational, administrative, and support tools that provide:

- Fault management
- Configuration and name management
- Performance management
- Accounting management
- Security management

The ISO looks at network management as an extension of the basic OSI Reference Model. Unfortunately, OSI network management is more a promise than a reality. In the meantime several vendors have been addressing one of the most demanding problems of the corporate information infrastructure: integration of many heterogeneous structures into an integrated network management system (INMS). Several INMS products have been available for some time, with IBM's Netview and AT&T's Unified Network Management Architecture (UNMA) being the most popular, at least in the Fortune 1000 community.

Here are some of the major concepts that are or will be commonly incorporated in INMSs:

- Addressing mostly the part of the network management system (NMS) integration that deals with connectivity
- Providing a consistent and transparent view of the INMS's total network management capabilities as if they were provided by a single system
- Accommodating tiered integration architectures that permit hierarchical network management authorities
- Supporting management services, such as configuration and fault management
- Allowing users to build their own management applications that drive, or create presentations from, their individual NMSs
- Using a modular approach to accommodate unforeseen changes in environment, user needs, NMS relationships, and so forth.

Even in an ideal OSI environment, there would be very few people who could understand in real time what is going on in a large internetwork, or interpret on-line the stream of management information provided by the INMS or individual NMSs, or just support normal internetwork operations around the clock. The solution to these problems is applying artificial intelligence (AI) technology.

In the next several years, AI will not only make integrated network management a reality, but it will also help integrate network and information management, providing the glue necessary for putting all pieces of the corporate information infrastructure together.

After the internetwork is designed and implemented, it should be managed. Network management provides the following:

- Adequate quality of network service in terms of bandwidth, transmission delay, error rate, user transparency, and reliability
- Network adaptability to ever-changing technology and user needs without service disruption

For many years network management has been provided by carriers and major computer vendors. However, with the advent of PCs, workstations, and LANs, as well as the proliferation of a multivendor environment, such a simplistic approach is becoming impractical for all but very simple internetworks. The fact is that users must take care of their internetworks or hire system integrators to manage network functions.

For most users network management is an extremely complex problem, and they seem to be ready to pay for its solution. According to recent research by Business Research Group, more than 75 percent of 300 Fortune 1000 companies intend to increase their budgets for network management by 48 percent from 1990 to 1992. In other research by Index Group, Inc., network management has been identified as an area of major concern for both IS and telecommunication managers (FIGS. 9-1 and 9-2).

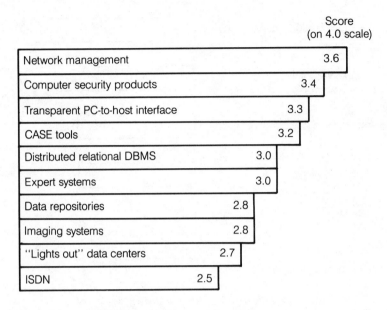

Score
(on 4.0 scale)

Network management	3.6
Computer security products	3.4
Transparent PC-to-host interface	3.3
CASE tools	3.2
Distributed relational DBMS	3.0
Expert systems	3.0
Data repositories	2.8
Imaging systems	2.8
"Lights out" data centers	2.7
ISDN	2.5

Source: Index Group, Inc. (*Computerworld*, February 5, 1990, p. 6).

Fig. 9-1. Areas of IS manager concern.

The ideal solution to network management problems is seen by users as so-called *end-to-end network management.* This method consists of a single internetwork operator console from which any component of the internetwork, including both subnet and host components, may be operated, troubleshot, controlled, and reconfigured remotely. End-to-end network management also implies significant involvement of on-site knowledge-based systems (KBSs) that provide assistance to network management personnel and keep the internetwork operator console from being overloaded with unnecessary details of internetwork operation.

The idea of end-to-end network management is far from implementation. Estimates for making it a reality range from four to ten years. In the meantime, internetworks have to be managed by using available management tools.

Facets of network management

Unfortunately, network management problems cannot be solved by purchasing more hardware or developing more software. The situation is complicated by the fact that network management is not just a technical problem. Rather, it

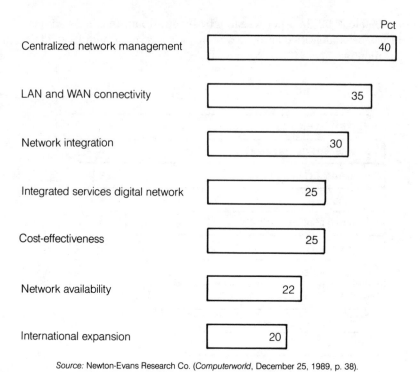

Pct

Centralized network management	40
LAN and WAN connectivity	35
Network integration	30
Integrated services digital network	25
Cost-effectiveness	25
Network availability	22
International expansion	20

Source: Newton-Evans Research Co. (*Computerworld*, December 25, 1989, p. 38).

Fig. 9-2. Key concerns of telecommunication managers.

comprises three separate but highly interrelated facets: organizational, technical, and functional. Let us look at these facets of network management in more detail.

Organizational facet

The main issue of the organizational facet is how to organize a network management process. This issue involves addressing and solving problems such as the following:

- Where to locate points of internetwork state control
- How to collect information about internetwork state and performance and make it accessible to management
- How to determine the minimum information that should be available to management to understand what is going on in the internetwork and how to deliver this information
- How to allocate network management personnel

From the organizational standpoint, network management should be considered in the context of the corporate information infrastructure that becomes increasingly decentralized, providing greater end-user freedom and information sharing and exchange. Managing an internetwork may mean managing hundreds of LANs, bridges, routers, gateways, backbones, and WANs that may be geographically remote and heterogeneous, reside in the subnet or the host, and be owned by different organizations within and outside the enterprise.

When corporate divisions and departments make networks an intrinsic part of their fiefdoms, control over the overall internetwork performance becomes more and more difficult. The situation is complicated by technical problems of isolating a problem in the internetwork to the customer or carrier equipment, or to a subnet or host. As a result, the trend is shifting from local to centralized network management.

It comes as almost a paradox that a more decentralized information infrastructure demands more centralized network management. Several important factors contribute to this paradox, making centralized network management a necessity:

- The entire enterprise relies more and more on its information infrastructure: hence, internetwork.
- Skilled network management personnel are hard to find and keep at each local site.
- No significant network management budget surge can be expected in the near future.
- Decentralized network management can hardly provide anything close to optimal internetwork utilization.
- The number of stations, such as PCs, workstations, and servers, that have to be networked rapidly increases.

The push for centralized network management is extremely strong, especially among IS managers. Centralized network management should provide a corporate-wide view of what is going on across the internetwork. The following operations are most often cited by IS managers as necessary to be carried out in centralized fashion:

- Access to a complex and constantly changing LAN/host network
- Utilization control and dynamic resource allocation
- Single-console monitoring and troubleshooting
- Traffic pattern analysis
- Performance measurement of heterogeneous networks for accounting and cost-justification purposes

As a result many IS managers want to remove operational autonomy from end-user divisions and departments and, sometimes, even from telecommunication departments. Users usually resist losing control of their network, and the conflict between IS and end-user organizations seems inevitable. In some cases top management resolves the conflict in a simple way: by outsourcing network management (see chapter 3).

Indeed, the reasons for which IS managers push centralized network management are not entirely altruistic. For them, centralization is an excellent chance to regain control over the computational resources (or what we call the corporate information infrastructure) they lost with the advent of PCs. Regaining this control is essential for the good of the enterprise. I have argued elsewhere in this book that building and managing the corporate information infrastructure is the business of IS organizations for the 1990s, and network management is obviously included.

Centralized network management, however, is not a panacea. TABLE 9-1 summarizes its advantages and disadvantages. When deciding on a network management organization, the IS manager must analyze these advantages and disadvantages; assign different weights to them, depending on business requirements; and select the most appropriate degree of network management centralization.

Table 9-1. Centralized Network Management Advantages and Disadvantages.

Advantages	Disadvantages
Concentrates scarce maintenance skills at one site.	Most faults occur at local sites (workstations, system and application software, etc.).
Standards and interfaces are easier to enforce and maintain.	For nonvoice communications, maintenance is actually end-user support rather than central engineering.
Security is easier to provide and enforce.	Frequent changes in traffic patterns and workstation locations are hard to handle.
Control over internetwork performance and utilization tighter.	Responsiveness to end-user needs is worse.

At any rate, network management calls for reconsidering the corporate organizational structure. Interrelationships among the IS department, the central telecommunication department, and on-site network management personnel have to be rectified; and the reporting structure has to be in accordance with the requirements for network management.

By all indications the new organizational structure will hardly be more robust than the old one. Some of the proposals to establish a matrix management structure, with some employees operating networks on-site but reporting to the "central authority," seem to confirm this grim prediction (Kerr 1988).

One interesting approach to resolving the trade-offs between centralized and local network management is *network partitioning*, with the corresponding changes in the corporate organizational structure. According to this idea the whole internetwork can be divided into an *access network* and a *transport network*.

The access network is building- or site-located and typically an LAN. It may be linked to other access networks by bridges. Each access network should have a manager who is responsible for user services and network operations, growth, and maintenance.

The transport network consists of geographically remote networks connected through a backbone. It is typically a WAN linked to other WANs (including public packet-switching networks) through routers or gateways. The transport network should be run by a central group responsible for network operation and maintenance, all-corporate security, and the issuance of guidelines for access network managers.

Technical facet

The evolution of computer and telecommunication technology has led to the development of extremely complex, heterogeneous, multivendor internetworks. As their complexity grows, so do the technical difficulties of managing these internetworks.

Managing an internetwork means controlling the performance and quality of service of hundreds of LANs, bridges, routers, gateways, Tx (x = 1, 2, 3) multiplexers, switches, backbones, and WANs that may be geographically remote and heterogeneous. Some of these internetwork components may be parts of the subnet, while others reside in hosts.

There are two sources of technical network management problems:

- Each internetwork component is a complex system with its own troubleshooting, configuration, and maintenance problems.
- The internetwork consisting of these components requires overall management that must concentrate on inter- rather than intracomponent problems.

Specific technical solutions to network management problems are in great degree dictated by organizational decisions. For example, the following LAN management functions are required regardless of what organizational decisions have been made:

- Monitoring and control of server activities
- Analysis of disk usage
- User access to resources
- Performance analysis
- Configuration and fault management

However, the method of providing these functions depends heavily on the organization of the network management process. In the case of completely centralized network management, all of the LAN management functions listed should be carried out from a remote internetwork operator console. If, however, only the first three LAN management functions need to be carried out locally, the last two would be remote.

As another example, even in centralized network management, just collecting all alarms and alerts from all LANs may not be enough. Instead, alarm analysis and interpretation should be done locally, and only the summary must be sent to the internetwork operator console.

Conversely, technological feasibility determines which of the desirable organizational network management options will really work. For example, even though end-to-end network management is well accepted and desirable, it is not feasible today; thus, more realistic trade-offs between desirable and feasible organizational solutions should be considered.

Functional facet

The final facet of network management addresses the issue of what should be involved in a typical NMS. From the functional standpoint, network management is a set of operational, administrative, and support functions and corresponding tools that:

- Keep the internetwork operational
- Adjust its architecture to current user requirements and traffic characteristics
- Fine-tune its performance
- Account for its utilization
- Protect it from unauthorized interference

In other words, to provide the internetwork service quality and adaptability, an NMS should support the following functions (Ericson, Ericson, and Minoli 1989; Brusil and LaBarre 1989):

- Fault management
- Configuration and name management
- Performance management
- Accounting management
- Security management

Let us look at these functions in more detail.

Fault management Fault management provides four basic services that promote continuous, reliable internetwork operation:

- Fault detection
- Fault diagnosis
- Fault correction
- Fault administration

The *fault detection* service detects fault messages in the network management data stream or receives such messages from other network management functions. Fault messages are converted in an internal format and passed to the fault administration service for logging and to the fault diagnosis or correction service for further actions.

The *fault diagnosis* service attempts to find the fault cause and initiate fault correction at the fault correction service. This service tries to do its job in a fully automated fashion by using active diagnostic tests and/or rules. However, it will provide on-line assistance to the human operator if it is unable to diagnose a fault on its own.

The *fault correction* service uses predefined fault correction rules to restore internetworking. This service also tries to do its job automatically—for example, by switching to the duplicate facility. However, if it is unable to do so, the fault correction service will provide on-line assistance to the human operator within the limits of its capabilities.

The *fault administration* service is used to build and maintain the fault diagnosis and correction rules and the fault history database. It also provides trend analysis and help for human operators.

Configuration and name management Configuration and name management is the fundamental part of network management responsible for all kinds of modifications of internetwork components, such as equipment, processes, and services. Whenever it receives a request for internetwork modification, it checks the current component state, confirms the modification validity, performs the modification, and finally validates it. Configurations may be modified to reduce congestion, avoid faulty equipment, or respond to changing user needs.

Configuration and name management functions include:

- Defining internetwork components
- Assigning names to internetwork components and managing them
- Initializing and terminating internetwork components as well as managing their states
- Defining control states and sequences for the entire internetwork
- Managing on-line state modifications for the entire internetwork and its components
- Providing on-line monitoring and reporting of modified states for the entire internetwork and its components
- Maintaining the current state and inventory of all internetwork components

Performance management Performance management is the third fundamental part of network management responsible for analyzing and requesting modifications of internetwork components to provide performance improvements in terms of throughput, delay, and resource utilization. Performance management functions include:

- Collecting performance statistics from all internetwork components, including those of the NMS
- Creating and maintaining the database of historical performance statistics
- Developing performance evaluation criteria and thresholds
- Analyzing current performance statistics aimed at performance fault detection and generation of performance alarms and fault events
- Analyzing long-term trends based on the correlation of current performance statistics and historical patterns
- Initiating internetwork components' operation mode and configuration modifications in response to performance fault events
- Monitoring on-line performance of the entire internetwork and its components

Accounting management   Accounting management provides a fair distribution of operating expenses among internetwork end users based on service usage. It also provides customization of routing and classes of service by the end-user request. Accounting management includes the following functions:

- Associating tariff schedules with use of internetwork resources based on system utilization statistics
- Calculating costs of internetwork services for users
- Organizing credible billing procedures for services used, based on billing audits
- Calculating combined costs for use of multiple resources.

Security management   Security management implements internetwork security policies. Its basic functions include:

- Distributing security-related information, such as encryption keys and access privileges
- Reporting security-related events, such as network intrusion, violation of access privileges, and access to and update of protected information or services
- Managing security-related mechanisms and services

Security is discussed in more detail in chapter 14.

OSI view of network management

The ISO looks at network management as an extension of the basic OSI Reference Model. The OSI Management Environment that consists of tools and services required to manage internetworks is discussed in terms of three underlying models (Brusil and LaBarre 1989; and Klerer 1989):

- Organizational model describing how OSI Management may be distributed administratively among management environments
- Informational model providing guidelines for a formal definition of internetwork components and their relationships
- Functional model describing network management functions and their interrelationships

Organizational model

The OSI organizational model is based on the concept of an *abstract object* and an object-oriented representation and computation model (Cox 1986). Abstract objects can communicate through *abstract ports*. Abstract ports may be symmetric or asymmetric with respect to services they supply or consume.

One of the fundamental abstract objects is called a *management domain*. The large internetwork can be divided into a number of management domains for administrative autonomy, accounting, or security reasons. For example, three major network management domains are the customer premises (host), the LANs, and the interexchange network (WAN).

Management domains may interrelate in a variety of ways, such as embedding or overlapping (FIG. 9-3). A management domain may consist of one or more *management systems*, zero or more *managed systems*, and zero or more *management subdomains*.

A managed system can be decomposed further into one or more *managed objects*. A managed object is a resource monitored and controlled by one or more management systems. In fact, a managed object is what we called previously an internetwork component, that is, a piece of equipment, a process, or a service. The concept of a managed object is recursive in that a managed object may be embedded in another managed object. For example, an LAN interface card is embedded in an end-user workstation. Both are managed objects.

A management system is a process that performs monitoring and controlling functions over managed objects and/or management subdomains.

A management subdomain is administered by an administrative authority that could be a public or private organization. The administrative authority is responsible for the creation, modification, and maintenance of managed objects, relationships among managed and management systems, relationships among managed systems and managed objects, and security mechanisms for access to managed objects.

Informational model

The core of the informational model is a management information base (MIB). The MIB is required to store and manage diverse information about the OSI

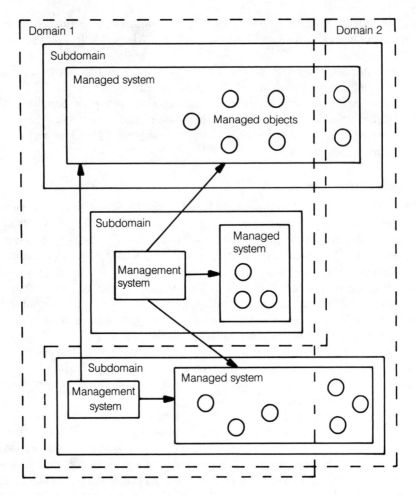

Fig. 9-3. Management domains.

system, such as its configuration, current and historic performance data, accounting information, and fault logs.

The MIB represents its information as a collection of *entries*, each describing a managed object. Entries are organized into a management information tree (MIT) shown in FIG. 9-4. The tree hierarchy represents decomposition of managed objects.

Each managed object is specified by three characteristics:

- A list of < attribute, value > pairs. Each attribute must have at least one operation defined for it: for example, read or modify. A value may have its own structure.
- A list of operations that can be performed on a managed object. Operation validity and failure may be included in the object specification.

- A list of messages that a managed object can issue or be reported on to one or more management systems. Messages can be triggered by error occurrence, exceeding parameter thresholds, elapsed timers, etc.

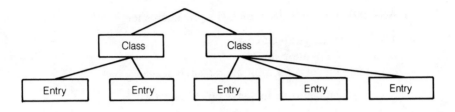

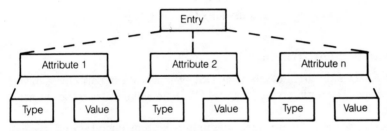

Fig. 9-4. Management information tree.

Functional model

The functional model defines the five underlying specific management functional areas (SMFAs) of network management similar to network management functions discussed in "Functional Facets" earlier in this chapter. In this section we will present the list of SMFAs with emphasis on the OSI procedures available for each of them.

- Fault management. Includes procedures for:

    a. Reporting fault occurrences
    b. Logging event reports
    c. Scheduling and executing diagnostic tests
    d. Tracing faults
    e. Initiating fault correction

- Configuration and name management. Includes procedures for:

    a. Collecting and disseminating data on current state of OSI system and managed objects
    b. Modifying OSI system, subnet, and layer attributes
    c. Changing the OSI system configuration

- Performance management. Includes procedures for:

  a. Collecting and disseminating data on current performance of OSI system and managed objects
  b. Maintaining and analyzing performance logs

- Accounting management. Includes procedures for:

  a. Informing users about costs
  b. Setting accounting limits
  c. Combining costs for multiple resource usage

- Security management. Includes procedures for:

  a. Authorization and authentication
  b. Access control
  c. Encryption and key management
  d. Maintenance and manipulation of security logs

OSI management structure

Figure 9-5 shows the architecture of an OSI system that can participate in OSI management. The architecture provides OSI management from the systems, layer, and protocol perspectives.

Systems management provides continuous system operation adapted to changing user requirements and environmental conditions. Systems management is responsible for managing the communication capabilities and communicating entities.

The systems management application process (SMAP) is the local process responsible for implementing systems management functions. It has access to an overall view of OSI system parameters and capabilities in the MIB and can manage all aspects of the OSI system.

The systems management application entity (SMAE) is the application layer entity. SMAE is responsible for communications between systems management entities using for that purpose application layer protocols.

Systems management functions are usually layer-independent or involve multiple layers. Examples include:

- Changing system or network configuration
- Transmitting accounting information
- Requesting comprehensive diagnostic tests
- Coordinating modification of parameters of several layers

(N)-layer management functions, $N = 1, 2, \ldots, 7$, provide the integrity of layer protocols and modification of layer parameters. These functions usually affect the overall operation of the layer and are not used for a single communication instance.

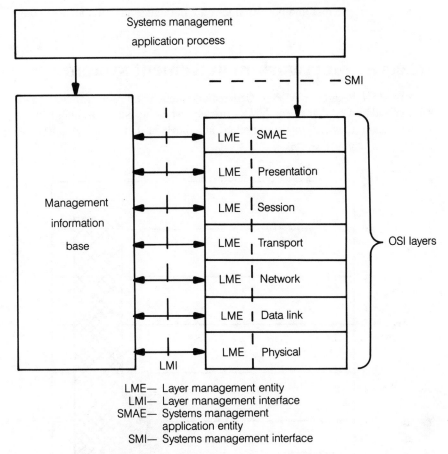

LME— Layer management entity
LMI— Layer management interface
SMAE— Systems management
application entity
SMI— Systems management interface

Fig. 9-5. OSI management architecture.

A *layer management process* may be a separate process or a process provided as part of the SMAP. *(N)*-layer management entities communicate through the systems management or *(N)-layer management protocol*. Examples of layer management functions include:

- Reading or modifying layer parameters
- Testing layers
- Activating layer services

(N)-protocol operations are used to manage a particular instance of communications so that the system will return to its previous state after this instance is finished. Examples of protocol management functions include:

- Modifying connection establishment parameters applicable to a particular communication instance

- Reporting errors and performance data obtained in the instance of communication

Integrated network management system

Like the OSI Reference Model, OSI management is more a promise than a reality. Today, OSI-compliant NMSs are almost nonexistent, although more vendors claim they will incorporate OSI standards in their products and prospects seem bright (FIG. 9-6).

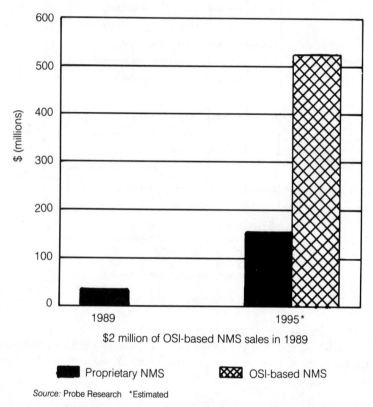

$2 million of OSI-based NMS sales in 1989

■ Proprietary NMS   ▨ OSI-based NMS

Source: Probe Research   *Estimated

Fig. 9-6. Network management system sales.

In the meantime, several vendors have been addressing one of the most demanding problems of the corporate information infrastructure: *interdomain management,* or integration of many heterogeneous NMSs into what is called an *integrated network management system* (INMS). Several INMS products have been available for some time, with IBM's Netview and AT&T's UNMA being the most popular, at least in the Fortune 1000 community (FIG. 9-7).

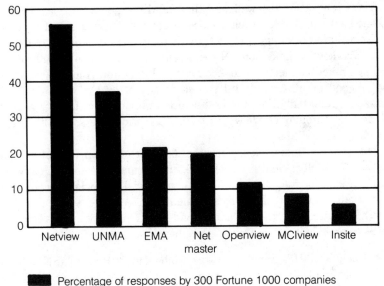

Percentage of responses by 300 Fortune 1000 companies
(multiple responses allowed)

Source: Business Research Group (*Computerworld*, March 5, 1990, p. 54).

Fig. 9-7. Integrated NMS choices.

The following concepts are or will be incorporated in INMSs (Brusil and LaBarre 1989):

- Addressing mostly the part of NMS integration that deals with connectivity
- Providing a consistent and transparent view of INMS's total network management capabilities as if they were provided by a single system (these capabilities are really a combination of many heterogeneous NMS capabilities)
- Concentrating on integration of monitoring and reporting of managed objects and events across individual NMSs
- Accommodating tiered integration architectures that permit hierarchical network management authorities
- Supporting management services similar to SMFAs (see "Functional Model" earlier in this chapter), namely configuration and fault management
- Allowing users to build their own management applications that drive, or create presentations from, their individual NMSs
- Using a modular approach to accommodate unforeseen changes in environment, user needs, NMS relationships, and so forth

AT&T and IBM, as well as other INMS vendors such as DEC and Hewlett-Packard, develop their INMSs gradually, offering specifications for interfacing other vendors' products with their own systems. For example, IBM's Netview/PC links non-SNA devices to Netview, and AT&T provides one-way limited connections to Accumaster Integrator. Another evidence of IBM's "good faith" toward OSI standards is that its OSI Communications Subsystem, reportedly the only OSI solution provided by IBM for accessing OSI devices through Netview until 1992, is priced at $300,000! (*Computerworld*, June 12, 1989).

The vendors' main excuse for the slow introduction of OSI-compliant INMSs is that OSI standards for network management are not yet ready or are too immature to be fully incorporated in commercial products. Indeed, there is a significant grain of truth in this statement.

While waiting for the advent of end-to-end network management and INMSs to provide it, internetwork users have few intermediate options:

- Using TCP/IP's Simple Network Management Protocol (SNMP), especially in a Unix environment and for internetworking LANs and WANs together
- Adding ad hoc features to existing NMSs, such as connectivity tools (for example, connecting Netview to any non-SNA box) or expert systems for fault and configuration management
- Using services of network management integrators, such as EDS; Network Management; Ernst & Young's Network Strategies; or major hardware vendors such as IBM, AT&T, DEC, and Hewlett-Packard
- Outsourcing, that is, letting other companies take over the entire network operation (the recent Merrill Lynch with IBM and MCI, or Eastman Kodak with DEC alliances are two examples of this option)

UNMA

In perhaps the most comprehensive attempt to comply with OSI management standards and to provide easy migration to an OSI INMS, AT&T has defined a UNMA (Klerer 1989). Its primary focus is to integrate a variety of independent, and sometimes even mutually hostile, NMSs. Accumaster Integrator is the first partial implementation of the UNMA.

The UNMA is a three-tiered architecture (FIG. 9-8). Network elements (NE), such as the customer premises (host), local exchange network (LANs), and interexchange network (WAN), make up the lowest level. Each NE may have its local management capabilities and is managed by an element management system (EMS).

The middle UNMA level comprises the EMSs. These systems may support different architectures and may be provided by different vendors. The UNMA currently accommodates existing NE-EMS protocols. The future evolution implies standardization of NE-EMS interfaces and protocols.

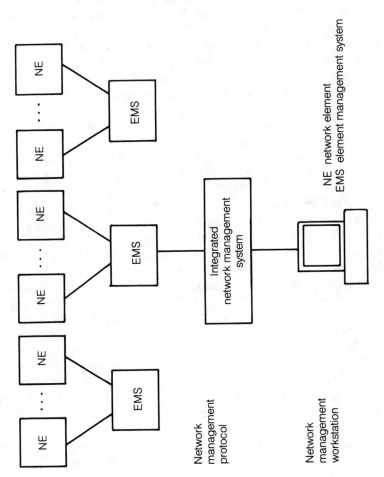

Fig. 9-8. Unified Network Management Architecture.

The highest UNMA level is an INMS that gathers together management functions from all EMSs. The flow between EMSs and the INMS is defined by a Network Management Protocol (NMP) based on the OSI Reference Model and Management.

The UNMA accepts both AT&T's and other vendors' EMSs. Integration of other vendors' EMSs into the UNMA is achieved by the vendors' compliance to the set of NMP specifications and messages.

Another important UNMA feature is that all network management information can be integrated and presented on either the customer premises or the service provider network. When the integration is made on the customer premises, the customer's portion of management information is passed from the provider to the premises. Conversely, when the integration is made at the service provider's site, customer management information is passed from the premises to the provider. In both cases the integrated information is viewed as a network management workstation (NMW).

The NMW provides the unified user interface, including help screens, input command screens, and graphic output. Using the NMW the network management personnel, whether on the customer or service provider premises, can access information about the network, analyze it, modify the network, and perform other network management operations.

The major goal of the NMW is *user transparency*. In other words, the user will view all management capabilities as provided by a single system. This view will not be affected by whether the user works with the INMS or a foreign EMS or with a customer's premises or a service provider's NMS.

As shown in FIG. 9-7, IBM's Netview and AT&T's UNMA are the two most popular INMSs on the market. They are also the subject of many competitive comparisons. (Actually, the two products are more complementary than competing.)

In the UNMA terminology, IBM Netview is an SNA EMS with some integrating features best developed for other IBM products. In its coverage of the IBM environment, Netview is fairly complete; and its only real competitor in terms of functionality is Net/Master. Its interface to non-SNA management systems is provided through another product, Netview/PC, which is incomplete and hard to use.

On the contrary, Accumaster Integrator is first of all an integrator that depends on individual EMSs to manage their NEs. Accumaster Integrator can be used in both IBM and non-IBM environments. In the first case, Netview may be considered as just another EMS hooked up to Accumaster Integrator. In the latter case, all information obtained by Netview is through the corresponding interface.

Summarizing, in the entirely-IBM environment, Netview and Accumaster Integrator do not compete at all and cannot even be compared. It is certainly a

Netview domain, with Net/Master, rather than Accumaster, being the major competitor.

In the entirely-non-IBM environment, Netview and Accumaster Integrator do not compete and cannot be compared either, because Netview is of no use in this environment. The decision whether to use Accumaster Integrator depends on many other factors, the major two being the number of different multivendor NMSs used and their mutual compatibility. The case for Accumaster Integrator is the strongest if the enterprise is using multiple independent and incompatible NMSs from various vendors.

Finally, in the mixed IBM/non-IBM environment, Netview and Accumaster Integrator complement one another. If the environment includes SNA, Netview (or Net/Master) is a must. The decision whether to use Accumaster Integrator depends on what portion of the entire environment is non-IBM. The case for Accumaster Integrator is again the strongest if the enterprise is using, in addition to IBM hardware, multiple non-IBM NEs and the correspondent independent and incompatible EMSs from various vendors. In this case, Netview or Net/Master will be used as one of the UNMA EMSs.

Such a position of Netview does not please some IBM executives. Speaking of IBM support for UNMA, Hellen Hancock, IBM vice president in charge of networking business, said: "Netview doesn't work well as a subsystem" (*Computerworld*, February 20, 1989).

Conclusion: AI and network management

The ultimate goal of network management is to provide an adequate quality of network service and network adaptability to changing technology and user needs without service disruption. OSI-based standardization of network management that follows OSI-based standardization of networks and internetworking should alleviate problems of continuous reliable internetwork operation.

However, networks have become so complex that, even in an ideal OSI environment, there would be very few people who could understand in real time what is going on in a large internetwork, or interpret on-line the stream of management information provided by the INMS or individual NMSs, or just support normal internetwork operations around the clock. The solution to network management problems comes in the form of KBSs (Ericson, Ericson and Minoli 1989) that can contribute to virtually every network management function discussed in this chapter (see "Functional Facet" and "Functional Model").

The most widely used area of AI applications in network management is fault management. Different forms of AI-based fault diagnosis systems are available today. For example, AT&T Accumaster Integrator uses a KBS that identifies a potential problem in an end-to-end network channel, based on the set of consolidated alarms coming from various EMSs. Other applications currently available include network layout, congestion control, on-line rerouting, and interpretation of performance information.

In the next several years, AI will not only make integrated network management a reality, but it will also help integrate network and information management, providing the glue necessary for putting all pieces of the corporate information infrastructure together.

Part III

Information management and protection

10

Business information: Basic requirements, kinds, and properties

Executive summary

Managing business information as a corporate asset means that information must be acquired and represented in such a way (or ways) that it can be used effectively and efficiently in a variety of applications. The information should be in a convenient form so that it can be presented to a diverse population of eligible users and kept consistent, safe, and secure.

Information management must meet four basic requirements:

- Information should be integrated.
- Information should be independent of any specific applications.
- Information sharing among many users should be provided.
- Centralized information management should be provided where possible.

There are five different kinds of information, each having unique characteristics:

- Voice
- Data
- Knowledge
- Text
- Images

In order to manage business information properly, one first has to assess it properly. The following information properties are the most important:

- Relevance: only information relevant to the current situation is obtained, and nothing else.
- Completeness: all information relevant to the current situation is obtained.
- Timeliness: all necessary information is obtained just in time.
- Accuracy: all necessary information is accurate and consistent.
- Conciseness: all necessary information is obtained in an understandable and immediately usable form.

Each of these properties may emphasize a supporting technology.

Information management: Basic requirements

As I pointed out in chapter 5, there are three major functions of the information infrastructure:

- Providing basic connectivity and user services
- Providing effective and efficient management of all kinds of information
- Providing the use of, and interfaces to, information sources, storages, processors, and the corporate network by diverse corporate users

The first function was described in chapters 7, 8, and 9. Starting with this chapter, we will discuss the second function of the information infrastructure: information management. This function implies building a coordinated collection of possibly distributed data, text, image, and knowledge bases and managing this collection as a corporate asset.

Managing business information as a corporate asset means that information must be acquired and represented in such a way (or ways) that it can be used effectively and efficiently in a variety of applications. The information should be in a convenient form so that it can be presented to a diverse population of eligible users and kept consistent, safe, and secure.

Basic requirements

Information management must meet four basic requirements:

- Information should be integrated.
- Information should be independent of any specific applications.
- Information sharing among many users should be provided.
- Centralized information management should be provided where possible.

Let us briefly describe each requirement.

Information integration

The *information integration* requirement implies that information used across several applications should be stored once, or at least its multiple occurrences must be explicitly coordinated. Failure to meet this requirement invites an information inconsistency disaster.

The explicit coordination of multiple occurrences of the same information implies a special information management facility that knows the locations of all these occurrences and, whenever one of them changes, propagates the change to all others. Usually, this facility is part of an integrity subsystem (see chapter 12).

Another information integration requirement implies that if the same information is presented in different forms (for example, symbolic and graphic), these forms must be explicitly coordinated. For example, if the user modifies a graphic image of an object, its symbolic representation should be appropriately modified.

The information integration requirement is valid only if information can change. If an information fragment is only accessed and read but never modified, it can be replicated in as many copies as one wants with no detriment to information consistency.

Information independence

The *information independence* requirement implies that information representation must be independent of any specific application. The inevitable effect of customizing information representation to a specific application is that this representation may be inefficient for future applications.

Even more dangerous (and therefore generally unacceptable) is the customization of information representation to a specific application after the information has already been used in previous applications. In this case, the correctness of each application can no longer be guaranteed, and users typically will have a hard time trying to find out why the application is all of a sudden incorrect.

Information independence must be provided at two levels: *logical* and *physical*. Logical information independence guarantees that existing applications will not be affected by information restructuring (for example, altering a data scheme or object specification). Physical information independence guarantees that existing applications will not be affected by information growth, modifications of information storage structure, or changes in information access strategy.

Typically, end users must be given authority to modify neither logical nor physical information representation. Such modifications are the business of specially assigned information administrators.

Information sharing

The ability for many users to access, manipulate, or develop new applications against the same information fragment at the same time must be provided as one of the information management functions. An important part of this ability is the *single-user illusion*—each user believes that he or she is the only one currently working with all the information, and there is no evidence to the contrary. In multiuser systems, information sharing is typically performed by the concurrency control subsystem (see chapter 12).

Centralized information management

Centralized information management within the enterprise must be encouraged as much as possible for the following reasons:

- Redundancy of information can be reduced.
- Consistency can be improved.
- Integrity can be better preserved.
- Security can be better enforced.
- Standards can be better enforced.

Fully centralized information management, however, may not be possible because:

- It contradicts the whole idea of information sharing and exchange in distributed environments.
- Information may have to be decentralized because of the geographical dispersion of the enterprise's components.
- Other factors may be in conflict with centralization of information management. These include information robustness through its replication, information query response time, and efforts to save the network bandwidth by placing information where it is needed.

For these reasons, I formulate the requirement for centralized information management as the following rule:

Decentralization of information should be avoided as much as possible unless the specifics of particular business requirements make centralized information management impossible or impractical.

Note that along with encouraging centralization of information management, one should encourage decentralization of information processing. Major arguments in favor of decentralizing information processing include:

- More effective and efficient problem solving
- More flexible flow of information and freer information exchange within the enterprise

- Higher availability of the information infrastructure and computational resources
- Higher potential for incremental growth of the information infrastructure as needed

Full decentralization of information processing may not always be possible for the reasons pointed out in "When Not to Downsize" in chapter 3. I formulate the requirement for decentralized information processing as the following rule:

Centralization of information processing should be avoided as much as possible unless the specifics of a particular application make decentralized information processing impossible or impractical.

Kinds of business information

Generally, there are five kinds of information (FIG. 10-1):

- Voice
- Data
- Knowledge
- Text
- Images

Let us briefly describe the kind of information from the viewpoint of its management. Chapters 11 and 13 provide additional information on the specifics of data, knowledge, text, and image management.

Voice

Voice is the oldest and still the most widely used kind of business information. Unlike other kinds of information, voice is mainly a human-to-human com-

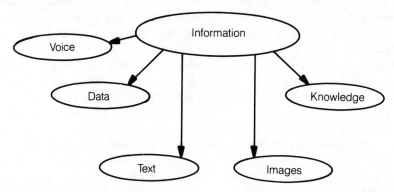

Fig. 10-1. Major kinds of information.

munication. For this reason, voice management is almost nonexistent, except for old-fashioned methods such as jotting down the talk content in a notebook or recording a message on the answering machine.

Genuine voice management will become feasible as soon as the entire voice communication cycle becomes technically and commercially available. The voice communication cycle is as follows:

1. Voice message transmission and reception
2. Utterance recognition and understanding
3. Indexing and storing the meaning of an utterance in symbolic form in a computer
4. Utterance retrieval and voice message generation
5. Voice message transmission and reception

Unfortunately, some elements of this cycle are not available yet. For example, in spite of fairly extensive research in the area of voice recognition and understanding, one may expect general-purpose, speaker-independent, large-vocabulary systems that can recognize and understand continuous speech only in the relatively distant future. Until such systems become commercially available, there is nothing to manage in the voice area.

Data

In terms of its computerization, voice and data are on exactly opposite ends of the spectrum. Data is the most computerized kind of information, and most commercial information management systems are, in fact, data management systems. Not surprisingly, data management is a much more advanced subject than management of any other kind of information. Moreover, many ideas about how to manage knowledge, text, and images come from the field of data management.

Data is an intrinsically structured kind of information. The fundamental structural unit of data is usually called a *record*, although the alternative terms "tuple," "table row," or just "row" are widely used in the relational database terminology. Data records consist of *fields*, alternatively called *attributes* or *columns*, and are organized in flat or hierarchical files (see "Virtual Filestore" in chapter 7).

The data representation model predominantly used today is a *relational data model*, although other, older models, such as the hierarchical, network, and inverted list models, are still in commercial use (Date 1987).

Simply put, all data represented in the relational model is seen by the user as a *table* consisting of rows and columns (FIG. 10-2A, -2B). Operations available to the user produce new tables from an initial one. A new table is essentially a *row subset*, a *column subset*, or a *row/column subset* (FIG. 10-3A, -3B, -3C). Figure 10-3D shows a new table which is a row/column subset of two concatenated tables shown in FIG. 10-2A, -2B.

A. Courses

COURSE#	CNAME	DURATION	FEE	AUDI	CLE
1	AI1	2	935	EXEC	BEG
2	KBS1	3	895	TECH	ADV
3	DATABASES	5	1395	TECH	WSH
4	SECURITY	2	695	GR	BEG
	SIS	2	935	MGR	ADV

B. Seminars

SEMI#	COURSE#	STARTDATE	SCITY	HOTEL	STUD_NUM
104	1	18-DEC-90	MIAMI	HILTON	
101	1	02-FEB-90	NYC	MARRIOTT	
102	1	14-APR-90	LA	HYATT	
103	1	19-JUL-90	DALLAS	SHERATON	
201	2	31-JAN-90	WASHINGTON	MARRIOTT	
202	2	28-SEP-90	CHICAGO	HYATT	
301	3	02-APR-90	ANAHEIM	HILTON	
302	3	23-APR-90	NYC	MARRIOTT	
303	3	10-JUN-90	TORONTO	HILTON	
501	5	12-FEB-90	LA	HILTON	
502	5	19-MAR-90	SYDNEY	HILTON	
503	5	30-MAY-90	NYC	SHERATON	

12 records selected.

Fig. 10-2. Typical data tables.

One of the most attractive features of the relational data model is its structural and visual simplicity. The *structural simplicity* lends itself to a relatively small set of basic operations over the relational table. The *visual simplicity* helps the user to understand data representation and anticipate the results of a query to the database.

Both the structural and visual simplicity of relational data representation significantly contribute to meeting the basic requirements for information management discussed at the beginning of this chapter—in particular, information independence. Indeed, meeting other requirements depends not only on data representation, but also on the quality of the information infrastructure and database design.

Not surprisingly, the structural simplicity of relational data representation limits the areas of its advantageous application. The rule of thumb is that the more structurally complex the information, the less it lends itself to relational

```
SQL>   SELECT *
  2    FROM COURSES
  3    WHERE FEE < 1000;
```

COURSE#	CNAME	DURATION	FEE	AUDI	CLE
1	AI1	2	935	EXEC	BEG
2	KBS1	3	895	TECH	ADV
4	SECURITY	2	695	MGR	BEG
5	SIS	2	935	MGR	ADV

```
SQL>   SELECT CNAME, FEE
  2    FROM COURSES;
```

CNAME	FEE
AI1	935
KBS1	895
DATABASES	1395
SECURITY	695
SIS	935

```
SQL>   SELECT CNAME, FEE
  2    FROM COURSES
  3    WHERE DURATION > 2;
```

CNAME	FEE
KBS1	895
DATABASES	1395

```
SQL>   SELECT CNAME, STARTDATE, SCITY
  2    FROM COURSES C, SEMINARS S
  3    WHERE C.COURSE# = S.COURSE#
  4      AND HOTEL = "MARRIOTT";
```

CNAME	STARTDATE	SCITY
AI1	02-FEB-90	NYC
DBS1	31-JAN-90	WASHINGTON
DATABASES	23-APR-90	NYC

Fig. 10-3. Typical operations over data tables.

data representation. For such information the use of *object-oriented* or hybrid *knowledge-representation models* (which are essentially the same from the representation viewpoint) is certainly preferable.

Knowledge

Unlike data records, which are structural data units that represent instances of entities and their interrelationships, structural knowledge units, called *conceptual descriptions*, represent entities themselves and their interrelationships.

Figure 10-4 illustrates a small knowledge base, an extended knowledge representation of a fragment of data tables shown in FIG. 10-2. Conceptual

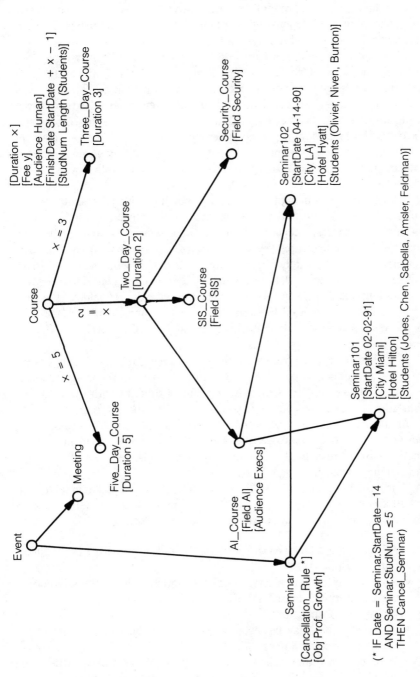

Fig. 10-4. Hybrid knowledge representation diagram.

descriptions, roughly equivalent to data records, are depicted in FIG. 10-4 by circles, while their slots, roughly equivalent to data fields, are square bracketed. Conceptual descriptions represent entities, and slots represent their features and relationships with other entities.

Although the knowledge base in FIG. 10-4 looks significantly more complex than the data tables in FIG. 10-2, it also represents significantly more. First, the knowledge base depicts not only data records (or, in AI terminology, instances of entities) like **Seminar101**, but also generic entities themselves. One example is the **Three_Day_Course** entity, which represents no specific course but, rather, any generic three-day course. Even more generic is the **Event** entity, which may include less generic (but still generic) entities of seminars, meetings, basketball games, receptions at the White House, etc., as its subclasses.

Thus, rather than being flat like a relational data table representing a particular data record, knowledge is a complex multirelational hierarchy of entities, their subclasses, subclasses of their subclasses, . . ., and finally their instances. In our illustration, the same knowledge base can be used practically unchanged for an absolutely different mix of particular courses and seminars.

Second, the value of slots belonging to more generic conceptual descriptions are inherited by less generic ones. For example, the *AI* value of the *Field* slot in FIG. 10-4 is inherited by both **Seminar101** and **Seminar102** from **AI_Course**. Therefore, both **Seminar101** and **Seminar102** are AI seminars.

Note that inheritance from more than one conceptual description, or multiple inheritance, is also possible. In FIG. 10-4, **Seminar101** is a subclass of both **AI_Course** and **Seminar**. As a result, it inherits both the *Field* slot value from **AI_Course** and the *Objective* slot value from **Seminar**.

An inherited value may be overridden. For example, the *Execs* value of the *Audience* slot in **AI_Course** overrides the same slot's *Human* value in the more generic **Course** conceptual description. In other words, only executives rather than all humans can attend an AI seminar.

Third, the knowledge base (FIG. 10-4), unlike the relational data table, permits all kinds of slot values rather than only atomic values as defined by the relational model. The slot value can be any of the following:

- A list of values (such as the *Students* slot of the **Seminar101** conceptual description)
- A reference to another conceptual description (such as the reference to the **Human** conceptual description in the *Audience* slot of the **Course** conceptual description)
- A variable that may be instantiated (such as the *Duration* slot of the **Course** conceptual description)
- A procedure (often called a *procedural attachment*) or a **rule** (often called a *demon*). (In object-oriented terminology, they are called a *method* and a *message*, respectively.)

An example of a procedural attachment is the *FinishDate* slot in the **Course** conceptual description. This slot whose value is a procedure is inherited by all instances of seminars, (**Seminar101**, **Seminar102**, etc.). In order to find out when **Seminar101** is finished, one may query the *FinishDate* slot through inheritance, and the attached procedure is evaluated, resulting in *02/03/91* (with substitution of *2* for *x*, and a startdate of February 2, 1991). By the same token, the number of students at each seminar can be found by evaluating the length of the list representing the *Students* slot value. The corresponding procedure is attached to the *StudNum* slot of the **Course** conceptual description.

A *rule* is a special procedure consisting of a set of conditions and a set of actions that are triggered (executed) when the set of conditions is satisfied. An example is the *Cancellation_Rule* slot of the **Seminar** conceptual description. The **Cancel_Seminar** action is executed when two conditions are satisfied:

- There are only two weeks left before the seminar.
- The number of enrolled students is equal to or less than 5.

The **Cancel_Seminar** action may involve a number of procedures: informing the instructor and the students that the seminar has been canceled, deleting the seminar from the knowledge base, moving the students to other seminars, etc.

The knowledge base shown in FIG. 10-4 is said to be in *hybrid knowledge representation* (Firdman 1988) because it combines two basic knowledge representations: *model-based* and *rule-based*. The model-based representation is the structure of conceptual descriptions and their interrelationships. The rule-based representation was illustrated by the *Cancellation_Rule* example.

Text

Unlike data and knowledge, text is an unstructured, linear kind of information. It may seem structured to the human, especially if it is split into parts, chapters, sections, and subsections, like this book. However, for the computer, a text is just a string of characters (sometimes a very long string). Text is stored in unstructured files (see "Virtual Filestore" in chapter 7).

Text management capabilities may be divided into two large categories:

- Text creation, editing, and composition, such as in word processing and electronic publishing
- Text search and retrieval, such as in large textual databases

Although practical applications usually include a mixture of both capabilities, the categorization is still helpful. In the first category, text will definitely change; in the second category, it stays unchanged (read-only). From a different viewpoint: in the first category, indexation and classification capabilities do not play an important role; in the second category, they do.

Text changeability   Text changeability directly affects the corporate information infrastructure. If a particular text stays unchanged, it can be replicated in as many copies as there are points of its use. No replication anomalies can occur. If the text is to be changed, trade-offs among factors such as the following can result:

- Local availability of the replicated text, resulting in savings of query cost and response time
- Increased robustness of the replicated text, resulting from having many identical copies at remote sites
- Potential inconsistency problems with the replicated text unless the consistency is explicitly enforced through file replication, resulting in additional costs and response time (see "Information Update Regimes" in chapter 6 and "Multiple Client/Multiple Server Architecture" in chapter 7)

The problem of unlimited immediate update discussed in chapters 6 and 7 is more complicated for text than for other kinds of information. Unlike data and knowledge with their high granularity, i.e., small size, of updatable units (for example data records or slots), the updatable text unit may be very large—actually,the entire file. Even in the case of a simple word processor, sending a 100 Kbyte file to the terminal may be noticeable. Sending routinely 10^4 to 10^5 bytes around the network can cause a serious problem, flooding the network for a relatively long time (1.5 to 15 seconds using a 56-Kbps T1 fraction). Thus, text replication must be handled with care, always considering the potential threat of network congestion or even crash.

Text indexation and classification   Indexation/classification is another main issue of text management. Selecting a relevant text from the sea of textual information may be a problem for at least three reasons:

- Text indexation/classification by key words and phrases is clearly insufficient.
- Creating a clear-cut classification of all textual documents beforehand is difficult, if not impossible. In most cases the text classification system is created incrementally as more new unexpected texts bring new index entries into being.
- Remembering the whole text classification system even if it is perfect is almost impossible and may require additional hierarchical index directories.

In order to improve text indexation and classification, different forms of search by text meaning, called *semantic search*, must be introduced. These searches include the following (listed in increasing order of their functionality and complexity):

- Search by synonyms (different words, same meaning) and antonyms (different words, opposite meanings)
- Search using most frequent combinations of words in phrases
- Search providing different levels of natural language understanding

The last solution is, of course, the most universal but the hardest to achieve.

A dynamically changing text classification system along with big index directories creates the same problems as those discussed previously in "Text Changeability," but in regard to an *index directory* rather than to text itself. If the index directory is large, frequently updated, and replicated at many sites for user convenience, the same problems and trade-offs we had with texts can result. Again, to avoid severe network congestion and overall performance degradation, one must not permit excessive index directory replication.

Images

Images are an exceptionally broad class of information. Such diverse kinds of information as the following fall under this class:

- Digitized images (documents, credit card slips, check stubs, etc.)
- Business graphics (graphs, trend charts, technical analysis charts, etc.)
- Iconics (general-purpose and problem-specific icons; graphic or schematic pictures on the screen)
- Geometrical data (engineering drawings, VLSI layouts, etc.)
- Three-dimensional graphics (simulated models and fixtures, facility plans, etc.)

Images are also diverse in their structure. For example, engineering drawings and three-dimensional graphics are highly structured classes of images. Their structure is much more complex than what can be effectively handled by the relational data model. The trend to using knowledge-based (object-oriented) representations for computer-aided engineering is strong.

At the other extreme, *digitized images* are represented as unstructured files since they are, in the final analysis, just a mass of 0's and 1's (or 1-byte digits in the case of gray scale). For this reason, most of the discussion regarding text is directly relevant to digitized images with one important exception.

A digitized image of a one-page document is much larger than one page of an ASCII text. While the latter is somewhere from 2K to 3K bytes, the former is about 300K bytes (at a resolution of 400 dpi)—a ratio more than one order of magnitude. This ratio has two important implications:

- Storing a large number of documents, such as in a government agency, or a big pharmaceutical firm, or a big law firm, even on the largest available magnetic disks, may be prohibitive. This restriction has brought to life a new technology: *optical jukeboxes*.

- The burden on the corporate network that accommodates imaged document transfer may be prohibitive. Consider that sending 10 pages of digitized documents along a 56-Kbps link would take more than 7 minutes! In the enterprise whose business relies on the effectiveness and efficiency of moving paper around, image traffic must be seriously studied before any premature decisions concerning the information infrastructure and imaging systems are made (see also War Story 1-1).

The large size of digitized image files reemphasizes the importance of separation between changeable and unchangeable images. It pays to replicate unchangeable images in all points of their use as long as memory costs remain lower than bandwidth costs.

For changeable images, the nature of changes should be carefully studied, keeping in mind opportunities of image traffic reduction. For example, in many cases, a new image can be represented as an old one plus a relatively little increment minus a relatively little decrement. In this case, only increments and decrements may be sent along the network, resulting in bandwidth savings. Consistency of resulting new images at various sites can later be rechecked off-line after hours.

In all cases of both image and text transfer, *data compression* has to be considered as a valuable feature. In the case of images, run length encoding may be an option. In the case of text, frequency dependent coding, such as Huffman or arithmetic coding, can be recommended (Tanenbaum 1988).

Properties of business information

In order to manage business information properly, one first has to assess it properly. For business information and from its user's standpoint, the following major properties seem most important:

- Relevance. This property implies that only information relevant to the current situation is obtained, and nothing else. Relevance eliminates, or at least alleviates, the situation of too much information.
- Completeness. This property implies that all information relevant to the current situation is obtained. Completeness eliminates, or at least alleviates, the situation of too little information.
- Timeliness. This property implies that all necessary information is obtained just in time. Timeliness eliminates, or at least alleviates, the situation of getting information too early or too late.
- Accuracy. This property implies that all necessary information is accurate and consistent.
- Conciseness. This property implies that all necessary information is obtained in an understandable and immediately usable form.

Each of these properties may emphasize a supporting technology. For example, data accuracy lends itself to relational database systems with more sophisticated integrity subsystems. Timeliness lends itself to real-time systems, while conciseness is naturally associated with intuitive, easily customized user interfaces.

For practical purposes, relative measures of each property should be assigned and attached to each more or less independent fragment of corporate information. These measures should then be associated with specific information management procedures. For instance, a higher degree of accuracy may mean a greater number of integrity and consistency checks put into a database engine or more frequent periodic integrity checks. A higher degree of relevance may imply a more sophisticated system of information classification and indexation. A higher degree of timeliness may imply more frequent information updates or use of the fastest workstations for processing.

Two trade-offs are intrinsic to information property measures. First, the higher the property measure, the more costly its associated information management procedures. Thus, high relative property measures should be assigned carefully, based on the real need for them. Second, some information property measures may be mutually conflicting. For example, requirements for high completeness or accuracy will likely conflict with those for high timeliness. Conflicts of this nature are application-specific. Here are some examples:

- For accounting/auditing applications, accuracy (not timeliness) has the highest priority.
- For real-time systems, timeliness may be more important than accuracy or completeness.
- For users with low computer proficiency, conciseness is more important than completeness.

As an extreme, the same information may or may not be acted upon depending on the relative importance of its properties. The relative importance rank of information properties should be determined and attached to each application using a certain information fragment.

For a given application, relative importance of information properties may additionally depend on several factors, including:

- Who is running the application
- What situation the application is to run in
- How regularly this application runs

11

Data management

Executive summary

Data are stored in databases and managed by DBMSs. DBMSs are used by three groups of people:

- End users who mostly run their applications, accessing and in some cases updating data in the database
- Application developers who develop applications against the database to make it usable by end users
- Database administrators (DBAs) responsible for all aspects of database management

For a variety of reasons explained in this chapter, the relational database is the predominantly used type of DBMSs; and the SQL is the predominantly used language for interfacing relational databases by both users and application developers.

Both American National Standards Institute (ANSI) and ISO have been trying hard to make SQL an international standard to provide portability of SQL applications and interoperability of various platforms supporting SQL. However, their goal has been attained only partially.

In spite of the requirement for centralized information management, business realities often dictate the opposite. The corporate information may reside at many remote locations, users of this information may also be dispersed, and still the user at any site may more or less regularly need information that is located at other sites. The corporate information infrastructure implies that information can be geographically dispersed but cooperatively used by users throughout enterprise. This discussion brings us to the concept of a distributed DBMS as a part of the information infrastructure responsible for corporate data management.

In spite of their popularity, DBMSs do not solve all problems of information management and processing. They have the following limitations that call for other systems capable of managing alternative kinds of information:

- DBMSs are inadequate for managing unstructured data such as text.
- DBMSs are equally inadequate for managing highly structured data. Management of highly structured data as well as data whose structure can often change should be addressed by knowledge bases or object-oriented databases (OODs).
- DBMSs describe data but fail to describe how it can or must be used. As a side effect of this deficiency, DBMSs support reusable data but do not support reusable applications. Combining the description of information and the ways in which this information can be used is provided by knowledge bases or OODs.
- Integrity preservation is a problem that is usually solved on an ad hoc basis. In knowledge bases and OODs, integrity preservation is an intrinsic part of a conceptual description because it combines descriptions of data and the ways it can or must be used. Once developed, an integrity check becomes a part of reusable software.

OODs address three of the four major DBMS limitations. However, OODs do not replace relational DBMSs; they complement them in important aspects listed. The object-oriented approach will undoubtedly revolutionize software development in general and data management in particular. The remaining questions are when and how.

DBMS architecture and functions

This chapter describes the DBMS architecture, relational and distributed databases, DBMS limitations, and the use of OODs to complement DBMSs. A typical DBMS architecture (FIG. 11-1) is divided into three levels: external, internal, and conceptual. The following paragraphs describe these levels, database administration, and DBMS functions and operations.

Levels of DBMS architecture

The external level deals with individual DBMS users. Each DBMS user has an interface to the DBMS. Two classes of users access the database from the external level:

- *End users* who mostly run their applications, accessing and in some cases updating data in the database. End users interact with the DBMS by means of a basic *query language* and an optional set of *application development tools*. In relational databases, the SQL is the query language of choice and the standard adopted by all national and international

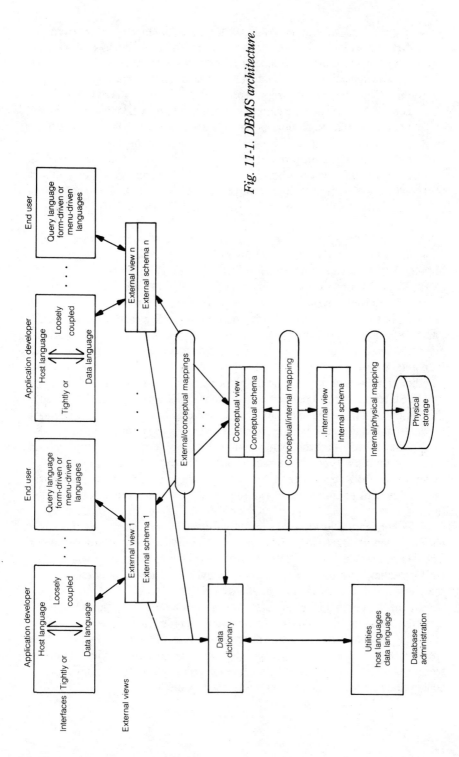

Fig. 11-1. DBMS architecture.

standard organizations. Application development tools vary from one DBMS vendor to another. However, form- and menu-based application development tools are typically offered by every vendor.

- *Application developers* who develop applications against the database to make it usable by end users. Application developers may access, and in some cases update, the data in the course of application debugging and testing. Applications developers may use (1) a *data language*, which is a combination of data definition and data manipulation languages defined for the DBMS in question (see "SQL" later in this chapter); (2) a host *language*, such as Cobol, which then must include a tightly coupled subset for data definition and manipulation; or (3) a combination of the first two, with the data language loosely coupled with the host language.

The third alternative is the one most widely used today, with SQL as a data language and a variety of host languages such as Cobol, C, Fortran, and high-level AI languages interfaced to SQL.

Individual users are usually interested in only a certain part of the entire database. Alternatively, someone may want them to be interested only in a certain part of the database for security reasons. In either case, this part of the database is called an *external view*. The external view is defined by means of an *external schema* that describes what is seen by a particular database user. Each individual user has the external view of the database; and one or more users, whether end users or application developers, may share the same one.

The internal level is concerned with the way the data are actually stored in the computer. Unlike the external level, which may have many external views, the internal level has only one view that represents the entire database.

At the internal level the database is seen as a collection of multiple occurrences of multiple types of stored records. The *internal view* is defined by means of the *internal schema* that describes various types of records, the way they are structured into stored fields, the way the records are indexed, and so forth.

The conceptual level is concerned with the representation of the entire database that abstracts itself from the way the data are stored in a computer. The conceptual view is equivalent to the external view of the user who is eligible for dealing with the entire database. Obviously, there is only one conceptual view which is the union of all external views.

At the conceptual level the database is seen as the collection of multiple occurrences of multiple types of conceptual records. In a somewhat simpler language, the database is the collection of multiple relational tables, like those shown in FIG. 10-2, each having multiple rows. The conceptual view is defined by means of the conceptual schema that describes each of the many types of conceptual records at the level of information contents.

In order to put the DBMS architecture together, three kinds of mappings (FIG. 11-1) are necessary:

- The *internal/physical mapping* defines the correspondence between stored records and disk pages and blocks.
- The *conceptual/internal mapping* defines how conceptual records are represented on the internal level. In order to support physical data independence (see "Information Independence" in chapter 10), the conceptual schema should be kept independent of all changes at the internal level. Conceptual/internal mapping should absorb such changes.
- The *external/conceptual mapping* defines the correspondence between individual users' external views and the conceptual view of the entire database. In order to support logical data independence (see "Information Independence" in chapter 10), the external schema should be kept independent of all changes at the conceptual level. External/conceptual mapping should absorb such changes.

Database administration

One of the most important parts of the DBMS architecture is the *data dictionary*. The data dictionary is a system database that contains data about data. Examples include descriptions of all tables and external views currently available in the database, descriptions of all users' rights of access to and update of each table, and its own description.

The data dictionary is a major tool for DBAs, the third group of DBMS users. (As a reminder, the first two groups are end users and application developers.) DBAs are responsible for all aspects of database management. C.J. Date (1987) defines the functions of DBAs as follows:

- Determining what business information must be stored in the database and how
- Developing the DBMS's conceptual schema
- Defining integrity and security checks
- Maintaining the data dictionary
- Communicating with users, analyzing their problems, and monitoring DBMS performance
- Determining and adjusting the DBMS storage structure and data access strategy
- Defining a backup and recovery strategy

As this list indicates, database administrative functions are diverse and complex. It is unlikely that a single person can handle all of them; thus, a team of DBAs may be needed. From the security viewpoint, it is even strongly recommended that the database administrative functions be split among several people. For example, the functions could be divided as follows:

- DBA1: functions associated with database design (the first four functions in the previous list). A DBA performing these functions is often called a *data administrator*.
- DBA2: functions associated with database performance (functions 5 and 6 in the list).
- DBA3: general administration functions (functions 3, 4, and 7 in the list).

The division of labor between DBA1 and DBA3 in performing the overlapping functions is fairly clear. While DBA1 oversees the design aspects of integrity, security, and data dictionary, DBA3 is responsible for day-by-day administration of the corresponding facilities.

An additional individual, called a *security officer* (administrator), also oversees database security. Database security is just a part of the security officer's overall responsibilities for the security of the information infrastructure.

DBMS functions

Let us look now at the functions of a typical DBMS. Most functions fall under one of three categories:

- Basic operations on data files (tables)
- Additional functions
- Transaction management functions

Here is a typical sample of basic database operations:

- Add a new file (table) to the database
- Delete a file (table) from the database
- Modify the structure of a file (table) in the database
- Insert new data into the file (table)
- Delete existing data from the file (table)
- Update data in the file (table)
- Retrieve data from the file (table)

Additional functions include view management operations, query optimization, and query editing operations. Transaction management functions are discussed in chapter 12.

Relational databases

As mentioned in chapter 10, the relational model is the data representation model that is predominantly used today. In one of his early papers (1974), E.F. Codd, the father of the relational model, makes the following statement of objectives for the relational approach (cited by C.D. Date's book, 1987):

1. To provide a high degree of data independence;
2. To provide a community view [conceptual schema, H.E.F.] of the data of spartan simplicity, so that a wide variety of users in an enterprise (ranging from the most computer-naive to most computer-sophisticated) can interact with a common model (while not prohibiting superimposed user views for specialized purposes);
3. To simplify the potentially formidable job of the database administrator;
4. To introduce a theoretical foundation (albeit modest) into database management (a field sadly lacking in solid principles and guidelines);
5. To merge the fact retrieval and file management fields in preparation for the addition at a later time of inferential services in the commercial world;
6. To lift database application programming to a new level—a level in which sets (and more specifically relations) are treated as operands instead of being processed element by element.

Although it is hard to highlight the relational model's merits better, I will try to elaborate on some of the issues addressed by Codd's statements.

As stated in "Data" (chapter 10), one of the most attractive features of the relational data model is its structural and visual simplicity, a slight modification of Codd's statement 2. The structural simplicity lends itself to a relatively small set of basic operations over the relational table. The visual simplicity helps the user understand data representation and anticipate the results of queries to the database. Data independence, Codd's statement 1, is, in fact, a direct consequence of the structural simplicity of the relational data model.

Another consequence of the structural simplicity pointed out by Date (1987) is that the relational model is a "minimum requirement, in the sense that any modern database system ought at least to support the facilities prescribed by the model." Today's relational DBMSs include many features that the relational model does not include. The relational model, however, influences and supports these features, directly or indirectly. These features include:

- Menu- and form-based interfaces and application development tools
- Transaction management capabilities (recovery, concurrency control, integrity, and security)

- Distributed and multiprocessor-based relational databases
- Ability to deal with the heterogeneous hardware problem (along with SQL standardization efforts aimed at portability and interoperability of SQL-based relational DBMSs and SQL applications)
- DBMS maintenance

Another point for discussion is Codd's statement 4. One may wonder why a theoretical foundation for database management is needed. The answer is simple. A concise and unambiguous theoretical foundation is a guarantee against the incorrectness of a DBMS implementation based on that model. Or, as C.J. Date states in volume 1 of his book on database systems (1987): the theoretical foundation reduces the likelihood of surprise—surprise for the user, that is.

Relational data model overview

With these issues in mind, I will briefly describe the relational model. It consists of three major parts:

- Data structure
- Data integrity
- Data manipulation

Data structure   Data structure includes two basic concepts: a *domain* and a *relation*. A domain is a set of values of the same type. For example, in FIG. 11-2 (a duplicate of FIG. 10-2), the domain for the *duration* column in the **COURSES** table (A) may be the set of all decimal integer numbers. Indeed, since 100-day seminars are a rarity, we can redefine the *duration* domain as a set of all one-digit decimal integers. The name of the domain (*duration*) in relational terminology is called an *attribute* attached to the domain.

In the relational model, all domains are single-valued; that is, each value belonging to the domain is atomic, or has no internal structure. For example, value 3 and value AI are atomic, while value (AI, SIS, DBMS) is a list of values, hence, nonatomic.

A relation of degree n on domains $D1, D2, \ldots, Dn$ is a set of n-tuples such that:

- Each tuple $d = \langle d1, d2, \ldots, dn \rangle$ consists of atomic values $d1$ that belong to domain $D1$, $d2$ that belong to domain $D2, \ldots, dn$ that belong to domain Dn.
- Each element di of tuple d, $i = 1, 2, \ldots, n$, is a value of attribute Ai attached to domain Di.

For example, the **COURSES** table (FIG. 11-2A) is a relation of degree 6 defined on domains with attributes *course#, cname, duration, fee, audience,* and *clevel*.

A. Courses

COURSE#	CNAME	DURATION	FEE	AUDI	CLE
1	AI1	2	935	EXEC	BEG
2	KBS1	3	895	TECH	ADV
3	DATABASES	5	1395	TECH	WSH
4	SECURITY	2	695	GR	BEG
	SIS	2	935	MGR	ADV

B. Seminars

SEMI#	COURSE#	STARTDATE	SCITY	HOTEL	STUD_NUM
104	1	18-DEC-90	MIAMI	HILTON	
101	1	02-FEB-90	NYC	MARRIOTT	
102	1	14-APR-90	LA	HYATT	
103	1	19-JUL-90	DALLAS	SHERATON	
201	2	31-JAN-90	WASHINGTON	MARRIOTT	
202	2	28-SEP-90	CHICAGO	HYATT	
301	3	02-APR-90	ANAHEIM	HILTON	
302	3	23-APR-90	NYC	MARRIOTT	
303	3	10-JUN-90	TORONTO	HILTON	
501	5	12-FEB-90	LA	HILTON	
502	5	19-MAR-90	SYDNEY	HILTON	
503	5	30-MAY-90	NYC	SHERATON	

Fig. 11-2. Typical data tables.

There is an obvious analogy between a relation and a table (file), a tuple and a row (record), and an attribute and a column (field). Here is a list of specific features of a relation in the relational mode (Date, *Database Systems* 1987):

- Each table contains only one tuple (record) type.
- Its attributes (fields) have no particular order, left to right.
- Its rows (records) have no particular order, top to bottom.
- Every attribute (field) is single-valued.
- Each table row (record) has an attribute (field) or attribute combination, called a *primary key*, that uniquely identifies it.

The last feature guarantees that the relation (table) does not have duplicate tuples (rows). Both tables shown in FIG. 11-2 have single-attribute primary keys: *course#* for **COURSES**, and *semi#* for **SEMINARS**.

Data integrity   In order to describe the data integrity part of the relational model, one should define the concept of a *foreign key*. A foreign key is an attribute (or attribute combination) in relation $R2$ whose values are required to match those of the primary key in relation $R1$. For example, the *course#* attribute in the **SEMINARS** relation (FIG. 11-2B) is a foreign key because its values must match those of the *course#* attribute, the primary key in the **COURSES** relation (FIG. 11-2A).

Two integrity rules make up the data integrity part of the relational model:

- Entity integrity. Each attribute participating in the primary key of a relation must be defined, i.e., have a nonnull value.
- Referential integrity. If relation $R2$ contains the foreign key matching the primary key of relation $R1$, every value of the foreign key of relation $R2$ must be either (1) equal to the value of the primary key in some tuple of $R1$; or (2) entirely undefined, i.e., have a null value in each of its attributes.

The entity integrity rule is intuitively obvious. Primary keys uniquely identify a tuple in the relation and thus are the only way of identifying and accessing it unambiguously. In fact, the primary key is an indicator of tuple existence.

To justify the referential integrity rule is also not very difficult. If some tuple $t2$ references tuple $t1$ through matching its foreign key against the primary key of $t1$, then $t1$ must exist. "Exist" means that there must be the tuple $t1$ whose primary key's value matches the value of $t2$'s foreign key. Sometimes, however, the foreign key must be allowed to be undefined. For example, one can imagine a special, one-time seminar that has no course number identifying it.

Following the two integrity rules, however, by no means solves the whole integrity problem. These rules touch just the tip of the iceberg, addressing only the generic issues inherent in the relational model. Unfortunately, most integrity problems are domain- or application-dependent and, therefore, must be addressed in the course of database design (see "Data Integrity Preservation" in chapter 12).

Data manipulation   The last part of the relational model is *data manipulation*, which provides the set of operators that facilitate various functions of the relational database. These operators include:

- Data retrieval: fetching a tuple (or a set of tuples) from the relation.
- Data insertion: inserting a tuple (or a set of tuples) into the relation.
- Data update: updating a tuple (or a set of tuples) in the relation.
- Data deletion: deleting a tuple (or a set of tuples) from the relation.
- View definition and manipulation: defining external user views and data manipulation operator overviews.
- Defining and using data access rights: defining which user can use which data and how.
- Defining integrity constraints: defining a set of rules that the database must satisfy at all times, in addition to the two integrity rules discussed in the previous section.

In the relational model all these and some other functions are provided by eight basic relational operators combined in two groups of four each:

- Since a relation is a set, the standard set of *set-theoretic* operations (union, intersection, difference, and Cartesian product) working on relations is necessary. These functions are defined as follows (refer to FIG. 11-3):

  a. Union: returns a relation that consists of all tuples appearing in either or both of the relations-operands.
  b. Intersection: returns a relation that consists of all tuples appearing in both of the relations-operands.
  c. Difference: returns a relation that consists of all tuples appearing in the first, but not the second, relation-operand.
  d. Cartesian product: returns a relation that consists of all possible concatenated pairs of tuples, one from each of the two relations-operands.

- The set of special *relational* operations, including restrict, project, join, and divide, is necessary to provide functionality that is not covered by

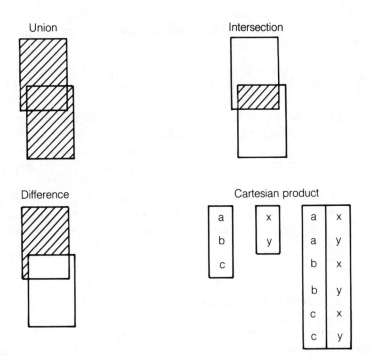

Fig. 11-3. Set-theoretic operations.

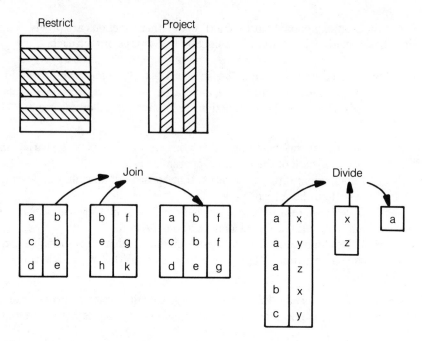

Fig. 11-4. Special relational operations.

set-theoretic operations. These functions are defined as follows (refer to FIG. 11-4):

a. Restrict: returns a set of specified tuples from the relation-operand.
b. Project: returns a set of tuples from the relation-operand, each of them including only specified attributes.
c. Join: returns a relation consisting of all possible concatenated pairs of tuples, one from each of the two relations-operands, such that in each pair, the two tuples satisfy some specified condition. In particular, for a natural join shown in FIG. 11-4, this condition is equality of values of concatenated attributes.
d. Divide: returns a relation consisting of all values of one attribute of the binary relation-operand (relation of degree 2) that match all values of another attribute of the unary relation-operand (relation of degree 1).

SQL

The SQL is a standard language for interfacing relational databases by both users and application developers. It is based on the eight set-theoretic and relational operations defined in the previous section. However, SQL operations are much more powerful and intuitive than operations of the relational model.

Note that the power of SQL operations has its negative side, however. There are almost always several possible ways of executing the same SQL statement that may differ significantly in their performance characteristics. To select a good (if not the best) SQL statement execution strategy independent of the quality of an application developer (which is not the case in nonrelational systems), all relational DBMSs have *query optimizers*. The optimizer is a critical part of a relational DBMS, especially for distributed databases, which will be discussed in the next section.

SQL may be directly used by a user who types SQL commands at the terminal and observes the results of their implementation. Most commands typed by end users are queries to the database so that their results are answers to users' questions. SQL is also used as an interlingua for communications among the relational database, development tools that generate SQL, and users of these tools.

Both ANSI and ISO have tried hard to make SQL an international standard to provide portability of SQL applications and interoperability of various platforms supporting SQL. However, their goal has been attained only partially. The SQL standard is severely deficient in many aspects, and most vendors proudly offer supersets of SQL, which in plain language means that vendor implementations of SQL are mutually incompatible. Suffice it to say that in the recent pageant of SQL-based relational DBMSs sponsored by *Computerworld*, compliance with the SQL standard was one of the comparison points. Oracle won, with DB2 and Informix being runners-up (*Computerworld*, March 5, 1990).

To further complicate the standardization problem, most vendors have developed menu- and form-based application development tools, and encourage application developers to use them and end users to run menu- and form-based applications. The problem that is often overlooked is that no standardization whatsoever exists at the level of these tools. Thus, even if the SQL standard were sufficient, its acceptance alone would not solve the problem of standardization in a way end users would like it to be solved. End users who have accumulated a critical mass of applications that are written using a vendor's application development tool will more likely be locked into this vendor's DBMS for the rest of their lives.

SQL consists of four interrelated sublanguages:

- Data query language
- Data definition language
- Data manipulation language
- Data control language

The *data query language* provides basic operations for retrieving data from relations (tables). It allows a selection of both rows and columns from a single table as well as two ways of working with multiple tables:

- Using join relational operations (see "Data Manipulation" earlier in this chapter)
- Writing queries within other queries (subqueries)

The data query language also provides data retrieval from one or more virtual tables or views.

The *data definition language* is used to create new relations (tables) and views as well as to modify or drop existing tables and views.

The *data manipulation language* provides basic operations for inserting tuples in data tables, updating data table content, and deleting records from data tables.

Finally, the *data control language* is used to sign up new and drop old users as well as to grant/revoke various privileges to/from users.

Distributed databases

In spite of the requirement for centralized information management (see chapter 10), business realities often dictate the opposite. The corporate information may reside at many remote locations, users of this information may also be dispersed, and still the user at any site may more or less regularly need information located at other sites. In other words, the corporate information infrastructure implies that information can be geographically dispersed but cooperatively used by users throughout the enterprise.

This discussion brings us to the concept of a *distributed DBMS* as a part of the information infrastructure responsible for corporate data management. According to C.J. Date, a distributed DBMS consists of a collection of sites, connected by means of a communication network, in which each site is a complete DBMS in its own right, but the sites have agreed to cooperate so that a user at any site can access any data in the network as if the data were stored at the user's own site (*Computerworld*, June 8, 1987).

The clear distinction between a distributed DBMS and systems with remote database access is that a true distributed DBMS is completely user-transparent—that is, the DBMS appears to the user as if the data were not distributed at all. On the contrary, in a DBMS with remote access capabilities, the user is always aware, to a greater or lesser extent, that the data are distributed and must take this fact into account.

Twelve rules for a distributed DBMS

C.J. Date formulates 12 rules for a distributed DBMS (*Computerworld*, June 8, 1987), which are given in the following paragraphs. The idea of these rules is that only the system that supports all of them can be called a full-scale, genuinely distributed DBMS. The system that supports only part of these rules or supports them only partially may have some problems if fully distributed operation is required.

Rule 1: Local autonomy   The sites in the distributed DBMS should be as autonomous as possible. This requirement implies that:

- Local data is locally owned and managed, with local accountability for data representation, integrity, security and other data and transaction management issues.
- Local operations remain purely local, with no penalties for the local DBMS users.
- All operations at a given site are fully controlled by that site, with no interference from any other site.

Complete local autonomy may not be possible. For example, local data may be duplicated elsewhere and therefore cannot be owned and managed completely locally. As another example, some components of the information infrastructure may temporarily work in the master/slave mode, with an obvious impact on local operation control. In all these cases, local autonomy anomalies must be explicitly identified and taken care of in an ad hoc fashion.

Rule 2: No reliance on a central site   The direct corollary of local autonomy is that no site must be central for any aspect of database management, such as centralized query processing, dictionary management, recovery, or concurrency control. Apart from local autonomy, the central site may also be undesirable because it may become a performance and reliability bottleneck.

Rule 3: Continuous operation   The downtime in a distributed DBMS should be as little as possible. In particular, incorporation of a new site or installation of a new release of the local DBMS should not affect the availability of the distributed DBMS.

Rule 4: Location independence   Users should be able to perform as if all the data they use were stored locally, without having to know which data resides where in the information infrastructure. Full location independence implies:

- Providing location independence for both retrieval and updates (the latter is much harder to provide than the former)
- Providing a distributed data-naming scheme including user reference by local name and its translation into a global address
- Using a data dictionary that specifies a site for each relation (table) in the distributed DBMS

Rule 5: Fragmentation independence   A distributed DBMS should support physical fragmentation of data tables for performance improvement so that data can be stored where they are most frequently used, and network traffic can thus be reduced. One classic example of such fragmentation is putting data about Los Angeles employees in the Los Angeles site and data about Tokyo employees in the Tokyo site.

As shown in FIG. 11-4 and "Data Manipulation" earlier in this chapter, relations (tables) may be split horizontally using the *restrict* operation or vertically using the *project* operation. Fragmentation may be done by any combination of restrict and project operations, but in such a way that the original table can be reconstructed by using a combination of *union* and *join* operations, the former for horizontal and the latter for vertical reconstruction. Note that the relational model provides basic operations for fragmentation and reconstruction.

Rule 5 states that users should be able to perform as if all the data they use were not fragmented at all. The same data may be fragmented and reconstructed in many ways many times as the application portfolio or its performance requirements change, but the user will not even notice.

Rule 6: Replication independence   A distributed DBMS supports replication if any relation (table) or its fragment is physically replicated at many distinct sites. Although relation replication improves DBMS performance and availability, it also causes an *update propagation problem* (see "Multiple Client/Multiple Server Architecture" in chapter 7 and "Information Update Regimes" in chapter 6). When a replicated relation or its fragment is updated, all copies of this relation or its fragment must also be updated.

Rule 6 states that users should be able to perform as if no data they use were ever replicated. Multiple copies of relations (tables) or their fragments may be dynamically created and dropped as the application portfolio or its performance requirements change, but, as in the case of fragmentation independence, the user will not even notice.

Rule 7: Distributed query processing   In "SQL" earlier in this chapter, we stated that the query optimizer is a critical part of the distributed DBMS. Query execution is a process involving CPU and input/output operation at several sites as well as data transmission across the network, with the latter being a potentially dominant performance factor, especially if the network is a WAN. Thus, query optimization should be done in two stages:

- *Global optimization* that minimizes the network traffic by figuring out what relations (tables) should be transmitted where for query execution, and how the result should be delivered to the site at which the query has been submitted
- *Local query optimization* that minimizes query execution time at each site where it is processed

As a simple illustration of this process, suppose that query Q is submitted at site X (Date, "Twelve Rules," 1987). Among other things, Q includes a join of relation Ry of 100 tuples at site Y and relation Rz of one million tuples at site Z.

The global optimizer should decide that Ry should be transmitted to Z because Ry is the shortest relation. (It would certainly make no sense to move a million-row table around.) As soon as Ry arrives at Z, the local query optimizer at Z should decide how to execute the join of Ry and Rz.

Rothnie and Goodman (1977) give an example that "dramatically illustrates the importance of choosing a good strategy for processing queries in a distributed environment" (Date 1985). They estimate the performance of six possible processing strategies for a simple query involving only two sites. The fastest (and smartest) strategy results in a 1-second response time. The dumbest strategy produces a response time of 2.3 days!

Rule 8: Distributed transaction management   In a distributed DBMS a single transaction may involve processing and updates at multiple sites which have to be coordinated by means of a transaction management mechanism, such as a two-phase commit (see "OSI Service Elements" in chapter 7). According to rule 2, each site must be prepared to serve as a transactional initiator or as a party. Transaction management is discussed in more detail in chapter 12.

Rule 9: Hardware independence   In a multivendor information infrastructure, the situation is common in which data from databases running on different hardware platforms have to be processed together. Therefore, interoperability of these hardware platforms and DBMS scalability across them are highly desirable to create a user's illusion of a homogeneous system. (See "Problems with Open Systems" in chapter 2 for definitions of *interoperability* and *scalability*.)

Rule 10: Operating system independence   In addition to different hardware platforms, there are different operating systems that run these platforms. DBMS interoperability is as important across different operating systems as it is across different hardware platforms.

Rule 11: Network independence   In addition to multivendor hardware and software, the enterprise may encounter different networks run by several carriers. Therefore, a distributed DBMS should support multiple LAN and WAN architectures and protocols.

Rule 12: DBMS independence   Under this title, one is asking for something that is hardly possible: DBMS compatibility. Here are two possible scenarios for DBMS independence.

First, if database vendors had really supported an SQL standard, and all the users had agreed to use it as the only application development tool, ignoring all menu- and form-based tools promoted by the same vendors, then the fact of using a particular DBMS would have been user-transparent. In other words, users would not have known and would not have had to know what particular DBMS they were using.

Second, if database vendors had left SQL standardization alone and switched to providing compatibility on the level of application development tools (or at least their interfaces), then the fact of using a particular DBMS would have been user-transparent. Again, users would not have known and would not have had to know what particular DBMS they were using.

Unfortunately, neither scenario seems realistic; therefore, rule 12 is hardly enforceable. However, the enterprise that needs to provide transparency between two particular DBMSs may do so on an ad hoc basis through developing a special two-way interface program. Its functions include as a minimum:

- Information exchange between databases
- Conversion of queries and responses in either database's language into another database language
- Two-way data dictionary mapping
- Conversion of either database's transaction definitions and management mechanisms into those of another database

Each of these functions is very far from trivial to implement.

Distributed database management

Let us summarize some specific features of distributed database management. The distributed environment may be described as follows:

- Communication channels are typically slower than storage devices, such as magnetic disks (however, this situation can change with the advent of fiberoptics backbones).
- Network systems typically have a high access delay time.
- Packet transmission and packet arrival acknowledgment takes a significant amount of CPU time.
- Different network systems or even different routes in the same network may have a broad variation of performance characteristics.

While the main performance criterion in a centralized DBMS is the number of disk accesses, in a distributed DBMS the volume of data and number of packets sent across the network play a much more important role. As a result, all traditional issues of data and transaction management, such as query optimization, update propagation, data recovery, concurrency control, and dictionary management, must be reconsidered from the viewpoint of network traffic minimization.

Query optimization was discussed briefly in the previous section. Update propagation was discussed in chapters 6 and 7. Data recovery and concurrency control are discussed in chapter 12. Dictionary management is addressed in the next section.

Dictionary management

As stated earlier in this chapter, the data dictionary is a system database that contains data about data. In addition to all the information that has to be stored and maintained in the data dictionary of the centralized DBMS, the distributed DBMS's data dictionary has to specify sites for each relation or its fragment in that DBMS. Indeed, it is these specifications that support replication, fragmentation, and location independence.

A major problem with the distributed DBMS's data dictionary is where and how to store it. The following four approaches suggest solutions to this problem, but none of them is free of drawbacks:

- Centralized approach. The entire data dictionary is stored at a single central site. Of course, this approach violates rules 1 and 2 (refer to "Twelve Rules for a Distributed DBMS" earlier in this chapter), which are critical to the whole concept of a distributed DBMS.
- Fully replicated approach. The entire data dictionary is stored at every site. This approach creates an update propagation disaster, seriously jeopardizing local autonomy (rule 1). It also makes the incorporation of a new site a serious endeavor, which may violate continuous operation of the distributed DBMS (rule 3).
- Partitioned approach. Each site maintains its local data dictionary for relations and other information stored at this site. The entire data dictionary can be obtained as a union of all disjoint local data dictionaries. This approach is good for local operations. However, for nonlocal operations, the broadcast to all sites to find out which one stores required data can quickly overload the network. If the number of nonlocal operations is big enough, the partitioned approach is unsatisfactory.
- Combination of centralized and partitioned approaches. As in a partitioned approach, each site maintains its local data dictionary for relations and other information stored at this site. However, there is additionally a central site that stores a unified copy of all local data dictionaries. Although more efficient than the partitioned approach alone (the broadcast is replaced by one message to the central site), this approach violates rules 1 and 2.

Because of the drawbacks pointed out, no existing system uses any of these approaches. All practical solutions are based on storing a certain subset of the data dictionary at each site. As a minimum, each site maintains its local data dictionary as in the partitioned approach. Different systems vary in what each site stores beyond this minimum.

As an illustration, the data dictionary can be treated as just another relation that can be fragmented and replicated in an arbitrary way. Data dictionary management is completely left to the DBA, who may change it as the need arises. Its drawback is that it requires a "meta" data dictionary that provides information about locations of data dictionary entries.

Some other approaches have also been investigated over the years. Refer to Date's book (1987) as an initial entry into the subject.

DBMS limitations

In spite of their popularity (at least one corporate DBMS is virtually a must for any company), DBMSs do not solve all problems of information management and processing. They have some severe limitations that call for other systems capable of managing alternative kinds of information given in chapter 10. The following discussion of DBMS limitations provides clues to the deficiencies that have to be addressed by these other systems.

First, DBMSs are inadequate for managing unstructured data such as text. The only DBMS facility that somehow addresses this issue is a data type allowing for a long string of ASCII characters (typically up to 64K bytes). However, managing processing ASCII files is completely left to the user. DBMSs are also inadequate for managing queries whose effect is a big file (such as ASCII text or a binary file representing a digitized image).

Management of unstructured data and queries producing big files should be addressed by special text or image management systems. These systems can be stand-alone or loosely coupled with traditional relational DBMSs, or built as the DBMS's component or just additional functionality.

Second, DBMSs are equally inadequate for managing highly structured data of various problem domain-specific types, such as engineering data in computer-aided design (CAD) systems. In this and many other cases, the structural simplicity of the relational model comes into conflict with the complex nature of information that has to be managed and processed. Representation of such information in "flat" relational tables is neither effective nor efficient.

The situation is even worse if the structure of data is not completely known or can often change. Although incremental modification of conceptual schema in relational DBMSs is possible, it certainly is not recommended.

Management of highly structured data as well as data whose structure can often change should be addressed by knowledge bases or OODs. They may be stand-alone systems that are loosely coupled with traditional relational DBMSs or built into the DBMS.

Third, DBMSs describe data but fail to describe how it can or must be used. Although some of the latest relational DBMS products, such as Sybase or Ingres Release 6.3, have begun to address this issue, its treatment is still far from sufficient.

As a side effect of this deficiency, DBMSs provide reusable data but do not support reusable applications. Reusability can come only as a result of joining the procedural description of data use with the declarative description of data itself.

Combining the description of information and the ways in which this information can be used is provided by knowledge bases or OODs. Again, these systems may be stand-alone or built into the existing relational DBMS.

The fourth DBMS limitation, integrity preservation, is a problem that is usually solved on an ad hoc basis. In the worst case, integrity preservation is an application developer's function. Application developers may build the same integrity checks in their application programs causing unnecessary duplication or, if checks are incorrect, further integrity violations.

In the best case, integrity checks are the business of DBAs (see "Database Administration" earlier in this chapter) who are trying to put problem domain-dependent integrity checks in the database engine rather than in application programs (see "Data Integrity Preservation" in chapter 12). Then database integrity relies on the quality of (1) data administration itself and (2) communications between data administrators and application developers. (The problem is how to let application developers know which integrity checks are in the database engine and which are not.)

In knowledge bases and OODs, integrity preservation is an intrinsic part of a *conceptual description* (*object* in OODs) because it combines descriptions of data and the ways it can or must be used. Once developed, an integrity check becomes a part of reusable software.

OODs

OODs address three out of four major DBMS problems discussed in the previous section. Let us look at some specific features of OODs and how they can be used in the commercial world.

Object encapsulation

First, OODs give the user complete freedom of defining new data types. No longer are users locked into a small world of DBMS data types, limited to numbers, characters, and dates. A new data type may be general-purpose, such as business graphics or annotated text, or specific to a particular class of problems, such as an account or a customer in banking applications. In object-oriented terminology, such data types are called *objects*.

An object may have an arbitrary complexity. There are no restrictions on the number of its attributes or their values. New attributes may be dynamically added, deleted, or modified at any time.

At any moment an object encapsulates all knowledge about the object that is currently available to the system, whether it is a declarative description of the object's features and relationships with other objects or a procedural description of how the object can behave or function and under which circumstances.

For example, the object named **Account** may have all typically relational attributes, such as *account#, customer_name, account_types* (joint or individual, checking or savings, etc.) account *opening_date*, and current account *balance*. These are declarative descriptions, also called *object properties* (sometimes, *state variables*).

In addition to declarative descriptions, the object **Account** may have a number of procedural descriptions, called *methods*. Here is a sample of methods that could be attached to the Account object:

- Transfer a prespecified amount of money, but no more than the account balance, from this account to any other account with the same *customer_name* by request from the customer whose name is *customer_name*.
- On the 15th of each month, transfer a prespecified amount of money to the customer's mortgage company.
- In the case of overdraft on this account, transfer the necessary amount of money from the customer's other account if so authorized; otherwise, send an overdraft notice to the customer.
- At the second anniversary of the account opening date, send a thank-you note to the customer and increase the interest rate earned by his account by 0.25 percent.

This list could go on and on, but the idea should be clear. *Object encapsulation* guarantees that the object description comprises all information concerning the object and only that information.

One major advantage of object encapsulation is that any modification of the object description does not affect other objects. Other objects may find out about these changes by sending messages to the object in question and observing changes in its behavior. In other words, other objects know what functions this object is capable of performing, but they never know how it is performing them.

Inheritance

Another advantage of encapsulation is that both properties and methods attached to a class of objects are valid for each member of the class unless otherwise stated. For example, if the overdraft procedure described in the previous section is defined for a generic, or any, checking account, it will automatically be enforced for each checking account currently in the database. This feature is referred to as *inheritance* because both the properties and the methods attached to a class of objects are inherited by all members (instances) of the class. Inheritance is a key feature of object-oriented and knowledge-based approaches for two reasons:

- It provides ultimate *information integration*: information that is common for all members of some class is stored only once in the description of that class. In addition to memory savings, inheritance makes integrity preservation a much easier task.
- Methods attached to generic objects are valid for a broad class of objects and therefore can be used repetitively and in different situations. In other words, such methods can be reused. Inheritance provides a mechanism (not the only one) for software reuse in object-oriented databases or knowledge bases.

Inheritance may be overridden by explicitly attaching an overriding property or a method to the object for which the inherited property or method must be overridden. For example, the overdraft procedure described previously is defined for the generic **Account** object. Therefore, it is inherited by all individual checking accounts for all customers, starting from Ms. Aaba and ending with Mr. Zyzund. However, Mr. Smith may be a notable exception. Since Mr. Smith has bought $1 million worth of certificates of deposit from the bank where he has a checking account, the bank may not want to bother him with annoying overdraft notices. Instead, Mr. Smith's customized overdraft procedure could look like this:

- No matter what the overdraft amount is, treat it as a short-term loan at 10.5 percent APR against the revolving credit line collateralized by certificates of deposit. Send an overdraft notice only when the loan amount exceeds this credit line.

This overdraft procedure must be explicitly attached to the object representing Mr. Smith's checking account. Then it will override the everyman's overdraft procedure described in the previous section. The former method is called overriding, while the latter is an inherited method.

Approaches to object orientation

OODs are not intended to replace relational DBMSs; they are to complement them in important aspects discussed in "DBMS Limitations" earlier in this chapter. For this reason, there are two possible approaches to incorporating object orientation in future commercial information systems:

- Developing specialized OODs, complementing them with necessary relational features and, perhaps, building interfaces between OODs and relational DBMSs
- Building object-oriented features into existing relational DBMSs, gradually bridging the gap between the two technologies

We refer to the first approach as more "religious" and to the second as more "pragmatic." This is not to say that the first approach is necessarily doomed to failure, nor that the second one will succeed no matter what. Just the opposite can also happen. The point, however, is that these two approaches are promoted by two very different communities.

The religious approach is pursued by small, aggressive, technology-driven companies, such as Ontologic, Servio Logic, Symbolics, and Graphael. A typical company of this class faithfully believes in a revolutionary role of object-oriented approach generally and OODs in particular. Its products have been successfully used in CAD and engineering applications, mostly in prototype systems. However, a typical OOD vendor has many obstacles to overcome before it can report significant commercial success. Here are some reasons for such a pessimistic view:

- A DBMS is generally a product with the highest *entry barrier* in the software industry because data is the biggest investment and the most conservative part of any IS. Therefore OOD vendors must demonstrate to their prospective customers that, in decreasing order of importance:
  a. The customers' installed base of data will be protected and effectively utilized.
  b. Their object-oriented products will be merged with the customers' installed base.
  c. Their products can effectively solve business problems that customers want to be solved and that older products cannot solve.

  (Unless OOD vendors stop talking technology and start talking business, they may have a hard time getting all of this done.)
- The object-oriented approach as preached by the "religious" vendors is not just another product or evolutionary step. It is a revolutionary change in the way people develop ISs, and changing their mindset may turn out to be more difficult than developing revolutionary products.
- In many respects OODs are currently solutions looking for problems. There are too few commercial applications and even less understanding of how this technology can be effectively used in combination with relational DBMSs.
- From the viewpoint of seasoned DBMS vendors and users, OODs are still an immature technology. For example, they do not address such traditional DBMS issues as multiuser operation and concurrency control, recovery, security, and interoperability across different hardware platforms.

The pragmatic approach is pursued by some of the major relational DBMS vendors. A typical company of this class believes in an evolutionary upgrade of its product by adding some of the easiest to implement object-oriented features. It does not introduce these features unless it is relatively new in the relational DBMS market or its business does not go very well. For example, IBM and Oracle do not have object-oriented features in their products (DB2 and Oracle Professional, respectively), but Sybase and Ingres do.

Pragmatic vendors understand that, for their customers, there are more important things than object orientation. They will offer it only if their installed base is seriously threatened by competition. So far, two object-oriented features have been offered by some relational DBMS vendors: triggers and user-defined data types.

Triggers are a particular case of OOD methods. Triggers are special procedures in a server's database engine that react to a set of predefined conditions and perform a set of predefined actions. For example, if the checking account could be opened with $500 minimum, and the data entry operator entered (for whatever reason) only $300, the DBMS would reject the insertion of the new record in the customer table and force the operator to fix the error or roll back a transaction.

An immediate advantage of using triggers is that integrity checks and similar procedures are put into the database engine and are not replicated in each application. As a result the development cycle becomes shorter, DBMS performance improves, and all procedure modifications are done only once, enforcing database consistency.

User-defined data types are a particular case of OOD objects. The user can define problem domain-specific data types in the database rather than in applications. Again, the result is development cycle reduction, DBMS performance improvement, and better database integrity enforcement.

Summarizing, I would like to stress that the object-oriented approach will undoubtedly revolutionize software development in general and data management in particular. The remaining questions are when and how.

12

Transaction management in DBMSs

Executive summary

A *transaction* is a logical unit of work that may either succeed or fail, with nothing in between being acceptable. Transactions must be managed for four major reasons:

- A transaction can fail. In this case, the consistent state of the database must be recovered, and the transaction must be restarted. This function of transaction management is called *data recovery*.
- Two or more transactions in a multiuser environment may interfere, trying to read or modify the same data at the same time. In this case, sequential transaction execution that guarantees consistent transaction effects must be provided. This function of transaction management is called *concurrency control*.
- A transaction may succeed, but for various reasons may still result in incorrect data. In this case, data correctness must be restored, based on DBMS knowledge about problem domain and data interrelationships in that domain. This function of transaction management is called *integrity preservation*.
- A transaction may undergo a deliberate unauthorized intrusion. In this case, sensitive information must be protected, and sensitive transactions must be permitted only if they are executed by authorized individuals. This function of transaction management is called *security protection*.

This chapter explains how these functions are implemented in today's DBMSs.

Transaction management functions

A DBMS carries out *transactions*. A transaction is a logical unit of work that, from the user's viewpoint, is indivisible, or *atomic*. The transaction may either succeed (its result is committed) or fail (its result is cancelled or rollbacked), with nothing in between being acceptable.

For example, if a banking transaction involves the transfer of funds from the checking to the savings account, the fact that it consists of adding some amount of money to the savings account balance and subtracting the same amount of money from the checking account balance is immaterial for the DBMS user and dangerous for the bank or account holder. The transaction effect in which the savings account balance is incremented but the checking account balance is not decremented is disastrous and must not happen.

Thus, the transaction transforms a consistent state of the database into another consistent state. (In our illustration, the total balance on two accounts must be the same before and after the transaction execution.) However, it does not guarantee consistency in the intermediate points, that is, inside the transaction. At some point the savings account balance could have been incremented and the checking account balance could not yet have been decremented, but this intermediate state would have been completely invisible to the user.

An application program may consist of one or more transactions. In FIG. 12-1 the program includes two transactions. The first one succeeds (is committed). The second one fails (is rollbacked). The transaction is then restarted and succeeds on the second attempt.

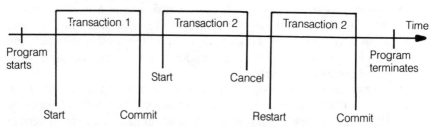

Fig. 12-1. Application programs and transactions.

Figure 12-2 shows the internal structure of a transaction. It includes:

- An input message that initiates the transaction
- The transaction body, which includes necessary queries and information processing operations
- An output message that supplies the user with additional information concerning transaction execution (for example, it can explain why the transaction has been canceled)

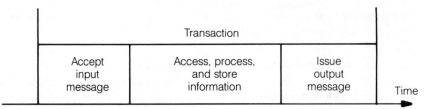

Fig. 12-2. Transaction structure.

Transactions must be managed. The goal of transaction management is to guarantee reliable transaction execution. More specifically, there are four major rationales for, and, accordingly, four major functions of, transaction management:

- A transaction can fail. In this case, the consistent state of the database must be recovered, and the transaction must be restarted. This function of transaction management is called *data recovery*. A recovery subsystem deals with transaction failures.
- Two or more transactions in a multiuser environment may interfere, trying to read or modify the same data at the same time. In this case, sequential transaction execution that guarantees consistent transaction effects must be provided. This function of transaction management is called *concurrency control*. A concurrency control subsystem deals with transaction interference.
- A transaction may succeed but, for various reasons, may still result in incorrect data. In this case, data correctness must be restored, based on DBMS knowledge about problem domain and data interrelationships in that domain. This function of transaction management is called *integrity preservation*. An integrity subsystem deals with data correctness.
- A transaction may undergo a deliberate, unauthorized intrusion. In this case, sensitive information must be protected, and sensitive transactions must be permitted only if they are executed by authorized individuals. This function of transaction management is called *security protection*. A security subsystem handles unauthorized intrusion.

The remainder of this chapter discusses the functions of transaction management.

Data recovery

Unfortunately, transactions do fail. Since the damage done by the failed transaction is usually unknown to the recovery subsystem, the best it can do is to restore the last consistent database state. In order to restore this state, the recovery subsystem must store it somewhere on a regular basis. There are two mutually complementary storages:

- Archive storage: stores the entire database copied (dumped) to it periodically (for example, at the end of each working day). An incremental dump of only those blocks that changed since the last dump can also be done.
- Log: stores changes made to the database as a set of records, with each record containing the old and new values of the changed data item. Since the log is perhaps the most critical component of the transaction management system, it is usually duplicated.

Local and global failures

Use of the archive storage and log is determined by the type of transaction failure. There are two types of transaction failures: local and global.

Local failure Local failure occurs within a single transaction. The local failure may be an *application failure*, caused by the application program; or a *general failure*, caused by the operating system.

An application failure implies that the abnormal situation is taken care of by the application program, and the recovery subsystem has nothing to do with it. An example of an application failure is an air ticket reservation transaction that fails with the output message "The flight is sold out" programmed by the application developer.

A general failure implies that the transaction terminates in an unplanned fashion so that the abnormal situation is taken care of by the recovery subsystem. An example of a general failure is a transaction that fails with the output system message "Arithmetic overflow in Statement X."

Global failure Global failure occurs for a reason beyond the transaction scope. There are two types of global failures:

- *System failures* (also called soft crashes) that affect all currently executed transactions but do not physically damage the entire database
- *Media failures* (also called hard crashes) that cause physical damage to the entire database and to at least some transactions

In the case of a general local failure, the recovery subsystem must force cancellation of the transaction in question. It has to analyze the log, looking for all log records pertinent to the failed transaction. For each such record, the recovery subsystem must replace the new value in the database with the old one. This process is called *undoing*.

In the case of a system failure, many transactions can fail, and at system restart the recovery subsystem has to know which transactions were affected by the system failure and what has to be done about them.

To handle system restart properly, the recovery subsystem periodically takes a *checkpoint*. Roughly, taking checkpoint Ci means that the recovery subsystem makes all database and log changes made since the last checkpoint $C (i - 1)$ final. (These changes could be temporarily stored in a buffer, cache memory, etc.) Therefore, the system failure that occurs after checkpoint Ci will not affect the state of the database and log set by Ci.

Figure 12-3 shows the recovery subsystem's alternative functions at system restart. Whenever the system fails, the recovery subsystem restarts it from the last checkpoint. For transactions that started and terminated before the last checkpoint (transaction T1), the recovery subsystem should do nothing because any changes to the database and the log were made final at the checkpoint.

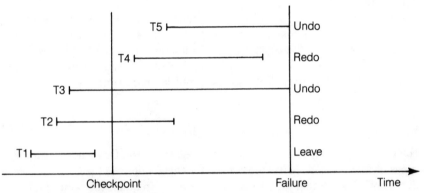

Fig. 12-3. Functions of recovery subsystem at system restart.

Transactions that terminated between the last checkpoint and the failure point must be redone, regardless of whether they started before or after the checkpoint (transactions T2 and T4). The reason is that although these transactions terminated, there is no guarantee that changes caused by them are actually in the database or the log file. Transactions that have not terminated by the failure point must be undone and restarted, regardless of whether they started before or after the checkpoint (transactions T3 and T5).

In the case of media failures, taking checkpoint would not help because the entire database could be damaged. Therefore, the database must be restored from the archive storage. All transactions completed since the last archive dump must be redone using the log.

Recovery in distributed systems

In the distributed DBMS, data recovery requires a *two-phase commit* protocol, a main transaction management mechanism for multiparty interactions (see "OSI Service Elements" in chapter 7). The two-phase commit protocol guarantees that all parties (sites) commit or roll back the transaction simultaneously. In order to see this protocol, let us consider the recovery subsystem's action in response to the transaction initiator or the party failure.

If the transaction initiator fails before it broadcast the failure (*rollback*) or success (*commit*) message to all parties, the recovery subsystem should send at system restart the rollback message to all parties. If the transaction initiator fails after it broadcast the rollback or commit message, the recovery system should resend the rollback or commit message, respectively, to all parties.

If a party fails before it reported success to the transaction initiator, the recovery subsystem should send at system restart the failure message to the transaction initiator. If a party fails after it reported success to the transaction initiator, the recovery subsystem must request the transaction initiator to rebroadcast commit or rollback and then to redo or undo the transaction at the party site.

Note that the two-phase commit provides coordination of multiple sites at the expense of local autonomy. Each party must do what the transaction initiator tells it to do—an obvious loss of local autonomy (see rule 1, "Twelve Rules for a Distributed DBMS," chapter 11). In other words, data recovery in distributed DBMSs is an intrinisically global problem that cannot be solved at the local level only.

Failure occurrence and recovery time

Haerder and Reuter (1983) provide data regarding the frequency of different types of failures and the recovery time for these failures (TABLE 12-1). These data show that Mother Nature is fair: the more frequent the failure, the less time it takes to fix it.

Table 12-1. Failure Occurrence and Recovery Time.

Type of Failure	Frequency of Occurrence	Recovery Time
Local	10-100 per minute	Same as transaction execution time
System	Several per week	A few minutes
Media	Once or twice per year	1-2 hours

Concurrency control

In a multiuser environment, several transactions may compete at the same time for access to the same data. The resulting mutual transaction interference could produce incorrect transaction effects even though the transactions would be correct if executed in isolation. The concurrency control subsystem should protect transaction execution from interference.

C.J. Date (1985) describes three basic concurrency control problems:

- Lost updates
- Uncommitted changes
- Lost consistency

These problems are described briefly in the following paragraphs.

Lost updates

Figure 12-4 depicts the lost update problem. For the sake of illustration, suppose that R is a record describing a certain flight, $R.QTY$ is its field having the number of available tickets as its value, and transactions A and B represent travel agents making reservations for that flight. For certainty, suppose that the initial value of $R.QTY$ is 50.

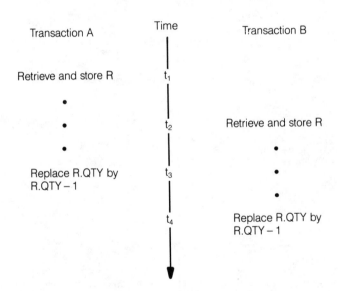

Problem: Neither A nor B sees the output of the other

Solution: • Force B to wait at t2 until A terminates (A may change R)
  • Deny A's update at t3 until B terminates (B has already seen R)
  • Deny B's update at t4 (B has an obsolete R)

Fig. 12-4. Lost updates.

At time $t1$, A retrieves and stores record R. At $t2$, B does the same. At time $t3$, A makes a reservation, bringing the number of available tickets down to 49. However, B does not know about it since B retrieved R earlier than A changed it. At time $t4$, B makes a reservation, bringing the number of available tickets down to 49 (instead of 48). *A*'s update is lost, and the flight is potentially overbooked.

There are several possible solutions to this problem that can be used by the concurrency control subsystem:

- *B* may be forced to wait at *t2* until *A* terminates.
- *A*'s update at *t3* may be denied until *B* terminates.
- *B*'s update at *t4* may be denied because *B* has an obsolete *R*.

Uncommitted changes

Figure 12-5 illustrates the problem of uncommitted changes. We will use the same example as in the previous section.

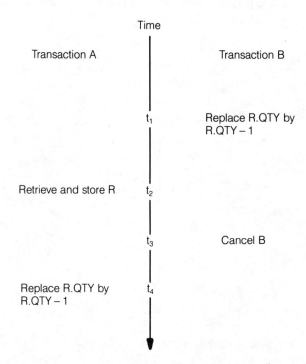

Time

Transaction A   Transaction B

t_1 Replace R.QTY by
                R.QTY – 1

Retrieve and store R t_2

t_3 Cancel B

Replace R.QTY by t_4
R.QTY – 1

Problem: transaction A does not see that transaction B has been canceled

Solution: Force A to wait at t2 until B terminates (B may fail)

Fig. 12-5. Using uncommitted changes.

At time *t1*, transaction *B* makes a reservation, bringing the number of available tickets down to 49. At *t2*, *A* retrieves record *R*. At time *t3*, *B* is canceled, and *A* does not know that it is left with the uncommitted change. At *t4*, *A* makes a reservation, bringing the number of available tickets down to 48 (instead of 49). Transaction *A* used the uncommitted change, and one ticket got lost.

The solution to this problem is to force *A* to wait at *t2* until *B* terminates.

Lost consistency

Figure 12-6 depicts the problem of lost consistency. To illustrate this problem, suppose that the bank customer has three accounts: *Acc1* with $40, *Acc2* with $50, and *Acc3* with $30. The customer wants to transfer $10 from *Acc1* to *Acc3* (transaction *B*). At the same time, another user (bank clerk or the customer's wife) wants to know how much money is in all three accounts (transaction *A*).

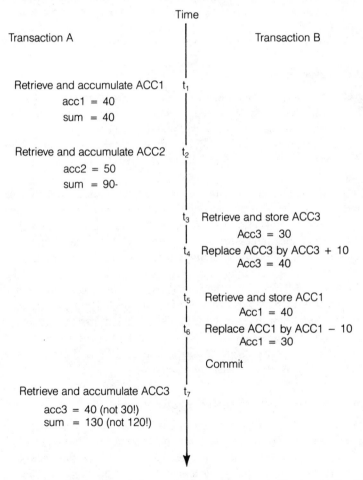

Time

| Transaction A | | Transaction B |

Retrieve and accumulate ACC1 t_1
    acc1 = 40
    sum = 40

Retrieve and accumulate ACC2 t_2
    acc2 = 50
    sum = 90-

t_3 Retrieve and store ACC3
    Acc3 = 30
t_4 Replace ACC3 by ACC3 + 10
    Acc3 = 40

t_5 Retrieve and store ACC1
    Acc1 = 40
t_6 Replace ACC1 by ACC1 − 10
    Acc1 = 30

Commit

Retrieve and accumulate ACC3 t_7
    acc3 = 40 (not 30!)
    sum = 130 (not 120!)

Problem: Transaction A does not see changes caused by transaction B
Solution: Force B to wait at t_3 until A terminates (B may cause inconsistency)

Fig. 12-6. Lost consistency.

At times *t1* and *t2*, transaction *A* retrieves records *Acc1* and *Acc2* and accumulates the sum of their balances. The sum is $90. At *t3*, *B* retrieves *Acc3*; and at *t4* it increments its balance by $10. At *t5*, *B* retrieves *Acc1*; and at *t6* it decrements its balance by $10 and commits. Now the balance in *Acc3* is $40, and the balance in *Acc1* is $30.

However, *A* does not know that the balances in *Acc3* and *Acc1* have changed. At *t7*, *A* retrieves *Acc3* and adds its new balance to the previously accumulated sum. The resulting balance is $130 (instead of $120)—a good news for the customer's wife but, unfortunately, wrong news.

Note that the difference between the lost consistency problem and the problem of using uncommitted changes is that, in the former problem, transaction *B* has committed. Nonetheless, it leaves the database in the inconsistent state.

The solution to this problem is to force *B* to wait at *t3* until *A* terminates.

Locks and deadlocks

The concurrency control problem exposes an intrinsic trade-off between DBMS performance resulting from parallel execution of multiple transactions and database integrity. As an extreme, a completely serial transaction execution would cause no problems that could result in integrity violation. The greater the degree of transaction parallelism, the greater the likelihood of integrity violation.

One of the most popular solutions to the concurrency control problem is to reduce transaction parallelism by *locking* data items, such as tables and records. Suppose that a transaction needs some data item. If the transaction wants the data item to stay unchanged, it acquires a lock on that data item. The lock prevents the data item from being read or updated by other transactions. When the transaction no longer needs the data item, it releases the lock.

The bad news about locks is that they can cause *deadlocks*. A deadlock is a situation in which two (or more) transactions wait for each other to release a lock on the records they want to work with. Figure 12-7 illustrates the deadlock situation. Transaction *A* requests a lock on record *R2* that currently is locked by transaction *B*. Transaction *B* requests a lock on record *R1* that currently is locked by transaction *A*. Neither transaction can proceed.

Concurrency control in distributed systems

In most distributed systems, concurrency control is also based on locking. However, if the data item to be locked is stored in a remote site, the request for a lock as well as its release turn out to be messages sent across the network. Moreover, to guarantee data integrity, these should be acknowledgment messages. The result is severe performance degradation that may reach two or more orders of magnitude compared with a centralized DBMS (Date 1985).

Any attempt to improve concurrency control performance in distributed DBMSs involves an inevitable trade-off between performance and local auton-

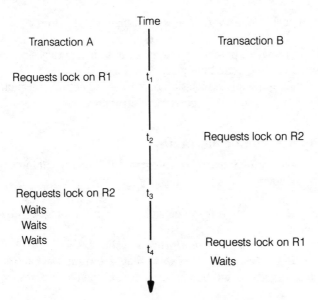

Fig. 12-7. Deadlock example.

omy. (See rule 1 of Date's "Twelve Rules for a Distributed DBMS" in chapter 11.) For example, some variation on the theme of the *master copy* that handles all concurrency control operations (lock request, lock acknowledgment, and unlock request) for a data item *D* can be used. (Master copies of different data items may be stored at different sites.) In this case the number of messages sent across the network can be significantly reduced. However, such a solution will result in a loss of local autonomy for all other sites storing *D*.

Another drawback of the master copy approach is the possibility of *global deadlock*, that is, a deadlock that involves more than one site. (To illustrate, imagine that record *R1* in FIG. 12-7 is stored at site *X* and record *R2* is stored at site *Y*.) The problem with a global deadlock is that it cannot be recognized by any single site based on the information available to it. Therefore, global deadlock detection requires information exchange between sites, hence, additional messages in the network that result in additional performance degradation.

Like data recovery, concurrency control in distributed DBMSs is an intrinsically global problem that cannot be solved at the local level only.

Integrity preservation

An integrity preservation subsystem is a collection of tools for protecting data accuracy (validity) and consistency. Data inaccuracy or invalidity may occur as a result of data entry errors, data scope violations, or invalid data updates. For example, the operator's entry "January 123" is invalid.

The integrity preservation subsystem has two functions:

- Monitoring all potential sources of data inaccuracy and inconsistency and detecting actual integrity violations
- Providing adequate violation responses (rejecting an update, reporting the integrity violation, correcting errors, etc.)

Integrity rules and constraints

Integrity preservation is based on integrity rules. A typical integrity rule consists of the following:

- A *trigger* condition that determines when an integrity check must be done
- A set of *integrity constraints* that all valid states of data must satisfy
- The *integrity violation response* that determines what must be done when a trigger condition is satisfied and the constraint is violated

Integrity constraints may be *general-purpose* and *problem domain-specific*. The entity and referential integrity constraints (see "Data Integrity" in chapter 11) are examples of general-purpose integrity constraints because each relational database must satisfy these constraints no matter what data are stored in it. The constraint that the sum of account balances must remain the same when funds are transferred from one account to another is an example of a problem domain-specific constraint (the problem domain is banking). The constraint that a Social Security Number must have a format XXX-XX-XXXX, where X is a decimal digit, is another example of a problem domain-specific constraint.

Defining integrity constraints as part of a database conceptual schema rather than an application program has several important advantages:

- Integrity constraints become part of a formal business definition and, as such, may be enforced across all applications potentially using them.
- Data integrity and consistency improve through enforcing integrity constraints.
- Application developers get free from specifying integrity constraints in their applications, which results in their improved productivity.
- Database performance improves through elimination of data transfer between the DBMS and an application program.
- Database maintenance is significantly simplified.

Problems of integrity preservation

In spite of these advantages, the current situation with data integrity is bleak. Integrity is undoubtedly the weakest point of virtually any DBMS. Several factors are responsible for this situation:

- Some DBMSs do not support even general-purpose integrity constraints, such as referential integrity.
- Most integrity constraints are problem domain-specific. They must be identified and accounted for at the stage of database design rather than application development. Traditionally, database designers do not define integrity constraints, believing the task to be beyond their scope of responsibilities.
- Most DBMSs do not provide a constraint definition language that could encourage database designers to define integrity constraints. This language could also alleviate the problem of putting constraints in the database engine rather than an application program.
- Comprehensive specification of all integrity constraints can take as much as 80 percent of a typical database conceptual schema (Date 1985), which changes the contents of the database design process and can affect both its deadline and performance of the resulting database.
- The experience of introducing referential integrity in DB2 has shown that even if integrity preservation facilities are available, it may be a long time before DBMS users actually start using them. Here are some reasons for this situation (Giovinazzo and Croft 1989):

  a. Inertia and procrastination. Since many DB2 systems have been installed and used without referential integrity, many users do not see the reason for fixing something that "ain't broken" even though they may regularly have integrity problems.
  b. Incorporation complexity. Incorporation of referential integrity into an already installed and used DBMS is by no means a trivial problem. In some cases, the effort may require a partial database redesign.
  c. Lack of qualified personnel. The enterprise may experience a shortage of personnel qualified to install referential integrity and to do preinstallation data and DBMS analysis and postinstallation DBMS administration.

Integrity preservation in distributed systems

If all the components of an integrity rule referred to local data items, no additional integrity preservation problems would arise in distributed DBMSs. Unfortunately, this is not always the case. Here are two potential sources of additional integrity preservation problems:

- One or more constraint constituents refer to data items stored in a remote site. Checking such a constraint constituent implies sending a message across the network and expecting the "True" or "False" response. This situation results in further performance degradation.

- The integrity violation response includes updates of data items stored in remote sites. At best, this situation causes additional performance degradation because a remote update is a message sent across the network. At worst, the updated data item may be replicated, resulting in an update propagation problem. (Refer to "Concurrency Control in Distributed Systems," chapter 12; "Twelve Rules for a Distributed DBMS," chapter 11; "Multiple Client/Multiple Server Architecture," chapter 7; and "Information Update Regimes," chapter 6.)

Security protection

Generally speaking, security protection activities include:

- Policy decisions
- Physical controls
- Technical solutions
- Audit trails
- Law enforcement

Security protection is a system-wide issue, and network security or DBMS security is just part of this problem. Thus, we postpone the discussion of security protection until chapter 14.

13

Specifics of knowledge, text, and image management

Executive summary

Four factors determine the specifics of knowledge management:

- Knowledge is distinct from any other kind of information.
- Its role in information management is to provide a natural "glue" for integration of all other kinds of information.
- Knowledge acquisition is much harder than data collection because knowledge is intrinsically subjective and distributed across many different knowledge sources.
- Knowledge must be validated before it is used, and the knowledge validation process is far from trivial.

The main feature of knowledge management is that it is a continuous process that may never end. This process leads the KBS development project through a series of incremental improvements. The most critical part of knowledge management is knowledge engineering, which provides incremental knowledge acquisition and validation.

Three factors determine the features of text management:

- Text is an unstructured, linear kind of information.
- Many texts may stay unchanged and, for the sake of sharing information and saving network bandwidth, should be replicated at all points of use.
- Sophisticated text classification and indexing are necessary for the effective use of multiple texts and should involve text meaning.

Text management can be provided according to three scenarios:

- Create—Store—Display: allows for a variety of word processing and desktop publishing applications.
- Scan—Locate—Display: involves scanning a textual file for some specific information, locating it, and representing it in a user-customized form.
- Create—Organize—Display: involves creating a complex text, organizing it according to a set of text relationships, and displaying the resulting document as an assembly of different kinds of information.

Specifics of image management are determined by an exceptionally broad variety of images including digitized images of documents, business graphics, graphic or schematic pictures on the screen, geometrical data, and three-dimensional graphics.

Text and image management provides significant potential benefits, such as greater productivity and efficiency, simultaneous multiuser access to the same document, reduced filing space, improvement in the quality of customer service, elimination of costly physical models and prototypes, and a short pay-off period.

Specifics of knowledge management

This chapter explores the differences between knowledge and data and discusses the knowledge management process, as well as the expected results at each stage of knowledge engineering. It also provides three scenarios of text management and processing and lists the potential benefits of image and text management.

Three crucial differences between knowledge and data determine the specifics of knowledge management. These differences concern:

- Distinct knowledge nature and role in information management
- Knowledge acquisition
- Knowledge validation

The following paragraphs discuss these differences in more detail.

Distinct knowledge nature

In chapter 10, we discussed some of the factors determining the distinct nature of knowledge compared with data. In this chapter, we will generalize and further elaborate on those findings.

The first underlying distinction between knowledge and data is that knowledge involves conceptual descriptions of not only specific entities (called *instances*), but also abstract entities (called *classes*). Moreover, the set of more and less generic classes and their instances may be represented as an *inheritance hierarchy* of conceptual descriptions.

For example, in FIG. 13-1 (a duplicate of FIG. 10-4), **Seminar101** and **Seminar102** are instances. These are conceptual descriptions of specific seminars with their dates, locations, lists of students, etc. Instances are similar to data records. **Seminar** and **Course** are classes of which **Seminar101** and **Seminar102** are instances. They represent abstract entities (concepts) of a seminar and a course, respectively. In turn, a seminar is a subclass of events; that is, **Seminar** is a less generic class than **Event**. Even a simple taxonomy, such as that of events and seminars, is beyond capabilities of any existing DBMS.

The second underlying distinction between knowledge and data is that a knowledge unit is normally an incomplete conceptual description of a class or an instance. One can represent in a knowledge base what one currently knows about a represented entity. However, one must not develop upfront a complete (more precisely, hopefully complete) conceptual schema before entering knowledge in the knowledge base. A class is the conceptual schema of itself and all its instances.

As a result, both class and instance descriptions may be developed incrementally, as a knowledge base designer's knowledge about the problem domain and entities in that domain evolves.

More knowledge in a database means inserting more records in a relation. More knowledge in a knowledge base means getting to know more specific entity features and relationships with other entities that make a previously incomplete conceptual description more complete. In other words, more knowledge means a richer and more complete conceptual model of the real world.

The third underlying distinction between knowledge and data is that knowledge involves conceptual descriptions of not only *declarative* entities, such as physical objects or ideas, but also *procedural* ones, such as processes, actions, events, constraints, dependencies, and data-driven rules. Today's DBMSs have very limited capabilities of this sort (see "DBMS Limitations" in chapter 11).

In FIG. 13-1, the *FinishDate* slot of the **Course** conceptual description exemplifies a procedurally defined value. The *Cancellation_Rule* slot of the **Seminar** conceptual description exemplifies a data-driven rule. (See "Knowledge" in chapter 10 for more discussion of these slots.)

The direct corollary of this distinction is that application programs written against the knowledge base can be stored in it as a procedurally defined slot in the relevant conceptual description and then repeatedly invoked (reused) by querying that slot. In FIG. 13-1, to evaluate the number of students enrolled for **Seminar101**, one has to query the *StudNum* slot of the **Course** conceptual description, which will invoke the **Length** procedure.

The fourth underlying distinction between knowledge and data is that a knowledge base represents a natural "glue" for integration of all kinds of

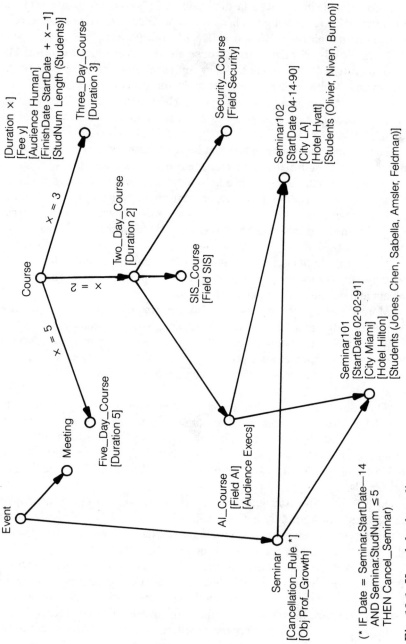

Fig. 13-1. Knowledge base diagram.

information defined in chapter 10 (voice, data, knowledge, text, and images). Data in the database may be dealt with as a collection of instances of some classes in the knowledge base. Some images, such as iconics, geometrical data, or three-dimensional graphics, may be represented very naturally as conceptual descriptions. Text, digitized images, and business graphics can be attached to the corresponding conceptual descriptions in the knowledge base as memos, annotations, documentation, etc.

When associations between knowledge and other kinds of information are represented explicitly in the knowledge base, it will provide a unified facility for automatic preservation of data, image, and text integrity. Indeed, this ability will be used in fuller degree as AI systems become capable of extracting meaning from the text and arbitrary three-dimensional scenes.

Knowledge acquisition

The previous section emphasized important advantages of using knowledge and data over using only data. However, in dealing with knowledge, one can run into some problems, and *knowledge acquisition* is one of them.

To put it simply, knowledge is much harder to collect than data. First of all, unlike data, which is mostly objective and concentrated in one or a few locations, knowledge is intrinsically subjective and distributed across many different knowledge sources:

- Domain experts
- Textbooks
- Magazine articles
- Documentation and manuals
- Case studies
- Other business folklore

Various knowledge sources may also have different quality so that the task of an individual who faces the problem of knowledge acquisition (i.e., collecting knowledge and putting it into a knowledge base) is challenging, if not formidable. The process of knowledge acquisition is often called *knowledge engineering*.

The knowledge-acquisition difficulties are multiplied by the fact that much knowledge is unquantifiable or fuzzy. In some cases, it is just intrinsic to a certain problem domain. In other cases, it is an effect of working with domain experts. Although domain experts know their business very well, they may have a hard time verbalizing their expertise, especially if they act on intuition or a hunch.

To summarize, knowledge acquisition is incomparable in its complexity, both technically and psychologically, with data acquisition and entry. It takes a team of professional knowledge engineers to do the job (Firdman 1988).

Knowledge validation

A broad variety of knowledge sources and their quality along with knowledge fuzziness make another activity, *knowledge validation,* also difficult. Acquired knowledge must always be put into a knowledge base and then validated in the context of a KBS running against this knowledge base. Practical approaches to knowledge validation include (Firdman 1988):

- Dry runs: having the KBS solve problems with known solutions and comparing the actual results with those solutions.
- Field tests: running the KBS in real-life conditions and evaluating the quality of the results.
- Panel of judges: putting together a team of domain experts whose task is to beat the KBS by offering it various problems of increased complexity.

Each approach (or combination of approaches) is highly recommended for KBS development projects. Nevertheless, none guarantees exhaustive knowledge validation, just as no debugging of a conventional program guarantees its validity. What makes knowledge validation even more difficult than validation of data and conventional programs is that knowledge validation criteria are often hard to formulate. The philosophical reason is that knowledge bases simulate the real world to a much higher degree than databases, and the best validation of the real world is the real world itself. In other words, the ultimate knowledge validation may well come as a result of many years of using the knowledge in field conditions and trying to bring it in accordance with the real world.

Knowledge management as a process

Specifics of knowledge discussed in the previous section determine certain features of knowledge management. The main feature is that knowledge management is a continuous process that may never end.

This statement does not mean that a usable KBS will never be delivered. What it does mean is that the KBS that is to solve a certain problem will go through a series of incremental improvements until it performs perfectly. Even if the state of perfect performance can be attained, which in many cases is questionable, the change in business environment and requirements may result in more complex KBS specifications, which will cause another round of knowledge acquisition and KBS development, and so forth. The cycle of bringing up additional requirements and meeting them may go on forever. So may the knowledge management process.

The most critical part of knowledge management is knowledge engineering defined earlier as a process of knowledge acquisition, that is, collecting knowledge and putting it into a knowledge base.

Effective knowledge engineering requires putting together the expertise and experience of two kinds of knowledge engineers: *specialists* and *generalists*. A knowledge engineer-specialist (specialist) is a knowledge engineer who may not be very proficient in KBS development but has extensive expertise and practical experience in the problem domain of interest. Likewise, a knowledge engineer-generalist (generalist) is a knowledge engineer who may not be very proficient in the problem domain but has extensive expertise and practical experience in KBS development. Knowledge engineers of both kinds should work as a team. The division of their responsibilities at different stages of knowledge engineering is described in the following sections.

Knowledge engineering is an iterative process that can be described as a sequence (not loop-free) of the following five stages (FIG. 13-2):

- Stage 1: observations and studies
- Stage 2: knowledge elicitation
- Stage 3: knowledge analysis
- Stage 4: knowledge synthesis
- Stage 5: performance evaluation and expertise validation

Let us describe these stages in more detail.

Observations and studies

At the stage of observations and studies, both specialists and generalists look at the problem domain and the set of problems to be solved from their specific vantage points. The results of their observations and studies are then compared and eventually merged into a single document. Main components of stage 1 include:

- Studying relevant business literature, such as textbooks, operational manuals, troubleshooting instructions, and regulations
- Looking into past case studies (if available), paying special attention to encountered problems, their solutions, and descriptions of who provided the solutions and how
- Conducting initial knowledge engineering sessions, mostly watching prospective users on the job to see what action scenario they undertake in which situation and what the first knowledge-elicitation sessions should involve

Here are the expected results of stage 1:

- The first partial problem model (PPM), which normally includes:

  a. A problem domain description, including professional slang used by domain experts and prospective users
  b. Product, information, and transaction flow diagrams (see Interlude 5-1)

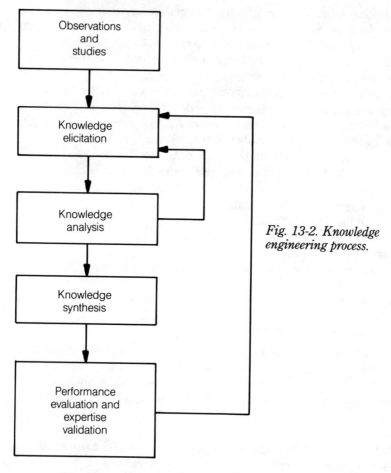

Fig. 13-2. Knowledge engineering process.

    c. Situation/scenario pairs obtained by watching prospective users on the job

- Preliminary ideas about the user interface component of the future KBS. User accounts and problem domain descriptions can play an important role at this stage of user interface design.
- List of observed deviations from canonized business documents. Essential questions to consider at a very early stage of knowledge engineering include:

    a. What are the differences between actual and normative user behavior?

    b. Why do these differences arise?

    c. How intuitive is the problem-solving process?

    d. What are the chances to simulate user activities?

Knowledge elicitation

Knowledge elicitation is provided by both specialists and generalists. Specialists are mostly involved in watching prospective users on the job (if still necessary) and directing domain expert interviews. Generalists are mostly involved in analyzing knowledge engineering sessions, structuring the PPM, and planning for subsequent knowledge engineering sessions.

Main components of stage 2 include:

- Interviewing domain experts, using standard interviewing techniques (audio and video recording if possible), and structuring the interview results to plan subsequent knowledge-elicitation sessions
- Running the current PPM against prospective users, soliciting their feedback, and modifying and correcting the PPM
- Conducting special question-and-answer sessions featuring advice and explanation extraction through "What if," "Why," and "How to" questions

Here is the list of expected results at stage 2:

- Transcripts of knowledge engineering sessions, including audio- and videotapes, if possible (domain experts sometimes resist this item)
- The modified and corrected PPM

Knowledge analysis

Knowledge analysis is provided by both specialists and generalists. Specialists are usually in charge of clarifying fuzzy or unclear domain expert statements and eliminating simple contradictions. Generalists structure the PPM, developing formal specifications for the first KBS prototype.

Main components of stage 3 include:

- Structuring the PPM based on transcripts and tapes
- Discovering gaps, missing information, and conflicts in the PPM
- Formulating plans and questions for the next knowledge-elicitation session (iterative loop)

Note that knowledge elicitation and analysis make up an iterative loop. Additional knowledge-elicitation sessions may be required as a result of knowledge analysis.

The results of stage 3 include:

- The structured formalized PPM and KBS prototype specifications
- Drafts of plans and questions for the additional knowledge-elicitation session with their justifications

Knowledge synthesis

Knowledge synthesis is mostly provided by generalists with assistance from specialists. Main components of stage 4 include:

- Selecting general-purpose and specific problem-solving methods
- Selecting a knowledge-representation formalism (KBS development tool)
- Completing PPM formalization in the selected knowledge-representation formalism

The result of stage 4 is the formal KBS specification document.

Performance evaluation and expertise validation

Performance evaluation and expertise validation are provided by both specialists and generalists. However, specialists mostly work with domain experts, while generalists mostly work with KBS designers.

Main components of stage 5 include:

- Evaluating performance of the current KBS prototype (for specialists, mostly in terms of the scope of KBS expertise and effectiveness; for generalists, mostly in terms of KBS efficiency)
- Validating the KBS prototype against validation criteria by using a combination of approaches described in "Knowledge Validation" earlier in this chapter
- Formulating plans and questions for the additional knowledge-elicitation session (iterative loop)

Note that performance evaluation/expertise validation and knowledge elicitation make up an iterative loop. Additional knowledge-elicitation sessions may be required as a result of the validation process.

The results of stage 5 include:

- KBS specification refinements
- Suggestions concerning performance improvements (in terms of the scope of expertise, effectiveness, and efficiency)
- Drafts of plans and questions for the next knowledge-elicitation session with their justifications

Specifics of text management

While the demand for knowledge management is dictated by the necessity to capture corporate knowledge as well as to represent and manipulate highly structured information, the push for text management comes from a different side: the quest for a paperless office. This is by no means a search for something exotic. Many businesses have a hard time managing an ever-increasing amount of various documents, and text and image management technology comes to the rescue.

In chapter 10, we discussed the specific features of text that make it different from other kinds of information. In particular:

- Text is an unstructured, linear kind of information.
- Many texts may stay unchanged and, for the sake of sharing information and saving network bandwidth, should be replicated at all points of use.
- Sophisticated text classification and indexing are necessary for the effective use of multiple texts and should involve text semantics (meaning).

With these features in mind, let us look at three main scenarios of text management and processing.

Scenarios of text management and processing

The following paragraphs describe the three scenarios of text management and processing:

- Create—store—display
- Scan—locate—display
- Create—organize—display

Scenario 1: Create—Store—Display This simple and widely used scenario of text management includes the creation and storage of an original document with subsequent display of this document on the screen or in hard copy.

Modifications of this scenario may include:

- Entry of an existing document as an alternative to document creation
- Compilation of a document from a set of existing or original documents as an alternative to document creation
- Storage of a formatted rather than an original document, for example, for a publishing purpose
- Storage of a compressed rather than an original document, especially if the document is frequently transferred over a WAN
- Display of a downloaded rather than an original document, for example, a document stored in a centralized repository and used at a user's workstation
- Display of an integrated document—an assembly consisting of the original text, pasted images such as business graphics or pictures from an image management system, and data tables imported from a relational DBMS

Scenario 1 is typically implemented by word processors of varying degrees of complexity. An alternative is an electronic publishing system, although the difference between the two is getting blurred.

Scenario 2: Scan—Locate—Display This scenario includes scanning a textual file for specific information, locating the information, and representing it in a user-customized form. Many variations of this basic scenario are possible. Typical variations include:

- Not one, but many textual files may be scanned for specific information. For instance, hundreds of files may have to be scanned to find anything that mentions shipping of a certain product. Or hundreds of an author's personal files must be scanned to find all notes concerning text management applications.
- The information sought may be indexed by a filename extension or keywords (such as a product name in the first example or "text" in the second). In order to increase the probability of finding the relevant texts only, key phrases may have to be used instead of keywords ("text management" instead of "text" in the second example).
- A located text may be annotated by the name of the volume and the file containing it, the time of its creation, its creator, the document the located text responded to, etc.
- The set of located texts may be displayed sorted by some criteria chronologically, by the number of keyword or phrase occurrences, etc.
- Located texts may be offloaded to the user workstation for a permanent use, such as reading, annotating, and processing (making a personal library of texts). For example, the offloaded texts might be searched for more specific information or restructured for specific purposes.

Scenario 2 is typically implemented by text management systems, also known as *text retrieval systems*.

Scenario 3: Create—Organize—Display This scenario includes:

- Creating a complex text (such as a text part of a book or a documentation manual) as a set of text fragments, not necessarily in the same order as they appear in the final document
- Organizing the text fragments according to a set of relationships, such as topical proximity or sequencing, so that the entire text is represented as a tree of related text fragments
- Displaying the resulting document, an assembly consisting of the organized text; supporting texts, such as the table of contents or index; pasted-in images, such as business graphics or pictures from an image management system; and pasted-in data tables imported from a relational DBMS

Like other scenarios, this one permits a variety of modifications and options. They include different ways of text fragment creation, variations in the set of admissible text fragment relationships, and different representations of the final document.

Scenario 3 is typically implemented by a combination of a word processor, a hypertext system, and an electronic publishing system.

INTERLUDE 13-1. HYPERTEXT

Hypertext systems deserve special attention. Hypertext is an attempt to reach beyond a traditional linear text structure by imposing an additional structure on text fragments (Conklin 1987). Conventional paper documents are linear both physically and logically. Physically, the paper document is a sequence of words from one line to another and from one page to another. Logically, the words are combined into sentences, paragraphs, sections, etc.

Even the seemingly hierarchical structure of this book (parts, chapters, sections, subsections, etc.) is actually linear. It is a special enumeration of parts, chapters, sections, and subsections that tells the reader what hierarchy the author had in mind writing this book. Still, the book is read (or at least is meant to be read) sequentially.

In a hypertext document, information is represented as a set of nodes connected with links. Each node contains an arbitrary text or an annotated graphic image. A link connecting two nodes represents a relationship between these nodes. A node may have several outgoing links. By following the link, the user can navigate through the hypertext network. To backtrack, the user follows the link in the reverse direction. Some of the nodes, called landmarks, are so important that they can be reached from every node.

Hypertext nodes and links can be changed dynamically. A user can at any time create new nodes and new links to new or existing nodes. Furthermore, information attached to nodes can be updated, annotated, commented, or further elaborated. Finally, users can define their own links to form new document organizational structures.

Each hypertext network node is associated with a screen window on a one-to-one basis. However, only open nodes are displayed in the window on the screen. A typical hypertext system supports standard window system operations, such as opening, closing, repositioning, and resizing.

The hypertext can be traversed in three ways:

- Through the navigation process described
- By searching the network for a keyword or by matching an attribute value
- By using browser, which displays the hypertext network graphically and provides a more global view of the hypertext

Using the hypertext to associate text and images is only the beginning. Future publications will integrate text, images, sound, animation, and video sequences, creating what is called a multimedia environment.

Text management applications

Text management has a number of promising applications. They can be divided into two groups:

- General office applications. This group includes:
    a. Personal information management
    b. Business records and mail administration
    c. General and corporate publishing
    d. Support of work group and enterprise-wide text management and communications

- Support of special business services. This group includes the following applications:

    a. Intelligent documentation. The demand for making technical documentation readable grows as does the complexity of documented systems. For example, the documentation for an advanced fighter is expected to be in the vicinity of one and a half million pages. New methods of documentation organization and use are certainly required.
    b. Business and government intelligence. The amount of information necessary to carry out effective intelligence operations is so huge that advanced methods of text management, processing, and packaging are absolutely necessary.
    c. Proposal preparation. Government contractors spend many weeks and millions of dollars to prepare a competitive proposal. At the same time, a big portion of any proposal is boilerplate textual information. Text management systems can be of great help in this area.
    d. Litigation support. A significant part of a law firm's business is text management and processing. Litigation support includes reading documents, finding relevant documents, sharing documents with other law firm members, etc. Text management systems may significantly increase lawyer effectiveness and productivity.
    e. Regulatory compliance. In the pharmaceutical business, a significant part of the new drug-approval process is text management, sharing, and processing. Text management systems can significantly alleviate the process and reduce the time to market new drugs, thus providing an obviously critical competitive advantage.

Specifics of image management

Images represent an exceptionally broad class of information, including:

- Digitized images of documents, such as letters, credit card slips, and check stubs

- Business graphics
- General-purpose and problem-specific icons (graphic or schematic pictures on the screen)
- Geometrical data, such as engineering drawings and VLSI layouts
- Three-dimensional graphics (simulated models and fixtures, facility plans, etc.)

Keeping in mind a broad interpretation of the term "image," we will identify the term "image" with the term "digitized image." There are two reasons for this focus:

- The document management and processing technology, based on digitized images, is available today.
- The demand for document management and processing systems is very high.

IDC (Framingham, Mass.) estimates that by 1992, about 1250 large-scale and 14,250 midrange image management systems will have been installed and operated. Many paper-intensive organizations, such as banks, insurance companies, government agencies, and law offices are implementing image management systems today to avoid handling millions of paper documents.

The following paragraphs discuss applications of document management and processing. Several war stories are included. One war story concerns three-dimensional image management and processing. The chapter concludes with a discussion of the potential benefits of text and image management and processing.

Image management and processing applications

One of the most popular document management applications is the *electronic file cabinet*, which includes document creation, entry, storage, and retrieval. The difference between text and image storage is that the electronic file cabinet allows the storage of a document image that may contain signatures, comments, and other similar information the ASCII text file would miss.

WAR STORY 13-1. ELECTRONIC FILE CABINET

The electronic file cabinet is one of the main applications for Wang Laboratories' Wang Integrated Image System (WIIS). One such application is for student records storage/retrieval (*MIS Week,* April 24, 1989).

Orange County Public Schools (OCPS), Orlando, Florida, installed a WIIS system to store and retrieve student records. According to OCPS, major benefits include:

- Increased efficiency and productivity
- Elimination of the need for filing and refiling

- Ability for several people to access the same document simultaneously
- Filing space savings

The system price is about $1 million, including software and consulting services.

WIIS is integrated with the OCPS's IBM mainframe so that WIIS users can access the mainframe database.

Another popular document management and processing application is check and credit card slip processing. This application includes high-speed document scanning; data compression; document storage, sorting, and processing; incorporation in customer statements; data decompression; and printing.

WAR STORY 13-2. CREDIT CARD SLIP MANAGEMENT AND PROCESSING

The joint IBM/Citibank project was initiated in February 1988. The resulting pilot of an ImagePlus system has been installed at a Citibank credit card facility in Sioux Falls, South Dakota (*MIS Week* April 24, 1989).

ImagePlus processes about 100,000 pages of correspondence from Citibank credit card customers per month. Each case document is digitized by scanners, stored temporarily in magnetic storage devices, processed by caseworkers at workstations, printed, and stored permanently on optical disks.

The system has a number of very impressive benefits:

- Retrieving a customer's case now takes 30 seconds compared with 24 hours that were necessary to retrieve an in-house file and up to three days for an off-site file.
- 25 rows of file cabinets have been reduced to two rows.
- Productivity increased 20 percent, while the need for manual filing and sorting tasks was practically eliminated.
- Quality of work improved, while the number of errors was reduced.

Based on the ImagePlus technology, IBM developed an ImagePlus High-Performance Transaction System (HPTS) that additionally includes (*Computerworld*, March 19, 1990):

- Image-capture front-end hardware and software supporting the capture speed of up to 2,400 documents per minute
- An image processor that recognizes printed and many handwritten check amounts, reducing the need for clerical support

If the amount on the check cannot be recognized, the image is sent via an LAN to operators who view the image and key in the amount.

A full-scale ImagePlus HPTS may cost "tens of millions of dollars" (*Computerworld*, March 19, 1990).

The third example of document management and processing is auditing tickets in a big airline. The ticket auditing operation employs several hundred people who do tedious work of sorting tickets and searching for tickets in cases of disputes (*Computerworld*, April 16, 1990).

WAR STORY 13-3. TICKET AUDITING

Andersen Consulting serves as a system integrator in the Passenger Revenue Accounting (PRA) project for Northwest Airlines. The system "will help Northwest audit 260,000 tickets it processes each day and currently stores in cardboxes." The project will cost "tens of millions" of dollars but "is expected to pay for itself in just six months" (*Computerworld*, April 16, 1990).

The system will let Northwest account for every ticket it sells instead of making a statistical sample of about 5 percent of its tickets, calculating the average price, and multiplying it by the total number of tickets sold. With the PRA completed, Northwest will have "six months of image data on-line at any time" (*Computerworld*, April 16, 1990).

The final example illustrates management and processing of three-dimensional graphics. This application exemplifies one of the major business advantages of three-dimensional image management: it elimates physical models and fixtures and provides rapid, flexible, three-dimensional "what-if" simulation.

WAR STORY 13-4. "NEXT GENERATION OF A CITY ON A 12-IN. SCREEN"

John Danahy and his group of students at the University of Toronto's Center for Landscape Research developed software that runs on Silicon Graphic's workstations and provides "what-if" simulation of "the exterior framework into which architectural teams must nestle their individual structures" (*Computerworld*, February 12, 1990).

Here is a sample of questions Danahy and his team can answer using their image management system:

- What if the buildings were six stories instead of eight?
- What if the trees on a central boulevard were placed 200 feet apart instead of 300?

The answer to these and similar questions come in a matter of minutes instead of days and weeks it used to take to redo drawings.

According to Danahy, three-dimensional "what-if" simulation not only improves architect productivity, but also changes the way architects work and think. "We're creating the next generation of a city on a 12-in. screen," Danahy said.

Benefits of text and image management

To conclude this chapter, let us look again at the potential benefits of text and image management:

- Text and image management systems provide greater productivity and efficiency. As only one example, these systems eliminate filing and refiling, a tedious process that often results in lost files. They also result in fewer errors in document processing.

- These systems allow simultaneous multiuser access to the same document, another productivity improvement factor for documents frequently used by many users.
- Text and image management systems significantly reduce filing space, providing another step toward the paperless office, which is so desirable.
- These systems improve the quality of customer service, making it prompt and error-free.
- Management of three-dimensional images eliminates costly physical models and prototypes, resulting in productivity improvement and savings at the same time.
- By incorporating the hypertext technology into text and image management systems, one can create a practical multimedia environment featuring integration and high flexibility.
- In spite of the high initial cost, text and image management systems have a surprisingly short payoff period (for most applications, within a year), another evidence that conventional text and image management are prohibitively expensive and should be automated in most businesses.

14

Security of the information infrastructure

Executive summary

Security is an intrinsic part of information management that deals with protection of both the infrastructure itself and information it manages against deliberate or accidental threats. It is a techno-managerial problem that should be solved on a system level.

Security protection may be defined as a set of provisions for application and information integrity and availability of the information infrastructure and ISs running against it. To provide a reasonable degree of information and application integrity, one first has to define the security environment in which the IS will operate.

A security environment is a triangle with assets, threats, and security measures as its nodes. Assets may have different value and be more or less vulnerable to threats. Security measures are developed to protect more valuable and vulnerable assets from potential threats. The risk management process is used to determine which assets must, and which may not, be protected. Thus, risk management creates a residual risk that must be consciously accepted by management.

The security environment is a basis and a prerequisite for an all-corporate security program. The security program pursues the following objectives:

- To establish a security planning process
- To establish a security management function
- To develop and enforce security policies
- To establish a budget review process

- To establish a risk management process
- To establish a formal procedure for security protection review
- To plan and execute corrective actions

Security of the information infrastructure usually refers to concepts, techniques, and measures used to protect both the infrastructure itself and information it manages against deliberate or accidental threats. As the involvement of SISs in all aspects of business grows, so does the importance of trustable security protection. Neglecting or underestimating the security aspect of information management may lead to disastrous results. Here are a few facts selected almost randomly:

- According to a report by Frost & Sullivan, Inc., a market research firm, "European corporations lost an estimated $10 billion in 1987 as a result of poor information systems security practices. About half of these losses can be attributed to deliberate fraud, while the rest come from accidental system failure and the loss or corruption of data" (*Computerworld*, April 2, 1990). Frost & Sullivan estimates that these losses will grow 9 percent annually, and maybe even more after 1992 with the integration of the European community.
- Ernst & Young estimates security losses in the United States at $3 to $5 billion. By one estimate, businesses report only 6 percent of all computer criminal acts for fear of publicity (*Computerworld*, March 12, 1990).
- A 28-hour computer software outage at the Bank of New York on November 21-22, 1985, forced the bank to borrow $22 billion from the Federal Reserve Bank (*Computerworld*, December 2, 1985).
- The trust officer of a bank moved $10 million out of 20 trust accounts and covered it up by suppressing the computer-generated customer statements and replacing them with hand-typed ones. The loss went undetected for a couple of years and was discovered only when the officer left the bank and the customers stopped receiving their statements. Trying to respond to their complaints, a new trust officer discovered the fraud (Chalmers 1986).

The lesson should be clear: security threats cannot be taken lightly. But how can security be provided? There is no single answer to this question. A good portion of this chapter is concerned with defining a framework, called a *security environment*, for understanding how to approach the security problem and what options for solving it are available.

Requirements for security protection

Before defining the security environment in detail, let us consider two generic and, therefore, intuitively clear requirements for security protection.

Security is a system-wide issue

Security is a system-wide issue that cannot be reduced to just a simple sum of database security and network security. The strictest security measures in one subsystem are pointless if they can be bypassed in another one. Security protection must be built into the information infrastructure so that any IS on top of it could at the same time perform the following functions:

- Provide necessary user services (what the IS has been designed for in the first place
- Close all security loopholes and sources of potential security leakage in such a way that the effort necessary to break up security would exceed the gains from breaking it up
- Avoid paranoia in the user community by creating awareness of security problems and security policy enforcement rather than just security enforcement

In order to meet all three requirements, the security protection program should be conceived, designed, and implemented as a part of the information infrastructure development process.

Security is a techno-managerial problem

Security is a techno-managerial problem. It used to be a managerial problem only—when having fences, guards, and badges was enough to protect the central computer room. With the advent of the information infrastructure, including PCs, networks, and remote access to computational resources from virtually anywhere in the world, a purely managerial approach to security problems no longer works.

On the other hand, security cannot be addressed as a technical problem only for a very simple reason: no purely technical solution to the security problem exists or will be found in the foreseeable future (if ever).

As a techno-managerial problem, security protection must involve a combination of technical solutions, policy decisions, security measures, awareness and educational programs, regular auditing, disciplinary actions, and law enforcement.

Military vs. commercial security

Although the name of the problem, security protection, is the same in both the military and the commercial environments, the essence of the problem is quite different.

In the military environment, the name of the game is prevention. Once disclosed, information is considered to lose its value completely or so severely that it can no longer be used. This approach has led to developing the concept of a *trusted computer system* and requiring the formally stated and enforced *security policy* (Department of Defense 1985; Bell and LaPadula 1976). Verification procedures have been developed to make sure that the security policy is not compromised.

It is believed that, in the military environment, criminal prosecution as a deterrent for security violations works poorly or insufficiently.

In the commercial environment, the name of the game is detection. Losses resulting from intrusion and information disclosure are considered to be recoverable completely or partly. For this reason the security system is considered to have accomplished its task if it can quickly detect and identify the perpetrator, providing enough information for criminal prosecution.

It is believed that, in the commercial environment, the threat of criminal prosecution and subsequent punishment works as a deterrent for security violations.

The different approaches to security protection in the military and commercial environments have caused differences in security enforcement methods. The main differences are shown in TABLE 14-1. Leslie Chalmers (1986) summarizes them as total security vs. cost-effective security.

Table 14-1. Comparison of Military and Commercial Approaches to Security.

Military Environment	Commercial Environment
Cost of information protection is included in cost of its collection or creation.	Cost of protection is extra, and information is protected only if this cost is less than the perceived cost of information loss.
Prevention from access to information is more important than from information modification.	Prevention from information modification is more important than from access to information.
Personnel must be cleared before they are allowed access to classified information.	Personnel are not cleared and are monitored for unusual behavior. Preemployment screening may even be illegal.

Two important points must be emphasized. First, there are some areas of security protection that are equally important in both the military and the commercial environments. These include:

- User authentication: the activity in which the user must prove his or her identity.
- Audit trail: a complete record of all activities by each IS user.
- Ongoing monitoring of employees: the activity aimed at detecting "when an individual has changed from a trusted employee to a potential problem" (Chalmers 1986).
- Cost-effectiveness: simply put, getting more security for less money.

Second, the military and commercial approaches to security are coming and will come closer to each other for the following reasons:

- As commercial information infrastructures and ISs play a more strategic role for the enterprise, they will contain more sensitive information and proprietary applications that make the difference between the enterprise and its competition. Therefore, some commercial information may have unrecoverable value, and the enterprise will use the prevention approach much more than before.
- As military budgets get squeezed, the military agencies and defense contractors will have to become more cost-effective—that is, get more security for less money. They will inevitably switch from prevention only to a mixture of prevention and detection simply because pure prevention is too costly.

The convergence of the two approaches may become an important consideration for both military and commercial planners of security protection systems of the future.

In the remainder of this chapter, we will mostly discuss commercial security protection. However, keep in mind that the differences between commercial and military security protection are becoming more and more blurred.

Basic definitions

In order to define the security environment, we must first define security itself. Security of the information infrastructure may be defined in a narrow and in a broad sense. In the narrow sense, *security protection* may be defined as a collection of security measures against unauthorized use and corruption of the information infrastructure and sensitive information.

This definition may be good for a technical person as delineating the scope of the security protection system functionality. However, for a business person or a manager in charge of corporate security, it may leave more questions than it answers. What information is sensitive? How does one know that a specific information fragment should be labeled sensitive? In which case is the information infrastructure considered corrupted? What is an unauthorized use?

The problem with the narrow definition is that it takes the answers to all these questions as a given. In fact, they are a part of security protection system specifications. However, the question that interests both business people and the security manager most is: How does one come up with these specifications in the first place? Obviously, the narrow definition cannot answer this question.

In the broadest possible sense, *security protection* may be defined as a set of provisions necessary to accomplish information system tasks in a specified time at the specified cost. At first glance, this definition seems to have nothing to do with security at all. Actually, it directly relates to security. Providing for the accomplishment of prescribed tasks in a specified time at the specified cost is exactly why the business community needs security protection.

For example, if valuable information were completely compromised, the system would not be able to accomplish some task. If, however, a sophisticated encryption algorithm that dramatically reduced IS performance were selected, so that the system could not accomplish its task in a specified time, it would not very much matter that information was well protected on its way through the network. By the same token, in the case of security overkill, it would not matter that information was well protected if the task could not be accomplished at the specified cost.

The point is that the broadest definition is relevant but insufficient. It is relevant because it interprets security as a cost/performance issue: one wants adequate security but does not want it to jeopardize IS performance or costs. The broadest definition is insufficient because it does not directly associate general system requirements with the security protection features that make up the security system specifications.

In order to correct this insufficiency, we first make a natural assumption that the IS could perform its tasks in a specified time at a specified cost without security, but would be vulnerable to certain threats. Indeed, security cannot improve IS performance or reduce its cost; but it can, and must, reduce IS vulnerability in such a way that IS cost and task accomplishment time are still within the specified limits.

There are three general ways to reduce IS vulnerability:

- Provide (or at least improve) information integrity
- Provide (improve) application integrity
- Provide (improve) availability of the information infrastructure and ISs on top of it

Information and application integrity

Let us more precisely define the three concepts for reducing IS vulnerability. We start by expanding the definition of *integrity*, given in chapter 12 as simply accuracy or validity of information. In the security context, information integrity is defined as a state of information that:

- has been obtained from the source believed to the correct and reliable; or
- was in the integrity state and has been modified legitimately, correctly, and consistently; and
- has not been exposed to malicious or uncontrolled accidental access, change, or destruction.

Obviously, this definition subsumes the one given in chapter 12.

A *level of information security* is the extent to which the information infrastructure is able to preserve information integrity and to protect information against unauthorized disclosure and use.

Application integrity is defined as a state of a program

- whose specifications have been obtained from knowledgeable and reliable sources and are believed to be complete and correct; and
- whose source and object code are believed to comply with specifications and are the same as originally developed, tested, verified, and certified/accredited; or
- which was in the integrity state and has been modified and tested in accordance with integrity-preserving standards and practices, and then retested, reverified, and recertified/reaccredited; and
- which has not been exposed to accidental or malicious access, change, or destruction.

A *level of application security* is the extent to which an IS is able to preserve application integrity and to protect it against unauthorized disclosure and use.

Security protection definition

Finally, *availability of the information infrastructure and ISs* is defined as their ability to provide a requested service at any time within acceptable time limits and with minimally admissible graceful degradation of performance. Information and application integrity as well as the availability of the information infrastructure and ISs may be considered as three major goals of security protection.

Now we are in position to redefine *security protection* in a broad sense in terms that relate directly to security. Security protection is a set of provisions necessary for:

- Application and information integrity
- Availability of the information infrastructure and ISs running against it

This definition tacitly implies that information and application integrity must be maintained continuously. This requirement is difficult to meet in its absolute sense because:

- Passive attacks, such as reading information or wiretapping a communication line, are difficult to detect.
- Deliberate program modifications (trapdoors) and dual-purpose programs (Trojan horses) are hard to preempt.
- Recovery operations following system and media failures (see "DataRecovery" in chapter 12) may be vulnerable to accidental and deliberate attacks.
- Errors and discontinuity of transmission are hard to prevent.

To provide a reasonable degree of information and application integrity, security protection objectives and priorities have to be clearly established and enforced. In order to accomplish this goal, one first has to define the security environment in which the IS will operate.

Security environment

As a first approximation, a security environment may be thought of as a triangle having the following nodes (FIG. 14-1):

- Assets that have to be protected
- Threats to those assets
- Security measures that should be taken to protect assets from threats

Let us look at these components of the security environment in more detail.

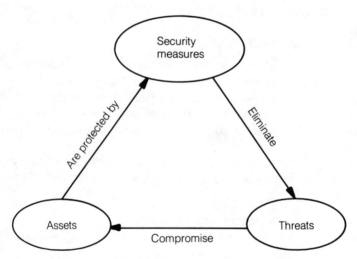

Fig. 14-1. Security environment (first approximation).

Assets

Four basic categories of corporate assets are pertinent to the security environment:

- Physical assets
- Intellectual assets
- Personnel assets
- Transactions and services

Physical assets include:

- Computers, including mainframes, minicomputers, PCs, and workstations
- Peripherals, including terminals, printers, and plotters
- Storage media, including magnetic tape and disk drives, optical jukeboxes, tapes, disk packs, and diskettes
- Network equipment, including all physical media components described in chapter 7 ("Physical Layer"), and internetworking components such as repeaters, bridges, routers, and gateways
- Supplies, including empty diskettes, paper, plotter pens, power supplies, and fire extinguishers

Intellectual assets include:

- Software including system software, such as operating systems, utilities, and DBMSs, application programs, and security software
- Information, including voice, data, knowledge, text, and images

Personnel assets include:

- End users
- Application developers
- Operators and maintenance personnel
- System programmers
- Database administrators
- Management
- Auditors

Finally, transactions and services include:

- Application runs, including transaction processing, batch processing, and ad hoc queries
- Operational services, including running a computer installation, tuning computer installation performance, expanding existing computer resources and facilities, and maintaining and supporting existing systems
- System services, such as customizing and tuning an operating system, and developing new utilities
- Database administration services, such as maintianing data dictionaries, monitoring DBMS performance, and defining integrity and security checks
- Audits

In addition to the four basic asset categories, there are intangible assets, such as company reputation or the ability to attract and keep key employees. However, we will not go into these intangible assets in detail to avoid needlessly complicating the main topic—the security environment.

Threats

Three general classes of threats may affect each of the four asset categories:

- Natural disasters, such as floods, earthquakes, hurricanes, and tornados
- Accidents, such as fire, power outages, water bursts or leaks, and traffic accidents
- Humans, such as employees, hackers, industrial spies, and enemies

Unlike natural disasters and accidents that act quite straightforwardly, humans may compromise security in a variety of ways, Here are the most common categories of threats caused by humans:

- Theft of assets, including:

  a. Theft of physical assets
  b. Finding sensitive information in trash
  c. Copying storage media
  d. Theft of information by accessing the IS

- Improper use of assets, such as:

  a. Using wrong data volume (disk pack, tape reel, etc.)
  b. Masquerading as an authorized user to penetrate the system
  c. Passing information through covert channels (unusual coding)

- Use of assets for other than business purposes, such as:

  a. Using corporate computer and network resources for personal purposes or private business
  b. Using public databases for personal purposes
  c. Unauthorized software copying and selling
  d. Making transactions on one's own behalf

- Unauthorized disclosure of information, including:

  a. Reading sensitive information
  b. Passing sensitive information outside to unauthorized people
  c. Replicating and disseminating sensitive information

- Interception of information by:

  a. Wiretapping communication lines
  b. Eavesdropping
  c. Picking up microwave or satellite transmissions

- Inadvertent or unauthorized corruption or modification of physical and intellectual assets, such as:

  a. Hardware failures
  b. Corruption of system programs because of inadequate hardware protection mechanisms
  c. Unauthorized change of information in memory and on disk
  d. Accidental or deliberate destruction of information
  e. Insertion of unauthorized messages in network traffic
  f. Information integrity violations
  g. Time-of-check-to-time-of-use (TOCTTOU) problems (information checked as valid is corrupted before it is used by a system)
  h. Residual problems, such as reading information left by the previous user
  i. Errors in system and application software
  j. Unintentional application corruption
  k. Application integrity violations
  l. Application infection with trapdoors, Trojan horses, or viruses

- Erroneous information infrastructure design, resulting in:

  a. Overloading memory and access mechanisms
  b. Frequent network congestion
  c. Loss of messages in the network
  d. Service breakoffs at the peak period
  e. Inadvertent denial or delay of service
  f. Violation of service continuity

- Enemy strikes, such as sabotage or a nuclear attack

Prioritization of threats

Not all potential threats described in the previous section are equally likely to happen. Robert Courtney and Mary Anne Todd ranked various threats by their plausibilities. Although their results were presented in 1984, they are still valid today.

The most widespread class of threats is human errors and omissions. As Courtney and Todd observed: "Criminals will never be able to compete with incompetents." I can only add that incompetents have immense opportunities for doing their job of compromising security well.

One of the notorious security threats is password abuses. They include:

- Passing the password to a peer
- Leaving the password on the terminal or nearby
- Using common, easy-to-crack passwords

Other threats in this class include:

- Keyboard entry errors
- Programming errors
- Submitting incorrect data to a database or program

The second most prevalent class of threats is dishonest employees. The most typical threats are embezzlement and fraud. These threats may appear in a variety of forms, such as:

- Taking advantage of flaws in manual or computerized procedures
- Taking advantage of access to privileged information
- Infecting the information infrastructure with viruses

The worst thing about this class of threats is that perpetrators usually work within their levels of authority (Chalmers 1986). No access rules are violated, no passwords are compromised, and even the technically ideal security system would be helpless against this class of threats. This situation provides further evidence that security is a techno-managerial rather than only a technical problem, and that the solution to this problem is a comprehensive security protection program rather than a bunch of technical solutions. Such a program will be discussed in "Formulating and Implementing a Security Program" later in this chapter.

The third most common security threat is fire, which, depending on its severity, can destroy all or only part of the assets. Obviously, fire can affect all categories of assets including intellectual assets and, indirectly, transactions and services.

The fourth most frequent security threat is disgruntled employees. As with dishonest employees, disgruntled ones may threaten the assets in a variety of forms, such as:

- Planting logic bombs, programs that will "explode" at a prespecified time in the future, causing damage to intellectual assets
- Corrupting information after they quit
- Passing user passwords to strangers, such as hackers or spies

The fifth most frequent security threat is water. Water damage may occur as a by-product of fire or as a result of burst pipes and leaks.

The sixth and last threat on Courtney-Todd's list is strangers, such as hackers and industrial spies. Although highly publicized, this threat is not as frequent as one might think. As with all human threats, strangers can compromise security in a variety of ways, including:

- Reading sensitive information through remote access to information
- Replicating and disseminating sensitive information

- Intercepting sensitive information by eavesdropping
- Infecting the information infrastructure with viruses

Security measures

Now that we have discussed assets and threats to those assets, let us focus on the security measures that protect assets from threats. Security measures may be considered from two complementary viewpoints:

- How to eliminate, or at least reduce, the likelihood of specific threats to assets (a *threat-driven* viewpoint)
- What has to be done to protect assets from threats (an *asset-driven* viewpoint)

The following subsections present both viewpoints of security measures.

Threat-driven security measures   In presenting a threat-driven viewpoint of security measures, we will follow the threat prioritization discussed earlier in this chapter.

Threat 1: Human errors and omissions   This class of threats may be diminished through a proper management response. It includes such measures as:

- Developing concise, consistent, and practically enforceable password policies and procedures
- Developing concise, consistent, and practically enforceable access control policies and procedures
- Providing security awareness training
- Determining responsibilities and duties
- Ensuring a system of mutual checks

Threat 2: Dishonest employees   To deal with this threat, an effective security policy is necessary, including:

- Team-based software development
- Peer code review
- Employee disciplinary procedures
- Violation detection and punishment
- Closed security environment (in some cases)

Threat 3: Fire   Some preventive measures against fire are as simple as they are necessary:

- Careful facility planning, including defining a location of physical assets relative to combustibles

- Controlling the quantity of combustibles, such as computer paper, in the vicinity of physical assets
- Installing and regularly checking fire extinguishing equipment

In addition to these simple measures, each enterprise has to have a comprehensive *contingency plan* that provides necessary information infrastructive and IS availability.

Threat 4: Disgruntled employees   To deal with this threat, a proper management response and an effective security policy are necessary. Management actions include:

- Understanding and accommodating personal needs of key employees
- Providing employee assistance programs
- Screening potential employees, especially systems programmers

If these actions do not help and the employee gets laid off or dismissed, the following administrative measures should be part of the security policy:

- Escorting the dismissed employee off the premises
- Immediately changing the employee's password and all other passwords the employee may have known as a part of his or her responsibilities

Threat 5: Water   Some simple preventive measures may work well—for example, having rolls of plastic sheeting handy near the equipment. In addition to this and similar simple measures, each enterprise has to have a comprehensive contingency plan that provides necessary information structure and IS availability.

Threat 6: Strangers   Two major security measures are effective against strangers:

- Developing concise, consistent, and practically enforceable access control policies and procedures
- Developing and maintaining a loophole-free user authentication system

Asset-driven security measures   In presenting an asset-driven viewpoint of security measures, we will follow the asset categorization given in "Assets" earlier in this chapter.

Security measures aimed at protecting *physical assets* include:

- Physical protection, such as fences, barriers, locks, alarms, and guards
- Control of access to sensitive areas, such as computer rooms and tape and disk storage areas
- Identification and authentication of entrants
- Buried transmission cables

- User and message authentication
- Access control

Security measures aimed at protecting *intellectual assets* include:

- User identification and authentication
- Access control
- Explicit policies for data classification
- Comprehensive backup procedures
- Audit trails

Security measures aimed at protecting *personnel assets* include:

- Environmental and safety control
- Protection against personnel threats (following up on tips, surveillance, etc.)

Security measures aimed at protecting *transactions and services* include:

- Access control
- Explicit policies for transaction classification
- Protected libraries of precompiled transactions
- User identification and authentication
- Audit trails

The lists of security measures given in this and previous sections are by no means comprehensive—nor are they meant to be. Rather, the objective is to show the breadth and complexity of the security problem and to emphasize once more that security is a techno-managerial problem. Only by a synergistic use of corporate policies, management responses, administrative actions, and technical solutions may one hope to achieve a really safe environment.

Classification of security measures From a security enforcement viewpoint, all the variety of security measures may be divided into four groups:

- Physical security measures
- Managerial security measures
- Administrative security measures
- Technical security measures

Physical security measures are usually organized as a set of concentric circles around the facility to be protected. Starting from outside, these may be:

- Perimeter controls
- Facility access controls

- Computer or communications center access controls
- Terminal room or remote terminal access controls
- Console or terminal access controls

All kinds of devices for physical security measures may be used. These include:

- Guards
- Electronic scanning
- Closed circuit television
- Controlled access doors
- Electronic badges

Managerial security measures represent a set of managerial decisions regarding the direction and control of the information infrastructure security. The key to successful security protection is integration of security measures into the overall enterprise operation.

In particular, trade-offs between normal operation criteria, such as system performance and response time, and security criteria, such as information and application integrity and the information infrastructure availability, must be carefully considered, agreed upon, and enforced.

Administrative security measures represent a set of procedures necessary to ensure that the physical, managerial, and technical security measures are not bypassed. Administrative procedures must be structured in such a way that, as the sensitivity of protected information increases, additional procedures could be added. All administrative procedures must be documented and disseminated within the enterprise, and the training program to enforce administrative procedures must be established on a permanent basis.

Technical security measures are primarily associated with both computer and network hardware and software operation. There are a number of documents developed by the National Computer Security Center (NCSC) and National Institute of Standards (NIST) that concern the degree of required security measures and formal verification of security mechanism correctness. In the government environment, these documents must be strictly followed. In the commercial environment, technical security measures should be modeled after those in federal documents but customized to the enterprise's particular security environment.

Security environment in more detail

We have defined a security environment as a triangle with assets, threats, and security measures as its nodes (FIG 14-1). Now we can see some deficiencies of this definition that are corrected in the more precise security environment scheme shown in FIG. 14-2.

First of all, not all assets are affected by all threats. Some assets are more

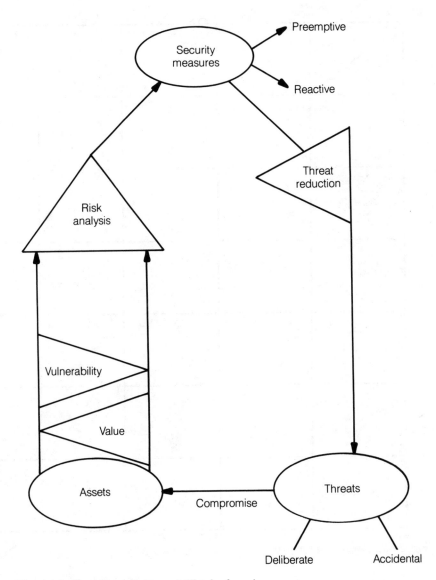

Fig. 14-2. Security environment (final scheme).

vulnerable to certain threats than to others, and some assets are more vulnerable than other assets. For example, in the commercial environment, personnel assets are not as vulnerable as intellectual ones. By the same token, the computer operator is more vulnerable to the fire in the computer room than to the hacker attack.

The concept of *asset vulnerability* is very important because it makes asset protection from threats selective; and the more selective the asset protection, the more cost-effective the security protection system.

Threats / Assets	Threat 1	Threat 2	⋯	
Asset 1	V_{11} $S_{111}, S_{112}, \ldots$	V_{12} $S_{121}, S_{122} \ldots$	⋯	
Asset 2	V_{21} $S_{211}, S_{212}, \ldots$	V_{22} $S_{221}, S_{222}, \ldots$	⋯	
⋮	⋮	⋮	⋮	
Asset i	V_{i1} $S_{i11}, S_{i12}, \ldots$	V_{i2} $S_{i21}, S_{i22}, \ldots$	⋮	
⋮	⋯	⋯	⋯	
Asset m	V_{m1} $S_{m11}, S_{m12}, \ldots$	V_{m2} $S_{m21}, S_{m22}, \ldots$	⋯	

Fig. 14-3. Threat/asset matrix.

Vulnerability of assets to threats may be studied in the context of a threat/asset matrix (TAM), each row Ai, $i = 1, 2, \ldots, m$, of which is an asset, each column Tj, $j = 1, 2, \ldots, n$, of which is a threat, and each cell $TAMij$ of which contains the degree of vulnerability, Vij, of asset Ai to threat Tj (FIG. 14-3). Cell $TAMij$ may also optionally include alternative security measures $Sijk$, with their cost estimates $Cijk$, $k = 1, 2, \ldots, l$.

Security measures may be *preemptive*, that is, aimed at security violation prevention; or *reactive*, responding to a security violation that has already occurred. All other things equal, preemptive security measures are more expensive than reactive ones.

	Threat j	$\cdots$	Threat n
	V_{1j} $S_{1j1}, S_{1j2}, \ldots$	$\cdots$	V_{1n} $S_{1n1}, S_{1n2}, \ldots$
	V_{2j} $S_{2j1}, S_{2j2}, \ldots$	$\cdots$	V_{2n} $S_{2n1}, S_{2n2}, \ldots$
	$\vdots$	$\vdots$	$\vdots$
	V_{ij} $S_{ij}1, S_{ij}2, \ldots,$ $S_{ij}k$	$\vdots$	V_{in} $S_{in}1, S_{in}\,2, \ldots$
	$\cdots$	$\cdots$	$\cdots$
	V_{mj} $S_{mj1}, S_{mj2}, \ldots$	$\cdots$	V_{mn} $S_{mn1}, S_{mn2}, \ldots$

Second, not all assets must be equally protected. For example, a clean floppy diskette does not deserve as much protection as the diskette that contains the only copy of this book's manuscript. (Actually, I have more than one). In other words, different assets have different *values*.

Calculating the value of some assets, such as physical ones, is fairly straightforward. For other assets, such as intellectual ones, the value calculation may not be trivial. Figuring out the value of information is one of the most difficult and subjective endeavors. Putting a value on a human life is not only difficult but also immoral. Nonetheless, making credible value estimates is necessary because it is the asset vulnerability and value that jointly determine if asset Ai should or should not be protected from threat Tj by one of the alternative security measures $Sijk$.

Third, under inevitable cost constraints, the managerial decision of whether or not to protect a certain asset may leave some other assets unprotected just because there is not enough money for security measures that could protect them. Management must decide which assets to protect and which to leave unprotected and realize a so-called *residual risk* resulting from its decisions. This process is called *risk management*.

Risk management does not allow assets to be left to intuition, which in many cases means to chance. If risk management is done correctly, more valuable and vulnerable assets will be protected better than less valuable and vulnerable assets.

Finally, approved security measures may not completely eliminate threats or, alternatively, may not give a 100-percent guarantee of threat elimination. Sometimes, they are even not intended to because of cost consideration. For example, it may be deemed better to reduce the probability of hacker attack to 10 percent for $1,000 than 5 percent for $10,000 or to 1 percent for $50,000. (Dollar values are not actual and are given just for illustration.)

In practice, one should always speak of security measures as reducing rather than eliminating a threat. This notion can be expressed through the *threat reduction ratio, Rijk*, provided by security measure $Sijk$ to reduce threat Tj to asset Ai.

Figure 14-2 represents the final scheme of security environment. For the purposes of security protection system development, one must always consider in the security environment scheme (FIG. 14-2) the particular assets, threats, vulnerabilities, values, risk assessments, and threat reduction ratios that are pertinent to the enterprise and the information infrastructure.

The following sections briefly describe three newly introduced elements of the security environment: vulnerability, information value, and risk management.

Vulnerability

Vulnerability is an asset feature that makes the asset affected by a threat. For example, insufficient fire protection or an unreliable power supply is a vulnerability of certain physical assets, such as computers or disk drives. Finding as complete a set of vulnerabilities as possible for all asset categories is a necessary step on the way to a better understanding of the security environment and, therefore, to more cost-effective security protection. This task is far from trivial, requiring a combination of intuition, experience, the ability to learn from other people's mistakes, and regular inspections of the current security environment. Complicating the task is the fact that the set of vulnerabilities and, especially, their relative weight, Vij, are unique for each enterprise and different even for the same enterprise today and, say, two years down the road.

In this section we will present examples of vulnerabilities for each asset category.

For *physical assets*, in addition to already mentioned insufficient fire protection and unreliable power supply, the following vulnerabilities are worth attention:

- Weak environmental control
- Frequent media crashes
- Insufficiently protected access to the computer room or magnetic tape storage
- Weak protection of LANs against tapping
- Possibility of jamming line-of-sight communication channels

For *intellectual assets*, vulnerabilities include:

- Insufficiently protected access to the computer room or magnetic tape storage
- Undetected bugs
- Weak antivirus protection of software
- Weak access control

For *personnel assets*, vulnerabilities include:

- Insufficient fire protection
- Shortage of database administrators in the area
- Personal weaknesses, such as greed or past criminal activity
- Low morale in the office
- Possibility of layoffs

Finally, for *transaction and services*, vulnerabilities include:

- Insufficient fire protection
- Incomplete contingency plan
- Insufficient network bandwidth, resulting in frequent network congestions
- Frequent system failures
- Shortage of database administrators in the area

As you can see from this sample, the same asset may have many vulnerabilities of a similar or quite different nature, and the same vulnerability may be had by various assets of the same or different categories.

Information value

As stated earlier in this chapter, calculation of the value of some assets is fairly straightforward, but, unfortunately, information is not among them. Assessing the *information value* is one of the most difficult and subjective endeavors because no uniform framework for doing so exists.

While no one would argue that information is a valuable asset, the value of a specific chunk of information is anybody's guess. The same information may have a dramatically different value for different parties. Whenever one talks about the information value, questions like the following are always appropriate: "Information value for whom?" or "Who established the information value?"

Furthermore, information value may change in time (usually it decreases) so the answer to the question "What is its value?" may be different today from what it was three months ago. Business plans and crop forecasts are obvious examples.

Finally, a variety of information integrity preservation situations (IIPSs) is so diverse that the best answer to the question "What is the information value?" is another question: "What situation do you have in mind?"

Let us look at six information value aspects that are caused by the following six IIPSs. In all of them, an information value is assessed in terms of costs.

IIPS 1: Information replacement or recalculation   In this case, information acquired from a public database, or obtained as a result of some operations over publicly available information, is lost. The information value is equivalent to the cost of information replacement or recalculation. This cost is relatively easy to quantify in terms of connection and CPU time or storage media costs.

IIPS2: Information recovery   In this case, nonsensitive information is lost or corrupted as a result of a disaster or a deliberate attack. The information value is equivalent to the cost of information recovery. Again, this cost is relatively easy to quantify in terms of personnel and CPU time as well as backup media costs.

IIPS3: Information loss   In this case, information that was previously created, gathered, rearranged, or repackaged is lost and cannot be replaced or recovered. Examples are books or business intelligence reports. The information value is more than just the cost of an information creator's time plus CPU time because:

- The material may never be recovered in its previous form, and some valuable ideas or conclusions may be lost forever.
- The value of lost information may decrease in time, so by the time it is re-created the part of its value may be lost forever.
- The frustration factor may result in complete project abandonment or in a re-creation time that exceeds prespecified time limits and makes the project pointless.

These factors should certainly be taken into account when assessing the feasibility of information re-creation. (The best recipe, of course, is to make information backups.)

IIPS4: Information disclosure   In this case, sensitive or confidential information is disclosed. The information value is equivalent to the cost of information disclosure consequences, as is the case with confidential military information. This situation is specific in that:

- The loss of information value may be up to complete even though there is no loss of information at all.
- The cost of information disclosure consequences is associated with prevention of an unauthorized access to information rather than with its replacement or recovery.
- The cost of prevention (confidentiality preservation) must be less than the cost of information disclosure consequences.

IIPS5: Information integrity violation   In this case, information was corrupted as a result of information integrity violation. The information value is equivalent to the cost of information integration violation consequences. This situation is specific in that:

- The loss of information value may vary widely, depending on what will go wrong as a result of information integrity violation, and the time and resources necessary to detect that information integrity violation has occurred.
- The cost of information integrity violation consequences is associated with prevention of an inadvertent or deliberate integrity-violating update of information rather than with its replacement or recovery.
- The cost of prevention (information integrity preservation) must be less than the cost of information integrity violation consequences.

IIPS6: Denial or delay of service   In this case, the service was denied or delayed as a result of an inadvertent or deliberate information infrastructure overload. The information value is equivalent to the cost of service denial or delay consequences. This situation is specific in that:

- The loss of information value may vary widely, depending on the kind of requested service, what will go wrong as a result of service denial or delay, and the degradation of information value as a function of time (if the service may be requested again).
- The cost of service denial or delay consequence is associated with the delayed or denied request for information rather than with its replacement or recovery.
- The cost of prevention (protection from service denial or delay) must be less than the cost of service denial or delay consequences.

Risk management

As stated earlier in this chapter, risk management is a process by which management consciously decides which assets must be protected, which assets must not, and what the residual risk resulting from such a decision is. The risk management process, as defined by Fred Tompkins (1984), involves six stages (Abrams and Podell 1987):

- Risk analysis
- Risk reduction analysis
- Management acceptance of the residual risk
- Development of risk reduction plans (RRPs) and action programs
- Implementation and maintenance of selected security measures
- Review and audit of the selected risk reduction action program

The risk management process is mostly a conceptual entity. Its first two stages coincide with the security environment definition, and the remaining stages appear as a natural part of the security program (see "Formulating and Implementing a Security Program" later in this chapter). Nonetheless, we intentionally present the risk management process as a separate entity in view of its paramount importance in the proper design of the security protection system.

Risk analysis The major purpose of risk analysis is to define the security environment, basically along the lines discussed in the previous section. The security environment should be defined as broadly as possible, using the TAM representation. (Refer to "Security Environment in More Detail" earlier in this chapter.) Recall that basic elements of the security environment include:

- All assets of all categories
- Potential threats to those assets, both intentional and unintentional
- Vulnerabilities of assets to identified threats
- Risk assessments based on asset values and vulnerabilities

After the security environment is defined, the risk occurrence impact should be assessed. This part of risk analysis implies conceiving and implementing a series of *security violation scenarios*. The process is akin to a brainstorming session in which synergistically working minds try to:

- Re-create events that can compromise the existing security environment
- Estimate the likelihood of each event
- Assess possible impacts of these events, such as damage or loss to assets
- Estimate costs associated with preventing these events

The expected result is that the participants eventually come up with practical recommendations for improvement of the security environment.

Risk analysis is most usefully applied prior to definitions of, and requirements for, the information infrastructure to take its result into account at the early stages of information infrastructure and IS implementation.

Risk reduction analysis   The risk reduction analysis process includes assessment of all available security measures. These measures may be considered from both threat-driven and asset-driven viewpoints and include:

- Physical security measures
- Managerial security measures
- Administrative security measures
- Technical security measures

Each security measure must be estimated and ranked in terms of the cost of its implementation and its threat reduction ratio.

Risk acceptance   At this stage, management must make the decision, selecting the subset of security measures for implementation. This decision must include certification/accreditation of the information infrastructure and the IS.

Certification implies that management realizes the level of residual risk and accepts it. *Accreditation* implies that management accepts the residual risk, understanding that the information infrastructure and IS must still provide required levels of (1) performance, (2) information and application integrity, and (3) availability of the information infrastructure and IS.

Development of RRPs and action programs   Now that the security measures have been selected, their implementation must be planned, and the resulting RRP must be executed. Typically, management develops a generic RRP, which is then taken by security professionals and expanded into a configuration of main and contingency RRPs of increasingly greater levels of detail (see also "Why Must the Strategic Plan Be Top-Down?" in chapter 1).

In the course of risk reduction planning, selected security measures should be discussed with all concerned parties, including users. The subset of selected security measures may have to be modified in a consensus-based fashion.

Implementation and maintenance of selected security measures   The most detailed RRP should then be further expanded into a comprehensive formalized action program (discussed in detail in chapter 1). Action programs must be scheduled into the general life cycle of the information infrastructure, and all ISs that work against it. Finally, responsibilities for action execution must be assigned. At the same time, a security awareness training program for users should be started.

An intrinsic part of the implementation of security measures is effective change management and maintenance. Maintenance must be organized as a dynamic process involving system modifications and enhancements while preserving the system availability.

Review and audit   Management must review the RRP execution periodically. The gamut of auditing techniques should be considered and applied wherever and whenever necessary, including:

- In-depth system testing
- *Tiger team penetration*, a technique by which penetrators (usually security consultants), who work under no constraints, attempt to circumvent the corporate security protection system
- Risk analysis updates
- Planning of new security measures and corrective actions
- Training of audit personnel

Formulating and implementing a security program

The optimal security environment just discussed is not the end; rather it is the basis and prerequisite for an all-corporate security program that takes care of the security part of the information infrastructure. The schematic relationship between the security environment, risk management, and the security program is given in FIG. 14-4.

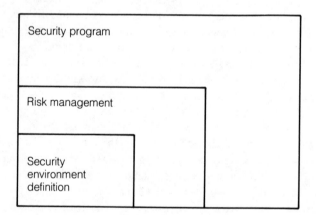

Fig. 14-4. Security environment, risk management, and security program.

Because security protection is a techno-managerial problem, the security program must involve a consistent and synergistic combination of:

- Technical solutions
- Policy decisions
- Security measures

- Awareness and educational programs
- Regular auditing
- Disciplinary actions
- Law enforcement

In this section, we will outline a prototypical security program, referring where necessary to the previous material describing the security environment and risk management. The security program should pursue the following seven objectives:

- To establish a security planning process
- To establish a security management function
- To develop and enforce security policies
- To establish a budget review process
- To establish a risk management process
- To establish a formal procedure for security protection review
- To plan and execute corrective actions

Let us discuss each of the objectives.

Security planning process

The security planning process is a necessary part of the SPPE process. As such, it should be organized along the lines discussed in chapter 1. Specifically, security planning must be based on the following:

- The corporate product, information, and transaction flows (see "Requirements for an Information Infrastructure" in chapter 5 and Interlude 5-1). For each chunk of information, the nature of its value should also be understood, based on relevant IIPSs (see "Information Value" earlier in this chapter).
- The security environment, which should be defined before this security planning process starts. In practice, however, the security planning and security environment definition processes go on concurrently, mutually enriching each other.
- The risk management process which, in turn, is based on the security environment definition. (In fact, its first two stages are the security environment definition.) The risk management process should produce the set of selected security measures that have to be planned and implemented as part of the security program.

As a part of the SPPE, the security planning process should include both short- and long-term security plans. It should also include elaborated contingency plans stemming from security violation scenarios obtained as a part of risk analysis. Indeed, the key to success of the security planning process is its timely expansion into a comprehensive formalized action program.

Security management function

As part of the security program, a security management function such as systems security officers (SSO) must be established. I call it a management function because the SSO is most likely not a single individual. For example, some SSOs may know how to eliminate or reduce certain threats (such as fire or hacker attacks) but may not be as proficient in how to provide system-wide security. Some other SSOs may be experts in the protection of certain assets, but not as good in risk analysis.

It is the security environment that dictates the organizational structure of the security management function. A typical structure may consist of the following:

- Chief security Officer (CSO) in charge of system-wide security who understands the virtual enterprise and the product, information, and transaction flows within it
- Supporting SSOs in charge of specific security issues

(For those of you who are sick of many different "Chief" officers, I can only say: "If there are so many of them, why not one more?")

The CSO coordinates the corporate-wide security program and assists line managers in interpreting and implementing the security program in their units. The CSO also makes sure that all aspects of the information infrastructure and IS security are properly addressed. Supporting SSOs are responsible for the planning and execution of specific components of the security program, such as the implementation of certain security measures.

Security policies

Establishing the set of comprehensive and, most importantly, consistent security policies is a cornerstone of the security program and, at the same time, a major endeavor. The security policy sets direction and guidance for both management and employees as to how security issues must be handled. It also defines responsibilities for functional management, information owners and users, and information service providers. The security policy should be presented to all line and staff units, reviewed regularly, and updated as necessary.

Two major issues are addressed by the security policy:

- How to handle information
- How to provide personnel integrity

Specific rules and guidelines that address these issues are referred to as the *information handling* and *personnel policy*, respectively.

Information handling policy The information handling policy sets standards and guidelines concerning the use of information. Initially, levels of information *sensitivity* should be defined, and each chunk of information should be assigned to one or another level. Information is then said to be classified according to its sensitivity.

The information value should also be defined, according to the six IIPSs introduced earlier in this chapter (see "Information Value").

The next important step is to define the rules of *information ownership* (see "Information Ownership and Management" in chapters 5 and 16). These rules are important because it is an information owner, not an IS organization, that has to be responsible for protection of information it owns. The information owner also has to define the rules for granting and revoking the rights of access to information it owns. The major goal for these rules is to maintain maximum information and application integrity.

The *access right rules* have to be discussed and agreed upon with the corresponding SSO in terms of balance between information classification, the user's need-to-know, and the user clearance, if applicable.

Personnel policy   Refer to "Prioritization of Threats" earlier in this chapter and you will immediately see why the *personnel policy* is so important. In particular, personnel proficiency and integrity are two of the most important aspects of the security program. The personnel policy must be unambiguous and address the following important issues.

Hiring and dealing with employees   New employee screening and some background investigation may be necessary, especially if the new employee is to be hired as a system programmer or a network management professional.

All new employees should go through a security awareness briefing. This briefing should not intimidate the employees; rather, it should make them aware of the security policies in the enterprise. It is very important to find an optimal trade-off between trust and reasonable suspicion.

All preventive investigations of actual or potential security risks and violations should be discreet and not insult the employee. Otherwise, the employee can easily turn from a loyal employee to a disgruntled one.

Coordination of personnel security and information classification   Personnel security and information classification must be closely coordinated. Screening and background investigations should not be the same for all employees. Rather, they should be accomplished, and access rights granted, in regard to the employee's need-to-know certain information and the classification of that information.

Security education and training   Continuous security education and training should be provided. Both present and newly hired employees as well as managers must go through the security education and training program. The program should address issues such as the following:

- Relationships between CSOs and the security program
- View of security as part of information management
- Corporate security requirements, policies, and procedures

- Administrative and technical solutions to a security problem, along with their advantages and disadvantages

As a result of security education and training, students must come to understand the need for security and must support security measures and policies. If the personnel policy should change, all employees must be immediately notified of the changes.

Administrative practices Security-related administrative practices should be strictly enforced. For example, vacations should be taken, and security-important assignments should be rotated using an unpredictable schedule.

Supervisors and managers must be trained to recognize the early signs of vulnerability such as drug abuse, alcoholism, and gambling. If any indication of such vulnerabilities occurs, counseling and assistance must always precede punishment.

Prevention of personnel dissatisfaction is also important. Periodic performance evaluations that offer clear explanations of their results must be conducted. Grievance channels allowing employees to discuss dissatisfaction without threat of punishment must be provided.

Security enforcement If no preventive measures help, security must be enforced, to the full extent of the law or the security policy, quickly and without hesitation. For example, if severe security policy violations are punished with dismissal, the employee who violates the security policy must immediately be dismissed. Embezzlement must always be prosecuted, although companies seldom enforce this policy.

Termination management Termination management is another important and subtle area of the personnel policy. Layoffs should be avoided by all means. However, if they are inevitable, terminations should be carried out fairly. Exit interviews are necessary to reduce employee stress and the likelihood of retaliation.

When the employee is dismissed for whatever reason, other employees must be notified and the employee password must be immediately changed. The employee should be walked out of the restricted area.

Formal security policy The information handling and personnel policies are sometimes (especially in a military environment) augmented by a *formal security model*. The formal security model allows one, at least in principle, to express security requirements precisely and, given an adequate formal *validation and verification* (V&V) process, guarantees that the security policy cannot be violated.

A security model has several advantages (Gasser 1988):

- It is precise and unambiguous.
- It is simple and abstract, and therefore easy to understand.
- It concerns only security features, leaving system functionality or implementation alone.

- It ensures that:
  a. No process can violate the security policy.
  b. Implementation completely and correctly represents specifications.
  c. No covert channels exist that allow a process to communicate with an unauthorized process.

For practical purposes, one can single out three major classes of formal security models:

- Compartment-based models
- Level-based models
- Information flow models

In *compartment-based models*, information is represented nonhierarchically; that is, objects that have to be protected are given compartment designations, such as salary information, performance evaluation, and technical information. Subjects are given clearance to access objects in some compartments. They may also be given a need-to-know for a specific object.

One of the best known compartment-based models is an *access matrix* (also called an *authorization matrix*) used in almost all DBMSs (Date 1985). An access matrix consists of six main components:

- Objects: anything that can be accessed, for example, segments of memory, files, data records, conceptual descriptions, programs, and the access matrix itself. In the access matrix (FIG. 14-5), column j represents object j.
- Subjects: active entities capable of accessing objects and other subjects, for example, programs, processes, and users. In the access matrix, row i represents subject i.
- Access rights: possible kinds of access to objects, such as read (SELECT in SQL parlance), delete, update, and write.
- Authorization rules: a set of rules describing conditions under which access is permitted and actions undertaken if the authorization rule is violated. In the access matrix (FIG. 14-5) each entry $A[i, j]$ is the set of authorization rules, applicable for a specific access right granted to subject i with respect to object j, and violation responses.
- Access control list: a list $L(i, a)$ of subjects i with access rights $A(i, a)$ they have for object a (who can access a certain object).
- Capability list: a list $L(b, j)$ of objects j, such that subject b has access rights $A(b, j)$ to each of them (what can be accessed by a certain subject).

Figure 14-5 shows an example of the access matrix. User 4 (Jerry Rice) is permitted to read information from information object 1. He is also permitted to delete information from this object but only after he makes 20 touchdowns.

Guarded objects / User	Information object 1	. . .	Information object m	
User 1: Montana	All	. . .	None	
User 2: Carter	All	. . .	Select	
User 3: Craig	All	. . .	None	
User 4: Rice	Select delete if touchdown = 20	. . .	None	
User 5: Lott	None	. . .	Select update	

Fig. 14-5. Access matrix.

User 1 (Joe Montana) is permitted to run program *n* but only if he negotiates his salary above $1 million. User 3 (Roger Craig) is permitted to run program 1 but only in work hours. Finally, user 2 (Dexter Carter) is permitted to read the access matrix itself. He is also permitted to update it but only if his weight is less than 300 pounds.

No violation responses are shown in FIG. 14-5. However, the scope of responses is fairly obvious. The illegal access must be denied, and any or all of

	Program 1	. . .	Program n	Authorization matrix
	Run if terminal 1 and blitz = true	. . .	Run if salary > $1M	None
	None	. . .	None	Select update if weight < 300
	Run if 9 am < time < 5 pm	. . .	Run	None
	Run if terminal 1 and speed > 50	. . .	None	None
	Run if terminal 1 and interception = 5	. . .	Run	None

the following results may occur:

- The violation response may be sent to the audit trail
- The SSO on duty may receive an immediate message about the violation, including the access in user's location or phone number
- The user password through which the request was attempted twice may be canceled

The access matrix must be permanently maintained. For instance, as subjects and objects are dynamically created, changed, and destroyed, access rights must be appropriately modified. As information ownership changes, access rights must also be appropriately modified.

In *level-based models* information is represented hierarchically. Objects are given *sensitivity levels*, such as unclassified, company proprietary, time sensitive, confidential, secret, and top secret. Subjects are given certain access rights (such as to read, to write, or to both read and write) through certain relationships between object and subject sensitivity levels.

One of the best known level-based models is the Bell-LaPadula model (1976). In this model both subjects and objects are assigned sensitivity levels, often called *clearances* for subjects and *classification levels* for objects. Sensitivity level A is said to dominate sensitivity level B if A's sensitivity level is greater than or equal to B's.

According to the Bell-LaPadula model, the system's secure state is determined by two properties:

- The simple security property

  For a Read access type, the subject's clearance must dominate the object's classification level.
- The *-property

  a. For a Read access type, the subject's clearance must dominate the object's classification level (no read up!).

  b. For a Modify access type, the object's clearance must dominate the subject's classification level (no write down!).

  c. For a Write (Read + Modify) access type, the subject's and object's sensitivity levels must be equal.

In *information flow models* the security policy is formulated in terms of information flow from one object to another object rather than subjects' access to objects. These models are especially useful for finding covert channels because neither compartment-based nor level-based models can find them.

Information flow analysis is a general technique for analyzing leakage paths in a system. It may be viewed as a security-related part of a study of product, information, and transaction flows (see "Requirements for an Information Infrastructure" in chapter 5 and Interlude 5-1), although it usually is much more detailed. The analysis can be done on the specification or implementation level.

Information flow analysis is less formal than the compartment- and level-based models (Gasser 1988). The rules for deciding when it is possible are complex and not completely formal. While information flow analysis can catch many potential flow violations, it can also miss some of the most interesting ones, especially if it is done on the specification level. Doing information flow analysis on the implementation level may be prohibitively complex.

Compartment- and level-based models can be combined to further restrict access. For example, subjects may be given clearance to access objects in some compartments, but only up to a certain sensitivity level. Either of these models can also be combined with information flow to eliminate the danger of covert channels.

Budget review process

Security costs money that may be hard to get because of a "it-won't-happen-to-me" syndrome typical for corporate management. To make the funding of security measures justifiable, one must establish a *budget review* process. The budget review process should account for shared and specific security costs. Shared security costs include costs necessary for both security and other purposes. The audit trail cost is one example. Specific security costs include those necessary only for security purposes. Some examples are SSO costs, encryption device costs, and access control software costs.

Risk management

The six-stage risk management process must be established to decide which assets must be protected, which assets must not, and what the residual risk resulting from such a decision is. Refer to "Security Environment in More Detail" and "Risk Management" earlier in this chapter for a discussion of the risk management process.

Formal review procedures

Formal review procedures are necessary to assess compliance of the information infrastructure and ISs with security policies and criteria. Each of the four kinds of security measures (physical, managerial, administrative, and technical) should have an appropriate set of formal review procedures. The level of review procedures should be determined by the security environment.

Corrective actions

Corrective actions are actions necessary to ensure that security plans and policies are in accordance with changes in requirements and the environment. These actions also result when an attack on the formal review procedure reveals weaknesses. Corrective actions must be approved by management and may include any or all of the following:

- Reinforcement of the importance of information and application integrity as one of the objectives for security protection
- Reevaluation of plans and procedures necessary to provide information infrastructure or IS availability
- Reconsideration of the whole risk management process or its components and, as a result, reselection of the set of security measures

- Reinforcement of personnel proficiency and integrity as the most important aspects of the security program
- Reevaluation of information classification and personnel clearances
- Correction of SSO functions and responsibilities
- Modification of security policies
- Modification of the current security plan

Conclusion

I have discussed security of the information infrastructure as a system-wide issue that cannot be reduced to just a simple sum of database security and network security. Building security protection into the information infrastructure is a strategically important choice because it ensures that any IS on top of it will have a certain (hopefully, sufficient) degree of security.

Indeed, each additional IS built on top of the information infrastructure will provide feedback regarding new security requirements that may be incorporated in the infrastructure. For example, some ISs might not need all security "bells and whistles" but would be hungry for raw computer and network performance. In this case, one should have built necessary flexibility into the information infrastructure to provide on-line switching from "more security" to "less security."

In the context of this chapter, the approach to security as a system-wide issue has its own price. Namely, I have stressed issues such as security environment definition, risk management, and security program development at the expense of more technical security problems, such as encryption or digital signatures. Given unlimited space, this might have seemed inexcusable. However, within practical book limitations (this is, after all, not a book on security), there is two-fold justification for my bias.

First, as I have emphasized repeatedly, security is a techno-managerial issue. It is the managerial rather than the technical security aspect that has been more often overlooked. Second, this book is for a business person rather than a computer science student. For a business person, encryption and digital signatures are security measures that have to be integrated into the "hole-free" fabric of security protection. Weaving this fabric and making it hole-free is more important, and thus the emphasis of this chapter.

Part IV

Human infrastructure

15

Human aspects of SISs

Executive summary

IT by itself does not give the enterprise a competitive advantage. People who properly use this technology do. Thus, a magic equation for developing an SIS is not complete unless one understands how IT and people should work together in a synergistic and mutually enhancing way.

The following human aspects of SISs are especially important:

- Organizational structure
- Teamwork and work groups
- Performance evaluation, incentive and reward (PEIR) systems
- Helping people to use IT

Organizational structures are currently in transition from highly hierarchical structures with opaque interdepartmental walls to flexible, project-oriented ones. They will become flattened; and small project-, problem-, and process-oriented work groups will replace rigid departments.

Changes in the organizational structure are possible only if the human aspects of SISs fully support these changes. The concept of a work group, its underlying element, must be understood and implemented. New job descriptions, performance evaluation methodologies, compensation criteria and schemes, incentives for people to stay in the company, and reward for contribution to the corporate bottom line and development have to be well thought out and implemented. In addition, a significantly higher level of computer proficiency has to be achieved for virtually all employees.

A lot of work has to be done before organizational structures similar to those discussed in this chapter become a reality. However, the technology necessary for making them a reality does exist and is available today, so the ball is in senior management's court. Without significant organizational changes, billions of dollars spent on computers, networking, and software will mostly be wasted. Technological and organizational innovation must be carried out concurrently to gain the competitive advantage.

In chapter 5, providing the use of, and interfaces to, information sources, storages, processors, and the corporate network by diverse corporate users was defined as the highest level of the corporate information infrastructure. This function may imply the creation of technological and organizational incentives for bringing the corporate organizational structure and the information infrastructure in accordance and providing synergy between the two.

Strategic triangle

The need for synergy between IT and people, which unfortunately is too often taken for granted and therefore overlooked, is reinforced in MIT's and Arthur Young's (now Ernst & Young) joint *Management in the 1990s* study. The report, representing Arthur Young's perspective, determines "alignment of strategy, business structure, and information technology" as a "key management concept for the 1990s" (Young 1989). MIT's study refers to this alignment as a *"strategic triangle."*

I present my version of the strategic triangle in FIG. 15-1. Its nodes correspond to three elements:

- CSOs (strategy in MIT terminology)
- IT
- Human aspects (business structure in MIT terminology)

Its sides represent interrelationships between the concepts attached to its nodes. For example, CSOs must explicitly address IT through building the information infrastructure and SIS on its top. Conversely, IT may (and should) determine CSOs (see "SIS Definition" in chapter 1).

Two sides adjacent to the human aspects node may be interpreted as the following relationships:

- Strategic objectives—human aspects: CSOs and the corresponding ASP have to be disseminated within the enterprise for discussion and feedback.
- Human aspects—strategic objectives: the consensus and then commitment to CSOs have to be generated before the enterprise begins to execute them (see "Consensus and Commitment" in chapter 1).
- IT—human aspects: IT promotes, and sometimes even forces, organizational changes in the enterprise.
- Human aspects—IT: people and the way they are treated determine the enterprise's ability to use IT effectively and efficiently.

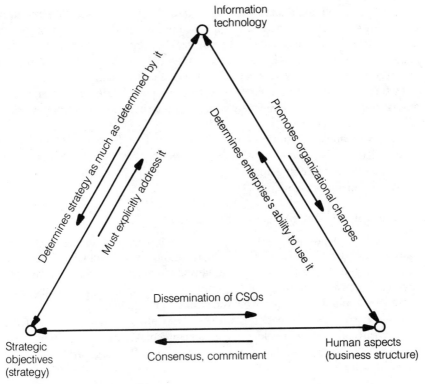

Fig. 15-1. Strategic triangle.

The last two relationships are the subject of this chapter. Specifically, the following four human aspects of SISs will be discussed:

- Organizational structure
- Teamwork and work groups
- PEIR systems
- Education and training in the use of IT

Organizational structure

It has been said many times and in many quarters that a deeply hierarchical organizational structure is counterproductive. It creates unnecessary vertical barriers between employees and impedes information sharing and exchange. It also creates fiefdoms whose main objective becomes self-preservation rather than maximum contribution to the enterprise business.

Apparently, fiefdoms are getting well entrenched quickly. In spite of the common recognition that hierarchical organizational structures must be flattened, there are still many big companies with 15 or more levels of reporting.

For years, the main justification for hierarchical organizational structures has been authority delegation. With this method, middle managers feel in charge of their own business. Furthermore, they analyze, filter, and package data they collect and pass it to senior management which, in turn, analyzes the packaged data and makes strategic decisions. Finally, middle managers interpret these decisions in the context of their responsibilities and disseminate information down to the employees, thus keeping them informed about what is going on in the company.

Unfortunately, this story is too close to a fairy tale. It works only in theory. In practice, the process of data analysis, interpretation, and dissemination in both directions is highly subjective, time-consuming, and causes significant delays and misunderstanding.

Flattening the organizational structure

Starting with a prophetic article in 1958, "Management in the 1980s" by Harold Leavitt and Thomas Whisler, many authors predicted what John Naisbitt calls "the whittling away of middle management"(1985). However, this prediction has not happened until recently because there was no adequate substitute for a middle manager. Now the situation is changing.

The corporate information infrastructure defined in chapter 5 and discussed throughout this book is an important contribution to flattening the organizational structure. Three major factors make flat organizational structures a reality:

- A better understanding of product, information, and transaction flows within the virtual enterprise, which is necessary for building the information infrastructure, helps to reduce costs, to streamline and simplify operations, and to increase information availability at the point of use.
- The information infrastructure provides significantly improved information sharing and exchange in all three directions: up, down, and peer-to-peer.
- The information infrastructure provides significantly improved information integrity and security, providing information validity and clearly defining rights of access to information for all IS users.

Does this mean that middle managers will soon be extinct? There is no single answer to this question. Managers who believe that their job is to attend meetings, supervise, report, and wait for promotion will definitely be "whittled away." One estimate claims that more than one million managerial and staff jobs have been eliminated since 1979 (Applegate, Cash and Mills 1988).

Managers who redefine their role in the enterprise, take more responsibility, and find ways of adding value to the corporate bottom line will thrive. Middle management jobs will become more technical, broader in scope, more advisory, and even educational. At any rate, the survival of a middle manager will depend on understanding IT and how it is affecting, or may affect, the enterprise.

As the number of middle managers decreases, senior managers will have to accept additional responsibilities that require computer proficiency. Most of these responsibilities will include ad hoc queries to the corporate data and knowledge bases as well as everyday use of text and image management systems. As information creators, senior managers will become owners of the information and thus responsible for its integrity and security.

The following war stories show that some of these predictions are already coming true.

WAR STORY 15-1. EXECUTIVE IS REPLACES MIDDLE MANAGERS

After a major reorganization that reduced management by 40 percent, the Big Oil Company's president requested an improved executive IS for his newly appointed senior management team. The system "did the work of scores of analysts and mid-level managers whose responsibilities had been to produce charts and graphs, communicate this information, and coordinate operations with others in the company" (Applegate, Cash, and Mills 1988). The president also introduced EM to streamline communications throughout the company.

WAR STORY 15-2. SENIOR MANAGERS USE A DATABASE

A large manufacturing company went through a major reorganization that involved layoffs, divestitures, and early retirements that reduced middle management by 30 percent. Senior managers became users of a "centralized corporate database, which integrated all aspects of the highly decentralized business," and a "sophisticated telecommunication network, which linked all parts of the multinational company" (Applegate, Cash, and Mills 1988).

Senior managers accessed the database to analyze, summarize, and display data concerning the virtual enterprise and let employees know what they should focus on.

Breaking through functional barriers

Vertical barriers are not the only ones that impede corporate productivity. Existing barriers between functional components, which I call *horizontal barriers*, are also counterproductive. Traditionally, functional components throw the results of their work over the wall to the next one in the product flow. The effect is lower product quality and unnecessary delays and loops in production and service.

Again, there is no shortage of papers and articles that predict the fall of horizontal barriers. In the manufacturing industry, for instance, there is a barrage of terms, such as "design for producibility," "design for manufacturability," "simultaneous engineering," and the like that describe the trend perfectly. However, only with the advent of information infrastructures and advanced technologies such as AI will breaking through the functional barriers become a reality.

The key, again, is understanding the product, information, and transaction flows within the virtual enterprise. Integration of adjacent functions becomes possible as result of the following:

- Further standardizing products and processes so that product families can share common components and processes
- Bringing regulations and constraints of later processes up front to previous ones to avoid time-consuming and expensive loops and feedbacks from later processes to previous ones
- Broadening the scope of both white- and blue-collar jobs

The corporate information infrastructure permits flexible rerouting of the information flow, including the authorization structure, for different products or services at different stages of the project. The effect is flexible and project-oriented organizational structures.

The paramount importance of flexible rerouting of the information flow and authorization structure is that it allows a large enterprise to operate like many small independent companies, thus combining the advantages of a large company (financial strength and sustainability) with the advantages of a small company (innovativeness and flexibility).

Organizational structure of the future

So what will an organizational structure of the future look like? First of all, as stated previously, it will be flexible and project- rather than function-oriented.

All employees will be gathered in pools classified by their professional expertise. This information as well as other personal employee characteristics will be stored and maintained in a corporate personnel database. When senior management decides to start a new project, the designated project manager will access the database to fill vacant positions in the project team with people from the corresponding pools.

Project teams will cross today's organizational boundaries and be responsible for a product or service for its entire life cycle. Project teams will be disbanded as soon as the project is finished, and all team members will return to the pool until they are selected for a new project.

With the exception of a small permanent senior management team, all reporting relationships will be determined by the current portfolio of projects. Project completion or termination may change existing reporting relationships. More permanent reporting relationships with senior management, including line management, will be based on motivation and encouragement to advance one's career through education and new experiences.

At all times information about who is working on which project, for whom, for how long, and with what responsibilities will be available to senior managers and other authorized employees. Progress reports for each project can be requested and obtained in a matter of seconds directly from the system without having to resort to human intermediaries such as middle managers and analysts.

The ability of senior management to monitor on-line the progress of all ongoing projects will make hierarchical authority delegation obsolete and will change relationships between senior management, line management, and project management. Both line and project managers will have more autonomy, control over their business, and responsibility.

Historical information about each individual's performance on prior and ongoing projects will be available to authorized personnel. This information will be the basis for PEIR and, therefore, all promotions.

Organizational structures like the one just described have been a subject of research and experiments for several years. Three major variations on the theme include:

- Adhocracy (Mintzberg 1988): a set of project-oriented teams that replace the hierarchy.
- Network organization (Eccles and Crane 1987): communication networks that connect all enterprise components and replace the hierarchy.
- Cluster organization (Mills 1991): a set of groups of people organized around a business problem to be solved, or a product or process to be developed and disbanded after the problem is solved or the product or process is developed.

Several corollaries of the organizational structure described in this section are worth special attention and further discussion. First, many management positions will become temporary. An individual who is a rank-and-file member of one project may become the manager of another if it fits well with the individual's performance during the previous project or professional expertise and experience. Conversely, the project manager may want to work as an implementor on another project to sharpen skills and prepare for managing the next, larger and more difficult project. As a result, the loss of managerial position will not necessarily be considered as a demotion, but rather as the next step in advancing an individual's career.

Second, multifunctionality will become a valuable (if not the most valuable) employee asset. Employees will have various incentives for mastering several skills. The employee with two or more skills will be more marketable within the enterprise, more quickly recruited for the next project, and more valued as a team member. Multifunctional employees will likely be rewarded more frequently because the demand for such employees will exceed their supply for years to come. As a result, the concept of career advancement will shift from climbing up the hierarchical corporate ladder to acquiring additional knowledge and skills.

Third, promotions and raises will be given for contribution rather than for moving up the corporate ladder or years of service. Performance evaluation systems will be connected with incentive and reward systems to determine the criteria for promotions, pay raises, bonuses, and the like.

Fourth, the personnel database may provide information about employees' fields of expertise, not only for senior management and project managers but also for other employees in the company who may need advice or help on a specific issue. As a result, a great deal of peer-to-peer interaction will arise, not only in the context of joint work on a specific project but also in on-request fashion. Ideally, this interaction may create the situation in which every employee, even in a large company, may communicate with any other employee. The MIT research calls such communications "weak links" because they are different from formal reporting or team communications (Young 1989). Senior managers in many companies dream about this situation but have not yet been able to attain it.

Fifth, an important side effect of extensive peer-to-peer communication augmented by the adequate proliferation of IT at an employee's desk will be a "grass roots" movement aimed at the complete redefinition or restructuring of the employee's job and at "raising productivity in ways initially unforeseen by management. . . . For example, one person gained his peers' admiration by reducing 30 hours of routine work to three automated hours" (Young 1989).

A lot of work has to be done before organizational structures similar to those discussed in this chapter become a reality. Two important points are worth noting:

- The technology necessary for making these organizational structures a reality does exist and is available today, so the ball is in senior management's court.
- Full utilization of the corporate information infrastructure is unlikely without the corresponding organizational change. Billions of dollars spent on computers, networking, and software may actually be wasted if the organizational structure does not match the information infrastructure. Technological and organizational innovation must be carried out concurrently. Or, as the MIT research states: "significant investment in new information technology without parallel organizational change is unlikely to yield good results" (Young 1989).

At the same time, changing the organizational structure is not the end. It is only the first step that has to be fully supported by three other human aspects: teamwork and work groups, PEIR systems, and education and training in the use of IT.

The new organizational structure has a project-oriented work group as its underlying element. Thus, the concept of teamwork, project-oriented work groups, and their interactions has to be thoroughly discussed, fully developed, and realized.

The new organizational structure also requires new job descriptions, new performance evaluation methodologies, new compensation criteria and schemes, and new incentives for people to stay in the company. Thus, PEIR systems have to be well thought out and implemented.

Finally, the new organizational structure requires a significantly higher level of computer proficiency for virtually all employees. Ignorance or lack of computer knowledge and skills may become a major stumbling block on the way to a new corporate identity. Various approaches for helping people to use IT have to be studied, developed, and implemented.

In the remainder of this chapter, we will discuss these three human aspects of SISs.

Teamwork

Teamwork, also called group work, is a major factor in providing high-quality products and services as well as adaptability to change, for example, in terms of time to market.

Teamwork relies on common understanding and consensus on:

- What information should be exchanged and shared
- What the information to be exchanged means
- How the information is to be exchanged and shared
- How the information exchange should be coordinated
- What the expected reaction to the information is

In addition to providing high-quality products and services as well as adaptability to change, teamwork has the following advantages:

- It breaks down organizational barriers.
- It unites the workforce.
- It provides information exchange in an orderly and secure way.
- It speeds up information transfer and exchange.
- It minimizes misunderstanding and information transfer errors.

In order to realize these advantages, the enterprise must first change some of its underlying assumptions concerning an employee's scope of knowledge and skills, and treatment by management. TABLE 15-1 (Mitroff 1987) lists old and new assumptions necessary to promote teamwork.

As its name suggests, teamwork is provided by teams, or (to use a more fashionable term) *work groups*. The following paragraphs discuss the work group.

Table 15-1. New Assumptions Necessary to Promote Teamwork.

Old Assumption	New Assumption
Employee skills do not have to be matched to the complexity of products; people perform best in highly specialized, narrowly defined jobs and must be paid for specific jobs.	Employee and management skills/systems have to be closely matched to the complexity of products. Since products are complex and diverse, employees must be multifunctional and paid for skills mastered.
Employees need not be knowledgeable about the business as a whole.	Employees must have an overview of the entire business and feel that they are a vital part.
There is no need for career development.	Education, training, and personal growth are the most important factors in teamwork.
Managers must deal with employees as individuals.	Teamwork is necessary for success in global competition. Managers must deal with employees as members of a team.
Assignment of overtime or transfer is done by the manager.	Teams cover all vacancies or shortages, and the manager does not have to be concerned with these matters.
Work must be closely supervised and evaluated by management.	Peer supervision and evaluation must be done by team members.

Work group definition and characteristics

For the purposes of this chapter, a work group is defined as a group having three important attributes (Hackman 1990):

- It is a relatively stable (and permanent during its lifetime) social system whose members are dependent on one another for some shared purpose and develop specialized roles within the group as that purpose is pursued.
- It produces an outcome (for which its members have collective responsibility) that may be measured and evaluated.
- It operates in the context of a larger social system, such as another group, department, division, or the entire virtual enterprise.

A work group may be created for any reasonable purpose. It may be *product-oriented*, that is, created with the goal to develop a new or modify an old product or service. The work group may also be *problem-oriented*, created to solve a certain problem; or *process-oriented*, created to develop or schedule a certain process. The work group may be functional or multifunctional; that is, it may serve one or more functional components of the enterprise.

The work group is disbanded after it has completed its job. All work group members migrate to another work group if the need exists and they have the knowledge and skills necessary for a job assigned to that work group.

No geographical proximity or location stability is required for successful work group operation. However, work group members typically have a constant need to access, exchange, share, and process certain common information on a regular basis. Therefore, product, information, and transaction flows as well as communication traffic within the group should be fairly well defined, and the information infrastructure supporting on-line interaction among work group members must be in place. Likewise, the consistency and continuity of user interface "look and feel" and workstation-to-workstation interface and protocols should be provided.

Work group size

Each work group must be self-contained. In other words, all functions and skills necessary to get the work group's job done must be represented. During the work group lifetime, its individual members can migrate from one functional assignment to another if they have the ability to carry out multiple functions.

The work group must be kept as small as possible for at least three reasons:

- The smaller the work group, the easier its coordination.
- The smaller the work group, the easier the recognition of individual contributions.
- The smaller the work group, the easier to achieve consensus, which, along with constant feedback on work group performance, is a crucial element of teamwork.

Advantages of work groups

Work groups have certain advantages. The major and strategic one is that they provide faster response to market changes and better coordination of new product/service introduction—two competitive necessities in the era of global markets and worldwide competition. Work groups also provide more effective crisis management, especially when the problem to be solved crosses multiple organizational barriers and requires a great deal of intercomponent coordination.

In addition, work groups increase productivity and provide better quality of work. They are relatively small, and the information they dwell on is well defined and realitively limited. Therefore, access to information is faster, as well as its manipulation and dissemination; the risk of an error is minimized; and security protection is improved.

As they function, work groups can discover new, previously unnoticed communication paths and information flows within the virtual enterprise.

Work group management

Work groups consist of people. Organizations that do not keep this seemingly trivial statement close to their hearts have no chance to succeed with work groups. They will just be bureaucratic units in disguise.

Whether a work group does or does not serve its purpose depends on the quality of work group management. Here are some major principles of work group management (Mitroff 1987):

- Facilitate rather than control.
- Encourage rather than constrain.
- Integrate rather than break down.
- Listen rather than order.
- Learn rather than teach.

To summarize, "rather than attempting to manage group behavior in real time, leaders might better spend their energies creating contexts that increase the likelihood that teams will prosper" (Hackman 1990).

Managing people in work groups   Even if people did not like teamwork, it would still be necessary because only a few trivial tasks can be accomplished by individuals in isolation. As a matter of fact, people do enjoy being in work groups for a variety of reasons:

- People expect to achieve in teams more than they would as individuals.
- People may exchange skills and build their knowledge.
- People can share big and small victories and celebrate them together.
- People can share disappointments and dilute blame.

Work group management must be sensitive to each of these reasons and always encourage joint work, on-the-job education, success celebration, and failure consolation sessions.

It has been proven that people want to be productive. Moreover, most people actively seek opportunities to excel. It is the bureaucratic system and managers protecting their turf that hold them back. For many people, the work group is a light at the end of the tunnel, and work group management must support people's desire to be productive.

The synergy in a work group, however, is not going to come automatically. Experiments have shown that an individual's performance in groups goes down (Sanders 1990). Researchers have also noticed that effort reduction is unconscious, and the individual output grows when team members are convinced that their effort is measured.

Individual performance can be dramatically improved if:

- There is significant specialization within the group.
- There is a sense of individual recognition.
- The teamwork is properly coordinated.
- Work group members adequately interact.

Recognition, interaction, and coordination   Of all the performance factors, recognition, interaction, and coordination are the most interesting (Sanders 1990). *Recognition* is a powerful form of feedback, one of the crucial elements of teamwork. Work group members want to know:

- How the work group is doing
- What they do right and how they can improve their performance

The main recognition component is letting a work group member control his or her environment and only then praising for performance.

The basis of *interaction* is information sharing. The value of information sharing should be constantly emphasized, and team members should be encouraged and motivated to inform peers of their individual contributions. In particular, quick dissemination of accomplishments alleviates coordination while providing immediate recognition and, hence, valuable feedback.

As paradoxical as it may seem, good *coordination* means giving people less information less frequently in a shorter time rather than more information more frequently in a longer time. In other words, coordination should provide opportunities and means for communication and information exchange; but the information infrasturcture must determine how much information is exchanged, how frequently, and for how long.

The most practical way to provide coordination is meetings. Meetings can stimulate creativity, facilitate brainstorming and idea generation, or focus work group members' attention on the highest-priority issues. No matter what the purpose might be, effective presentation of information is a must (Sanders 1990).

Meetings may be both *in-person*, with all work group members getting together in one room; and *on-line*, using various available work group communication tools, or *groupware*. In-person meetings are especially good for immediate individual recognition, although on-line meetings can also be used for this purpose.

Checklist for work group management   Let us summarize principles of work group management as a checklist for further references (Sanders 1990):

- Keep work groups small.
- Maintain an on-line skills inventory of group members.
- Focus on people, not technology.
- Create the working environment rather than directly manage.
- Support a work group member's desire to be productive.
- Recognize team members' individual accomplishments.
- Encourage education and skill multifunctionality.
- Practice good team coordination.
- Balance information sharing and privacy.
- Use IT to support work group activities.

PEIR systems

As stated earlier in this chapter, the new organizational structure requires new performance evaluation methodologies, new compensation criteria and schemes, and new incentives and rewards that make people stay in the company and perform well.

In order to develop a new PEIR system, the enterprise should address four interrelated issues:

- How to assess work group effectiveness
- How to tie principles of performance evaluation to work group effectiveness parameters
- How to develop the incentive and reward system
- How to troubleshoot PEIR systems

Let us discuss each issue in turn.

Dimensions of work group effectiveness

The first issue that should be addressed in the context of this section is how to assess work group effectiveness. J. Richard Hackman (1990) suggests three dimensions:

- The degree to which the work group's product, no matter what it is, meets the standards of quality, quantity, and timeliness established by group clients. Hackman stresses that "reliable, objective performance measures are rare" in organizations. Depending on what the work group is to accomplish, these standards can be established explicitly as a set of product requirements and specifications or implicitly as general market requirements dictated by competitive considerations.
- The degree to which normal work group operations enhance the capability of work group members to work together in the future. The point is that a "one-job stand" performance, even if successful, does not constitute an effective work group.
- The degree to which the work group experience results in the personal growth and well-being of its members. If personal growth does not happen, the whole idea of work groups will fail because its members will see no difference between the work group and old, rigid departments and will lose trust in this sort of "innovation."

The relative weight of each of the work group effectiveness parameters is dictated by specific objectives set for the work group and circumstances in which it operates. For example, for a group of students enrolled in a seminar on SISs, the third parameter is probably most important because the personal growth of students was the reason for the seminar. For a group of kamikazes created with the goal to destroy an American aircraft carrier, the second and third parameters are not that important, while the first one is the reason for creating the group. For a work group doing enterprise modeling, a job that can be broken up into relatively independent pieces and thus is highly iterative, the second parameter is indeed important, but so are the other two. At some point in this project, the level of work group member frustration may be so high that the third parameter will become, at least temporarily, of paramount importance.

Principles of performance evaluation

Agreeing upon the weight of each group effectiveness parameter and then developing a performance evaluation system has to be done at the stage of work group creation and, apparently, for each new work group. Although performance evaluation criteria may be very different for different projects and work groups, some general principles for the performance evaluation system may be formulated as follows:

- Pay for the quality (degree of customer satisfaction, for example) and timeliness (time to market) more than for the quantity (effectiveness parameter 1).
- Pay for teamwork rather than only individual accomplishments (effectiveness parameter 2).
- Pay to the work group and let its members decide on a consensus basis who contributed what and who deserves how much (effectiveness parameter 2).
- Pay for the rapport among work group members and their willingness and readiness to work together again (effectiveness parameter 2).
- Pay for the professional and personal growth, for example, for additional functional skills acquired by a work group member in the course of the project (effectiveness parameter 3).

In addition to general principles that hold true for practically any industry or field of endeavor, some specific principles should also be formulated. For example, in the manufacturing industry, achieving maximum worker utilization (as opposed to maximum machine utilization) or estimating and tracking total labor and cost (rather than direct/indirect labor ratios) may be considered parameters of significant importance in the performance evaluation system.

Incentive and reward systems

Performance evaluation based on principles discussed in previous sections should be augmented by special incentive and reward systems. These systems must be closely associated and coordinated with CSOs and successful actions that support the CSOs (see "Formulating CSOs" and "Action Program" in chapter 1). Moreover, it is the priority of a certain action or project that determines the level of the incentive and the corresponding reward for its successful completion. The incentive and reward system without CSOs leads to anarchy in which people may be rewarded for participating in someone's pet projects rather than for contributing to the important ones.

As discussed in chapter 1, step 5 of the SPPE process consists of implementing and monitoring action programs, evaluating their ongoing results, and changing them if necessary. Incentive and reward system development should be tightly coupled with this part of the SPPE process because the latter may dramatically change the priorities of various actions and projects and, hence, switch the enterprise's interest to employee contributions from one field of endeavor to another.

The important conclusion is that, while principles of performance evaluation are fairly permanent and stable, the incentive and reward system is dynamic and volatile. If the enterprise is to be flexible and adapt to changes, so too must its incentive and reward system.

Information about the incentive and reward system currently in effect and its updates must be widely advertised and disseminated within the enterprise as a strong signal of what is important to the enterprise and how it is ready to reward its employees for their accomplishments. By the same token, information about the people who have actually been rewarded, including what they were rewarded for and why, must be made available to everyone in the enterprise.

Here are a few examples of what could fall under the umbrella of the incentive and reward system:

- The enterprise starts a grass roots program, trying to uncover and solve quality problems in manufacturing. It creates incentives for all those who can come forward with a problem that previously was not identified and perhaps (but not necessarily) its possible solution.
- The enterprise wants to close the gap between its marketing, sales, and service people and its product definition and development people. It creates incentives for those in marketing, sales, and service who can identify customer needs, requirements, and complaints that have not been considered by a product definition work group. Additional incentives could be created for those who can suggest how to incorporate necessary modifications into the existing line of products.
- The enterprise is going to standardize on the OS/2 operating system for its PCs. It anticipates OS/2 support problems and creates incentives for all application programmers to learn OS/2 as an additional skill and provide on-demand support for end users should any problem arise.
- The enterprise needs to penetrate a new international market (for example, the Soviet Union). It creates incentives for those who can provide useful information about the specifics of the Soviet market, the Soviet culture, and the Soviets' ability to pay in hard currency.

For each of these examples, a flexible scale of monetary and other rewards could be developed, putting the reward in direct dependence on the significance of the submitted material as determined by the client.

Troubleshooting work group management and PEIR system

In order to check if work group management and the PEIR system perform properly, one has to understand the factors that determine work group performance, how these factors may be affected as the work group proceeds with its project, and how to diagnose the arising problems.

Work group performance is determined by three factors (Hackman 1990):

- Sufficiency of the level of effort put forth to accomplish the work group task (the *effort factor*). If this level is insufficient, the work group has an *effort problem*.
- Adequacy and sufficiency of available knowledge and skills relative to knowledge and skills necessary to accomplish the task (the *talent factor*). If knowledge and skills are inadequate or insufficient, the work group has a *talent problem*.
- Adequacy of task performance strategies relative to the work to be done and the environment in which it is to be done (the *strategy factor*). If the task performance strategy is inadequate the work group has a *strategy problem*.

These factors cannot be affected directly, for example, by ordering work group members to get more knowledge and skills. The only way to affect the effort, talent, and strategy factors, and consequently solve the corresponding problems, is to create *organizational conditions* that could increase the likelihood that the effort, talent, and strategy are adequate and sufficient.

Hackman (1990) suggests three such organizational conditions:

- Group structure
- Organizational context
- Coaching and assistance

Each of these organizational conditions can indirectly affect each of the three work group effectiveness factors, resulting in a three-by-three matrix (TABLE 15-2). In TABLE 15-2, rows are work group effectiveness factors, columns are organizational conditions, and each matrix cell C_{ij} contains the remedy that organizational condition j brings to improve factor i.

Each remedy implies a set of questions that a PEIR system troubleshooter should ask to improve work group effectiveness in an indirect way, through improving work group management of the PEIR system.

Table 15-2. Effectiveness Factors and Affecting Organizational Conditions.

Work Group Effectiveness Factors	Group Structure	Organizational Condition		Coaching and Assistance
		Organizational Context		
Effort	Building motivating potential	Developing an adequate incentive and reward system		Obtaining commitment and providing coordination
Talent	Providing adequate group staffing	Providing education and training		Fostering expertise sharing and cross-training
Strategy	Establishing work group behavior norms	Providing adequate information		Fostering creative strategy development

Building motivating potential implies asking questions like these:

- Do the work group's purpose and task match?
- Do all work group members want to work on the task and accomplish it?
- Do all work group members share responsibility and accountability for what they do?
- Do all work group members know how well they perform relative to the task?

Questions concerning adequacy of the incentive and reward system include:

- Does it provide proper recognition of performance?
- Is the whole work group rewarded or its individual members?
- Do incentives encourage group collaboration and performance?

Ian Mitroff (1987) provides the following guidelines for troubleshooting a PEIR system:

- Ask work group members if the project they are on is going well and how they estimate their personal contribution. If the majority say that the project is not doing well, but they are doing a great job, one encounters a typical "other-guy's-fault" syndrome. This syndrome is a clear indication of poor teamwork. If, however, only one member thinks the project is not doing well, the work group has a "black sheep" problem, and this individual needs to polish his or her social and teamwork skills.
- Ask work group members how they personally benefit from the work group's success. If the response is "not much," it is a clear indication of a poor performance evaluation system, one of the three cornerstones of work group effectiveness (see "Dimensions of Work Group Effectiveness" earlier in this chapter).

- Ask human resource department people how much employees are paid. If the answer is that they make as much as similar people do in this and other companies, it is a clear indication that employees in this company are treated as competitors for a limited resource of money rather than as contributors in the corporate bottom line.
- Ask people how much their performance in the work group contributes to the rewards they get. If the answer is "little," it is an indication of a poor performance evaluation system. Most likely, performance criteria have not been defined, and the work group management does not really know who has done what for the work group.

Obtaining commitment and providing coordination implies a set of questions like these:

- Do all work group members believe that the task can be accomplished?
- Are all work group members committed to accomplishing the task?
- Are work group members given less information less frequently in a shorter time rather than more information more frequently in a longer time? (See "Recognition, Interaction, and Coordination" earlier in this chapter.)
- Do work group meetings stimulate creativity, facilitate idea generation, and focus work group members' attention on the highest-priority issues?

Providing adequate group staffing implies the following questions:

- Does the work group have the staff it needs to accomplish its task?
- Is the work group not too big?
- Do work group members have enough knowledge to accomplish the task?
- Do work group members have sufficient professional and interpersonal skills?
- Does the work group have a necessary balance between too much homogeneity and too much heterogeneity of skills and experiences?

Providing education and training implies the following questions:

- Are relevant education and training available to work group members?
- Are education and training available on work group members' demand or only when someone else deems them appropriate?
- How well are education and training tuned to work member needs?
- Is the quality of education and training sufficient?

Fostering expertise sharing and cross-training implies questions like these:

- What is the status of education and training in the enterprise? Are education and training considered necessary or excessive overhead?

- Are work group members properly assisted on when and how they should improve their knowledge and skills?
- Do work group members share their expertise and experiences? How?
- Is worker multifunctionality encouraged and properly rewarded?

Establishing work group behavior norms implies questions such as these:

- Are there clear standards of behavior in the enterprise?
- Do work group members share the same set of behavior norms?
- Do behavior norms encourage strategy development and strategic planning?
- Do behavior norms allow for and encourage regular performance evaluation?

Providing adequate information implies the following questions:

- Do work group members have enough information for strategy development?
- Do they have relevant and correct information?
- Is information about changes in the environment available?

Finally, fostering creative strategy development implies the following questions:

- Do work group members have problems executing the strategic plan?
- What problems do they have?
- How comfortable are they about modifying the strategy if the changing environment demands modification?

This list of troubleshooting questions is certainly incomplete and could go on and on, but the idea should be clear. Work group success is impossible if it is not complemented by proper management and a PEIR system that is closely associated with CSOs and tasks assigned to the work group.

Proficiency gap

As stated previously, the new organizational structure requires a significantly higher level of computer proficiency for virtually all employees. This requirement creates a problem that I call a *proficiency gap* (FIG. 15-2).

IT advances by leaps and bounds. However, people's ability to absorb new technologies and acquire practical knowledge about a huge variety of hardware, software, and ISs is as limited as it has ever been. People are the most conservative component of the strategic triangle (FIG. 15-1).

As a result, the proficiency gap—gap between the current level of IT and

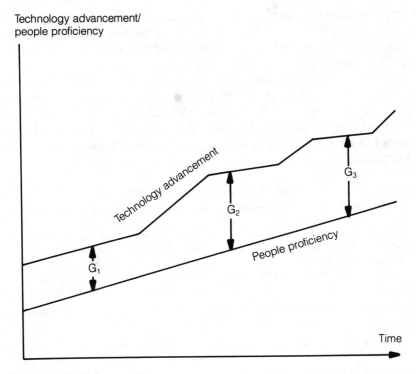

Fig. 15-2. Proficiency gap.

people's ability to use it effectively—is widening. The situation becomes threatening because the normal reaction of humans to a technology they do not understand is to ignore it. The consequences may be devastating from the perspectives of both the single enterprise and the whole IS market. Corporations will not be able to take full advantage of available ITs. The IS market can eventually collapse if the demand for products stops following its supply.

The solution to the proficiency gap problem may come from two sides:

- People should get closer to IT by becoming more proficient in its use.
- IT should get closer to people by being easier to use.

The first solution implies a massive education and training effort. The second solution implies developing genuinely user-oriented interfaces with ISs. These solutions are discussed in detail in the following paragraphs.

Education and training

Perhaps nothing is more important to successful incorporation of IT and SISs than employee education and training. However, with few exceptions, this area of corporate activity is highly underrated and underfinanced. Education and training must be organized as an ongoing process fostered by the enterprise.

Before going into details of the education and training process, let us look at the distinctions between education and training.

Education vs. training   Education and training are different as shown in TABLE 15-3. Education broadens and deepens an individual's knowledge, while training typically improves the individual's skills that relate directly to job responsibilities. In other words, training is a short-term investment, while education is a long-term investment for both the enterprise and the employee.

Table 15-3. Education vs. Training.

Education	Training
Addresses "What is" and "Why"	Addresses only "How" concerns.
Concerns "What to teach."	Concerns "Why we need to teach it."
Gives people basic knowledge that they may or may not use.	Tells people what the next step is in applying what they have just learned.

Two typical mistakes concerning education and training are as follows:

- Neither is viewed as an investment at all.
- Since training provides a short-term result, it is part of the American short-term business hysteria and is preferred to education, which provides results that are longer term and not so obvious.

However, education is as important as training for at least the following reasons:

- Market forces are changing the structure of virtually every industry and thus affect the corporate future.
- Change in the way the enterprise does its business is the only way to catch up with (or, even better, to anticipate) market changes.
- This change is impossible to carry out without IT.
- Education is necessary to understand IT, its linkages with business strategies and its impact on the workforce of this decade and beyond.

Only a few companies, such as Andersen Consulting, IBM, and Xerox, spend enough money for education. According to some sources, an average American company spends on both education and training as little as $100 per employee per year! It comes as no surprise, then, that many companies have difficulties managing IT.

Myths about corporate education   One reason for the lack of attention to education is the variety of myths about corporate education. Here are the most common myths:

- There is not enough money for education. This myth fits well with an enterprise that looks at education as an expenditure rather than an investment in the future of both the corporation and the employee. At the same time, it is not uncommon that such an enterprise wastes millions of dollars purchasing hardware and software or contracting ISs that it does not need or does not know how to use.

  Education can and should be viewed as an investment and considered in a broader context of corporate strategic plans, action programs, and corresponding knowledge and skill requirements. Investment in effective focused education will pay off many times.
- Education is a kind of perk for employees. This myth is common in an enterprise that sends its employees to seminars and conferences as a bonus for good performance or because now is their turn to go. This type of enterprise does not have an education plan that supports corporate strategic plans and action programs. Again, education should be considered in a broader context of corporate strategic plans, action programs, and corresponding knowledge and skill requirements.
- Employees get educated and leave for other companies or, even worse, for an enterprise's competitors. This myth is a typical confusion of a cause and an effect. People do not get educated in order to jump to another company. However, they leave because they do not grow personally. Salary and bonuses are only one component of personal growth; the opportunity to acquire new knowledge and skills, and to keep up with the pace of technological progress, is another very important one.

  Research shows that one of the major reasons for leaving a company is a lack of exactly this component of personal growth, and education is indeed its foundation. In enterprises that care about employee education and see it as one of the important factors in corporate development, the employee turnover is lower than in those that put education at the bottom of their priority list.
- Education is not an enterprise, but a college or U.S. government business. This myth is a typical example of the "other-guy's-fault" syndrome. IT develops so rapidly that no college program can give a student adequate education for the next ten or even five years of his or her business activity. Continuing education is not a luxury but a competitive necessity. As for the U.S. government, one may argue that it has to participate in continuing education, training, and retraining much closer; but a lack of such participation cannot be used as an excuse for corporate ineptness.

Education and training budget In addition to the previous myths, there are more objective obstacles to corporate education. One difficulty is that the definition of education expenditures is vague. Try to answer the following questions unambiguously, and you will understand what I mean:

- Does education include only the time spent in attending formal courses or also the time spent away from the job at a local college?
- Does it include education of only white-collar employees or both white- and blue-collar employees?
- Does it include travel expenses?
- Does it include facility costs for in-house education?
- Does it include books, hardware, and software used in education?
- Does it include the time spent in informal work group cross-training?

What really is necessary is to develop an all-inclusive education and training budget, based on CSOs and planned specific action programs and projects. Accounting systems should be modified accordingly to itemize the education and training budget rather than to hide it in overhead annals. This budget should be viewed as an investment, and the ROI should be estimated.

One additional difficulty in singling out the education and training budget is the fairly common practice of saving education and training money to offset overspending in other areas. Some managers use this method to look good at the next performance review. Some disincentives against this practice should be created.

Corporate education and training requirements Both education and training must be focused on a specific audience. For example, education and training programs can be developed for:

- Key decision makers, such as top corporate management
- Middle management
- Other white-collar employees
- Blue-collar employees

Even programs on the same subject should be presented differently for these groups of students, with a different breakdown between education and training. For example, an IT program for senior management should emphasize the impact of this technology on the enterprise business rather than technicalities of the subject. This program should be almost 100 percent education. The program on the same technology for end users should emphasize its application aspect. It should provide about 20 percent education and 80 percent training.

Generally speaking, the lower the student level, the more detailed, specific, product-oriented, and training-oriented the program. Conversely, the higher the student level, the more generic, strategically oriented, and educational the program. From the psychological viewpoint, the lower the student level, the more important the student motivation and building of self-confidence.

Continuity and quality of education and training are especially important.

Each student should be familiar with the education and training path, including follow-ups and their regularity.

Education and training are only as good as the instructors providing them. Requirements for a good instructor include:

- Knowledge of the subject matter
- Practical experience
- Communication and interpersonal skills
- Understanding of students and their needs and ability to adjust the presentation level accordingly

What constitutes good education and training? Good education and training may take many different forms, with wide variations in results and time and money spent. For example, reading trade magazines and newsletters is one for the most inexpensive ways of self-education; spending time regularly on this activity, however, requires sufficient background, resolve, continuous commitment, and a strong will.

Attending trade shows and multispeaker conferences provides valuable information on the subject in one place and at one time. This activity gives attendees the opportunity to compare different views, products, and system solutions and, hopefully, to come up with their own views and solutions pertinent to specific enterprise situations. The problem is that trade shows and conferences are usually short events, and inexperienced attendees may be overwhelmed by the amount of information that has to be digested in a very short time.

Regularly scheduled on-site education or training courses are an easy way of acquiring new knowledge and skills. An inexpensive alternative to on-site courses is attending classes at local colleges or vocational schools. Both on-site and school-based courses are well complemented by self-paced videotaped or computer-based education or training courses, which are especially good for people who need to build self-confidence in a private setting.

Attending vendor-provided educational and training curricula and courses is also an excellent way of getting focused education and training. These courses give best results if the student has the ability to separate the essence from sales pitches or if the decision to buy the vendor's products has already been made.

Visiting other companies and industries shows how peers apply new ideas, approaches, and techniques. Such visits can provide excellent education or even training if they are well thought out in advance and if the goals for the visit are clearly understood by all visitors.

Finally, extending regular invitations to top consultants can make digesting new ideas, approaches, and techniques easier, especially for top management. Inviting consultants to off-site brainstorming management sessions is also a good idea. If consultants are selected properly, senior managers may gain a wealth of information and significant changes in their strategic views and objectives in a very short time.

Sample curricula   This concluding section on education and training briefly describes a set of four curricula that constitute a common denominator for corporate education and training. The idea here is to avoid specifics and to show what is common for many enterprises in practically all industries.

Personal development   This curriculum should include courses on motivation, innovation, leadership, learning, and similar topics. Each course should be customized for specific audiences: senior management, middle management, staff, etc.

Quality   The curriculum on quality is a must not only for the manufacturing and pharmaceutical industries, but for all industries. After all, quality is abused in all industries, and service industries are not an exception. This curriculum should include courses on quality deployment, assurance, control, and costs; methods for achieving customer satisfaction; and preventive failure avoidance or maintenance.

Advanced information technologies   This curriculum should include courses of general interest, such as computers, networking, database technology, and AI. Depending on the particular industry, courses in CAD, computerized futures trading, or electronic data interchange can also be included.

Project implementation and management   This curriculum should include courses on competitive market and product analysis; new product service, and process definition and development; project management; teamwork; and communication in small work groups.

User-oriented interfaces

The quality, simplicity, and intuitiveness of user interfaces and tools provide another way of reducing the proficiency gap. Each IS has two aspects: *functionality*, or problem-solving capabilities; and *presentation*, or user interface (Firdman 1988, vol. 2). These two aspects are equally important.

The function of the presentation component is to present the IS for different classes of users who may have different purposes for using the IS. Thus, a class of users and a purpose for the system use make up two dimensions of user interface design.

The following discussion of classes of IS users and purposes for IS use presents a broad concept of a user interface, including a screen-based interface (operational windows, menus, on-line help, prompts, advice, explanations, tutoring, etc.), hard-copy documentation (tutorials, manuals, user guides, etc.), and auxiliary visual aids (slides, random-access compact videodisks, etc.).

Classes of users   In analyzing classes of potential IS users, keep in mind two factors. First, there is no such thing as (absolute) user-friendliness; thus, there is no way to provide a single interface for all classes of IS users. Users have both professional and individual preferences—and sometimes even idiosyncrasies—concerning a user interface. For example, some users like menus; some do not. Some like icons; some do not, and so forth. But that is not all.

The same user may have different ideas of user-friendliness depending on his or her proficiency in using a specific system. For a simple illustration, consider a recent buyer of a PC software package. Right after the purchase, the buyer would probably like a menu-driven interface that would not require reading the documentation manual. However, a few days later, the same user may figure out how to use the system. From then on, the user would like to type one macrocommand to have the system perform desired functions. At this stage, users may hate a menu-driven interface.

The point is that users need variable interfaces. Ideally, we could think of a special KBS that builds a model of its user as he or she uses the IS. Based on this model, the IS could customize its interface to a specific class of users, taking into account their proficiency in using the system.

I view the IS of the near future as a system with a single core functionality but many different user interfaces, each targeting a specific segment of the user community or even individual users who use the system frequently.

The second factor in analyzing classes of potential IS users is that users differ in their levels of understanding the IS and operating it. The level of understanding and level of operating skills make up two almost independent parameters of a user class.

Consider individual A with a strong background in AI who wants to learn a new, sophisticated KBS development tool. This individual has a high level of understanding of the tool and therefore does not need extensive tutoring in how the tool works. However, A does need tutoring in how to run the tool.

The user interface for individual A is different from the one for individual B, who does not have sufficient background in AI. Individual B does need tutoring on how the tool works because B's level of understanding is not as high as A's.

With an understanding of the two factors discussed, we now can look at one possible way of defining a class of users. We should somehow quantify level of understanding and level of operating skills and then define classes of users through different combinations of values of these two parameters.

As an illustration, we can define four gradations of both the level of understanding and the level of operating skills (none, low, moderate, and high) and then define four classes of users as follows:

- Naive user

  a. Level of understanding is none.
  b. Level of operating skills is none.

- Novice

  a. Level of understanding is low.
  b. Level of operating skills is none.

- Competent user

  a. Level of understanding is moderate.
  b. Level of operating skills is moderate.

- Expert

  a. Level of understanding is high.
  b. Level of operating skill is high.

A *transition curve* that displays how to provide transition from the naive user to a novice to a competent user to an expert is shown in FIG. 15-3. This curve consists of four states, each requiring its own interface; and three segments, each requiring its own training methodology.

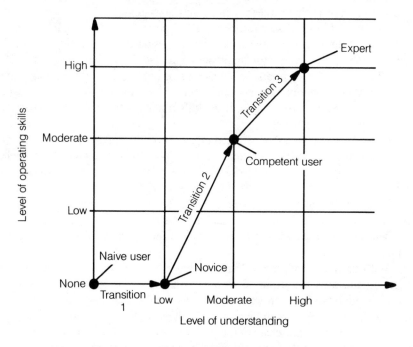

Fig. 15-3. Transition curve for classes of KBS users.

Indeed, one could quantify the parameters, or name or define classes of users differently. The point is that one should understand who the users are, what kinds of interface are needed for each class, and how transition from one class to another can be provided as users gain proficiency in understanding and running the system.

Purposes for IS use The second dimension of user interface design is purposes for IS use. There are four possible purposes:

- Learning the system
- Operating the system
- Getting help from the system
- Understanding the system

Each purpose requires a specific interface different from those required for other purposes.

At the stage of learning, which is a necessary initial investment by the IS user, we need *procedural* presentation of the IS. In other words, we would like for the IS to take the initiative and offer the user a set of simple keystroke-based operations (primitives), which are necessary to boot and run the system, and to explain what these operations accomplish. The IS should also give the user some exercises and check the user's understanding of system primitives.

At the stage of operating the system, which is necessary in our user classification (FIG. 15-3) for transition from novice to competent user, we need *scenario-based* presentation of the IS. In other words, we would like the IS to supply the user with a list of typical situations and meaningful scenarios that should be used in each situation to solve typical problems. Each scenario can be a sequence of keystrokes, menu choices, mouse movements and clicks, etc. The scenarios can later make good macros.

Getting help from the IS is necessary unless the user is already an expert. (Sometimes even experts need help.) The need for help may be casual or even rare, but desperate. Whenever such a need occurs, the IS should realize the specific reason for the help request and supply the user with an effective solution to the problem.

Unfortunately, most of today's ISs respond to the request for help, by providing on-line documentation, which is absolutely inadequate. The last thing a user wants when he or she needs help is to read a manual. Help must be focused on the user's current need and must address a specific problem encountered by the user. Help also has to provide advice and sometimes explanations of what actually happened.

A key to solving this problem is to supply the IS with a conceptual model of itself. In other words, AI technology can be used to describe the IS as a set of its components and the relationships among them, thus providing the IS with knowledge about itself and how it operates (see "Specifics of Knowledge Management" in chapter 13).

In this case, whenever the user does something (for example, makes a menu selection or a keystroke), the conceptual model of the IS simulates the user action and always knows where the user is, what the user options are, how to undo an erroneous action, and so forth. With the proliferation of SISs, I firmly believe that using their conceptual models for help will become necessary for proper SIS operation.

Building a conceptual model of the IS while it is under development also solves the problem of understanding how the IS works. In terms of the illustration (FIG. 15-3), understanding the IS is necessary for transition from a novice to a competent user and especially from a competent user to an expert. In order to understand the IS, users could simulate its problem-solving capabilities on the conceptual model using tutoring facilities for learning and operating the system.

Principles of interface design   Based on our discussion of classes of IS users and purposes for the IS use, we can formulate the principles of interface design as follows:

- Architecture of a user interface must be a changing function of the underlying functional IS structure and user proficiency in running the IS. The IS must support multiple user models and, accordingly, multiple user interfaces for different classes of users.
- All user activities at the terminal must be followed by the IS's conceptual model in order to provide immediate help that focuses on the user's current need and addresses a specific problem encountered by the user. All user activities must also obey a predefined control structure that provides the necessary nesting and undoing of IS user actions.
- The user interface must include a proper mixture of menu-driven tools, visual presentations (such as icons and animation), pointing facilities, and natural language (in the future, speech). A share of each of these presentations in an IS must be determined by the particular characteristics of users (including proficiency in doing their jobs) and the problem to be solved. A study of prospective IS users and how they accomplish their jobs may have to precede IS and, specifically, user interface design.
- The user interface must be mixed-initiative with the gradual shifting of the initiative from the IS to the IS user as user proficiency in understanding and running the IS grows (or, in terms of our user classification illustration, FIG. 15-3, as users move from the class of naive users to the class of novices to the class of competent users to the class of experts).
- A visual presentation component must be as close to (or at least consistent with) the existing working environment (consoles, cockpits, etc.) as possible.
- Specific software ergonomic requirements (depending on the problem domain, user proficiency, load, level of responsibility, and similar factors) must be accounted for.

Giving users what they want   Based on the principles of interface design presented in the previous section, we can outline major user requirements and show how these requirements can be met by IS developers. There are two facets of interaction between the IS user and the IS itself:

- Learning the IS
- Operating the IS interactively

At the stage of learning the IS, the major user concern is to make the learning curve as fast as possible; that is, IS users want the following:

- To get something done immediately. It is hard to overestimate the psychological impact of this concern on user acceptance of the IS. In order for users to get involved early with the IS, it should provide:

  a. On-line tutoring initiated and led by the IS
  b. Problems and tests with answers and explanations of user mistakes

- To operate the IS in a meaningful way within a few hours. In other words, users do not want to spend weeks and months playing with the system before they can do something useful. In order for users to operate the IS in a short time, it should provide:

  a. Self-explaining menus and graphic facilities
  b. Effective focused help
  c. Scenario-oriented and scenario-indexed documentation (hardcopy or on-line)

- To grasp the smallest meaningful subset of IS capabilities first and then gradually expand their understanding and operating skills necessary to run the IS in expert fashion. In order to provide incremental learning of the IS, it should include:

  a. A structured set of manuals and on-line documentation that gradually leads the user from learning and using the smallest set of controls necessary to operate the IS to full-scale expert system operation
  b. An expandable library of scenarios of basic IS uses and applications

At the stage of IS operation, the major user concern is to get as much interaction and help from the IS as possible. IS users want the following:

- A system response when it is needed and at the level expected. In order to provide such a response, the IS should include:

  a. A conceptual model of itself that can be accessed at different levels of abstraction and from different viewpoints
  b. A help facility that focuses on the current user need and addresses a specific problem encountered by the user, including (but not limited to) undoing erroneous user actions

c. An explanation and advice facility capable of answering "Why," "What if," and "How to" questions in various situations of operating the KBS.

- Quick reference capabilities that are based on semantics of the problem domain rather than only indexing by keywords. In order to provide such capabilities, the IS should have advanced text management capabilities such as natural language understanding limited to a problem domain sublanguage and professional jargon.
- The IS ability to memorize frequently used sequences of primitive actions and provide the user with the set of macros customized to the user and the range of problems to be solved. In order to provide this capability, the IS should have macrogeneration facilities for both user actions at the terminal and typical IS procedures.
- Time- or skill-dependent exclusion of excessive tutorials and help facilities as user proficiency grows to a higher level of understanding and operating skills. User proficiency grows along with the complexity of problems that the proficient user wants to solve. In this situation, memory requirements also grow, leaving no room for excessive facilities required by less proficient users.
- Crash recovery capabilities to help the user, especially an inexperienced one, operate the system under disastrous circumstances. In order to provide these capabilities, the IS should include:

  a. Built-in crash recovery utilities
  b. Advising and warning messages with "What if" explanations
  c. History maintenance facility to keep the recent history of IS operations

- Visual aids for higher productivity (especially important in real-time operation) and clear understanding of what is going on in the IS. In order to provide such visual aids, the IS should include:

  a. Graphic representation of IS data and knowledge bases with dynamic follow-up of the IS's problem-solving activities
  b. Domain-specific icon and animation facilities
  c. Interface with random-access compact videodisks for focused presentation and tutorials

16

Corporate IM/SD policy

Executive summary

Many issues involved in the corporate information infrastructure are a matter of policy. The IM/SD policy is a part of the corporate policy pertaining to information management and ISs.

This chapter itself is like an executive summary. It provides an outline of a generic IM/SD policy with the understanding that each enterprise will end up with its own unique policy matching its vision and culture. The outline is presented as a set of questions to be answered by the IM/SD policy. The issues include:

- Linking information management and system development to the corporate vision and CSOs
- Information ownership and management
- Information value estimation
- Information storage, access, manipulation, and protection
- IS development, certification, and maintenance
- Reducing the proficiency gap
- Making outsourcing decisions
- Defining corporate culture and personnel policies

Many issues involved in the corporate information infrastructure are a matter of policy. This chapter summarizes the previous discussion of policy issues, complementing it with other policy issues that were referred to earlier but not discussed. The IM/SD policy is part of the corporate policy pertaining to information management and ISs.

The goal of this chapter is two-fold:

- To ascertain that each enterprise has to develop, maintain, and enforce its IM/SD policy
- To provide an outline of an IM/SD policy with the understanding that each enterprise will end up with its own unique policy matching its vision and culture. The outline provides only a statement of direction for IM/SD policy development.

Why an IM/SD policy?

Why does an enterprise need an IM/SD policy? The first reason is that the IM/SD policy has a critical impact on the corporate information infrastructure. I cannot imagine building the information infrastructure without first resolving policy issues. These issues include:

- Ways of, and approaches to, linking information management and system development to the corporate vision and CSOs discussed in chapter 1. For example, although chapter 1 outlines a generic methodology for linking business strategies and IT, deciding on the particular methodology best suited to a certain virtual enterprise is mostly a matter of policy.
- Principles of information ownership and management, including guidelines for information value estimation. These issues were already discussed on a preliminary basis in "Impact of IM/SD Policy" (chapter 5) and will be reinforced in "Information Ownership and Management" later in this chapter.
- Principles and methodologies of information storage, access, manipulation, and protection. This issue includes the security program development and enforcement (see chapter 14, especially "Security Policies").
- Guidelines for IS development, certification, and maintenance. Although IS development is beyond the scope of this book, these guidelines are mentioned here as a necessary policy issue.
- Guidelines for reducing the proficiency gap, including education and training programs and principles of user interface development (see "Proficiency Gap" in chapter 15).

The second reason for having an IM/SD policy is that it has a critical impact on all outsourcing decisions. In order to alleviate these decisions in each situation, an enterprise has to develop methodologies, guidelines, and checklists for the following issues:

- Make-or-buy decisions
- System integration project procurement and management
- Cost estimate and risk sharing strategies

The third reason for having an IM/SD policy is that it has a critical impact on corporate culture and personnel policies. Indeed, the corporate culture is completely a policy matter. An enterprise has to develop methodologies, guidelines, and checklists for the following issues:

- Risk/benefit analysis
- Work group creation, operation, management, and disbandment
- PEIR programs
- Professional and personal growth programs (including continuing education and training)

IM/SD policy questions

The following is a sample checklist of questions that have to be answered for each issue in the IM/SD policy.

Linking IM/SD to the corporate vision and CSOs

The following five-step SPPE process (chapter 1) translates the corporate vision of the future into the set of implementable action programs:

- Formulating the list of CSOs
- Putting together a capable strategic planning team responsible for translating CSOs into implementable action programs
- Developing a set of alternative strategic plans with rough estimates of their cost-effectiveness
- Expanding the selected strategic plan into a hierarchy of increasingly detailed action programs
- Implementing and monitoring action programs, evaluating their ongoing results, and changing them if necessary

The SPPE process has to be supported by policies describing how this process should be carried out in the enterprise. In particular, the following questions have to be answered:

- What is the corporate vision of the future?
- How is this vision disseminated across the enterprise?
- What process is used to translate CSOs into an implementable IM/SD program?
- How is this process organized?
- How are action program priorities and sequencing defined?
- What are the practical steps for obtaining consensus about strategic plans and their implementation and then committing to them?

Information ownership and management

As mentioned in chapter 5, people like to own information, but they do not like the responsibilities naturally stemming from information ownership. Establishing policies and guidelines for information ownership definition and the information owner's information management responsibilities is an important part of the IM/SD policy.

Two information ownership guidelines dictated by technology are very simple:

- Information can be accessed only by people who are explicitly authorized to do so by its owner.
- Information can be updated only by its owner or by people who are explicitly authorized to do so by its owner.

The rest of the information guidelines are fairly arbitrary, and each enterprise should establish them as its corporate IM/SD policy. Here are some of the issues that have to be addressed by this policy:

- Information owner's rights and liabilities

  a. Who owns which information?
  b. What are general ownership rights?
  c. How can rights of access be granted to, or revoked from, those leasing information?
  d. What are the information lease conditions and terms?
  e. What are the lessee liabilities for violating these conditions and terms?
  f. What are the limits of information owner liabilities?

- Management of geographically dispersed information

  a. Who makes the decision to duplicate information at different sites?
  b. May the information owner's decision not to duplicate information be overridden? By whom?
  c. Who is liable for information management at remote sites where information duplicates reside?

- Integrity and consistency preservation measures

  a. What basic integrity/consistency checks and controls are available to the information owner?
  b. How can these checks and controls be certified?
  c. If these checks and controls are put into an application rather than into a database engine, who is responsible for information integrity and consistency?

- Security measures

  a. What basic security controls are available to the information owner?
  b. How can these controls be certified?
  c. What trade-offs between information security and flexibility of information sharing and exchange are possible?

- Conflict resolution

  a. How are the potential conflicts between information owners and users or between information owners and centralized information administrators and security enforcers to be resolved?
  b. Who makes up a reasonable conflict arbiter?
  c. What are the normal arbitrage procedures?

Information value estimation

In chapter 5 we discussed the importance of information value assessment. The issue of information value is often ignored, with the excuse of its subjectivity. However, subjective information value assessments are better than none, and both the quality and cost of the corporate information infrastructure may be significantly affected by these assessments.

Information value assessment is mostly a matter of the corporate IM/SD policy. The policy has to answer the following questions:

- How is the information value defined? (A commonly accepted methodology of information value definition is presented in "Information Value," chapter 14.)
- What information integrity preservation situations are accepted? (See "Information Value" in chapter 14.)
- How is the corporate information ranked in terms of its value?
- How does the value of corporate information change in time?
- What are the ways of increasing the information value?
- How is information replaced or recalculated (including disaster recovery procedures)?
- What is the impact of information value on security measures?
- How is information disclosure prevented?

Information storage, access, manipulation, and protection

Information is stored to be used. At the same time, it is protected so as not to be misused. This simple dilemma is not so simple to resolve. The IM/SD policy has to define the trade-offs between information dissemination and security. The questions that have to be answered by the IM/SD policy include:

- How can people be encouraged to use information and, at the same time, enforce its integrity, consistency, and security?

- How can information vulnerability to threats be reduced without violating free information sharing and exchange?
- What information should be stored on workstations, file servers, mainframe, etc.?
- How is important information residing on a workstation locked?
- How are access rights granted to (revoked from) users?
- How can application integrity be provided?

System development, certification, and maintenance

The following questions concerning system development, certification, and maintenance have to be answered by the IM/SD policy:

- What methodologies, languages, and tools are to be used for system development?
- What restrictions are imposed on system developers?
- Are users allowed to develop their systems?
- What is a planned product's life cycle and what are the deliverables at each stage?
- How should business experts, users, system analysts, and programmers cooperate and interact?
- How are specifications developed and maintained?
- How is the fast prototyping process organized?
- What are the testing and quality assurance procedures?
- What are the requirements for system certification?
- What are the maintenance policies and procedures?

Reducing the proficiency gap

The IM/SD policy should address the proficiency gap problem in two directions: through continuous education and training (see "Education and Training," chapter 15) and through enforcing principles of user interface design (see "Principles of Interface Design," chapter 15). Questions that have to be answered by the IM/SD policy include:

- How can business managers improve their technical knowledge and skills?
- How can IS personnel improve their business skills?
- How is the corporate mission disseminated within the IS organization?
- How is the technology update briefing for employees organized?
- How can users be classified in terms of their computer proficiency?
- What are the user interface requirements for different classes of users?
- What is the corporate process for the discovery, assessment, management, and incorporation of emerging technologies?

Making outsourcing decisions

As I pointed out in chapter 4, the choice of balance between the IS customer's and outside contractor's involvement in IS development is the most critical issue in system integration. In many respects this choice is a matter of corporate policy—more precisely, the IM/SD policy. The following major factors underlie the outsourcing policy:

- Technical and project management expertise and capabilities
- Cost-effectiveness
- Project confidentiality
- Risk sharing with a system integrator
- Internal politics

Thus, the IM/SD policy should answer the following questions:

- What is the relative weight of each factor of the outsourcing policy?
- What are the criteria for making an in-house vs. outsourcing decision?
- What are the criteria for the system integrator selection?
- What is the cost estimate methodology?
- What are the critical risk factors?
- How should qualities be considered when selecting an appropriate partner to share risk?
- What must the contract include?
- How should payments, bonuses, and penalties be tied to IS performance and deadlines?
- What are the contingency plans for failure?

Corporate culture and personnel policies

In chapter 1, I noted that the naive or excessive faith in traditional ROI assessments can result in unjustified investments, inflated expectations, preference for ISs that contribute little to the bottom line, and undermining of the strategic impact of IS on the business because it is always harder to estimate the impact of cost elimination or reduction.

MIT's and Arthur Young's (now Ernst & Young) joint *Management in the 1990s* study says that standard benefit/risk assessments of information technology "are applicable when the goal is to automate an existing function. However, more varied assessment methods are needed when the goal is to disseminate information throughout an organization or to transform whole functions or businesses" (Young 1989).

Providing guidelines for the benefit/risk analysis of investment in IT is certainly one of the components of the corporate IM/SD policy. In particular, the IM/SD policy has to provide methodologies for a more qualitative approach to ROI assessments and for benefit/risk analysis at the strategic, operational, and cost elimination, rather than only cost-elimination, levels.

The IM/SD policy has to answer the following questions concerning benefit/risk analysis:

- What qualitative approaches to benefit/risk analysis are used in the enterprise and how?
- How should standard benefit/risk analyses be complemented with more qualitative ones?
- How can benefit/risk analyses at the strategic, operational, and cost-elimination (reduction) levels be differentiated?

In chapter 15, work groups were described as a major element of the information infrastructure. Work groups provide:

- Faster response to market changes
- Better coordination of new product/service introduction
- More effective crisis management
- Increased productivity and better quality of work

The way work groups are organized and operated is completely a matter of the corporate policy. The IM/SD policy specifies the corporate policy in areas where IT is an intrinsic part of work group operation or a work group is created for the purposes of information management or system development.

The IM/SD policy has to answer the following questions concerning work groups:

- How and for what purpose is a work group created?
- How and when is it disbanded?
- How is the work group staffed?
- How do work group members interact when working on a problem?
- How are work group members recognized for their contributions?
- How does the work group promote professional and personal growth?
- What are the principles of work group management and coordination?
- How is work group effectiveness defined?
- What are the principles of individual and work group performance evaluation?
- How are the principles of performance evaluation tied to work group effectiveness parameters?
- How is the incentive and reward system developed, maintained, and modified?
- What methods are used to troubleshoot PEIR systems? (Refer to "Troubleshooting Work Group Management and PEIR System" in chapter 15 for more detailed questions.)

17

A look into the future

No one has a crystal ball that can predict the pace of technological progress. Look at the speed with which technological inventions have burst into our lives. People of my generation still have a hard time accepting the fact that a Boeing 747 can get off the ground, let alone fly around the globe, or that they can see live all the action of a soccer game being played in Italy. Neither was possible when I was young. My children, however, are not at all surprised by these and similar facts of life.

Likewise, in the information systems industry, very few people could predict the PC revolution, even in the early 1970s. (I knew one who did, but he could not even come close to predicting its scope and size.) Today, very few people can believe that 50 million transistor chips will be feasible by the year 2000. By the way, I know of nobody who can clearly say (beyond projecting the memory size or mumbling about redundacy on the chip) what kind of functionality will be put on this chip. As of today, we just do not know how we are going to use these huge numbers of transistors.

An interesting part of science- and technology-related crystal ball business is that, at all times, everything that could be invented seems to have already been invented. Yet everyone who once said that there is nothing more to invent has been proven wrong.

With all this in mind, I feel reluctant to forecast the state of IT in 10 years. In addition to the fear of making mistakes (understandable because of my hope that people will still read this book, or its revision, in 10 years), there is another reason for my reluctance. IT has already produced so much that I would not mind if the next 10 years were spent exclusively putting everything available today to real-life use. We then would have at least eliminated the proficiency gap problem.

The point is this: why don't I take IT in its current state and try to predict how it will be used in this decade? My hidden thought is that such a prediction could come close to a self-fulfilling prophecy. After all, it is easy to predict IT applications because IT has to be applied the way I suggest if we are not to admit that the information infrastructure and systems are just a waste of time and money.

I see two major sources of IT application trends. The first source is the process of strengthening linkages between business strategies and information systems that support them. In other words, success breeds success. As soon as senior management starts seeing real advantages of using SISs, it will encourage the transition from automating existing corporate functions (typical of the MIS era) to changing the way the enterprise does its business and then automating the new way (typical of the SIS era).

The second source of IT application trends is the process of strengthening linkages between the corporate information and human infrastructures. As significant changes in workforce demography, availability, set of values, and attitudes already under way become more visible, enterprises will have to spend much more on employee education and training but, at the same time, bring IT to people rather than people to IT as before.

Here is a sample of major trends for the 1990s caused by linkages between business strategies and information systems that support them:

- Planning and design of the corporate information infrastructure will become a necessity and a main component of corporate investment in IT.
- As part of the information infrastructure, information resources for various kinds of information rather than only data will become transparently available at all authorized points of use. Most information storage and management functions will be done on mainframes and other centralized servers.
- End-user computing resources will become even more powerful and less expensive. Most information processing functions will be highly distributed and done on workstations and PCs.
- The demand for SISs will significantly increase as companies formalize their understanding of business through enterprise modeling and develop the information infrastructure as an SIS foundation.
- Transition from MIS to SIS development will lead to increased complexity which, in turn, will increase the demand for system developers, software reusability, and better system development tools.
- Increased system complexity will be accompanied by the increasingly desperate need to hide this complexity from end users and hence create more genuinely user-oriented interfaces.
- Proliferation of SISs will lead to increased IS expenditures and be accompanied by greater accountability for these expenditures.
- IS expenditures will shift from hardware aquisition to enterprise modeling, customized software development, and system integration.

In order to see trends caused by linkages between the corporate information and human infrastructures better, it is worthwhile to look first at the major workforce changes currently occurring in the American business. Towers Perrin and the Hudson Institute, which conducted a survey of 645 companies, identified six such changes (*Computerworld*, August 20, 1990):

- Increased labor shortages, especially in certain parts of the country.
- Greater cultural diversity. The increasing number of minorities and immigrants will create a work environment with less homogeneous value systems.
- Increased number of women who demand shorter work weeks, more flexible job schedules, or even telecommute.
- Shift in worker values to more independence, flexibility, challenge, and quality of life.
- Aging of the workforce, partially because of labor shortages that result in calling retirees back to work.
- Skill mismatch and shortage, with an especially big demand for technically proficient workers.

"How is an American enterprise going to cope with these workforce changes?" The answer to this question is unanimous: "By using IT." There is a strong belief that "technology and human resources are the two strategic resources that will separate one company from its competitors during the next 10 years" (*Computerworld*, August 20, 1990).

The next question is: "How is IT going to help businesses cope with workforce changes?" I propose the following set of IT application trends caused by the linkages between the information and human infrastructures:

- The corporate information infrastructure will cover the increasing number of employee homes and their interconnections. More people will work for companies from their home offices, using computers, telecommunications, and videoconferencing and will come to the "office office" only occasionally, primarily for in-person meetings with their peers. The cost of hardware and software installations at home will be offset by savings in corporate office space.
- Peer-to peer information sharing and exchange will become necessary for the enterprise's effective and efficient operation. Stronger support for peer-to-peer communications will be accompanied by stricter requirements for information protection.
- The number of application software products aimed at offsetting the shortage of labor will significantly increase. In particular, more application software will be developed to take routine work away from workers, leaving them more time for creative work that currently cannot be computerized.

- Knowledge-based and expert systems technology will be increasingly used for at least three purposes:

  a. To capture scarce or fading expertise so that newcomers get up to speed faster and do their jobs better

  b. To provide on-the-job training for employees through structured computer-assisted instruction and knowledge/hypertext-based documentation

  c. To help educationally disadvantaged people become part of the workforce through developing "wordless," yet intuitively clear and unambiguous, graphic interfaces that direct them through the sequence of simple steps to get the job done

I realize that this list is incomplete and invite you to stretch your imagination and add something really exciting to it, or just wait until today's hardly visible trend becomes tomorrow's reality.

Acronyms

ACSE	Association Control Service Element
AI	artificial intelligence
ANSI	American National Standards Institute
AP	action program
ASN	Abstract Syntax Notation
ASP	aggregate strategic plan
BABB	basic architectural building block
CAD	computer-aided design
CASE	computer-aided software engineering
CBEMA	Computer and Business Equipment Manufacturers Association
CCITT	Comite Consultatif International de Tèlègraphique et Tèlèphonique
CCR	commitment, concurrency, and recovery
CEO	chief executive officer
CICA	centralized information/centralized applications
CIDA	centralized information/distributed applications
CM	operation management
CPU	central processing unit
CSMA/CD	carrier sense multiple access with collision detection
CSO	chief security officer
CSO	corporate-specific strategic objective
CSP	corporate strategic plan
CTO	chief technology officer
DARPA	Defense Advance Research Project Agency
DBA	database administrator
DBMS	database management system
DEC	Digital Equipment Corporation
DICA	distributed information/centralized applications
DIDA	distributed information/distributed applications

DIS	document imaging system
dpi	dots per inch
EDS	Electronic Data Systems
EM	electronic mail
EMS	element management system
ESA	Enterprise System Architecture
FDDI	fiber distributed data interface
FEM	formal enterprise model
FSFA	first sent, first arrived
FTAM	file transfer and management
GSO	generic strategic objective
HDLC	High-level Data Link Control
HPTS	High-Performance Transaction System
IDC	International Data Corporation
IEEE	Institute of Electrical and Electronic Engineers
IIPS	information integrity preservation situation
IM/SD	information management/system development
IMS	information management system
INMS	integrated network management system
IS	information system
ISO	International Standards Organization
IT	information technology
JTM	job transfer and management
KBS	knowledge-based system
LAN	local area network
LED	light-emitting diode
MAN	metropolitan area network
MIB	management information base
mips	million instructions per second
MIS	management information system
MIT	management information tree; Massachusetts Institute of Technology
MOTIS	Message-Oriented Text Interchange System
NCSC	National Computer Security Center
NE	network element
NFS	network file system
NIST	National Institute of Standards
NMP	Network Management Protocol
NMS	network management system
NMW	network management workstation
NPDU	network protocol data unit
OOD	object-oriented database
OS	operating system
OSF	Open Software Foundation
OSI	Open Systems Interconnection

PBX	private branch exchange
PCM	plug-compatible mainframe
PEIR	performance evaluation, incentive, and reward
PIPA	protected information/protected applications
PISA	protected information/shared applications
PPM	partial problem model
PSN	packet switch node
RDBMS	relational database management system
RISC	reduced instruction set chips
ROI	return on investment
RPC	remote procedure call
RRP	risk reduction plan
SAA	System Application Architecture
SDLC	Synchronous Data Link Control
SIP	system integration pyramid
SIPA	shared information/protected applications
SIS	strategic information system
SISA	shared information/shared applications
SISPD	strategic IS planning and design
SMAE	systems management application entity
SMAP	systems management application process
SMFA	specific management functional area
SNA	System Network Architecture
SNMP	Simple Network Management Protocol
SP	strategic plan
SPARC	Scalable Processor Architecture
SPPE	strategic planning/plan execution
SQL	structural query language
SSO	systems security officer
TAD	tools and applications development
TAG	technology assessment group
TAM	threat/asset matrix
TCP/IP	Transmission Control Protocol/Internet Protocol
TOCTTOU	time of check to time of use
TSAP	transport service access point
UNMA	Unified Network Management Architecture
USO	universal strategic objective
V&V	validation and verification
VLSI	very large-scale integrated circuit
WAN	wide area network
WIIS	Wang Integrated Image System

Bibliography

Abrams, M.D., and H.J. Podell. *Computer and Network Security: Tutorial*, 64–65. Washington, D.C.: IEEE Computer Society Press, 1987.

Applegate, L.M., J.I. Cash, Jr., and D.Q. Mills. "Information Technology and Tomorrow's Manager." *Harvard Business Review* (November–December 1988).

Baran, P. "On Distributed Communication Networks." *IEEE Transactions on Communication Systems* CS-12 (March 1964): 1–9.

Bell, D.E., L.J. LaPadula. "Secure Computer Systems: Unified Exposition and Multics Interpretation." MTR-2997, rev. 1 (March 1976). Bedford, Mass.: MITRE Corporation.

Birrell, A.D., and B.J. Nelson. "Implementing Remote Procedure Calls." *ACM Transactions on Computer Systems* 2 (February 1984): 39–54.

Brusil, P.J., and L. LaBarre. "Managing Networks." In *ISDN, DECnet, and SNA Communications*, edited by Thomas C. Bartee, 255–95. Indianapolis, Ind.: Howard W. Sams & Co., 1989.

Business Week (May 23, 1988).

_____ (November 7, 1988).

Chalmers, Leslie S. "An Analysis of the Differences Between the Computer Security Practices in the Military and Private Sectors." *Proceedings of the 1986 Symposium on Security and Privacy*, IEEE (1986): 71–74.

Coad, Peter, and Edward Yourdon. *Object-Oriented Analysis*. Englewood Cliffs, N.J.: Yourdon Press, Prentice-Hall, 1990.

Codd, E.F. "Recent Investigations into Relational Data Base Systems." *Proceedings of IFIP* (1974).

Computerworld (January 29, 1990), 16, 23

_____ (February 5, 1990), 1, 6, 90, 145

_____ (February 12, 1990), 1, 122

_____ (February 20, 1989).

_____ (March 5, 1990), 54, 88

_____ (March 12, 1990).

_____ (March 19, 1990).

_____ (April 2, 1990).

_____ (April 16, 1990).

_____ (June 12, 1989).

_____ (August 20, 1990).

_____ (November 20, 1989).

_____ (November 27, 1989).

_____ (December 2, 1985).

_____ (December 25, 1989), 36, 38, 88

Conklin, J. "Hypertext: An Introduction and Survey." *IEEE Computer* 20, no. 9 (September 1987).

Courtney, Robert H., and M.A. Todd. "Problem Definition: An Essential Prerequisite to the Implementation of Security Measures." Second International Congress and Exhibition on Computer Security, Toronto, September 10–12, 1984.

Cox, B. *Object-Oriented Programming*. Reading, Mass.: Addison-Wesley Publishing Co., 1986.

Date, C.J. *An Introduction to Database Systems*, vol. 1, 4th ed. Reading, Mass.: Addison-Wesley Publishing Co., 1987.

_____. *An Introduction to Database Systems*, vol. 2. Reading, Mass.: Addison-Wesley Publishing Co., 1985.

_____. "Twelve Rules for a Distributed Data Base." *Computerworld* (June 8, 1987).

Department of Defense Trusted Computer System Evaluation Criteria, National Computer Security Center, December 1985.

Eccles, R.G., and D.B. Crane. "Managing Through Networks in Investment Banking." *California Management Review* (Fall 1987): 176.

Ericson, E., L. Traeger Ericson, and D. Minoli, eds. "Expert Systems Applications in Integrated Network Management." Norwood, Mass.: Artech House, 1989.

Firdman, H.E. *Putting Artificial Intelligence to Work*. Vol. 1: *Understanding the Technology*. Fallbrook, Calif.: Henry Firdman & Associates, 1988.

_____. *Putting Artificial Intelligence to Work*. Vol. 2: *Developing Practical Knowledge-Based Systems*. Fallbrook, Calif.: Henry Firdman & Associates, 1988.

Gasser, M. *Building a Secure Computer System*. New York: Van Nostrand Reinhold, 1988.

Giovinazzo, M., and J. Croft. "Right Data, Wrong Time?" *Computerworld* (May 8, 1989).

Gundon, Tony. *Infrastructure: Building a Framework for Corporate Information Handling*. London: Prentice-Hall, 1989.

Gunn, Thomas G. *Manufacturing for Competitive Advantage: Becoming a World Class Manufacturer.* Cambridge, Mass.: Ballinger Publishing Co., 1987.

Haerder, T., and A. Reuter. "Principles of Transaction-Oriented Database Recovery." *ACM Computer Surveys* 15, no. 4 (December 1983).

Kerr, S. "Politics of Network Management," *Datamation* (September 15, 1988).

Klerer, S.M. "The OSI Management Architecture: An Overview." In "Expert Systems Applications in Integrated Network Management," edited by E. Ericson, L. Traeger Ericson, and D. Minoli. Norwood, Mass.: Artech House, 1989.

Leavitt, H.J., and T.L. Whisler. "Management in the 1980s." *Harvard Business Review* (November-December 1958).

Lind, Barbara. Personal communication with author.

Meyer, Herbert E. *Real-World Intelligence.* New York: Weldenfeld & Nicolson, 1987.

Mills, D.Q. *Rebirth of the corporation.* New York: Wiley, 1991.

Mintzberg, H. "The Adhocracy." In *The Strategy Process*, edited by J.B. Quinn, H. Mintzberg, and R.M. James. Englewood Cliffs, N.J.: Prentice-Hall, 1988.

MIS Week (April 24, 1989).

_____ (June 19, 1989).

Mitroff, Ian I. *Business NOT as Usual.* San Francisco, Calif.: Jossey-Bass Publishers, 1987.

Naisbitt, J., Aburdene P. *Re-inventing the Corporation: Transforming Your Job and Your Company for the New Information Society.* New York: Warner Books, 1985.

Nelson, B.J. "Remote Procedure Call." Ph.D. diss., Carnegie-Mellon University, 1981.

Perlman, R., A. Harvey, and G. Varghese. "Choosing the Appropriate ISO Layer for LAN Interconnection." *IEEE Network Magazine* 2 (January 1988): 81–86.

Porter, Michael E. *Competitive Advantage.* New York: The Free Press, 1985.

_____. *Competitive Strategy.* New York: The Free Press, 1988.

Rothnie, J.B., Jr., and N. Goodman. "A Survey of Research and Development in Distributed Database Management." *Proceedings of Third International Conference on Very Large Data Bases* (October 1977).

Sanders, B.D. "Making Work Groups Work." *Computerworld* (March 5, 1990).

Tanenbaum, Andrew S. *Computer Networks.* Englewood Cliffs, N.J.: Prentice-Hall, 1988.

Tompkins, Fred.G. "NASA Guidelines for Assuring the Adequacy and Appropriateness of Security of Safeguards in Sensitive Applications." MTR-84W179 (September 1984). Falls Church, Va.: MITRE Corporation.

"Unix—Opening the Door to Business Solutions," IDC White Paper (1990), 5, 8.

Wiseman, Charles. *Strategic Information Systems*, 106. Homewood, Ill.: Richard D. Irwin, 1988.

"Work Teams in Organizations: An Orienting Framework." In *Groups That Work (and Those That Don't)*, edited by J.R. Hackman. San Francisco, Calif.: Jossey-Bass Publishers, 1990.

Young, Arthur. *The Landmark MIT Study: Management in the 1990s*, 1989.

Index